HAWAII
ACCESS

W9-CHT-346

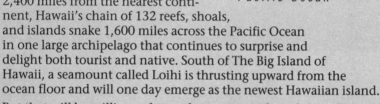

Hawaii Orientation

Surrounded by the world's largest body of water, the islands of Hawaii are both protected and enhanced by their geographical isolation. Some 2,400 miles from the nearest continent, Hawaii's chain of 132 reefs, shoals, and islands snake 1,600 miles across the Pacific Ocean in one large archipelago that continues to surprise and delight both tourist and native. South of The Big Island of Hawaii, a seamount called Loihi is thrusting upward from the ocean floor and will one day emerge as the newest Hawaiian island.

But that will be millions of years from now, and until then the varied landscapes of the eight major Hawaiian islands are enough to attract 6.9 million visitors each year. **Oahu**, where 836,000 people live, is 618 square miles in size and is divided by two major mountain ranges, the Waianaes and Koolaus. This largely underrated island has much natural beauty to offer the tourist who takes the time to escape the crowds. **Kauai**, home to 51,000 people, is the oldest and northernmost of the islands, and features the most memorable lush scenery. Mount Waialeale, which has more rainy days per year than any other place on Earth, is also on Kauai. Most of this island's 558 square miles are inaccessible by car, making this a mysterious island with a vast, waterfall-streaked interior that is frequently viewed by helicopter.

Hawaii island, also called **The Big Island**, is the behemoth of the lot—a pulsing, throbbing, 4,035-square-mile wonderland where volcanoes still erupt and snow-capped peaks can be seen from remote rain forests and black sand beaches. This island is more than three times the size of the state of Rhode Island; it's also the second most populous island in Hawaii, with more than 120,000 residents.

Much smaller is **Maui**—an island whose golden-goddess allure is being tempered by extensive resort and condominium development. More than 91,000 people live on Maui's 735 square miles. The 10,023-foot-high Mount Haleakala and the older West Maui Mountains divide this island into five sections, each with its own character. However, resort developments continue apace all over the island, from Kapalua to Wailea to the ongoing success of West Maui's Kaanapali Beach Resort, Hawaii's first and most extensive master-planned resort.

The islands of **Molokai** and **Lanai** are technically part of Maui County and remain—except for the privately owned **Niihau** and the unpopulated **Kahoolawe** islands—the least explored of the major Hawaiian islands. Aside from its only tourist development on the western shoreline, Molokai's 264

square miles are hardly developed and many of the island's 6,700 residents want to keep it that way. On tiny Lanai, the privately owned "pineapple island," recent developments have charted a new course for the future of this 141-square-mile island. Pineapple production is being phased out, jet service is being added, and two pricey hotels are now in business, making it clear that Lanai's laid-back days are numbered.

Together, the Hawaiian Islands comprise one of the world's most fragile ecosystems. With less than 25 percent of the state's original forests remaining and 40 percent of its native bird species extinct, Hawaii itself is an endangered species. The encroachment of nonindigenous plants into native habitats have decimated many bird species that existed only in Hawaii, and foreign investment and rampant development, many believe, threaten a similar fate for the people and lifestyle of all the Islands. Visitors should take care of Hawaii's environment while they enjoy its bountiful pleasures, just as the state's leaders would do well to conserve and preserve the natural resources that remain.

Getting to the Islands: Who Flies Where

American Airlines: Honolulu International, Oahu; and Kahului Airport, Maui 526.0044, 800/433.7300

Canadian Airlines: Honolulu International, Oahu 922.0533, 800/426.7000

Continental Airlines: Honolulu International, Oahu 532.0000, 800/231.0856

Delta Airlines: Honolulu International, Oahu; and Kahului Airport, Maui 800/221.1212

Hawaiian Airlines: Honolulu International, Oahu (One bonus—they don't charge extra to hop onto one of their inter-island flights when you reach Honolulu.)..537.5100

Northwest Airlines: Honolulu International, Oahu 955.2255

Pan American World Airways: Honolulu International, Oahu 800/221.1111

Trans World Airlines: Honolulu International, Oahu 800/221.2000

United Airlines: Honolulu International, Oahu; Lihue Airport, Kauai; Kahului Airport, Maui; and Keahole, The Big Island 547.2211

Getting around the Islands: Inter-Island Carriers

Commuter planes fly between the islands with the frequency of a big-city bus service. **Aloha Airlines, Aloha IslandAir,** and **Hawaiian Airlines** are the Islands' three major passenger carriers. They all share an inter-island terminal at Honolulu International Airport. Aloha and Hawaiian make regular hops on full-size jets to Honolulu, Oahu; Maui; Kauai; and Kona and Hilo, The Big Island. Hawaiian also flies to Lanai, Molokai, and the West Maui-Kapulua airport. **Aloha IslandAir,** owned by Aloha Airlines, flies to Honolulu, Oahu; Waimea-Kohala, Kahului, and Hana, Maui; Hoolehua, Molokai; and the Lanai airport.

Air Molokai is another small commuter service that flies to Honolulu, Oahu; Kahului and Hana, Maui; Molokai and Kalaupapa, Molokai; and the Lanai airport.

These commuter airlines have their own passenger terminals and in some cases offer small savings over the major airlines. However, the flights take longer and there are stricter limitations on baggage. You should arrange for airport-to-resort transportation since your hotel will probably be a considerable distance away. Some hotels offer shuttle services, but there are few limousines and no public bus services from any of the island airports except Oahu.

Air Molokai 834.0043

Aloha Airlines 836.1111, 800/367.5250

Aloha IslandAir 833.3219, 800/323.3345

Hawaiian Air 537.5100, 800/367.5320

Major Airports

Big Island: Hilo and Keahole
Kauai: Lihue
Maui: Kahului
Molokai: Hoolehua (also known as Kaunakakai)
Oahu: Honolulu International

Minor Airports

Big Island: Waimea-Kohala and Upolu
Kauai: Princeville
Lanai: Lanai City
Maui: Hana and West Maui-Kapalua
Molokai: Kalaupapa

Ground Transportation

Buses On every island, senior citizens may obtain free bus passes from the county; check with each island's county information office.

Oahu's very efficient bus system, **TheBus** (848.5555), covers the entire island every day for 60 cents one way. It's one of the best deals in Hawaii.

On the island of **Kauai,** the new **Kauai Bus** (246.4622) runs on weekdays between the Kauai Community College in Puhi and the far reaches of Kapaa, for $1 one way.

There is no public transportation on **Maui,** but **Trans-Hawaiian** (877.7308) transports people from the Kahului Airport to Kaanapali and back every hour from 7AM-6PM; no reservations are needed upon arrival at the airport, but reservations are recommended for departure from Kaanapali. Pick-up time for departure is at least three hours before flight time; $13 one way. **Akina Tours** (879.2828) takes passengers from the airport to the South Maui, Kihei, and Wailea areas, leaving the airport every hour on the half-hour from 7:30AM-7:30PM. Reservations are required for departures, and there's a courtesy phone at each baggage claim area; $10 per person one way, $8 per person for two or more going to the Kihei/Wailea area, ages seven and under are free.

On **The Big Island,** the **Hele-On Bus** (935.8241) runs 7AM-6PM from Hilo to Ka'u, and from Hilo to Honoka'a, Waimea, and Kailua-Kona. This is a *big* island; most visitors rent a car.

No matter which island you're on, ask your hotel whether it provides shuttle service; all the major resorts offer it.

Car Rentals The major car rental companies have booths at the major airports throughout the state, even on Molokai. On the island of Lanai, The Lodge at Koele and Manele Bay Hotel provides shuttle service for their guests, and although there is no car rental agency at the airport, the two car rental operations, **Lanai City Service** (565.6780) and **Oshiro Service and U-Drive** (565.6952), provide taxi service.

Driving On most of the islands, the roads skirt the coastline. Rush-hour traffic has intensified on **Kauai, Maui, The Big Island,** and **Oahu,** so be prepared, as there usually are no alternate routes to the main roads.

Oahu has the heaviest traffic and is the hardest island to navigate. Two major freeways (H-1 and H-2) traverse the island and are the major commuter corridors, so avoid them at all costs during commute hours, especially in these times of heavy road work and construction. Kalanianaole Hwy leading east to Hanauma Bay, Sandy Beach, Makapuu, and windward Oahu, is undergoing a three-year, road-widening process.

Taxis Taxi service is available on all the islands you can visit. You can hail a cab at the airport or look in the yellow pages of the phone book for the local taxi services. Fares differ on each island and in some cases, particularly for long distances, a cab driver may give you a ride for a flat fee.

FYI

Climate There are basically two seasons in Hawaii: April through November is the warmer season, when temperatures float comfortably in the 75 to 88° F range, except during August and September, which are the hottest, most humid months, and temperatures frequently soar to the 90s. The coldest months are usually December through February, when evening temperatures can dip into the high 50s and 60s. Although *mauka* (from the mountain) showers dampen the gardens on many summer nights, the heaviest rainfall months throughout Hawaii are December through February. The water temperature for all the islands is usually about 80° F.

Newspapers The two dailies statewide are *The Honolulu Advertiser* (the morning paper) and the *Honolulu Star-Bulletin* (the afternoon paper). Some islands also have their own periodicals: *Maui News, Hilo Tribune Herald* (The Big Island), *West Hawaii Today* (The Big Island), *Garden Island* (Kauai), and *Kauai Times.*

Telephone *The area code for all the Hawaiian Islands is 808.*

For inter-island phone calls, dial a 1 before the number (don't dial the area code). Calls are charged by the minute.

Television The major TV stations statewide are KGMB/CBS, KITV/ABC, and KHON/NBC, all broadcasting from Honolulu.

Time Hawaii does not follow Daylight Savings Time (DST) and is therefore two hours behind the West Coast and five hours behind the East Coast when the mainland states are on DST. When the mainland goes off DST, Hawaii is three hours behind California and six hours behind the East Coast.

Tourist Seasons Peak tourist season is from June through August and December through January, and reservations for everything from hotel rooms to rental cars are much harder to come by. The rest of the year is off season.

Visitor Information The central office of the Hawaii Visitors Bureau (HVB) is on Oahu at 2270 Kalakaua Ave, No. 801, Honolulu HI 96815, 923.1811.

The HVB's neighbor island offices are:

Maui Visitors Bureau, 380 Dairy Rd, Kahului HI 96732, 871.8691.

HVB in Hilo (The Big Island), 180 Kinoole St, Suite 105, Hilo HI 96720, 961.5797.

HVB in Kailua-Kona (The Big Island), 75-5719 W. Alii Dr, Kailua-Kona HI 96740, 329.7787.

HVB on Kauai, 3016 Umi St, Lihue HI 96766, 245.3971.

Phone Book

The area code for the state of Hawaii is 808.

Emergency: fire, police, ambulance	**911**
Directory Assistance	411
Hawaii Visitors Bureau	923.1811
Inter-Island Directory Assistance	555.1212
Weather	961.5582

How to Read this Guide

HAWAII ACCESS® is arranged by island and then broken down into neighborhoods so you can see at a glance where you are and what is around you. The numbers next to the entries in the following chapters correspond to the numbers on the maps. The type is color-coded according to the kind of place described:

Restaurants/Clubs: Red	Hotels: Blue
Shops/ 🌺 Outdoors: Green	Sights/Culture: Black

Rating the Restaurants and Hotels

The restaurant ratings take into account the service, atmosphere, and uniqueness of the restaurant. An expensive restaurant doesn't necessarily ensure an enjoyable evening; however, a small, relatively unknown spot could have good food, professional service, and a lovely atmosphere. Therefore, on a purely subjective basis, stars are used to judge the overall dining value (see star ratings below). Keep in mind that the chefs and owners change, which sometimes drastically affects the quality of a restaurant. The ratings in this book are based on information available at press time.

The price ratings, as categorized below, apply to restaurants and hotels. These figures describe general price-range relationships between other restaurants or hotels; they do not represent specific rates.

★ Good	$ The price is right
★★ Very good	$$ Reasonable
★★★ Excellent	$$$ Expensive
★★★★ Extraordinary	$$$$ A month's pay

Map Key

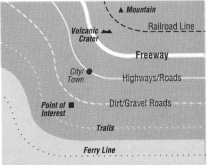

5

The Big Island

The latest news about **The Big Island** of Hawaii is that it's getting bigger—it's now 290 acres larger than it was in 1983, twice the size of all the other Hawaiian islands combined. Since January 1983, the ongoing and vigorous eruption of **Kilauea Volcano** has pumped great volumes of lava through underground lava tubes and down the island's eastern slopes, restructuring the topography and wreaking havoc as it traveled toward the sea. Several homes and major attractions have been buried by what many see as the fury of **Pele**, the volcano goddess of Hawaiian legend. Among the destroyed sights and shops are the **Kalapana Store**, the popular **Queen's Bath** swimming hole, the **Wahaula Visitors Center** in the **Hawaii Volcanoes National Park**, and the **Black Sand Beach** at Kaimu.

The Big Island has the only two active volcanoes in Hawaii: **Kilauea**, active since 1983, and **Mauna Loa**, which last erupted in 1984. But these fiery craters tend to misrepresent the entire island. Both are grouped on the east side of the island, yet too many potential visitors are led to believe (perhaps by poorly informed travel agents) that the whole Big Island is a vast formation of hard, black lava.

The truth is that the Big Island has lava rock as well as rain forests, virtual deserts, sandy beaches, grasslands, and even a snow-capped mountain, **Mauna Kea.** Some of the island's prominent features gave rise to its nicknames: Volcano Island, Orchid Island, and The Big Island (which alludes to its size and is commonly used to avoid confusion between its formal name, Hawaii, and the chain of islands that make up the state). To better understand the geography of the Big Island, imagine it divided into two sides: the east has the active volcanoes, Hawaii Volcanoes National Park, and the town of **Hilo;** the west

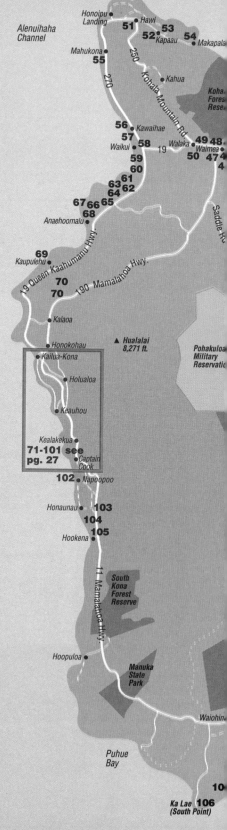

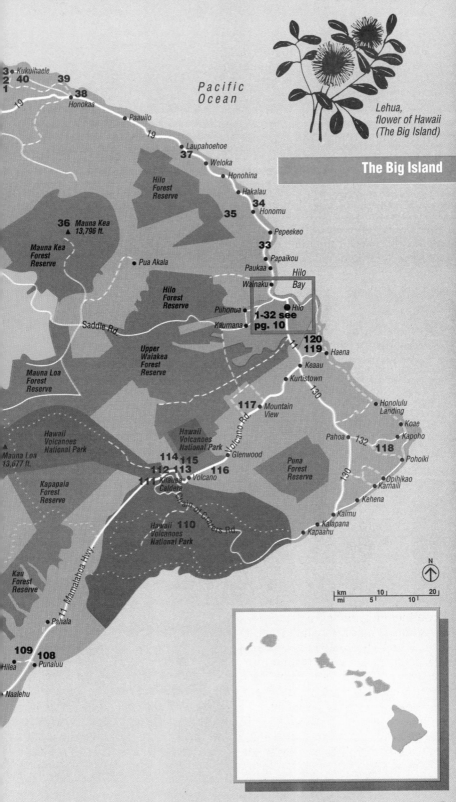

Pacific
Ocean

Lehua,
flower of Hawaii
(The Big Island)

The Big Island

3 • Kukuihaele
2   **40**   **39**
1
38
Honokaa
Paauilo
19
Laupahoehoe
37
Weloka
Honohina
Hakalau
34
35   Honomu
Pepeekeo
33
Papaikou
Paukaa   Hilo
Wainaku   Bay
Piihonua   • Hilo
Kaumana   **1-32 see**
pg. 10

Hilo
Forest
Reserve

36 Mauna Kea
▲ 13,796 ft.

Mauna Kea
Forest
Reserve

Pua Akala

Hilo
Forest
Reserve

Saddle Rd.

Upper
Waiakea
Forest
Reserve

120
119   • Haena
Keaau
Kurtistown

Mauna Loa
Forest
Reserve

117 • Mountain
View

Honolulu
Landing
Koae

Pahoa   Kapoho
132
118   Pohoiki

▲
Mauna Loa
13,677 ft.

Hawaii
Volcanoes
National Park

Hawaii
Volcanoes
National Park
Glenwood

Puna
Forest
Reserve

130

Opihikao
Kamaili
Kehena

114 **115**
112 **113**   **116**
111 Kilauea
Caldera   Volcano

Kapapala
Forest
Reserve

Hawaii
Volcanoes
National Park

110

Ocean of Craters Rd.

Kaimu
Kalapana
Kapaahu

Kau
Forest
Reserve

11 Mamalahoa Hwy.

Pahala

109 **108**
Hilea   • Punaluu

Naalehu

N
↑

km   10   20
mi   5   10

7

region is filled with resorts, extending from **Keauhou Bay** to **Kailua-Kona** and north along the **Kohala Coast.**

Hilo's unusual propensity for heavy rainfall (more than 200 inches in 1990) is yet another reason the east side of the Big Island is unfairly maligned. Although the town is not oriented to tourists, it's a friendly fishing and agricultural community only 27 miles from the volcanoes. Locals refer to it as "Hawaii's last old town."

Except for volcano-watchers who may spend one or two nights in Hilo or at the sadly declining **Volcano House** hotel in **Volcano**, most visitors are drawn to the luxurious, sun-kissed resorts on the west side. Unlike Hilo, West Hawaii is usually dry as a bone, with Kohala Coast rainfall averaging under nine inches a year. Those who can handle the

price tag stay at the **Mauna Lani Bay Hotel, Kona Village Resort**, the newly opened **Ritz-Carlton Mauna Lani**, or the **Mauna Kea Beach Hotel**— collectively recognized as the crème de la crème. Other highbrow hotels include the **Four Seasons**, the **Hyatt Regency Waikoloa**, and the **Royal Waikoloan**. Another popular center of activity is the area between Keauhou Bay and Kailua-Kona. Plenty of sight-seeing cruises, party boats, fishing charters, and an extensive roster of dining, shopping, and entertainment establishments give Kailua-Kona a lively, tacky, honky-tonk quality that tends to obscure the town's historic features.

About 1,500 feet above Kailua-Kona you'll find **Holualoa**, an erstwhile coffee-growing town that has since become sanctuary to Big Island artists. The tiny main street is dotted with studios and galleries mingled with ancient storefronts and small businesses. Down the hill and heading north, the Kohala Coast resorts—Waikoloa, Mauna Lani, and Mauna Kea—offer golf, fine dining, tennis, water sports, and helicopter tours against a backdrop of spectacular ocean and mountain vistas. North and east you'll have a better perspective of the imposing profile of the 13,796-foot-high **Mauna Kea** before coming to the grasslands above the Kohala Coast, where you'll find the **Parker Ranch** and the charming *paniolo* (cowboy) town of **Waimea**. Note the haunting beauty of the North Kohala District as you approach **Hamakua Coast**, which stretches from Hilo to Waimea, running between the sea and a series of waterfalls. Northeast of Waimea, the **Waipio Valley** lures nature lovers who don't mind the incredibly steep drive down for a glimpse into a place that was a major cultural center almost a thousand years ago.

The Big Island calls for big energies. You can, of course, devote yourself to sunning at one of the beach resorts (though the beaches are fewer in number and of lesser quality than on the other Islands). But to discover the best of the Big Island, make a few road trips—and leave room for serendipity.

Helicopter Tours What better way to see an active volcano, especially since tours from the ground are now hindered by lava flows? Helicopter flights cover the island, from the volcanoes to the beaches of Puna and Ka'u— and you can even help map out the flight course.

Helicopters departing from **Waikoloa Heliport:**

Kenai	329.7424, 800/622.3144
Mauna Kea	885.6400
Papillon	329.0551, 800/367.7095

Helicopters departing from Kailua-Kona's **Keahole Airport:**

Big Island Air	329.4868
Classic Aviation	329.8687
Hawaii Airventures	329.0014
Papillon	329.0551, 800/367.7095

Helicopters departing from **Hilo International Airport:**

Hawaii Island Hoppers	969.2000
Hilo Bay Air	969.1545
	969.1547, 800/776.6137

'Io Aviation 935.3031

Kainoa Aviation 961.5591

Kenai 969.3131

1 Hukilau $ This restaurant has literally survived four tidal waves, so it must be here to stay. Your choice of the complete dinners of steak, lobster, crab legs, and abalone are bargains; the waterline marks add a whole new dimension to the Polynesian decor. Strictly local style, though; so don't expect any fancy dishes. ♦ Eclectic ♦ Daily 7AM-1PM, 4-8:30PM. 136 Banyan Dr, Hilo. 935.4222

2 Harrington's ★★$$$ Seafood lovers come for the chowder, catch of the day, fresh shellfish, and pasta-seafood combinations, and the view overlooking tranquil **Reed's Bay.** ♦ Seafood ♦ Daily 5:30-9:45PM. 135 . Kalanianaole Ave, next to Banyan Dr, Hilo. 961.4966

3 Arnott's Lodge $ Although Arnott's isn't listed with the American Youth Hostels, it's very much a backpacker's lodge. The walk-up offers single private rooms, rooms for double occupancy, semi-private rooms for single travelers, and a two-bedroom suite. Great for budget-conscious travelers, and close to a beach with tidal pools. ♦ 98 Apapane Rd, Hilo. 969.7097

 4 Leleiwi Beach Park This beach has tidal pools, snorkeling, surfing, and picnic facilities. ♦ Off Hwy 12, near Hilo Airport

 5 James Kealoha Beach Park Locals call it "Four Miles," which is the distance from the downtown post office building to the park. Swimming, picnics, surfing, and spearfishing. ♦ Off Hwy 12, near Hilo Airport

6 Onekahakaha Beach Park Great for children because of its shallow, calm swimming area protected by a breakwater. Picnics and camping. ♦ Off Hwy 12, near Hilo Airport

7 Hawaii Naniloa Hotel $$$ The best of the limited choices of hotels in Hilo, the Naniloa commands a fine location on Banyan Dr, with views of Hilo Bay, the beginnings of the Hamakua coastline, and the adjacent Coconut Island. Three wings with 325 rooms, and a new health spa. Recent renovations have added a decidedly Japanese flavor (lots of pink marble and a Japanese restaurant). ♦ 93 Banyan Dr, Hilo. 969.3333, 800/367.5360; fax 969.6622

7 Uncle Billy's Hilo Bay Hotel $$ Uncle Billy Kimi (who also runs the Kona Bay Hotel) believes in keeping prices down in a homey atmosphere. The 150 rooms serve the purpose, but don't expect anything special. Some have a refrigerator and kitchen sink. Pool, shops. ♦ 87 Banyan Dr, Hilo. 961.5818, 800/442.5841 (HI), 800/367.5102 (US); fax 935.7903

7 Hilo Hawaiian Hotel $$ A 290-room hotel that won't win any awards, but is a serviceable base for exploring Hilo and the volcano country. The banyan tree in front of the hotel was planted by **Babe Ruth,** the baseball legend. Pool, restaurant, cocktail lounge, and shops. ♦ 71 Banyan Dr, Hilo. 935.9361, 800/272.5275 (HI), 800/367.5004 (US); fax 961.9642

 8 Banyan Drive Fronting a chain of hotels along Reed's Bay in Hilo, the drive is named for the numerous banyan trees planted here by visiting dignitaries and celebrities during the 1930s. Recognizable names on the

plaques include **Babe Ruth** and **Amelia Earhart.** ♦ Off Kamehameha Ave near the Hilo International Airport

9 Naniloa Country Club A flat, 9-hole course across from the Hawaii Naniloa Hotel. Par 35, 3,156 yards. Cheap green fees, but watch for rain. ♦ Starting time required on weekends. 120 Banyan Dr, Hilo. 935.3000

10 Liliuokalani Gardens You'll swear you're in the Far East when you visit this elaborate, 30-acre Japanese garden. The manicured grounds contain footpaths, pagodas, stone lanterns, a ceremonial tea house, bridges, and tidal pools. A popular picnic site and backdrop for wedding portraits. Follow the footpath to tiny, palm tree-covered **Coconut Island,** with a sweeping view of Hilo Bay. ♦ North end of Banyan Dr

11 Nihon Restaurant and Cultural Center $$ Authentic Japanese decor but rather basic fare. A sushi bar and Japanese beer and sake round out the menu, and there's a view of Hilo Bay and Liliuokalani Gardens from the lanai bar. The art gallery features Japanese cultural and art exhibits. ♦ Japanese ♦ M-Sa 11AM-2PM, 5-9PM. 123 Lihiwai St, Hilo. 969.1133

12 Suisan Fish Market For early risers, this is a chance to watch Hilo's multilingual fishing fleet unload its catch at what the old-timers know as **Sampan Harbor.** The auctioneer uses a patois of English, Hawaiian, Japanese, and a bit of pidgin. Hilo's thriving bastion of local color. ♦ Free. Auction M-Sa 8AM. Lihiwai St at the end of Banyan Dr

13 K.K. Tei ★$$ If you have more than six people in your party, reserve one of the *ozashiki* rooms overlooking the Japanese garden; otherwise, the main dining room will suffice. Try the sukiyaki, the *yosenabe* (cook-it-yourself soup in an earthenware pot), or the seafood specialties. ♦ Japanese ♦ M-Sa 11AM-2PM, 5-9PM. 1550 Kamehameha Ave, Hilo. 961.3791

Restaurants/Clubs: Red   **Hotels:** Blue
Shops/ ♣ Outdoors: Green   **Sights/Culture:** Black

14 Ken's Pancake House $$ This local representative of the California chain is near the airport, reliable, and the only 24-hour restaurant in Hilo. Try the macadamia nut pancakes or one of the wild waffle combinations. ◆ American ◆ 24 hrs. 1730 Kamehameha Ave, Hilo. 935.8711

15 Fiasco's ★$$$ The large selection of American, Chinese, and Italian food, including a salad bar, burgers, and lobster in season. A nightclub (with taped fifties, sixties, and seventies music) draws late-night dancers. ◆ Eclectic ◆ M-W 11:30AM-10PM;

The Big Island

Th 11AM-10PM; F-Sa 11:30AM-11PM. Nightclub Th-Sa 8:30PM-1AM. Waiakea Square Warehouse, 200 Kanoelehua Ave, Hilo. 935.7666

16 Prince Kuhio Plaza This $47.5-million shopping complex in the Kanoelehua area brings **Liberty House, Sears, Safeway, Longs** and many other retailers to Hilo. ◆ Off Kanoelehua Ave, Hilo

17 Hilo Orchidarium A quarter-acre tropical garden of splendid orchids and a gift shop that sells orchid plants, some of which are very rare. ◆ Donation requested. M-Sa 9AM-5PM. 524 Manono St, Hilo. 935.8318

18 Waiakea Villas $$ This former Sheraton hotel was converted into condominiums in 1985. Now a three-story walk-up on 14 acres bordering the **Wailoa Pond Freshwater Reserve.** Some of the 141 units (from standard rooms to one-bedroom suites) come with kitchenettes. A bargain if you don't mind the dark, dank corners and slightly offbeat location. Pool and tennis courts. ◆ 400 Hualani St, Hilo. 961.2841, 800/367.7042; fax 961.6797

18 Miyo's ★★$ Japanese-food lovers (and Hilo is a great town for it) flock to this charming eatery at the edge of the Wailoa Pond. The no-smoking dining room overlooks the ponds, with parks and curved bridges in the distance. Specialties include *soba* (buckwheat noodles), *shabu-shabu* (cook-it-yourself vegetables in an earthenware pot), and *miso* soup with fresh mushrooms. Top off the meal with poha berry ice cream by Hilo Homemade. ◆ Japanese ◆ M-Sa 11AM-2PM, 5:30-8:30PM. Waiakea Village, 400 Hualani St, Hilo. 935.2273

19 Dick's Coffee House ★$ A local hangout marked by its low-priced, wholesome food in a humorously kitschy atmosphere. Green Bay Packers pennants, deer antlers, and oversized currency hang from the walls, while waitresses serve up *mahimahi* with eggs, omelets, and all the coffee shop classics. ◆ M-Th, Sa 7AM-10PM; F 7AM-11PM; Su 7-10:30AM. Hilo Shopping Center, 1261 Kilauea Ave, Hilo. 935.2279

19 Restaurant Miwa ★★★$$ Miwa's seasonal menu includes fresh Kona crab available year-round except during the summer months. (The chef recommends swishing some sake in the crab's cavity for added flavor.) Other dishes to try include the ever-popular Bangkok shrimp, tempura, sushi, and the best *haupia* (coconut) cream pie in the world. ◆ Japanese ◆ M-Sa 11AM-10PM; Su 4:30-10PM. Sushi bar M-Th 11AM-2PM, 5PM-midnight; F-Sa 5PM-1AM. Hilo Shopping Center, 1261 Kilauea Ave, Hilo. 961.4454

The Big Island

20 Sun Sun Lau ★$$ This mammoth restaurant provides plenty of elbow room for chowing down sweet-and-sour pineapple shrimp, chop suey, or watercress pork. The Cantonese menu is extensive. The Chinese munchy specialty, cracked seed, is a favorite with Island kids and warrants a big display here. If you have an adventuresome palate, take along some shredded mango or salted lemon seed for the road. ◆ Chinese ◆ M-Tu, Th 10:30AM-8PM; F-Su 10:30AM-9PM. 1055 Kinoole St, Hilo. 935.2808

21 Restaurant Fuji ★$$ A high-ceilinged, pleasant Japanese oasis in a businessperson's hotel, offering *soba* (buckwheat noodles), grilled fish, and *nabeyaki* (vegetables and noodles cooked in an earthenware pot). ◆ Japanese ◆ Tu-Su 11AM-2PM, 5-9PM. 142 Kinoole St, Hilo. 961.3733

22 Sig Zane Designs Designer **Sig Zane** takes the simplest Hawaiian motifs, such as the *ti* leaves, breadfruit, or taro leaf, and prints them on his fabrics to create Island wear that is elegant and educational. Each T-shirt, aloha shirt, muumuu, quilted jacket, and *pareu* (cloth worn as a sarong) imparts the spirit of Hawaii. Zane's wife, **Nalani Kanaka'ole,** is a revered hula master, and their son, **Kuha'o,** is launching his own line of children's clothing, KZD. Look for their shop with the yellow awning, an Island experience not to be missed. ◆ M-Sa 9:30AM-4:30PM. 140 Kilauea Ave, Hilo. 935.7077

23 Hilo Farmers Market Local color abounds at this festive fair. Come early for the best buys in fresh vegetables, flowers, and plants, baked goods, and arts and crafts from more than 80 vendors. Truly an ethnic bonanza, with *malasadas* (Portuguese donuts), pickled turnips, *warabi* (fern shoots), exotic orchids, wing beans, papayas, corn, and various obscure Island offerings. A number of artists got their start here, too, so check out the artwork. ♦ W, Sa 6AM-noon. Kamehameha Ave (Mamo St) Hilo

24 Bears' Coffee ★$ It's amazing that so many people choose this tiny coffee shop to begin their mornings. Always bustling, this classic establishment offers waffles, eggs, croissants, muffins, and bagels, accompanied by espresso and other coffee favorites. Deli sandwiches and salads make this a quick and satisfying midday stop. ♦ M-F 7AM-5PM; Sa 8AM-4PM. 106 Keawe Shop, Hilo. 935.0708

Coffee Country

Along the western slopes of the Big Island's twin volcanoes, Mauna Loa and Mauna Kea, and on the smaller Hualalai, the hillsides are sheltered from wind and sun and the soil is a rich, porous mixture of vegetation and lava rock. These volcanic peaks catch the clouds and hold them until midmorning, creating lush conditions ideal for growing Kona beans—some of the world's finest coffee beans.

Kona coffee (named for the region it's primarily harvested in) is the only coffee grown commercially in the US. Because the coffee's growing conditions are restricted and the beans have to be picked by hand (the red berries holding the two beans ripen at different intervals), Kona is an expensive (but delicious) treat for coffee connoisseurs.

ERIC J.W. LEE

25 Lehua's Bay City Bar and Grill ★★$$ Hilo's hippest gathering place for lunch, dinner, and after hours. The friendly staff serves up excellent soups (especially the chicken curry and clam chowder), *ahi,* and the burger are real crowd-pleasers at lunch. For dinner there's spinach lasagna, grilled prawns and chicken, fresh fish, scampi, and a light medley of east-west specials, including vegetarian dishes. The nightclub offers live contemporary and Hawaiian music. ♦ Continental ♦ M-Sa 11AM-9:30PM; live music F-Sa until 1AM. 11 Waianuenue Ave, Hilo. 935.8055

26 Big Island Gallery The best of the island's artists are represented in this gallery, run by prominent potter **Chiu Leong**. Works include **Hiroki Morinoue's** prints and paintings, **Franco Salmoiraghi's** photography, **Ira Ono's** Trashface collages, **Clayton Amemiya's** wood-fired ceramics, **Henry Bianchini's** bronze sculptures; and **Leong's** designs are all sold here. ♦ M-Sa 10AM-5PM. 95 Waianuenue Ave, Hilo. 969.3313

27 Roussels ★★★$$$ New Orleans-born brothers **Spencer** and **Andrew Oliver** got together with **Herbert Roussels** and opened this fine French-Creole restaurant in 1985. It's located in the historic Masonic Temple Building (meetings are still held upstairs), with 16-foot-high columns and hardwood maple floors. Chef Andrew is a genius with fresh Hawaiian fish, traditional Louisiana gumbo, shrimp remoulade, and roast duck. The Cajun-style blackened fish is legendary, and the lemon mousse a must. ♦ Creole ♦ Daily 5-10PM. 60 Keawe St, Hilo. 935.5111

28 Dolphin Bay Hotel $ Economical and clean, this hotel is one of Hilo's best-kept secrets. The rooms are plain but inviting, and the grounds are lavishly landscaped with bananas, orchids, ginger plants, and a dense tropical forest. There are four types of units in the two-story walk-up, each with a kitchen, TVs, and fans (there's no air-conditioning, and the telephone is in the lobby). You'll love the convenient location and intimate ambience—and the warmth of owners **Margaret, John,** and **Larry Alexander.** ♦ 333 Iliahi St, Hilo. 935.1466

"I think Kona coffee has a richer flavor than any other, be it grown where it may and call it by what name you please."

Mark Twain, 1866

Restaurants/Clubs: Red
Shops/ 🌴 Outdoors: Green

Hotels: Blue
Sights/Culture: Black

29 Lyman Museum and Mission House

The Mission House (pictured below) was among the first wood-frame structures in Hilo, built in 1839 for the **Reverend David Lyman** and his wife **Sarah.** Visitors can still see their 19th-century furnishings, clothing, and other artifacts. The adjoining Lyman Museum, completed in 1973, is one of the least exhausting of Hawaii's museums. The **Island Heritage Gallery** features a *pili* grass house, *kapa* (bark cloth), and carvings and cultural artifacts of Hawaii's ethnic groups. The **Earth Heritage Gallery** displays volcanic and mineral formations, including land shells. ♦ Admission. M-Sa 9AM-5PM; Su 1-4PM. 276 Haili St, Hilo. 935.5021

30 Rainbow Falls Early risers can watch as

the sun peeks over the mango trees, forming a rainbow in the mist of the thundering falls that cascade into the Wailuku River gorge. ♦ Wailuku River State Park, Waianuenue Ave, Hilo

31 The Hilo-Area Mamalahoa Highway Scenic Drive If you're not in a rush, take this scenic drive into the past. Beginning at Wainaku St on the north side of Hilo, occasional signs will direct you to the old wooden-bridged Hamakua Coast road called the Mamalahoa Highway (Hwy 19). You'll pass the ancient, river-mouth surfing spot **Honolii,** then turn off onto the four-mile **Pepeekeo** route overlooking **Onomea Bay,** where sailing ships anchored during the 19th century. This rural road was once filled with sugarcane trains and bullock carts passing to and from markets and mills. Before you get back on the main highway and head toward Kamuela-Waimea and cowboy country, linger at **Akaka Falls,** a 420-foot waterfall into a verdant gorge just off Rte 220 near the town of Honomu. This beautiful spot is celebrated in ancient chants and contemporary love songs. ♦ From Hilo to Waimea Town, about 60 miles, approximately an hour and fifteen minutes driving time

32 Hamakua Coast Drive From Hilo to

Kailua-Kona or vice versa, this drive is for long-distance enthusiasts. North of Waimea, the highway follows a coastline resplendent with mountain greenery and plunging waterfalls. This makes a lasting impression of the Big Island's massive beauty. Roadside attractions include the **Macadamia Nut Factory** in Honokaa and sight-seeing spectacles at **Akaka Falls, Laupahoehoe Point,** and **Waipio Valley.** ♦ From Hilo to Kailua-Kona, approximately 90 miles; about three-hours driving time

33 Hawaii Tropical Botanical Gardens For

a lush botanical experience on the wet Hilo-side of the Big Island, take a small group tour of this rain forest and nature preserve above Onomea Bay. **Daniel J. Lutkenhouse,** a retired California trucking executive who had long been charmed by the rain forests of the Hilo area, formally opened the foundation to the public in 1986. The one-and-a-half- to two-hour tours provide informative tidbits about some of the 1,600 endemic and imported plants, but you can walk around the large lily and *koi* (carp) pond, the giant mango trees, the pungent guava orchard, or the jungle of huge Alexander palms on your own. The exotic plant collection comes from Fiji, Peru, Madagascar, Indonesia, and other parts of the world. Cars are not allowed inside the gardens, so prepare to meander outdoors. Tours begin at a small restored church about a half mile from the garden's entrance on the Mamalahoa Hwy, just off the Hawaii Belt Hwy. Bring mosquito repellent. Parking and restrooms are available. ♦ Donation requested. Tours daily, 8:30AM-4:30PM. On the Scenic Drive to Onomea Bay, seven miles north of Hilo. 964.5233

Lyman Mission House

Nature's Necklaces

When the Polynesians first came to the Hawaiian Islands around AD 500, they brought along remnants of their Asian homeland, and leis were among their most precious keepsakes. The exotic garlands were used in many aspects of Hawaiian daily life and were lovingly refined into an art form. Not only were they ornamental, they displayed rank in religious and spiritual rites. The designs of leis reflected various backgrounds, and historians used to study them to help define emigration patterns.

The Big Island

Today, the art of making leis continues to flourish. The materials used to make leis are either strung together by hand, braided with flowers or greens, sewn to heavy fabric, or wound with cord. And not all leis are made of flowers. Many leis are fashioned out of shells, seeds, feathers, or animal teeth—and these leis last for years, if not forever.

Royalty used to value feather leis, especially bright yellow ones. Royal women wore *lei hulu mans* (bird feather leis) to indicate their high social standing.

Feather leis are more expensive than the shell or nut leis because they take a long time to construct and the most prized feathers are from exotic birds, and they're not readily available. Nowadays, pheasant, geese, peacock, or duck feathers are generally used to make such leis.

More temporary leis are made with fruit, vines, berries, flowers, or leaves. Jasmine, plumeria, orchids, carnations, and ginger are the flowers of choice. The *lei hala*, made from the pandanus tree, has been worn since ancient times. It's considered an aphrodisiac, as well as a symbol of love and the end of bad luck.

The *maile* lei and *mokihana* lei (pictured below) are often worn at important ceremonies. *Maile* is a fragrant, vinelike plant grown in the Hawaiian mountains, and leis made of *maile* are traditionally untied, rather than cut, at opening ceremonies. The *maile* lei was created to honor Laka, the goddess of dance, and is still widely used today. If green *mokihana* berries, grown in the mountains of Kauai, are added to the lei, that signifies a special honor—one reserved for newly married couples or special guests.

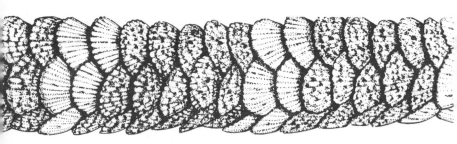

Lei olepe

Peacock lei

Lei mokihana

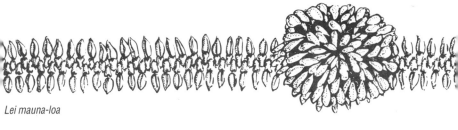

Lei mauna-loa

Lei awapuhi melemele

Lei of mamane, lehua, a ali i, ukae-nene, oa, and palapalai

Tonga

Lei pupu o Niihau

34 Kolekole Beach Park Follow the sign on Hwy 19 to Kolekole Beach Park and your reward will be a cool, freshwater pond fed by Kolekole Falls. A playing field, two picnic pavilions, and camping are also available. ♦ Off Hwy 19, just past Honomu, going north

35 Alaka Falls What sets this 420-foot cascade and its 400-foot companion, **Kahuna Falls**, apart from other waterfalls is the lush 65-acre park that surrounds them. Plants and flowers were brought in from all over the world to create the dense rain forest atmosphere. Sprays of orchids, bamboo groves, carpets of moss, bougainvillea bushes, gin-

gers, azaleas, ferns, and countless other exotic plants will perk up your senses. The moist air and deafening roar of water follow you on the 20-minute hike along the paved path to the waterfalls. ♦ Rte 220 off Hwy 19

36 Mauna Kea A dormant volcano in the northern half of the island, Mauna Kea rises 13,796 feet above sea level. It is the highest point in the Pacific, and its uppermost slopes are generally covered with snow from January through May. Weather permitting, it's quite possible to ski Mauna Kea early in the day and return to the hotel in time for a sunset swim. You may be surprised to learn there's an official **Ski Association of Hawaii,** whose local and mainland members you'll recognize by their *Ski Hawaii* T-shirts. You won't find lifts (or lift lines) at Mauna Kea. Instead, skiers travel 20 miles up a paved road through black lava and cinder cones to reach the snow (which generally starts at 11,000 feet), and then continue up to the start of several runs. Once you've enjoyed one of the three- to five-mile runs, you can hop back into a vehicle and it's back to the top again. Not only are there no ski lifts, there's no snow-covered lodge and no après-ski drinking around a roaring fireplace (nor is there biting wind or dangerous underbrush). Short of hickory skis, this is skiing at its most basic. The gritty texture of the snow is a lot like sand, although veteran skiers compare it to the crisp corn snow of New England. Locals call it "pineapple powder." The long and fast ski runs are natural with snow depths generally ranging from five to six feet, and they have Hawaiian names like **Alii's Run, Pele's Parlor, King Kamehameha's Run,** and **Prince Kuhio's Run. Poi Bowl,** a quarter-mile-wide stretch starting at the **Mauna Kea Observatory** at the summit, is excellent for beginners, while the other runs are steeper and more challenging. If you're interested in skiing, contact the Ski

Association of Hawaii (Box 8327, Honolulu HI 96813—no phone). **Ski Guides Hawaii** on the Big Island provides guides, transportation, and equipment rental (Box 1954, Kamuela HI 96743. 885.4188). ♦ If you don't have a four-wheel drive, the observatory offers tours to the summit on Sa evenings, reservation only. Call Mauna Kea Support Services, 935.3371 for information, M-F 7AM-noon, 1-4PM

37 Laupahoehoe Beach Park This pleasant grassy peninsula is distinguished by a memorial to the 24 students and teachers who lost their lives here in the 1946 tidal wave. The park is on the former Laupahoehoe village site. Picnics and camping. ♦ Off Hwy 19, Laupahoehoe

38 Hotel Honokaa Club ★$ Lobsters in season are fresh and cheap here. Locals come for meals at prices that won't break the bank. The fare is decent and standard—steak and lobster, seafood platters, *mahimahi*—and the large room is accented with vinyl tablecloths and a TV in the corner. Not the most chic place (a bit weird, and strangely lit), but very practical, with loads of local color. ♦ American ♦ M-F 9:30AM-2PM, 5:30-8PM; Sa-Su 7:30-11AM, 5:30-8PM. On Hwy 240 (Mamane St) Honokaa. 775.0678

39 Macadamia Nut Factory You can watch through the large windows of this processing plant as macadamia nuts are made into delicious snacks. The kernels are separated from their hard, brown shells, roasted in coconut oil, and then packed (unless, that is, they aren't first smothered in chocolate, twirled into macadamia nut butter, baked into cookies, or blended into jams). You'll see just how far this designer nut has come since an Australian introduced it to Hawaii in 1881. Free, freshly roasted samples. ♦ Free. Daily 8AM-6PM. Just off Hwy 240, Honokaa. 775.7743

40 Waipio Valley Artworks A remote showcase for Big Island artists, with a pleasing amalgam of paintings, native-wood carvings and bowls, sculptures, furniture, and crafts. The bamboo vases, Mundorff collectibles, Jay Warner koa boxes, Tutuvi T-shirts, and other works stem from Hawaiian motifs. ♦ Daily 8:30AM-5:30PM. Old Village Rd, Kukuihaele. 775.0958

41 Waipio Valley The Hamakua Coast ends at this valley, once favored by Hawaiian royalty. Also known as the **Valley of the Kings** or **The Land of Curving Water,** this was once home to 40,000 Hawaiians, according to oral tradition. Before Captain Cook arrived, Waipio was the cultural and political hub of the island, a pastoral community of taro (from which poi is made) farmers and fishers who left behind many artifacts. Ancient temple sites, stone terraces, waterfalls, and steep valley walls make this an awesome and spiritually inspiring site. The few taro farmers who remain cling to a lifestyle immortalized in the songs and chants of ancient Hawaii. They survived the 1946 tsunami (tidal wave) that wiped out the villages that once thrived in this distant valley. ♦ Waipio Valley Overlook at the end of Hwy 240, just past Kukuihaele

42 Waipio Hotel $ If you like roughing it, nothing can equal the original Waipio Valley hostelry, **Tom Araki's** barrackslike "hotel" with no electricity. The five-room retreat is a haven for reclusive seekers of a paradise without phones, restaurants, and other comforts. Bring your own food, flashlights, and towels—everything else is here, including taro fields in the front yard and a view of waterfalls, clean shelter, and a more-than-adequate communal kitchen. ♦ 25 Malama Place, Waipio Valley. 775.0368

Nuts for Macadamias

The macadamia nut is a native of Australia, where **Dr. John Macadam,** an Australian chemist, gave his name to the Queensland nut. The first macadamia seeds were sent to Hawaii in the 1880s for the planting of ornamental trees. By 1921 the commercial potential of the macadamia was realized as it became a popular snack food, and the first plantation was started near Honolulu. By the eighties, more than 29 million pounds of macadamia nuts (which resemble filberts) were being harvested on the Islands annually—almost all for export.

The dark green macadamia tree is a subtropical evergreen that can grow as tall as 40 feet. Many species have spiked leaves similar to holly that are used as holiday ornaments. The tree bears fruit in five years, reaching its peak of productivity after 15 years. Inside the green, oval-shaped shell, the macadamia meat rests within another hard shell, which is difficult to break without crushing the tender nut. The long maturation period and limited supply contribute to the nut's not-so-cheap price, but the macadamia is holding its own among its snack nut competitors.

For a firsthand look at how macadamia nuts are made into exotic snacks, visit the **Macadamia Nut Factory** in Honokaa on the Big Island. They'll even give you free, freshly roasted samples (see page 16 for details).

ERIC J.W. LEE

43 The Tree House $$$ A 30-foot-high monkeypod tree with all the comforts. **Linda Beech's** Tree House is an exotic offering, a one-room cabin with one double and one single bed, a refrigerator, hot plates, electricity, and running water. A waterfall and mountain pool are just down the trail, and a Japanese hot tub simmers nearby. Standard rental cars can't make it down to the Waipio Valley, so you'll need to make transportation arrangements through **Waipio Shuttle** or Linda Beech. One warning: For about 10 days every year, the cottage is inaccessible because of high river water. If guests are stranded, their

accommodations during the delay are complimentary. This is a good base for trail rides and wagon and horseback-riding tours that can be arranged in the valley. ♦ Off Hwy 240, Waipio Valley. 775.7160

44 Parker Ranch Broiler ★$$$ The Parker name is everywhere in this neck of the woods, and since the **Parker Ranch** people own this handsome western-style restaurant, you'll be cutting into their Big Island beef (not to be ranked with Iowa corn-fed beef). Big appetites will enjoy the buffet lunch. ♦ American ♦ Daily 11AM-2PM (bar only 2-3PM) 5-10PM. Parker Ranch Shopping Center, Waimea. 885.7366

45 Waimea This town's 2,500-foot elevation provides a cool, crisp climate that you may find refreshing after baking on the hot beaches of West Hawaii. Volcanic cinder cones long covered by greenery are dotted with grazing cattle. **Mauna Kea** looms in the distance, flower and vegetable farms abound, and *paniolos* (cowboys) in boots and hats add a real western flavor. Few people realize that Hawaii's *paniolo* (a derivative of the word Español) predate the American West, having come from Spain and Mexico at the request of **Kamehameha III** in the 1830s to teach the Hawaiians how to ride, rope, and herd cattle. Today Hawaiian cowboys may be Filipino, Portuguese, Chinese, Japanese, or any and all mixtures therein.

Waimea is cowboy country thanks to **John Parker,** a seaman from New England who jumped ship in 1809, settled on the Big Island, and domesticated a herd of wild cattle that British captain **George Vancouver** had given to **Kamehameha the Great.** The King, who gave Parker some land in exchange, also had a granddaughter that Parker married. The Parker Ranch dynasty was born. Today Parker Ranch consists of 225,000 acres, with 50,000 head of cattle. You can tour the ranch, visit its original two-acre homestead, or walk through owner **Richard Smart's** historic home, **Puuopelu,** and his extensive Impressionist art collection.

Waimea is a friendly town, checkered with funky-looking buildings, grazing horses and cattle, and the stately homes of the landed gentry. It is also a boomtown, growing rapidly (too rapidly for some). Considering the number of signs with the name "Parker" on them—Parker Ranch Shopping Center, Parker Ranch Broiler, Parker Ranch Visitor Center, Parker Ranch Lodge, and Parker School (private)—it doesn't take long to figure out who runs the town. Curiously out of step with the Parker monopoly is the **Kahilu Theatre,** the $2.5 million baby of Richard Smart (great, great, great grandson of John

Parker). Many Big Islanders regard the Kahilu as the Island's cultural magnet, drawing people in their up-country finery to plays, concerts, and various other cultural events. Some may wonder why the town isn't called Kamuela, which is Hawaiian for Samuel (after **Samuel Parker,** the grandson of John Parker), because Kamuela is the official post office address for Waimea, to avoid confusion with the other Waimea on the island of Kauai. By whatever name, this town is a fine place to visit. ♦ From Kailua-Kona, take Hwys 19 or 190 north (39 miles, an hour and a half drive); from Hilo, take Hwy 19 north (59 miles, two-hour drive)

Parker Ranch

46 Parker Ranch Visitor Center and Museum A narrated slide show depicts the history of the 225,000-acre Parker Ranch, the largest privately owned ranch in the US (only the corporate-owned King Ranch in Texas is larger), and describes the life of the Hawaiian cowboys. Parker family memorabilia and photographs on display. ♦ Admission. M-Sa 10AM-5PM. Parker Ranch Shopping Center, Waimea. 885.7655

47 Aloha Luigi $ Pastas, pizza, and homemade sausages and sauces served in unpretentious surroundings in the middle of town. Small, busy, and redolent with the smell of garlic and cheese. You can order takeout or sit at one of the handful of tables, often crowded at lunchtime with students from the nearby school. ♦ Italian ♦ M-Sa 11AM-9PM. Junction of Hwys 19 and 190, Waimea. 885.7277

47 Edelweiss ★★$$ German-born chef/owner **Hans-Peter Hager** opened Edelweiss in 1984. It's a small place (only 15 tables in a rustic, *paniolo*-style setting of hewn, open beams), but on any given night, chef Hager offers 14 to 18 house specials, ranging from roast duck Brigarade to Molokai venison, and a superb rack of lamb basted in garlic, mustard, and fine herbs. Also recommended are the *hasenpfeffer* (roast rabbit) and his state-of-the-art weinerschnitzel. The desserts—homemade Bavarian pudding, cheesecake, and fruit pies—are worthy finales to the feast. A caveat: No reservations are accepted, so expect long lines. ♦ German ♦ Tu-Sa 11:30AM-1:30PM, 5-9PM. Hwy 19, Waimea. 885.6800

47 Gallery of Great Things This selection of artifacts from Hawaii, Indonesia, Papua New Guinea, and throughout the Pacific leans toward the tribal. Jade carvings, chopsticks made of native and exotic woods, Indonesian baskets, koa furniture, coconut-fiber hats, watercolors, oils, lithographs, and jewelry make for interesting shopping. ♦ M-Sa 9AM-5PM. Parker Square, Hwy 19, Waimea. 885.7706

48 Bread Depot Just follow the aroma of breads and cinnamon rolls to find this popular venue for freshly baked breads, such as caraway rye and *paniolo* (a variation of French sourdough), passion fruit muffins, cheese brioches, and deli sandwiches and soups. Plan on the clam chowder for lunch, but get there early—it goes fast. Salads change daily and desserts seasonally, which means that if you're here during *lilikoi* (passion fruit), mango, or guava seasons, expect hints of them in the coulis and tropical cheesecakes. Very small, with seating for 14, and a brisk take-out business. ♦ Daily 6AM-3PM. Opelo Plaza, Hwy 19, Waimea. 885.6354

48 Merriman's ★★★$$$ Chef/owner **Peter Merriman** pioneered the development of Hawaii's regional cuisine, giving new meaning to the word "fresh." His innovative use of seaweed, *opihi* (limpets), sea urchin (sometimes he dives for it himself), and Island-raised beef, lamb, and veal is legendary. The *mahimahi* and *ono* are in his kitchen soon after they're caught, the veal is naturally raised in Waimea, the goat cheese is made in Puna, and the strawberries and tomatoes are grown down the road. Specialties include the wok-charred *ahi*, Kahua lamb, lokelani tomato salad, and for dessert, passion fruit mousse. ♦ Hawaiian ♦ M-F 11:30AM-1:30PM, 5:30-9PM; Sa-Su 5:30-9PM. Opelo Plaza, Hwy 19, Waimea. 885.6822

49 Hale Kea This former Parker Ranch manager's home, built in 1897, is now a beautifully restored, 11-acre complex with English gardens, a museum, a restaurant, and a shopping center. ♦ Daily 10AM-10PM. Kawaihae Rd, Waimea. 885.6095

Within Hale Kea:
Hartwell's ★$$$ A high-ceilinged lodge with a fireplace and several cozy dining alcoves, each with its own character. Ranch memorabilia provides the backdrop for hearty pastas, lamb, *lilikoi*-glazed duckling, fresh Island catch, and breakfast flapjacks (Su only). ♦ Continental ♦ M-Sa 11AM-8:30PM; Su 10AM-8:30PM. 885.6095

MAYA GALLERY

Maya Gallery Works by nationally renowned artists such as **Dorothy Dehner** and **Herman Cherry** are represented here. Fine arts, including furniture, fill half of the gallery, and the other half is devoted to crafts and folk arts, such as handmade paper, exotic Japanese soaps, handcrafted jewelry, and native wood bowls. Clothing and accessories made of kimono silk also featured. ♦ Daily 10AM-6PM. 885.9633

Noa Noa You'll want to linger in this shop if only to marvel at the Indonesian goods, including batiks, jewelry, drums, antiques, quilts, and vases. ♦ Daily 9:30AM-8PM. 885.5541

New Vintage Country Store Tropical **Dreams,** makers of nut butters and ice cream, expanded their line with this store. They offer fine cotton dresses and men's shirts by Komil, Caswell-Massey soaps, and dainty country accoutrements that correspond with the rustic feeling of Waimea. Don't forget the macadamia and mocha nut butters at the rear of the store. ♦ Daily 10AM-6PM. 885.2133

Trail Blazers

If you want to experience the Big Island's *paniolo* (cowboy) country, there's no better way than to saddle up on a horse. **Ironwood Outfitters** offers trail rides into the pastures and highlands of the Kahua Ranch, a 30,000-acre, cattle-raising spread in the Kohala foothills. Owner/operator **Judith Ellis** will set you up with a fine quarter horse, thoroughbred, or Morgan for the leisurely journey up the 4,000-foot elevation of the Kohala Mountain range. Choose from Ironwood's Top of the Mountain Ride (daily 10AM to 1PM), late-afternoon horseback tours (one- to one-and-a-half-hours long), and private equestrian rides. Make reservations at least a day in advance, especially during August and around Christmas. For more information, call 885.4941.

Waipio Na'a'apa Trail Rides offers horseback tours along the Black Sand Beach. You start at the Waipio Lookout parking lot, just outside the town of Honokaa, by hopping into their four-wheel-drive vehicle, which takes you down a thousand feet (on a treacherously steep road) and across the valley to their stables. The two-and-a-half-hour ride follows Waipio Beach. For more information, call 775.0419.

Restaurants/Clubs: Red   Hotels: Blue
Shops/ ♦ Outdoors: Green   Sights/Culture: Black

49 Waimea Gardens Cottage $$ **Barbara Campbell** knows all about hospitality. She is a longtime resident of Waimea, where she has combined the advantages of a lovely cottage in a wonderful location with her professional savvy (Campbell worked for the Kona Village Resort for more than 20 years). Her cottage is ensconced among geraniums, ferns, roses, Easter lilies, and a graceful willow tree in the front yard. A charming bed and breakfast—immaculate—with full kitchen, desk, and all the conveniences. Campbell handles a referral service to the best B&B operations on the island, so if hers is full

The Big Island

she'll know where to book you instead. ♦ Off Kawaihae Hwy, Waimea. 885.4550, 800/262.9912

50 Kamuela Museum A very unorthodox museum whose founder, Big Island native **Albert K. Solomon,** says his Hawaiian grandmother predicted when he was eight years old that he would open a museum. It took several decades, but she was right. The museum represents 54 years of former Honolulu policeman Solomon's collection of international items, some of them antiques and some just plain junk. Opened in 1968 by Solomon and his wife, who continue to operate it (their home is in the same building), the museum ranks somewhere between an institution and a weekend flea market. Undocumented and unorganized, there's everything from a Model-T tire remover to an old Japanese harp and ancient Hawaiian feather money. ♦ Admission. Daily 8AM-4PM. At the junction of Hwys 19 and 250 in Waimea. 885.4724

51 Ohana Pizza & Beer Garden ★★$$ A good North Kohala place to stop for a pizza when driving around this side of the Big Island. Outdoor beer garden with chilled imports and sandwiches, salads, and fresh fish. ♦ Pizza ♦ Daily 11AM-10PM. Hwy 270, Hawi. 889.5888

52 Original King Kamehameha I Statue This statue may have a less dazzling setting than the Honolulu replica across from Iolani Palace, but its history is richer. For $10,000, American sculptor **Thomas R. Gould** was commissioned in 1878 by the Hawaiian Legislature, at the urging of **King Kalakaua,** to do a statue of the mighty warrior king in commemoration of the centennial anniversary of Captain Cook's arrival in Hawaii. Gould studied a photograph of handsome Honolulu businessman **John Baker,** a close friend of King Kalakaua, who posed in loincloth, feather cloak, spear, and helmet as inspiration for Kamehameha. Gould's clay figure was finished in Florence, Italy; sent to Paris, France for bronze casting; and eventually shipped from Bremen, Germany, to Hawaii. Nearing Cape Horn, the ship burned and sank at Port Stanley in the Falkland Islands, carrying the statue and its nine-ton shipping crate to the bottom of the sea, presumably lost forever. Gould agreed to do another statue for $7,500. This one reached Honolulu intact and was unveiled on 14 February 1883, during Kalakaua's coronation. A few weeks later, to everyone's surprise, the original Kamehameha statue arrived in Honolulu on a British ship whose skipper had bought it for $500 from a salvage yard. The skipper's asking price was $1,500. Since one hand was broken off and the spear was missing, Kalakaua talked him down to $875 and

The Big Island

then had the statue repaired and sent to the sleepy town of Kapaau, in North Kohala, where Kamehameha was born. The Honolulu statue is more fanciful, but the original is more honest, an appropriate homage to the great Kamehameha, whose name means, literally, The Lonely One. ♦ Off Hwy 27, in front of the Kapaau Courthouse in Kapaau, North Kohala District

53 Tropical Dreams Tropical Dreams macadamia nut butters and gourmet ice creams have a strong following on the island, and this is where they're made. Stop here for a *lilikoi* sorbet or papaya ice cream (the coconut and macadamia nut ice creams are also exemplary. Most of the island's upscale restaurants serve Tropical Dreams ice cream; you'll soon know why. ♦ M-F 9AM-5PM; Sa 10AM-5PM; Su 11AM-5PM. Off Hwy 270, Kapaau. 889.5386

54 Keokea Beach Park Picnic and camping facilities on a cliff overlooking the ocean. ♦ Northwest end of Hwy 270, Niulii

55 Lapakahi State Historical Park This restored ancient Hawaiian fishing village is a dramatic seaside setting. Take a casual self-guided tour among the stone enclosures, stone-house sites, canoe sheds, fishing shrines, and stone games displayed here. You will learn about the local legends, fishing customs and techniques, salt gathering, and the honest, simple life of the sea centuries ago. ♦ Daily 8AM-4PM. Off Hwy 270, Mahukona. 889.5566

Hawaii from Top to Bottom

The eight major Hawaiian Islands illustrated below lie 2,400 miles off the coast of North America and cover about 400 miles of the Pacific Ocean. Nearly all of Hawaii's population live on these islands, although there are another 124 islands and atolls northwest of Niihau that complete Hawaii's archipelago.

All the Islands are actually tips of enormous volcanoes. Centuries ago, these submerged volcanoes erupted over and over, building up lava until they finally emerged above the ocean surface. The summits of these major islands, which are the youngest islands in the chain, range from 13,796 feet on the Big Island to 1,477 feet on Kahoolawe.

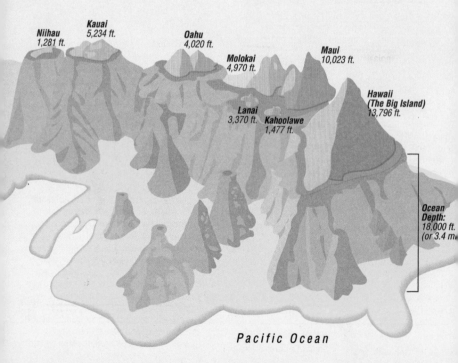

Niihau 1,281 ft.
Kauai 5,234 ft.
Oahu 4,020 ft.
Molokai 4,970 ft.
Maui 10,023 ft.
Lanai 3,370 ft.
Kahoolawe 1,477 ft.
Hawaii (The Big Island) 13,796 ft.
Ocean Depth: 18,000 ft. (or 3.4 m.

Pacific Ocean

56 Cafe Pesto ★★★$$ Unobtrusive, down-to-business, and unequivocally the best pizza house on the island. Even from the parking lot the smell of garlic seductively hints at the smoked salmon-and-basil pizza, and the oriental mushroom-and-artichoke pizza with rosemary Gorgonzola sauce, all baked in New York-style crusts. The pastas and salads (with fresh rosemary, arugula, and Waimea greens) hold their own, too. ♦ Pizza ♦ M-Th, Su 11AM-9PM; F-Sa 11AM-10PM. Off Hwy 270, Kawaihae Center, Kawaihae. 882.1071

56 Harrington's ★★★$$$ Informal ambience with a sunset view, and good pastas and seafood—a memorable restaurant. Pasta jambalaya, linguine with scallops in pesto sauce, and capellini with escargots are some of the specials that have earned Harrington's a loyal following. ♦ Seafood ♦ M-Sa 5:30-10PM. Off Hwy 270, Kawaihae Center, Kawaihae. 882.7997

57 Samuel M. Spencer Beach Park A white sand beach with swimming, and picnic and camping facilities around a large, old stone pavilion. ♦ Off Hwy 270, Kawaihae

58 Pu'ukohola Heiau National Historic Site This mammoth structure of carefully placed lava rocks and boulders is the largest restored *heiau* (temple) in Hawaii. Built in 1550 and rebuilt by **King Kamehameha** more than two centuries later, it serves as a powerful reminder of the practice of human sacrifice in the ancient Hawaiian religion. At its dedication in 1791, Kamehameha invited his archrival to the ceremony and then offered him up as a human sacrifice. A prophecy of the time held that Kamehameha would conquer and unite the islands if he erected a temple to his family war god on the hill at Kawaihae; the prophecy was fulfilled after the erection of Pu'ukohola. The fortress-like structure is also a marvel of engineering, with waterworn lava rocks and boulders set together without mortar. It measures 224 feet by 100 feet. ♦ Daily 7:30AM-4PM. Hwy 270, south of Kawaihae. 882.7218

59 Mauna Kea Beach Hotel $$$$ Although nothing can diminish the Mauna Kea's flawless and legendary **Robert Trent Jones Jr. Golf Course,** the accommodations, service, and dining appear to have lost some of their luster. **Laurance S. Rockefeller** chose this isolated locale for its pristine, crescent-shaped beach and consistently sunny weather. The classic design of the hotel, built in 1965, gives it a graceful appearance as it recedes from the sea into the mountains. The terraced buildings maximize the ocean views. More than a half-million plants of nearly 200 varieties were brought in from other Islands to landscape the spacious grounds and courtyards. Mauna Kea is literally an art museum without walls, with more than 1,600 art objects from throughout Pacific-Polynesia, Thailand, Japan, Sri Lanka, New Guinea, China, and Hawaii. Framed Hawaiian quilts hang on the walls. Mauna Kea offers the modified American Plan (room rates include breakfast and dinner) and the European Plan (room only) year-round. There are 310 rooms, no TVs, and 13 plexipave tennis courts. On his first

visit, **Merv Griffin** proclaimed, "Now I know where old Republicans come to die." ♦ One Mauna Kea Beach Drive, Kohala Coast. 882.7222, 800/882.6060; fax 882.7552

Within the Mauna Kea Beach Hotel:

Mauna Kea Buddha This seventh-century Indian Buddha (pictured below), a 1,500-pound pink granite form, sits on a solid block of Canadian black granite in the shade of a bodhi tree.

Cafe Terrace ★$$$ The fresh ingredients used for the cafe's buffet have made the Mauna Kea a major proponent of regional cuisine and supporter of local farmers, fishers, and ranchers. Hawaiian fern shoot salad, many varieties of sashimi, and mounds of fresh Island specialties share billing with the ocean view. ♦ Continental ♦ Daily noon-2:30PM. 882.7222

Mauna Kea Buddha

Batik Room, The Dining Pavilion, The Garden $$$$ The Batik Room (where only dinner is served) offers Pacific and Far East specialties in the hotel's most formal setting. The Dining Pavilion serves breakfast and, California-style cuisine for dinner, with alfresco dining during the day. The Garden's new menu honors fresh local ingredients such as Big Island-raised abalone, *mahimahi,* and *ohelo* berry mousse. ◆ Batik Room: daily 7-10PM. The Dining Pavilion: M 6:30-11AM; Tu-Su 6:30-11AM, 6:30-9PM. The Garden: call for dinner schedule. 882.7222

The Big Island

Mauna Kea Luau ★★$$ A very upscale luau, with Hawaiian delicacies (and some non-Hawaiian alternatives) served on the hotel's grassy oceanside gardens. The feast includes *hulihuli* (spit-roasted) pig, *kalua* pig on special occasions, poi, *lomilomi* salmon, and baked taro as well as steaks, chicken, ribs, and crab claws. ◆ Hawaiian ◆ Tu 6PM. 882.7222

59 Mauna Kea Golf Course Generally credited, or cursed, as Hawaii's toughest course, this land was reclaimed from ancient lava flows, and designed by **Robert Trent Jones Jr.** Other than a few refinements, particularly the dome-shaped greens, the course remains an ego bruiser for even the above-average golfer and a severe threat to misdirected shots. It is also a beautiful layout, with the ocean always in sight. Ranked among America's 100 greatest golf courses and designated "Hawaii's finest" by *Golf Digest,* the course hosts two tournaments annually, the Pro-Am in July and an Invitational in early December. An 18-hole course, par 72, 7,000 yards. ◆ Expensive green fees; preferred starting times and rates for hotel guests. Off Hwy 19. Pro shop. 882.7222

60 Hapuna Beach State Park This long white sand beach is great for bodysurfing that can border on the treacherous when the currents are especially strong. Follow the warnings posted when swimming is hazardous. Sorry, no camping (but the State Parks Department rents A-frame cabins nearby). Picnic facilities are available. ◆ Off Hwy 19, south of Mauna Kea

---

Mauna Kea and **Mauna Loa** on the Big Island are the tallest mountains in the world when measured from the ocean floor. They are both more than 30,000 feet high.

With an elevation of 13,020 feet, **Lake Waiau,** on the Big Island's Mauna Kea, is the third highest lake in the US and the highest in Hawaii. Niihau's **Halalii Lake** is the largest in the state.

Restaurants/Clubs: Red
Shops/ 🌴 **Outdoors:** Green
Hotels: Blue
Sights/Culture: Black

61 Puako Petroglyph Archaeological Park
One of the largest—3,000 units—clusters of petroglyphs in Hawaii, officially placed on the State and National Historic Registers in 1982. The Mauna Lani Resort established this public park mainly to protect the petroglyphs, which have been subjected to vandalism, theft, foot traffic, and even damage from bulldozers after recent fires in the area. A natural trail system with controlled access is posted with signs that describe the archaeological sites at the newly opened **Holoholokai Beach Park** at the north end of the resort. Viewers are asked not to step on the stone carvings or make rubbings from them (an area has been provided where you can make rubbings from replica petroglyphs). Damaged petroglyphs are open to public view so visitors can realize the consequences. ◆ Off Mauna Lani Dr; entrance in the Mauna Lani Resort

62 Francis H. Ii Brown Golf Course Since it opened in 1981, these emerald fairways and greens, carved out of a 16th-century lava flow, have received worldwide attention. Two 9-hole courses have been added to the original **North Course** and **South Course.** All 36 holes look like sculptured masterpieces flowing brilliantly through the black *a'a* and *pahoehoe* lava fields lined by groves of twisted *kiawe* trees. Ocean views are almost secondary. Both courses are par 72, 7,015 yards. ◆ Expensive green fees. Preferred starting times and rates for Mauna Lani Resort guests. Off Hwy 19. Pro shop. 885.6655

63 Ritz-Carlton Mauna Lani $$$$ The signature cobalt-blue vases and china contrast nicely with the crimson blooms of the roses the hotel had specially cultivated in Waimea. The decor is old-world elegant, with antique armoires filled with rare china. More than 1,000 works of art grace the walls and hallways. The 19th-century English and American paintings set the tone of excellence that pervades the 542-room hotel. Chandeliers of Baccarat crystal (and quartz crystal too, an unusual touch) light up the dining rooms and hallways done in padded silk-brocade wall coverings, koa paneling, Italian marble, and Renaissance-inspired upholstery. The 32-acre property has two six-story wings facing the ocean. The comfortable rooms have celadon-green walls and marble bathrooms with separate showers and tubs. Outside you'll find a 10,000-square-foot swimming pool adjacent to an artifically constructed, but inviting, white sand lagoon. The manicured grounds feature myriad plantings selected for color, cultural integrity, and fragrance. The **Ritz-Carlton Club** tops the Kohala wing with its own lounge, tea service, elevator key, and special privileges. Tennis buffs can choose from 11 courts, and golfers are very near the Mauna Lani's fabled **Francis H. Ii Brown Golf Course.** ♦ Deluxe ♦ One North Kaniku Dr, Kohala Coast. 885.2000, 800/241.3333; fax 885.5778

Within the Ritz-Carlton Mauna Lani:

The Dining Room, The Grill Restaurant and Lounge, The Cafe Restaurant and Lounge $$$$ Executive chef **Philippe Padovani** brought his considerable talents here from the Halekulani Hotel (and its stellar La Mer) on Oahu and lost no time earning a reputation on the Big Island. The Dining Room offers *kiawe*-smoked (mesquite) Norwegian salmon, duck liver terrine, and lamb loin medaillons with artichoke jardiniere. The Symphony of Desserts, a seduction of strawberry sunburst, chocolate Saint Remon, and fresh pear tart makes for a grand finale. The Grill's masculine, clublike atmosphere suits the menu of fresh seafood and steaks—classics with an innovative regional twist. A plush private dining room is available for parties of up to 14 people. The Cafe, however, is Padovani's creative statement, with Asian specialties highlighting fresh seafood and local produce. ♦ Dining Room: daily 6-10PM. Jacket required; reservations recommended. Grill: daily 6-10PM. Cafe: daily 6:30-11AM; 11:30AM-10:30PM. 885.2000

Inter-Pacific Some of the finest shopping in Hawaii is located right here. The **Giorgio Armani** boutique offers ties, suits, and high-priced sportswear by the Italian designer, with American designs by **Ralph Lauren Polo** next door. Swimwear and casual wear are also available. Women also can choose from **Bottega Veneta, Anne Klein, Nina Ricci, Adrienne Vittadini,** and more. ♦ Daily 9AM-10PM. 885.2000 ext 7162

64 Mauna Lani Bay Hotel and Bungalows $$$$ The only five-diamond Hotel on the Big Island, and one of but four in Hawaii. The $80-million hotel opened with a world-class flourish in 1983 and soon began winning

accolades and awards—for its historic preservation, golf course, and overall excellence. This distinctively Hawaiian landmark combines the highest standards of European and Hawaiian hospitality: grace, style, architectural excellence, and a charming aloha spirit. Inside the blue-tiled courtyard, you'll find a waterfall leading to the Grand Atrium, filled with fish ponds, rare orchids, and the chatter of Kona Coast birds. Rooms (built at a cost of $200,000 each) include teak and rattan furnishings, color TVs hidden away in armoires, roomy baths with twin vanities, and wide verandas. More than 90 percent of the 354 rooms have ocean views, and 27 rooms face the Mauna Kea and Mauna Loa mountains. Deep pockets may prefer the five $2,500-a-day, 4,000-square-foot bungalows with private pools and 24-hour butler service. Families may prefer the luxurious one- and two-bedroom ocean villas within the 80-unit **Terrace** condominium complex. The grounds feature prehistoric Hawaiian fish ponds and a 16th-century lava flow with shelter caves and petroglyphs. Golfers can play the newly expanded 36-hole **Francis H. Ii Brown Golf Course,** and tennis buffs can volley in the 10-court **Tennis Garden.** There's also wind-

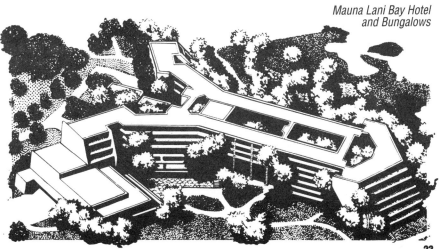

Mauna Lani Bay Hotel and Bungalows

surfing, canoeing, and scuba diving just off-shore. Daily classes in Hawaiian fishing techniques and hula-aerobics are highly recommended. An exceptional experience. ♦ Deluxe ♦ Off Mauna Lani Dr, Kohala Coast. 885.6622, 800/367.2323; fax 885.6183

Within the Mauna Lani Bay Hotel and Bungalows:

The Canoe House ★★★★$$$ A rare match of ambience and consistently impressive cuisine fired by the imagination of chef **Alan Wong**. Dine indoors, where a large koa canoe dangles from the high ceiling; or out-

doors, where the sea is always lit—if not by the setting sun, then by the night lights shining on the white lines of waves. Specialties include seared rare *ahi* with fern shoots and Chinese sausage, lobster won-ton ravioli, bamboo-steamed *mahimahi* (flawless), and *poha* (berry-glazed rack of lamb with Island sweet potatoes). The *pupu* (appetizer) assortment is also worth trying. ♦ Pacific Rim ♦ Daily 5:30-10PM. 885.6622

Le Soleil ★★★$$$$ The exceptional wine list here won *The Wine Spectator's* Award of Excellence in 1990 (a first among Big Island restaurants). The high-priced, small, and select menu includes steak, lamb, venison, seafood, duck, and veal in classic preparations with a local twist. Soothing dark green and amber tones, piano music, candlelight, and a garden view make this a romantic dining experience. Menu changes regularly. ♦ Continental ♦ Daily 6:30-9:30PM. Jackets required. 885.6622

Bay Terrace ★★$$$ Pleasant alfresco dining—three meals a day—with *malasadas* (Portuguese donuts) for starters, and pastas and sandwiches at lunch. Candlelight and an à la carte menu of international cuisine make for romantic dinners. ♦ Continental ♦ M-Sa 6-11AM, 11:30AM-2PM; Su 11:30AM-2PM, 6-9PM. Jackets required for men. 885.6622

The Gallery ★★$$ Renowned chef **Peter Merriman** got his start here. The informal dining room serves mostly American fare, with an emphasis on the fresh seafood caught and cultivated on the Big Island. Daily fish selections can be prepared four ways including sautéed with Island *lilikoi* (passion fruit) and cilantro beurre blanc, and vegetarian black bean chili and shrimp phyllo add an international flavor. ♦ American ♦ Daily 6:30-9:30PM. 885.7777

Knickers ★★$$ Four seasons pasta, and *soba* (buckwheat noodles), sandwiches, hamburgers, seafood, and steaks round out the luncheon menu. For dinner, the selections are upgraded to bouillabaisse, prime rib, London broil, and sautéed Hawaiian

snapper. ♦ Continental ♦ Daily 6:30-9:30AM, 11AM-3PM, 5:30-9:30PM. At the Mauna Lani Golf Course. 885.6699

65 The Kings Course, Beach Course, Waikoloa Village Golf and Country Club The newest and most challenging of these is the par 72, 7,064-yard Kings Course, adjacent to the Royal Waikoloan. Designed by **Tom Weiskopf** and **Jay Morris**, it opened in 1990 with six lakes, nine acres of water, 83 sand traps, and a 25,000-square-foot clubhouse. The par 70, 6,507-yard Beach Course is also adjacent to the Royal Waikoloan, and the par 72, 6,687-yard Waikoloa Village Golf and Country Club is just six miles north of the hotel. These courses were both designed by **Robert Trent Jones Jr.** ♦ Kings Course: 885.4647. Beach Course: 885.6060. Waikoloa Village Golf and Country Club: 883.9621

66 Hyatt Regency Waikoloa $$$ Described as a Disneyesque-mega resort by those who favor more intimate settings, the challenge here is finding your room via the labyrinth of walkways, tramways, and waterways that wind through the 62-acre site. The gargantuan three-building complex has more than a mile of waterways (traveled by a dozen 24-passenger canal boats), a mile-long museum walkway, and endless paths and gardens.

Developer **Chris Hemmeter** and partners pulled out all the stops with this super resort. The $360-million hotel is more like a small city, with two main swimming pools, waterfalls, waterslides, 19 meeting rooms, and the largest health spa on the island. The 25,000-square-foot spa offers European herbal treatments, fitness classes, nutrition counseling, steam rooms, saunas, whirlpools, and Jacuzzi tubs. Resident astronomer **Eddie Mahoney** leads picnic tours to the Mauna Kea summit, where he explains (in nonbaffling lingo) the workings of the powerful telescopes. The hotel's restaurants include **Spats, Donatoni's,** and the **Kona Provision Co.** ♦ Deluxe ♦ One Waikoloa Beach Dr, Kohala Coast. 885.1234, 800/228.9000; fax 885.5737

67 Anaehoomalu Bay This crescent-shaped beach fronting the Royal Waikoloan is an inviting playground (with public access) for windsurfing, scuba diving, swimming, and sunning. The ancient royal fish ponds behind the beach are preserved by the hotel. ♦ Off Queen Kaahumanu Hwy, 18 miles north of Keahole Airport

Kona Village Resort Hut

68 Royal Waikoloan $$$ This smaller, more modest neighbor to the flamboyant Hyatt Waikoloa is for those who favor a more intimate Hawaiian ambience. Recent renovations (to the tune of $10 million) have spruced up the 543 rooms. The wide, generous **Anaehoomalu Bay,** essentially in the front yard, is a key attraction along with the **Royal Cabana Club,** a 16-room, two-story structure on the lagoon, Sunday luaus, a fitness center, six tennis courts, and two nearby championship golf courses. ♦ Off Queen Kaahumanu Hwy, Kohala Coast. 885.6789, 800/537.9800; fax 885.7852

Within the Royal Waikoloan:

Tiare Room $$$$ Dinner is served in this romantic room of rich woods, etched glass, and crystal. The menu includes Molokai venison, roast duckling, and a plantation platter of lobster medallions, filet mignon, sautéed fresh Island fish, and baked stuffed shrimp. ♦ Continental ♦ M-Sa 6:30-9:30PM

69 Hale Moana ★★$$$ Chef **Glenn Alos** has made this room his own creative playground. The luncheon buffet, with elegant samplings of Island favorites, is a splendid seaside repast. Dinner selections include fresh *opakapaka* broiled with saffron and orange butter, *ono* sautéed with lime and macadamia nut beurre blanc, boneless quail in Cajun spices, and many other hearty offerings. Five panels displayed in this high-ceilinged Polynesian *hale* (house) pictorially describe Captain Cook's voyages to Hawaii. The panels, entitled *Les Sauvages de la Mer Pacifique,* are made of perfectly preserved 18th-century French wallpaper. They were rolled up and stored in a Paris attic for more than 100 years before an American collector discovered them. ♦ Reservations for non-guests. Daily 7:15-9:30AM, 12:30-2PM, 6-9:30PM. 325.5555

69 Kona Village Resort $$$$
Paradise for those seeking solitude, romance, and the best of Polynesia: thatched bungalows, reflective lagoons, turtles in the clear offshore waters, and lazy days on the beach. A two-mile drive from the front gate takes you through a black desert of lava to the hotel. (Nothing even vaguely resembles the standard hotel experience here.) Lean over a *lauhala* (woven pandanus) desktop to the cash register, then ride to your *hale* (thatched A-frame bungalow) on a jitney. You will have reached the seashore, where there are lagoons, swaying palms, peacocks that roam freely, and comfortable accommodations without TVs, telephones, or other distractions. The 125 thatched bungalows, sprawling over 82 acres, are replicas of New Zealand, Samoan, Tahitian, Hawaiian, and other Polynesian structures. The expensive price tag includes three meals, snorkeling gear, catamaran rides, and all the amenities. Casual dress is the rule. ♦ Off Queen Kaahumanu Hwy, Kailua-Kona, about six miles north of Keahole Airport. 325.5555, 800/367.5290

Kona Village Resort

Within the Kona Village Resort:

Kona Village Luau ★★★★$$$ The best luau in the Islands. Guests and nonguests begin with a 5:30PM tour of the luau grounds, then witness the unveiling of the *imu* (earthen oven) that has roasted the pig and sweet potatoes. With the ohia-log table, the malo-clad men chipping away at the *imu,* and the steam rising from the pit, this is a dramatic event. The feast is as authentic as a commercial luau gets, with *opihi* (limpets, a Hawaiian delicacy), banana pudding, sushi, *laulau* (steamed pork with taro leaves), *poisson cru*

The Big Island

(raw fish), and a show of delicacies from Hawaii and the South Pacific. The program, held across a lagoon from the thatched luau pavilion, is fiery and beautifully lit, with chants of Pele, Hawaii's volcano goddess, and ancient and modern dances. Look for Hawaiian artist **Herb Kane's** brilliant paintings on the back wall. ♦ M, F 6:30PM; tour at 5:30PM. Reservations required. 325.5555

Hale Samoa ★★$$$$ The newest and fanciest of the two dining rooms at the Kona Village, and highly recommended whether you're a guest or not. (Guests pay a surcharge to dine; nonguests must make reservations.) The menu includes blackened sashimi, entrecote of Kona yearling beef, loin of lamb with lobster medallions, and a sprinkling of Asian specialties served in a romantic room. ♦ Polynesian ♦ Tu, Th, Sa-Su 6-9:30PM. 325.5555

70 Kailua-Kona to North Kohala Drive

Don't miss this scenic drive through cattle country, lava fields, and a vast mountain range (see "Driving Destinations" on page 28).

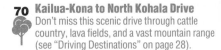

71 Kona Ranch House ★★$$$ The patio bar and homey atmosphere of this delightful, plantation-style restaurant are much loved by the local families who have made this a Kona favorite. There are two dining rooms: the **Paniolo Room,** offering family dining (hearty eaters are directed to the Paniolo Platter); and the **Plantation Lanai,** filled with elegant turn-of-the-century wicker furnishings. The emphasis is on Big Island beef, plus fresh fish and tasty Island specialties. ♦ Hawaiian ♦ Daily 6:30AM-9PM. Kuakini Hwy, just south of the traffic light at Palani Rd and Kuakini Hwy. 329.7061

72 Quinn's $$ This little local hideaway, around the corner from Alii Drive, serves reasonably priced salads and sandwiches, vegetarian specialties, fresh fish, and beef in a small patio setting. Quinn's just celebrated its 12th anniversary, so you know it's a solid Kona oasis. ♦ American ♦ M-Sa 11AM-1AM; Su 11AM-11PM. 75-5655 Palani Rd, across from the Hotel King Kamehameha. 329.3822

Hale Samoa

73 Ahuena Heiau In his final years, **Kamehameha the Great** ruled the newly united Hawaiian kingdom from this cove, known as **Kamakahonu** (eye of the turtle). Kamehameha died here in 1819, and his remains were taken to a secret resting place. The compound of thatched huts, plants, fish ponds, and an oracle tower includes the historic **Ahuena Heiau,** a refuge for the king in his final days. Dedicated to **Lono,** the Hawaiian god of fertility, this was an area of peace and prosperity. After Kamehameha's death, the entire old order was toppled when the queen regent **Kaahumanu** and her foster son **Liholiho** sat down and ate together, thereby breaking an ancient taboo. This picturesque historic site was restored by the Hotel King Kamehameha under the direction of the Bishop Museum of Honolulu. ♦ Free. Directly behind the Hotel King Kamehameha

74 Hotel King Kamehameha $$$ At the head of Kailua Village's main street, Alii Dr, within easy walking distance of **Kailua Pier** and the town's myriad shops, restaurants, and historic sites. The hotel's twin buildings have 460 rooms with lanais. Adjoining the lobby is Kailua-Kona's only fully air-conditioned shopping mall, containing some 30 shops (grant-

ed, its presence detracts from the hotel's identity) and a small museum of Hawaiian artifacts. The hotel offers visitors —and nonguests, too—free tours of the grounds. Ask about the outstanding **Hula Experience** (M, W 10AM), which traces the history of the ancient hula, and the **Ethnobotanical Tour** (Tu, Th, Su 10AM). Pool, tennis courts, and a modest strand of beach along Kamakahonu Bay. ♦ Off Alii Dr, Kailua-Kona. 329.2911, 800/733.7777

Within Hotel King Kamehameha:

Moby Dick's ★$$$ Specialties from Kona waters dominate the fare, from the sashimi

appetizer to fresh *opakapaka* (red snapper), *mahimahi* meunière, and sandwiches. Stick with the catch of the day, since it's delivered fresh daily from Kailua Pier. ♦ Steak/Seafood ♦ Daily 5:30-9PM. 329.2911

Hotel King Kamehameha Luau ★$$$ The beauty of the historical grounds gives this typical hotel luau added appeal and atmosphere. ♦ Tu, Th, Su 6PM. Reservations required. 329.2911

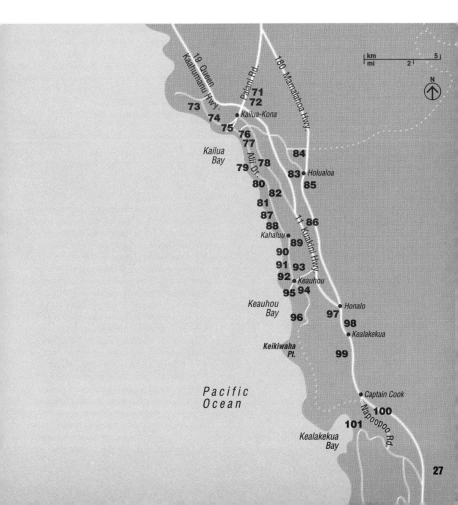

Atlantis Submarine A touristy but thoroughly enjoyable underwater trip in a comfortable, air-conditioned, 65-foot high-tech submarine, one of two in Hawaii. Looking out the large view ports at a hundred feet deep, you can watch huge *papio* (trevally), *nenue* (pilot fish), live coral, and multitudes of tropical fish. They devour the food they get from the crew. ♦ Six dives daily. Office and

logo shop in the Hotel King Kamehameha. 329.6626

75 Kailua Pier The heartbeat of Kailua Village, which still retains its flavor as a fishing community. Charter fishing boats, glass-bottom boats, and catamarans come and go from Kailua Pier, and in the late afternoons, marlin and other Kona fish are hoisted onto the scales, weighed, and photographed with jubilant anglers. You can also see the many Kona Canoe Club members gliding out of the bay for late-afternoon practice runs in the ancient Hawaiian sport of outrigger canoe racing.♦ Off Alii Dr

Driving Destinations

There's ample room on this island, which makes it the best to explore by car. To reach the scenic and historic North Kohala District, you can take the high road or the low road. The high road, the Mamalahoa Hwy (Hwy 190), winds along the slopes of Mauna Kea, through the cattle country of the giant Parker Ranch, and into the misty *paniolo* (cowboy) town of Waimea; you can then take Kohala Mountain Rd (Hwy 250) through the scenic Kohala Mountains (the highest peak is 3,564 feet). The low road, straight as an arrow, is the Queen Kaahumanu Hwy (Hwy 19), which slices through lava fields, and parallels the coast for 34 miles from Kailua-Kona to the old harbor at Kawaihae. From Kawaihae, Hwy 270 follows the coastline, where you'll see magnificent ocean views as you head for the old plantation towns of Hawi and Kapaau. At the far northern tip of the island is Upolu Point, where you can see Maui across the channel. The Pololu Valley lookout at the end of the drive is the grand finale—the isolated, rugged childhood neighborhood of Kamehameha the Great. Historic sites on this invigorating country drive include the Mookini Heiau near Kamehameha's birthplace, Lapakahi State Historical Park, Pu'uko-hola Heiau, and the original Kamehameha the Great Statue in Kapaau. From Kailua-Kona to Upolu Point, the distance is approximately 60 miles, about 90 minutes driving time.

Restaurants/Clubs: Red **Hotels:** Blue
Shops/ 🌳 Outdoors: Green **Sights/Culture:** Black

76 Ocean View Inn ★$$ The unchallenged answer to the inevitable question: Where do the locals eat? This landmark inn has an ocean view, if you look really hard through the louvered windows, but the big attraction for nearly half a century has been Island home-cooking at nontourist prices. If Kona had a truck stop, this would be it. The menu is longer than a stuffed marlin—everything from steaks and seafood to curry and stuffed cabbage, Hawaiian and Chinese food, and quite possibly Kailua-Kona's only Vienna sausage omelet. There's even an old soda fountain that looks like it was shipped intact from Main Street USA. ♦ Eclectic ♦ Tu-Su 6:30AM-2:45PM, 5:15-9PM. Alii Dr, across from Kailua Pier, Kailua-Kona. 329.9998

77 Marty's Steak and Seafood Restaurant ★$$$ This used to be **Buzz's,** part of the reliable Honolulu chain. The menu is the same: great steaks, fish, and Korean-style ribs, plus a good salad bar with hot bread. The upstairs, open-air dining room above Alii Dr offers a romantic view of the bay. ♦ Steaks/Seafood ♦ M-Sa 11AM-3PM, 5-10:30PM; Su 5-10PM. Alii Dr, across from Hulihe'e Palace, Kailua-Kona. 329.1571

77 Cafe Sibu ★★$ Affordable Indonesian food in a small cafe with indoor and outdoor tables. It's casual and pleasant, with a variety of piquant curries, *satay* dishes in spicy peanut sauces, and barbecued meats and vegetables. The classic *gado gado* salad with peanut and lime dressing has a big following, as do the vegetarian stir-fries. Balinese masks, batiks, and artifacts give great ambience to the tiny place. Highly recommended. ♦ Indonesian ♦ Daily 11:30AM-9PM. Kona Banyan Ct, 75-5695 Alii Dr, Kailua-Kona. 329.1112

78 Mokuaikaua Church Built in 1837 by the first missionaries, this is the oldest church in Hawai'i. Its lava rock walls and ohia beams look the same as they did then. ♦ Daily 6AM-6PM. Off Alii Dr, opposite Hulihe'e Palace

79 Hulihe'e Palace Hawaiian alii (royalty) spent their summer vacations at this Victorian-style, two-story structure constructed of coral and lava in 1838 by Big Island governor **John Adams Kuakini,** brother-in-law of **King Kamehameha. King Kalakaua** also favored the palace as a summer retreat. Operated as a museum by the **Daughters of Hawaii,** it is simple but impressive, with a massive koa dining table, **Queen Kapiolani's** four-poster bed, and fabulous 19th-century cabinetry and mementos. ♦ Admission. Daily 9AM-4PM. 75-5718 Alii Dr, Kailua-Kona. 329.1877

80 Kona Inn Restaurant $$$ Fondly remembered as the site of the wonderful old Kona Inn, which had rooms overlooking a manicured lawn that swept all the way down to the sea wall. Unfortunately, the Kona Inn was torn down in favor of yet another touristy shopping center with restaurants and shops. The Kona Inn Restaurant got the best of the deal—overlooking the lawns with a million-dollar ocean view. The proprietors did the site justice by building a beautiful bar, patio cocktail area, and open-air dining room, with lots of rich koa wood. Less imagination went into the menu, which relies on the unfailingly repetitive of catch the day (expensive here), a few other seafoods, plus steaks and prime rib. ♦ Continental ♦ Daily 11:30AM–midnight. Kona Inn Shopping Village, 75-5744 Alii Dr, Kailua-Kona. 329.4455

80 Fisherman's Landing $$ The best thing about this gargantuan restaurant is its location—on the water with a bay view on each side. Indoor and outdoor dining rooms, with a lengthy menu heavy on the local ethnic favorites. *Poke* (raw fish), stir-fried vegetables, and seafood and steak dishes are some of the offerings. The view outshines the food by far. ♦ Eclectic ♦ Kona Inn Shopping Village, 75-7544 Alii Dr, Kailua-Kona. 326.2555

80 Yong Yong Tree ★$$ When Yong Yong Tree opened in 1982 with an enormous menu of Mandarin, Cantonese, and Szechuan dishes, the *haole* (Caucasian) waiters and waitresses had their work cut out for them. The complications of ordering have eased, however, and it is possible to settle down to a forthright meal at Kona's No. 1 Chinese restaurant, which offers Peking duck, *mu shu* pork, lobster in black bean sauce, and lots more. ♦ Chinese ♦ M-Sa 11AM-9PM; Su 4-9PM. Kona Inn Shopping Village, 75-5744 Alii Dr, Kailua-Kona. 329.7100

Reel 'Em In

Unlike many deep-sea fishing excursions, the fishing off the coast of Kailua-Kona begins minutes after your boat leaves the dock. The charter boats cruise within a mile or two of the Kona shoreline (all that's needed to make a good catch here) and the captain provides the equipment (no fishing licenses needed), plus expert advice and assistance if necessary. All you need to bring are food, drink, and sunscreen. Half-day charters leave just after sunrise and return by noon; all-day charters are back in time for cocktails. Parties of up to six people can hire charters (with a captain and a mate) for exclusive use, or you can share charters and pay on a per-person basis. One excellent service (and the oldest) is the **Kona Charter Skippers Association** (329.3600, 800/367.8047), which books 26-foot to 54-foot boats. Other recommended charter-boat companies include the **Kona Coast Activities Center** (329.2971), **Phil Parker's Kona Activities Center** (329.3171), and **Charter Locker** (326.2553).

80 Hula Heaven Kitschy collectibles from Hawaii's halcyon days, the 1920s to the 1950s, that produced raffia-skirted hula dolls, handpainted neckties, and the coveted Mundorff prints and Matson cruise liner menus. Hula girl lamps, silk aloha shirts, and muumuus can cost hundreds of dollars, but the charm bracelets and salt-and-pepper shakers are much less. Great for browsing. ♦ Daily 9AM-9PM. Kona Inn Shopping Village, 75-5744 Alii Dr, Kailua-Kona. 329.7885

80 Flamingo's T-shirts, silk sportswear, evening dresses, and a few choice items of antique clothing can be found here. ♦ Daily 9AM-

9PM. Kona Inn Shopping Village, 75-5744 Alii Dr, Kailua-Kona. 329.4122

80 Don Drysdale's Club 53 $$ This is owned by the former Los Angeles Dodger pitching great, but don't expect to find Drysdale here often. What you will find is a relaxed atmosphere with indoor and outdoor tables, an ocean view, cheap drinks, great bartenders, good service, and some say, Kailua-Kona's best cheeseburger—the Big D Burger with grilled onions. This is a lively, comfortable spot where sports fans can nosh on soups, nachos, and buffalo burgers while watching their favorite sports events on TV. ♦ Daily 10AM-1AM. Kona Inn Shopping Village, 75-5744 Alii Dr, Kailua-Kona. 329.6651

81 Phillip Paolo's $$$ The popular Honolulu eatery expanded to waterfront row with this split-level restaurant, with sliding doors opening to the deck and ocean. There are some nice touches here, but it can be pretentious, and the food—Northern Italian with some French touches—is heavy and inconsistent. *Mahimahi* scampi and sautéed fresh scallops with snow peas are two of the specialties. ♦ Continental ♦ M-F 11AM-2:30PM, 5-10PM; Sa-Su 5-10PM. Waterfront Row, 75-5776 Alii Dr, Kailua-Kona. 329.4436

81 Jolly Roger Kona Restaurant $$ In the Jolly Roger chain, Kona's establishment is superior, largely because of its ocean view and hefty roster of fresh fish specials. Steak and lobster at a good price, and sandwiches, pastas, burgers, and the usual family standbys at affordable prices. ♦ Eclectic ♦ Daily 6:30AM-10PM. Waterfront Row, 75-5776 Alii Dr, Kailua-Kona. 329.1344

82 Uncle Billy's Kona Bay Hotel $$ This one-time annex to the old Kona Inn was converted into a 125-room hotel run by the bargain-minded **Uncle Billy Kimi** clan (he has 11 kids). Kailua Village's shopping and historic attractions are right outside the front door, and the **Banana Bay Buffet** offers unspectacular but reasonable food. Pool. ♦ 75-5739 Alii Dr, Kailua-Kona. 329.1393, 800/442.5841 (HI), 800/367.5102 (Mainland US)

This Little Piggy Went to a Luau

The luau is a native ritual and a feast of celebration, worship, and thanksgiving. Ancient Hawaiians celebrated the crowning of a chief or the victorious end of a battle with a luau. Today, a luau may be held to rejoice in the birth of a first child, to bless a new house or marriage, or to pay tribute to the gods for their gifts of taro, fish, or a bountiful harvest. The feast not only reinforces the sense of community, it also is viewed as a gift from the luau host to all his or her friends and family.

The Big Island

Authentic luaus are rare today; the traditional foods of raw fish (*aku, ahi, uhu*), raw shellfish (*opihi*), raw Island crab (*aama*), and raw river shrimp (*opae*) scared off so many tourists that a modified tourist luau is now the standard. But even the watered-down luau is a plethora of sensual pleasures, from the fine native dancing and singing to the festive decor and, of course, the star attraction, the roast pig (called the *kalua* pig).

The luau pig roasting takes place in a native Hawaiian barbecue pit called an *imu*—an earthen oven lined with lava rocks, *kiawe* wood, and banana stalks. The pig is covered with *ti* leaves and allowed to simmer in its own juices for several hours. The high point of the celebration comes when the roast pig is raised from the *imu* for all to see. Then the feast begins, which traditionally includes these Hawaiian treats:

Chicken long rice Long, transparent noodles (evidence of Hawaii's rich Asian influence) boiled with shredded chicken.

Haupia Rich pudding made from coconut milk.

Laulau Steamed spicy meats (beef, pork, or fish) wrapped in taro leaves.

Lomi Salmon Salted and shredded salmon mixed with tomatoes and green onions.

Poi A pasty pudding made from pulverized taro root. (A longtime staple of the Hawaiian diet, *poi* is definitely an acquired taste not easily adopted by newcomers. The bland diet is best combined with salted meat or fish.)

From the Pit to the Pig: The Mechanics of the Hawaiian-Style Barbecue

Building the Imu The luau host first chooses an area for the earthen oven that has good drainage, and digs a pit big enough to accommodate the lava-rock lining and the pig. A pole is inserted in the middle of the pit and its base is covered with bricks (one to two dozen) to retain heat. Kindling-size wood (*kiawe* wood) is stacked around the pole, and the pit is lined with about a hundred lava stones. The pole is then pulled out and replaced with a kerosene-saturated jute rope. Once the fire is started, it takes at least three hours for the rocks to get sufficiently hot, at which point the unburned wood is carefully removed and the hot rocks are covered with banana stalks and *ti* leaves.

Prepping the Pig The entire body of the pig is cleaned and split open lengthwise. The insides are salted, and with long cooking tongs, 15 hot stones are placed inside the animal. The feet are bound with a rope and the pig is put into a mesh cage and set into the pit. A thick layer of *ti* leaves is spread over the entire mound, and then covered with wet jute, canvas bags, and a thin layer of earth. The mound is lightly wet down, and any holes that allow steam to escape are plugged with leaves and dirt. The pig then roasts (approximately five hours for a one hundred-pound pig). Finally, the layers of dirt, canvas, and leaves are removed with poles. The pig is brought out and the stones are removed from the inside of its body. The roasted pig is displayed on a platter, and, after sufficient oohing and aahing by the luau guests, is carved into generous portions of tender pork.

83 Eclipse ★★$$$ A refined, mainland-style bar and dining room with a sophisticated menu: pâté, oysters Rockefeller, salmon in puff pastry, steak Oscar, beef Wellington, scampi Provençal, and veal wrapped around prawns. Dine and leave early if you're not interested in late-night disco-style dancing; this is a real hot spot. ◆ Continental/French ◆ M-F 11AM-2PM, 5-9PM; Sa-Su 5-9PM. 75-5711 Kuakini Hwy, Kailua-Kona. 329.4686

84 Holualoa Inn $$ Gleaming hardwood floors, intriguing architecture, great art, and flawless taste make this cedar estate a place to remember. Far from the commercialism of Kailua-Kona, this B&B is run professionally and pleasantly, featuring a fireplace and large, open-beamed living room; a suite and three rooms in Polynesian and Asian themes; quilts; lots of windows; and *lauhala* mats on the floors. The pool and deck look down the slope to the ocean, and there are a number of quiet spots for solitude and scenery. ◆ Mamalahoa Hwy, Holualoa. 324.1121

85 Studio 7 This gallery, owned by artist **Hiroki Morinoue,** is small and serene, with a quality much like a Zen garden or a tasteful, unpretentious Japanese inn. Morinoue's own paintings and prints share space with the Big Island's best in all media. ◆ Tu-Sa 10AM-4PM. Mamalahoa Hwy, Holualoa. 324.1335

85 The Kona Hotel $ The large, ramshackle pink building has been a Holualua landmark for nearly 65 years and now attracts a steady stream of artists, hikers, sportfishers, students, and adventurers from all over the world. Clean and charming with communal bathrooms, no telephones, a widow's walk to the world's most scenic outhouse, and 11 rooms, a few with views over the coffee fields some 1,500 feet below. A great find and very inexpensive. ◆ 76-5908 Mamalahoa Hwy, Holualoa. 324.1155

86 Kimura Lauhala Shop You must see the *lauhala* (woven pandanus) items **Tsuruyo Kimura** has been selling since the days when hala trees were abundant in Kona and the Kimuras traveled around the island bartering. The shop is awash in the warm browns of woven fiber goods from Hawaii and the South Pacific—hats, mats, kitchen goods, purses, and hangings. Ask for the Kona lauhala; it's the best. ◆ M-Sa 9AM-5PM. Corner Hualalai Rd and Mamalahoa Hwy (Hwy 190) 324.0053

Where the Ironmen Meet

The North and South Kona districts, on the western side of the Big Island, are world-renowned for sportfishing, resorts, gourmet coffee, and potent marijuana (called *pakalolo* in these parts). But in recent years Kona has garnered attention from all around the world as the site of the **Ironman Triathlon.** This highly competitive, physical competition, launched in 1979 by long-distance runner and swimmer **John Collins,** consists of three major endurance events: a 2.4-mile rough-water, ocean

The Big Island

swim; a 112-mile bicycle ride; and a 26-mile run. The Ironman swimmers begin en masse in Kailua Bay, then ride bicycles from Kona to Kohala and back, and finish with a marathon from the Kona Surf Hotel to the Keahole Airport and back to the Kailua Pier. This grueling test of physical and mental strength is a big crowd-pleaser every November. The ABC network show *Wide World of Sports* usually airs a tape-delayed version. For more information, contact Ironman Triathlon, 75-170 Hualalai Rd, Suite D-214, Kailua-Kona HI 96740, 329.0063.

87 Huggo's ★$$$ If you had this location—virtually hanging over crashing surf—you wouldn't worry much about the food either. Hard to top for sunset cocktails, after which the big, black manta rays will come out to play in the floodlights. Sandwiches and such at lunch; prime rib, steaks, and seafood at dinner, including (when available) fresh lobster and prawns. ◆ Steaks/ Seafood ◆ M-F 11:30AM-10PM; Sa-Su 5:30-10PM. 75-5828 Kahakai Rd, Kailua-Kona. Just north of the Kona Hilton. 329.1493

88 Kona Hilton Beach and Tennis Resort $$$ It's hard not to like the Kona Hilton, recently brightened up by $2.2 million in renovations. With its landmark saltwater lagoon and lava peninsula, it manages to be romantic, even for a somewhat large hotel. There are hammocks under coconut trees and an open-air dining room with a sweeping view of the Kailua coastline, all the way down to the Ahuena Heiau at the northern end. The 445 rooms are in two towers at the south end of Kailua-Kona. Private lanais landscaped with bougainvillea look out at the ocean, mountains, or village. The Hilton's close proximity to Kailua Village is also desirable. Four lighted tennis courts, a pool, saltwater lagoon, and a nearby small beach. The hotel's luau is held oceanside M, W, F 6-9PM. ◆ Off Alii Dr, Kailua-Kona. 329.3111, 800/HILTONS; fax 329.7230

Within the Kona Hilton Beach and Tennis Resort:

Hele Mai $$$ Dine in their open-air dining room with a view of the sun bouncing off the lava rocks in Kailua Bay. The outside tables practically hang over the water, which is nice if the wind isn't blowing. Short menu of beef and seafood. The oceanfront **Windjammer Lounge** within the restaurant has a nautical motif, and the fish mounted on the walls attest to Kona's stature as a world fishing capital. Nightly entertainment at the Windjammer. ♦ Steaks/Seafood ♦ Hele Mai: daily

5-9:30PM. Windjammer: daily 11AM-midnight. 329.3111

89 Tom Bombadil's Food & Drink ★$$ This watering hole near Alii Dr, named after a character in **J.R. Tolkien's** popular *Hobbit* trilogy, is a favorite hangout for local fishers and triathletes. The fishers are partial to the strong mai tais, and the triathletes, who converge in Kona each November for the Ironman Triathlon, come here for proper and specially priced carbo-loading, with pasta, pizza, beer, and the usual fish, chicken, and meat specials. The roasted chicken here is legendary, and the restaurant is complemented by a graciously rowdy outside patio. Full cocktail lounge. ♦ American ♦ Daily 11AM-10PM. 75-5864 Walua Rd (Alii Dr) Kailua-Kona. 329.1292

90 Aston Royal Sea Cliff Resort $$$ These large, attractive condominiums are ideal for families who prefer to be self-sufficient. The stark, angular white structure stands out along the lava coastline of Alii Dr. Studios, and one- and two-bedroom suites with lanais, washer/dryer, cable TV, and full kitchen with dishwasher and microwave. Two pools and tennis. ♦ 75-6040 Alii Dr, Kailua-Kona. 329.8021, 800/922.7866

91 Kona by the Sea $$$ One- and two-bedroom suites with double baths in a four-story resort between the Kailua-Kona and Keauhou resort areas. Complete kitchens, pool, Jacuzzi, and the **Beach Club** restaurant ($$$). ♦ 75-6106 Alii Dr, Kailua-Kona. 329.0200, 800/922.7866

92 Jameson's by the Sea ★★$$$ The location sets it apart—on the ocean at **Magic Sands Beach,** Kona's only white sand beach. The menu is equally pleasing: fresh *opakapaka, mahimahi,* and *ono* are always available in several preparations, along with scallops, pasta, and an especially delicious scampi. With the professional, pleasant service, Jameson's is a hard-to-beat combination. ♦ Continental ♦ M-F 11AM-3PM (5PM for appetizers) 5-10PM ; Sa-Su 5-10PM. At Magic Sands Beach, 77-6452 Alii Dr, Kailua-Kona. 329.3195

92 Keauhou Beach Hotel $$$ The most historic and genuinely Hawaiian of the Kona hotels. Hawaii's monarchs once played here, and the beauty of the area hasn't changed. The seven-story, 318-room hotel, adorned with cascading bougainvillea, is set amidst a coconut grove. The grounds include stone idols and a 150-foot-long pond, fed by a freshwater spring and the ocean, that **King Kalakaua** used to fatten fish for his table. Tall, stately monkeypods, lush plantings, petroglyphs, and the former home of King Kalakaua are among the attractions. Be sure to ask for a room in the renovated wing (garden rooms are all unrenovated). Music lovers should sample the jazz at the **Makai Bar** where the **Hawaiian Jazz Club** congregates Sundays 4-8PM (**George Naope'** has been known to make the occasional appearance). The seafood and Chinese buffets—affordable and extensive—draw long lines of local folks. ♦ 78-6740 Alii Dr, Kailua-Kona. 322.3441, 955.7600, 800/367.6025; fax 322.6586

92 Pahoehoe Beach Park This small beach, bordered with *kiawe* trees, is not good for swimming, but sportfishers and picnicking families often retreat to here. ♦ Off Alii Dr, three miles south of Kailua-Kona

92 Magic Sands Beach The sand here disappears seasonally—usually in March or April—leaving a rocky shoreline (hence the name). Swimming, bodysurfing, and good whale sighting. ♦ Off Alii Dr, south of Pahoehoe Beach Park

Sail the Seas

Captain Beans' Polynesian Cruises combines dinner and entertainment with the beauty of the Kona sunset. Morning snorkeling cruises are available, too. For more information, call 329.2955.

Fair Wind, at Keauhou Bay near the Kona Surf, Kona Hilton, and Keauhou Beach hotels, offers two daily cruises on a 50-foot, glass-bottomed trimaran. A full bar, snorkeling gear, instruction, and a side trip to the Captain Cook's monument at Kealakekua Bay are also offered. For more information, call 322.2788.

Royal Hawaiian Cruises provides four-hour trips from Kailua Pier to the marine preserve at Kealakekua Bay for swimming and snorkeling. Continental breakfast, barbecue lunch, and snorkeling gear are included. For more information, call 326.2999.

Captain Zodiac is the high-speed alternative. Their highly maneuverable, inflatable rafts take you on a four-hour excursion along the Kona coastline and into exciting sea caves and grottoes. Snorkeling gear and a light lunch are included. For more information, call 329.3199.

92 Little Blue Church Officially named **St. Peter's Catholic Church,** this church is nicknamed for its blue tin roof. Built in 1889 on a *heiau* (ancient temple) site that has recently been restored. ♦ Off Alii Dr, directly in front of Kahaluu Beach Park

92 Kahaluu Beach Park Swimming and snorkeling in a protected bay and reef, but the salt-and-pepper sand is somewhat rough. ♦ Off Alii Dr next to the Keauhou Beach Hotel

93 La Bourgogne ★★$$$ A few years ago, duck à l'orange, pâté, and pheasant would have been wishful thinking in this seafood-oriented town. Thanks to owner/chef **Guy Chatelard,** the Gallic pleasures of sweetbreads, steak tartare, and classically prepared game are available in this intimate atmosphere of hushed tones and velvet banquettes. Small—only 10 tables. ♦ French ♦ M-Sa 6-10PM. 77-6400 Nalani St, Kuakini Plaza South, Hwy 11. 329.6711

94 Kona Country Club Cut out of black lava rock, the course overlooks the ocean and borders the **Kona Surf Hotel**—an excellent and convenient choice for golfers staying in the Kailua-Kona and Keauhou Bay area. Splendid ocean views, a well-maintained course, and some of Hawaii's most consistently sunny weather. Now 27 holes, with a fourth nine in the making. Par 72, 6,165 yards. ♦ Expensive green fees. Kona Surf and Keauhou Beach Hotel guests extended preferred starting times and rates. Pro shop. 322.2595

95 Kanaloa at Kona $$$ These low-rise villas, with full kitchens, private lanais, and private Jacuzzi tubs, rank among the most spacious accommodations in Kona, ideal for self-sufficient families. The resort, slightly off the beaten track, is extremely quiet, comfortable, and well-managed. The 37 villas are immaculate and tasteful, sprawling over 17 acres in a cul-de-sac near Keauhou Bay. Some of the split-level units have great views of the ocean, golf course, or mountains. Ceiling fans make up for the lack of air-conditioning, and the indulgent bathrooms all have Jacuzzi tubs, double vanities, and separate showers with double

The Big Island

heads. Tennis courts, three pools, and an outstanding terrace restaurant overlooking Heeia Bay and bordered by the **Kona Country Club.** Great value if couples or families share a unit, which is invariably large. ♦ 78-261 Manukai St, Kailua-Kona. 322.2272, 800/777.1700; fax 322.3818

96 Kona Surf Resort $$$ A striking example of hotel architecture, all the more impressive because its five four- and seven-story wings were erected on top of rugged lava fields formed centuries ago at the ocean's edge. Unfortunately, the Kona Surf is in dire need of renovations. The rough-around-the-edges look dominates. The rooms are large, though, and the lack of a sandy beach is eased by the surf crashing against lava and vistas of sparkling Kona seas. The manta rays that

Kona Surf Resort

gather here at the point at night are something to behold. Two swimming pools (including a great saltwater pool with ocean views), a massage room, tennis courts, and several shops. Nearby is the championship **Kona Country Club** and **Keauhou Bay,** departure point for several daily sight-seeing and snorkeling cruises. ◆ 78-128 Ehukai St, Kailua-Kona. 322.3411, 800/367.8011; fax 322.3245

Within the Kona Surf Resort:

S.S. James Makee $$$ Roast rack of lamb, chicken, pasta dishes, and the Kona

standard, fresh seafood, served in a room with a nautical motif. A limited menu, but pleasant enough for a dress-up evening. ◆ Continental ◆ Daily 6-10PM. Reservations required. 322.3411

97 Aloha Theater Cafe ★★$ This old theater converted to a health food restaurant is a worthy stop at any time of day. Excellent vegetarian soups and sandwiches, bagels and lox, tempeh burgers, lasagna, fresh-squeezed juices and smoothies, carrot cake, and brownies. For breakfast, the pancakes, French toast, and corn bread are meant to be enjoyed with abandon. Great ambience, with a veranda that wraps around the old theater. ◆ Health Food ◆ M-Sa 8AM-8PM. Off Hwy 11, Kainaliu. 322.3383

98 Kona Coffee Roasters You'll know by the blue awning and aroma of fresh-brewed coffee that you're here. Kona's best coffee—espresso, cappuccino, and all variations—is roasted and ground on the premises and sold with gourmet teas and gifts. ◆ M-F 8AM-5PM. Off Hwy 11, Kainaliu. 322.9196

99 Canaan Deli $ High-rise sandwiches, bagels, and even pasta—for dinner—to go, or sit at the outdoor counter and monitor daily life in charming Kealakekua. ◆ M-F 7AM-7:30PM; Sa 7AM-2PM. Off Hwy 11, Kealakekua. 323.2577

100 Manago Hotel $ Who needs luxury when you have a clean, modest hotel with character, a good view, and a restaurant with an Island-wide following? The Manago Hotel is 74 years old and still going strong, with **Mrs. Manago's** picturesque gardens flourishing beneath the lanais. The second and third generation of Managos now run the hotel. Cheap and quiet, with private or shared baths. ◆ Off Hwy 11, Captain Cook. 323.2642

Within the Manago Hotel:

Manago Hotel Dining Room ★$ Folks come from up and down the coastline for the fresh fish and pork chops. Budget prices, a luxury view, and **Mrs. Manago's** Japanese-style home-cooking distinguish this as one of West Hawaii's landmarks. ◆ Hawaiian ◆ Tu-Th 7-9AM, 11AM-2PM, 5-7:30PM; F-Su 7-9AM, 11AM-2PM, 5-7PM. 323.2642

101 Kealakekua Bay and Captain Cook Monument Hawaii's first European visitor, **Captain James Cook,** was killed here in 1779, a year after he'd been greeted royally by the Hawaiians. The site is marked by a 27-foot white pillar, accessible only by boat but visible from the south shore of Kealakekua Bay, a marine preserve popular with snorkelers and scuba divers. ◆ Take Hwy 160 from Kuakini Hwy

102 Royal Kona Coffee Mill and Museum Sampler Taste the brew that made Kona famous and observe the mill in seasonal operation (call for specific months). Old roasting equipment and photographs of past harvests displayed. ◆ Daily 8:30AM-4:30PM. Napo'opo'o Rd, between Captain Cook and Napo'opo'o. No phone

103 The Painted Church Officially **St. Benedict's Church,** this Gothic place of worship is known as The Painted Church because of the biblical scenes painted here in 1900 by **Father John Berchmans Velghe** of Belgium. For Hawaiians who couldn't read or write, the priest illustrated Christianity with Island motifs. Open to the public. ◆ Off Hwy 160 near Honaunau

104 Pu'uhonua o Honaunau When ancient Hawaiians broke a sacred law, or were being chased by the enemy in times of war, their only escape was to swim or run to the nearest *pu'uhonua* (place of refuge) where they were absolved by a *kahuna pule* (priest). They hid there until the war or conflict blew over. Pu'uhonua o Honaunau was such a sanctuary and now is a National Historical Park. Most impressive is the **Great Wall,** a massive, mortarless barrier of lava rock 1,000 feet long, 10 feet high, and 17 feet wide constructed around 1,550 *heiaus* (temples). Thatched huts, wooden idols, petroglyphs, palace grounds, and cultural demonstrations on six fascinating acres within a 180-acre park dotted with tidal pools at the ocean. ◆ Admission. Daily 7:30AM-5:30PM. Off Hwy 160, about a 40-minute drive south from Kailua-Kona. 328.2326, 328.2288

Green Sand Beach near South Point on the Big Island got its name from the greenish tint of the olivine crystals in the sand.

Restaurants/Clubs: Red   Hotels: Blue
Shops/ 🌳 Outdoors: Green   Sights/Culture: Black

105 Hookena Beach Park Salt-and-pepper beach with swimming, much favored by local families in the area. The road to the beach is narrow and steep, off the beaten track. ◆ Turnoff from Hwy 11 to Hookena

106 South Point It's an 11-mile drive from Mamalahoa Hwy to South Point, or **Ka Lae,** in the Ka'u District. The barely passable road and flat, treeless surroundings discourage all but the most intrepid, but those who complete it can claim they've been to the southernmost point in the US. This is believed to be where the first Polynesian discoverers of Hawaii landed. ◆ Turn off Hwy 11 near Waiohinu

107 Green Sand Beach Volcanic olivine crystals created the color and inspired the name of this beach on Mahana Bay, about three miles east of South Point. Accessible only by four-wheel drive or by hiking. Bring a guide, and swim only if it's exceptionally calm—currents can be treacherous. ◆ South Point, Ka'u

108 Punalu'u Black Sand Beach Park One of the Big Island's best-known black sand beaches, with picnic and camping facilities and a broad bay with concrete foundations, vestiges of its former days as a significant shipping point for Ka'u. Palm trees and spring-fed lagoons add to the beauty here, but the rocky bay is not recommended for swimming. ◆ Off Hwy 11, Punalu'u

109 SeaMountain Golf Club Because of its remote location in Punalu'u on the southeastern rim of the island, SeaMountain receives little recognition and only limited play. Though it doesn't compare to Kona Coast Golf, it is interesting and scenic, taking golfers gradually from sea level into the mountains. Par 72, 6,492 yards. ◆ Moderate green fees. Located midway between Kailua-Kona and Hilo near Punaluu Black Sand Beach at SeaMountain Resort. Pro shop. 928.6222

The Big Island

110 Hawaii Volcanoes National Park The best known of all the Big Island attractions (see map below), with a volcano that just won't quit. **Kilauea's** record-breaking eruptive phase—since January 1983—has destroyed 178 homes, more than half in 1990 alone. Prominent landmarks such as: **Kalapana Village, Walter Yamaguchi's Kalapana Store,** the **Wahaula Visitors Center, Mauna Kea Congregational Church, Harry K. Brown Park,** and **Kaimu Black Sand Beach** are buried under lava. Established in

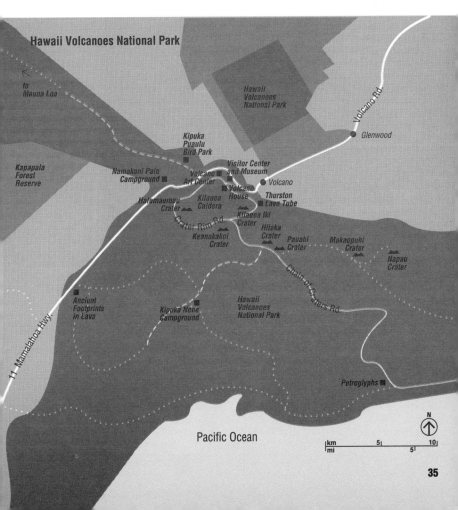

Hawaii Volcanoes National Park

to Mauna Loa

Hawaii Volcanoes National Park

Volcano Rd.

Glenwood

Kapapala Forest Reserve

Kipuka Puaulu Bird Park

Namakani Paio Campground

Volcano Art Center

Visitor Center and Museum

Volcano House

Volcano

Halemaumau Crater

Kilauea Caldera

Thurston Lava Tube

Kilauea Iki Crater

Crater Rim Rd.

Keanakakoi Crater

Hiiaka Crater

Pauahi Crater

Makaopuhi Crater

Napau Crater

Ancient Footprints in Lava

Kipuka Nene Campground

Hawaii Volcanoes National Park

Chain of Craters Rd.

Petroglyphs

11 Mamalahoa Hwy.

Pacific Ocean

N

km / mi   5   10 / 5

1916, the 377-square-mile park begins at **Mauna Loa** near the island's center, narrows eastward, then fans south around Kilauea volcano to the seacoast near what was Kalapana. Volcano novices can view a short film shown hourly at the **Kilauea Visitors Center** (or the extended one shown nightly at **Volcano House).** The center has a museum and displays maps of eruptions and road hazards.

Mauna Loa, now 13,667 feet above sea level, devoted two of its three million years to reaching the ocean surface. It sleeps for long spells between eruptions—the last one was in 1984. Kilauea, younger and more active, is

The Big Island

4,000 feet above sea level and still growing. Its eruptions have added nearly 300 acres to the island's land mass since 1983, running over a large section of the **Chain of Craters Road.** The road is closed slightly east of the **Kamoamoa Campground** on the Kalapana side, with a roadblock below the intersection of Hwy 130 (Kalapana Bypass Rd) and the road to Kaimu. You can't hike to the active vent because it's on state land, but you can view it from the air by helicopter. Check with park rangers for current conditions.

Past eruptions have also left marks on the area. A 1977 eruption sent lava less than a half mile from the now-devastated Kalapana, while in 1960 the town of Kapoho was destroyed. That eruption added some 200 acres to the island, and Kapoho's lavascape served as a training ground for American astronauts to walk on the moon. Although hundreds of warriors battling **Kamehameha the Great** died in a 1790 eruption of Kilauea, only one person has been killed by an eruption in modern times (an amateur photographer killed in 1924 by a falling block of lava and hot ash when he got too close to a steam explosion). **Crater Rim Road** has metal barricades that can be erected to stop motorists within minutes of an alert.

The park's network of roads and trails allows visitors the option of driving for several miles, then parking and exploring specific sights. **Bird Park** is an easy unpaved path through forest and meadows filled with birds. The **Halemaumau Trail** into the Kilauea caldera, leading across fresh lava flows, is for the hardier hiker. The self-guided, 6.4-mile hike takes five hours round-trip, or you can meet a friend with a car at the Halemaumau parking area to save the hike back. A shorter trek is **Mauna Iki** (Footprints Trail)—a 3.6 mile, two-hour round-trip. The paved path crosses the Ka'u Desert to the footprints made by those fleeing warriors of 1790. **Pele,** the volcano goddess, doesn't like it when visitors take lava rocks home as souvenirs. The park annually receives rocks in the mail from travelers besieged with bad luck. Stay on the trails, heed warning signs, and leave the

rocks alone! ♦ Admission to the park. Visitor Center daily 7:30AM-5PM. Off Hwy 11 from Hilo. Volcano eruption information: 967.7977

Within Hawaii Volcanoes National Park:

Thurston Lava Tube Lava tubes form when a crust of lava hardens and a river of lava continues to flow beneath the surface. A 1975 earthquake temporarily closed this tube when a wayward boulder blocked the entrance. It is named for **Lorrin A. Thurston,** the Hawaii publisher who pushed for a Volcanoes National Park and was on the expedition that discovered the tube.

 Devastation Trail This eerie landscape looks like a science-fiction film locale. Dead ohia trees, burned clean of their leaves by cinders from a 1959 Kilauea eruption, stand like skeletons in a bed of black pumice. A wooden boardwalk crosses the region for one-half mile. ♦ Trailhead on Crater Rim Rd

 Chain of Craters Road Winding through the parks interior passes, this road passes several huge craters formed in prehistoric and modern times. The latest series of eruptions have closed parts of the road, so you will run into a dead end a couple of miles east of Wahaula. The road passes the Hilina Pali Road turnoff, leading to an overlook and picnic area above some 50 miles of southeast coastline, possibly the longest stretch of wild seascape in the state. The side trip to the lookout is 45 minutes from Chain of Craters Road. ♦ Southeast from Crater Rim Rd

111 **Volcano Golf and Country Club** An unusual location for a golf course, with the biggest, hottest bunker on earth—a live volcano. This high-altitude course is laid out along the rim of an active volcano—great for golfers who seek out novel experiences. Par 72, 6,119 yards. ♦ Moderate green fees. Hawaii Volcanoes National Park. Starting times. 967.7331

112 **Volcano House** $$ There have been a succession of Volcano Houses since 1846, from grass shacks to board-and-timber structures, and all have offered something no other inn in the world can match: the opportunity to eat, drink, and sleep on the rim of an active volcano. **Mark Twain** was one of the early Volcano House guests. **Kilauea** is the hotel's backyard, and many a guest has sipped a cocktail in **Uncle George's Lounge** (named for **George Lycurgus,** the Greek who wound up in Hawaii because of a poker game and owned and operated Volcano House from 1895 to 1960), watching the volcano in comfort. The present Volcano House was built in 1941, replacing an 1877 structure that became the **Volcano Art Center,** a gallery of paintings, sculptures, and photographs. There has been a decline in the service here, something several changes in management have not been able to remedy. The accommodations and restaurant (regularly besieged by tour buses) are eclipsed by the new lodges and B&Bs in the area. The main structure has the feel of a hunting lodge, with a floor-to-ceiling lava rock fireplace. The fire in it has burned continuously since the 1870s, kept alive by glowing embers moved from one fireplace to another. Volcano House offers views of the fiery volcanic pit from the bar and dining room. Hotel features include a steam bath generated by natural volcanic vents; movies twice nightly of past eruptions; close proximity to the roads and hiking trails through the **Volcanoes National Park;** and the nearby **Volcano Golf Course.** ◆ Hawaii Volcanoes National Park. 967.7321

Within the Volcano House:

Ka Ohelo Dining Room $$$ The best thing about this restaurant is the view of **Halemaumau Crater.** Haunting and otherwordly, it far outshines the mediocre food that is served up daily to mobs of tourists bussed in on charters. Try breakfast or early dinner to avoid the rush, but don't expect gourmet fare. ◆ American/Seafood ◆ Daily 7AM-2PM, 5:30-8:30PM. 967.8419

113 Hale Kilauea $$ The nine rooms are named after the siblings of owner **Morris Thomas,** who built this two-story, walk-up on three acres. The fireplace in the lobby adds a nice touch, and the friendly service keeps it intimate, but you can remain anonymous here if you prefer it. Although Hale Kilauea lacks the character of some of the B&Bs, it offers the opportunity for more privacy in spite of its small size. All rooms face the fern and ohia forests, but the corner room named **Heidi** has a balcony and the best view. ◆ Off Kilanea Rd, Volcano. 967.7591

114 Chalet Kilauea $$ A two-story, cedar-shingle home in the misty Volcano forests. Owners **Brian** and **Lisha Crawford,** the consummate hosts at this B&B, are international travelers who know the art of hospitality. You can stay in the **Out of Africa Room,** the **Oriental Jade Room,** the **Continental Lace Room,** or the **Treehouse Suite.** There's also a large communal living room (with hundreds of CDs to choose from), a deck with a redwood hot tub, and surroundings of ohia trees, hapu'u ferns, and healthy brilliant hydrangeas. Lisha's gourmet breakfasts are served on fine china and linen in a cheerful Art Deco breakfast room with black-and-white tile floors and French windows looking out onto a flower-fringed yard. Her warmth, gracious-

Chalet Kilauea

EAST ELEVATION.

ness, and insider's tips on the island are worth the price of admission. The Oriental, Jade, and Lace rooms share a bathroom, but what a luxurious bathroom it is. And there are no mosquitoes at this 3,800-foot altitude. Heartily recommended. ◆ Off Wright Rd at Laukapu Rd, Volcano. 967.7786, 800/937.7786

KILAUEA LODGE

115 Kilauea Lodge ★★$$$ This splendid estate was built in 1938 as a camp lodge for the YMCA. It's now a stellar attraction in Volcano, with seven charming rooms, each with its own bath, and a new wing, called **Hale Aloha,** soon to be unveiled. The fine accommodations are matched by the cuisine—the best in Volcano, attracting diners from all over East Hawaii to the beef, chicken, and seafood specialties (and wonderful soups) concocted by owner/chef **Albert Jeyte.** The large, high-ceilinged dining room was the gathering place of the YMCA, which left its mark in the Fireplace of Friendship that was built with rocks, coins, and memorabilia from civic and youth groups around the world—32 countries in all. Every room has a fireplace—a classic touch that somewhat redeems the thin walls. Just beyond the window is a large, manorial front yard with bright blue hydrangeas and stone pillars at the entrance. A wonderful experience. ◆ Off Old Volcano Rd, Volcano. 967.7366

The word "volcano" was derived from Vulcan, the Roman god of fire, whose underground forge powered the volcanoes of the Lipari Islands near Sicily. Lava temperatures reach 2,200°F (1,200°C), not hot enough to melt land but 12 times the heat needed to boil water.

116 Carson's Volcano Cottage $$ Tom and **Brenda Carson** rent out three units and a separate cottage amidst a mix of azaleas, and camellia, ohia, maple, and cedar trees. A short path winds through the foliage to the English cottage with Victorian interior, and the three connected studios, each with its own cheerful personality. Dark cloth cushions, old Hawaiian photographs, fresh flowers, a veranda, and large windows looking out to the pines and plum trees add to the experience. The Carsons have given a personal, homey touch to each rental—provisions include homemade breads and fruit

The Big Island

preserves, coffeemakers, and small refrigerators, as well as heaters and electric blankets for the chilyl Volcano air. ♦ Off Sixth St, at Mauna Loa Estates, Volcano. 967.7683

117 Akatsuka Orchid Gardens Stroll through showy gardens of orchids of all sizes, varieties, and colors. You can order plants and cut flowers, and have them shipped back home; many are already certified and ready to roll. All visitors receive a free orchid. ♦ Free. Daily 8:30AM-5PM. 22½ miles south of Hilo. 967.7660

118 Lava Tree State Park The 1790 eruption that resulted in lava footprints also coated the trees with lava. Those torched trees are gone, but the lava molds still stand in this lush, captivating park. ♦ Off Hwy 132, near Pahoa

119 Mauna Loa Macadamia Nut Corp Owned by **C. Brewer & Company** of Honolulu, this is the world's largest producer and marketer of the macadamia nut. The visitors center offers a slide show, viewing stations of the mill's processing and packing, and a few free samples. But don't make the mistake of thinking you can save money by buying macadamia nuts from the source; there are no bargains here, and usually you can get the nuts cheaper at a convenience store. ♦ M-F 8:30AM-5PM. Off Hwy 11, about 6 miles south of Hilo. 966.9301

Macadamia nuts

120 Nani Mau Gardens A botanical showpiece, with about half of its 66 acres landscaped and open to the public. Waterfalls, streams, a one-acre rose garden with 21 varieties, and thousands of orchids and bromeliads are among the attractions. You can take a narrated tram tour, drive around in a golf cart, or stroll at your own pace along paved walkways. A pleasant outing on a sunny day. ♦ Free for children and senior citizens. Daily 8AM-5PM. 421 Makalika St, Hilo. 959.3541

Party Boats

See the Big Island while you're wined and dined on your own luxury cruise. Captains **Bob** and **Carol Hogan** of **Discovery Charters** have built boats, written about them, and sailed them extensively. Their 45-foot yacht, *Discovery*, carries two to six passengers on upscale sailing, snorkeling, and party cruises along the Kona and Kohala coastlines. For more information, call 326.1011.

The Big Island's Highlights

A misty day in Waimea.

Driving through the ironwoods of the Kohala Mountains, between the towns of Waimea and Hawi, via Kohala Mountain Rd 250.

Skiing or playing in the snow on top of Mauna Kea.

A luau or buffet lunch at Kona Village Resort.

A drive along Hamakua Coast between Hilo and Waimea.

Looking out from the Kona Surf Hotel at the manta rays swimming in the ocean at sunset.

Snorkeling or scuba diving at Kealakekua Bay.

Touring Hawaii Volcanoes National Park.

Sitting by the Friendship Fireplace at Kilauea Lodge.

Hiking through the Thurston Lava Tube.

Noelani Whittington
Executive Director, Kohala Coast Resort
Association, the Big Island

Volcano Village, on the Big Island. This quaint village just outside **Hawaii Volcanoes National Park** must be about 3,000 feet above sea level. Nights are great for curling up with a good book or enjoying lively conversations around a fire; days give way to picking *ohelo* berries in native forests, bicycling, and spending money on local art.

Four-wheel-drive treks with members of the **Kona Historical Society** into very inaccessible areas on the Big Island. Their historian's narration is superb—I always come away with a deeper appreciation of the Big Island.

Horseback riding in the **North Kohala** mountains, beautiful Big Island country.

Spending time in **Waipio Valley,** at the end of the Hamakua Coast on the Big Island, walking along unpaved roads and watching wild horses roam in streams or frolic at the beach.

Peter Merriman
Chef, Merriman's Restaurant, Kamuela,
the Big Island

Moonlight strolls on **Hapuna Beach,** south of the Westin Mauna Kea on the Big Island.

A breakfast of granola and fresh Hayden mangos.

Mai tais in the afternoon at the Big Island's **Mauna Lani Beach Club.**

Kalua pig at the **Ocean View Inn** in Kailua-Kona on the Big Island.

A **Waipio Valley Wagon Ride** on the Big Island.

Barbara Campbell
President, Hawaii's Best Bed & Breakfasts,
the Big Island

Bird Park at Volcano on the Big Island. Beautiful, quiet, peaceful...a great way to spend an hour or so.

The **Bread Depot** in Kamuela on the Big Island for muffins and fresh cinnamon rolls in the morning, and a quick, good, and reasonably priced meal in the afternoon.

Hulihee Palace in Kona on the Big Island.

Brian and Lisha Crawford
Owners, Chalet Kilauea at Volcano, the Big Island

Lava flowing into the ocean at sunset at **Kilauea** on the Big Island.

Swimming in the Big Island thermal tide pools at **Kapoho.**

Hiking the Kilauea Iki Trail in **Hawaii Volcanoes National Park** on the Big Island.

A full-moon picnic at **Kamoamoa Black Sand**

Beach on the Big Island's southeast coast.

Visiting the observatories atop the Big Island's **Mauna Kea.**

Kaui Goring
Public Relations, Hawaii Prince Hotel, Honolulu, Oahu

Ulupalakua Ranch, Maui, a nontouristy historic ranch on the slopes of Haleakala with a sense of the true Hawaiian past. Beautiful views.

Honolulu Academy of Arts. An oasis of serenity in the city with an outstanding museum shop and garden lunches.

The **Contemporary Museum** in Honolulu.

Windward Oahu (Waimanalo to Punaluu). Gorgeous scenery and a leisurely Hawaiian lifestyle still exist on the island of Oahu. The mountains (Koolau) are spectacular.

Old plantation towns (Koloa, Kauai; Hanapepe, Kauai; Makawao, Maui; Holualoa, Hawaii; and Waimea, Hawaii).

The Willow's in Honolulu is the best Hawaiian restaurant.

Top activities: **Adventures on Horseback** in Maui; hiking through Maui's **Haleakala Crater;** a helicopter ride through Haleakala or the **Na Pali Coast** on Kauai; and snorkeling at **Molokini Island,** off Maui.

Daniel Penhallow
Speech Instructor, Kauai Community College

A hike on the **Napali Cliffs** on Kauai—the most spectacular hike in the world.

A swim at **Poipu Beach,** especially at sunset—the cleanest, most refreshing ocean water off Kauai.

Dinner at **A Pacific Cafe** on Kauai—the finest and freshest food in the islands; informal but first class.

Watching the sunrise (weather permitting) from **Haleakala Crater** in Maui is unbelievable; a spiritual experience (bring a warm coat!).

A morning swim at Oahu's **Waikiki Beach** in front of the Halekulani Hotel (you'll have no problem understanding why the Hawaiians used to come here to regain their health).

Hawaii's *paniolos* (cowboys) were riding on the Big Island even before American cowboys tamed the Wild West. The first *paniolos* were brought to the islands by **Kamehameha III** around 1830. Primarily Mexican, Spanish, and Indian, they were called *vaqueros* until *paniolo* evolved from the word *español.*

Restaurants/Clubs: Red	**Hotels:** Blue
Shops/ Outdoors: Green	**Sights/Culture:** Black

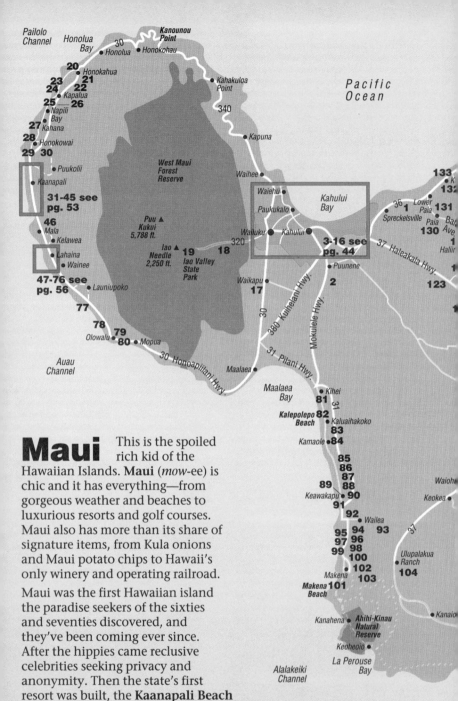

Maui

This is the spoiled rich kid of the Hawaiian Islands. **Maui** (*mow*-ee) is chic and it has everything—from gorgeous weather and beaches to luxurious resorts and golf courses. Maui also has more than its share of signature items, from Kula onions and Maui potato chips to Hawaii's only winery and operating railroad.

Maui was the first Hawaiian island the paradise seekers of the sixties and seventies discovered, and they've been coming ever since. After the hippies came reclusive celebrities seeking privacy and anonymity. Then the state's first resort was built, the **Kaanapali Beach Resort**, which paved the way for the tourist industry, making this once obscure island a household name worldwide.

In 1990, 2.3 million people visited Maui—more than any other Hawaiian island except Oahu, which attracted 5.3 million visitors. While these numbers attest to the popularity of this seductive island, they also hint at a possible problem. For many people, Maui has too much allure—and too many people and too much traffic. According to the 1990 US Census, Maui was the state's fastest-growing county in the past decade, with a countywide

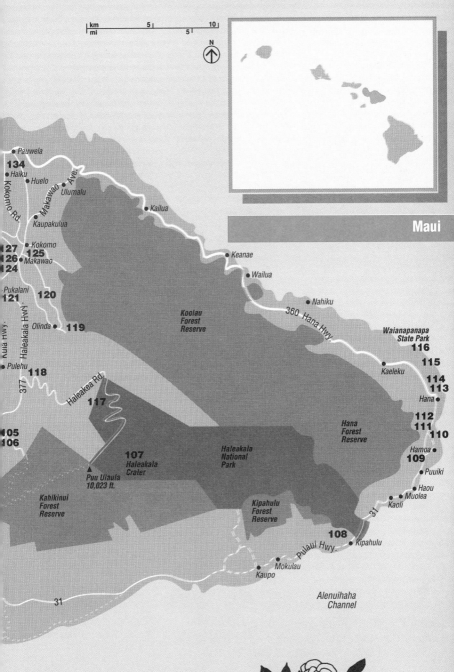

km | 5 | 10
mi | 5 |

N

Pauwela
134
Haiku
Huelo
Makawao Ave.
Kokomo Rd.
Ulumalu
Kailua
Kaupakulua
Kokomo
127
126
125
Makawao
124
Keanae
Wailua
Pukalani
121
120
Nahiku
360 Hana Hwy.
Olinda
119
Koolau
Forest
Reserve
Waianapanapa
State Park
116
115
Kaeleku
Pulehu
118
114
113
Hana
Haleakea Rd.
377
Haleakala Hwy.
Kula Hwy.
117
112
111
110
105
106
Hana
Forest
Reserve
Hamoa
109
Puuiki
107
Haleakala
Crater
Haleakala
National
Park
Puu Ulaula
10,023 ft.
Haou
Muolea
Kaoli
Kahikinui
Forest
Reserve
Kipahulu
Forest
Reserve
31
108
Pulaui Hwy.
Kipahulu
Mokulau
Kaupo
31
Alenuihaha
Channel

population of 100,374 (Maui's county borders include the islands of
Molokai and **Lanai**). That's a 42 percent increase over 1980, and even
then, many thought Maui County,
with its 70,847 residents, was
growing precariously fast.

Lokelani,
flower of Maui

Why do people keep coming? This is the island where you can easily sail across the channel and anchor off neighboring Molokai and Lanai. This is the island where you can drive up-country and hike in **Haleakala Crater,** the world's largest dormant volcano, and this is where you can discover the splendors of the **Hana Hwy,** one of Hawaii's most popular coastline roads. In short, the attractions on Maui are numerous, and if you don't like one part of the island, you can easily visit another.

Maui can be divided into five general regions: **West Maui,** containing the old whaling port of Lahaina, Kaanapali, Kapalua, Napili, and by far the highest concentration of tourists; **Southwest Maui,** anchored by the Kihei condominium strip and the ever-expanding Wailea Resort; **Central Maui,** the heart of the island's commerce and government, which encompasses the towns of Kahului and Wailuku and the main airport; **Up-Country Maui,** farming and cattle country on the slopes of Haleakala; and the **Hana Coast,** located on the beautiful, undisturbed east shores. West Maui or Southwest Maui is where you will probably stay, but you can play anywhere. And no matter what you're looking for, you are not likely to find Maui wanting in any of the categories that lure people to the tropical Islands.

Maui

▶▶▶▶▶▶▶▶▶▶▶▶▶▶▶▶▶▶▶▶▶▶▶▶▶▶▶▶▶▶▶▶▶▶

Helicopter Tours For a bird's-eye view of Maui's rain forests, hidden waterfalls, and moonlike crater landscapes, the following helicopter companies offer a variety of unforgettable tours. **Sunshine Helicopters** (871.0722, 800/544.2520) has 14 trips available, from simple to deluxe, and is the only service with a beach landing on the island of Lanai. Their deluxe Haleakala-Hana tour with a champagne toast in beautiful Ulupalakua offers views of Molokai, Kahoolawe, and Molokini. **Papillon** (669.4884) tours include a half-hour West Maui special, an all-day Hana package, a three-island (West Maui, Molokai, and Lanai) tour that touches down in Kalaupapa on Molokai, and the very popular Hana-Haleakala Odyssey that lands in Hana. **Kenai Helicopters** (871.6463, 800/622.3144) is another popular company, and **Blue Hawaiian Helicopters** (871.8844, 800/247.5444) offers five tours, including the "Sunset Spectacular," an hour-and-40-minute flight over Hana and Haleakala that lands on a private, remote site on the slopes of the volcano. Other reliable helicopter companies include **Hawaii Helicopters** (877.3900, 800/346.2403), **Cardinal** (877.2400), **Maui Helicopters** (879.1601), and **Alexair** (871.0792, 800/462.2281).

Cruises When the ocean is calm and the sky exceptionally clear, the islands of Molokai and Lanai appear so close to Maui it seems you could reach out and touch them. The **Pailolo Channel** separates the island from Molokai, which is only six miles away, and the **Auau Channel** separates it from Lanai, located eight miles away. Both are certainly close enough to

visit in an afternoon or a day, whether you're aboard a rigid-hull inflatable, a catamaran, or a large yacht. Numerous cruises are available to these islands, including scuba diving and sportfishing trips. Other boat rides feature snorkeling adventures at **Molokini,** the crescent-shaped islet off South Maui; sunset and party cruises; and whale-watching tours in the winter months. Cruise companies to choose from include **Trilogy Excursions** (661.4743, 800/874.2666); **Stardancer** (871.1144), an elegant, 150-foot floating restaurant and nightclub; the six-passenger **Cinderella Yacht Charters** (242.2779); **Ocean Riders Adventure Rafting** (661.3586, 800/657.7960); **Windjammer Cruises,** which runs the glass-bottom boat, *Coral See* (661.8600); **Blue Water Rafting** (879.7238), which gets you from Maalaea to Molokini in 10 minutes; **Lin Wa Cruises** (661.3392), offering glass-bottom boat tours; **Idle Wild** (572.8964); and the **Pacific Whale Foundation** (879.8811).

Whale Watching Hawaii's official state mammal is the whale, and Maui provides splendid views of these creatures. Each year in late November, gentle humpback whales begin arriving from their northern feeding grounds in the Bering Sea off the coast of Alaska to mate, give birth, and nurse their young in Maui's warm offshore waters. They remain until early June. **Lahaina,** once the whaling capital of the world, is now the whale-watching capital. Each year thousands of visitors to Maui find themselves caught up in the spectator sport during the peak months of January through April. Whether you live here or are visiting, the sight of a 40-ton giant whale breaching alongside its calf never fails to thrill. Whale-watching vessels are required by federal law to remain at least a hundred yards from the whales, and the better charters carry scientists and naturalists with underwater cameras and microphones to record the sight and song of the huge mammals. Their commentary can make the difference between a good sighting and a great one. Be aware that there have been a couple of arrests for harassing whales, which underscores the importance of judicious viewing and respectful treatment of these winter guests. Skippers who chase whales and get too close to them may be thrilling their passengers, but they're also harassing the whales and committing a crime.

1 Hana Road With its 53 miles of horseshoe turns, bridges, and narrow shoulders, this is one of Hawaii's most popular—and notorious—drives. It should be tackled at a very leisurely pace, and only those with steel nerves, supernatural endurance, and an unquestionable thirst for scenic motoring should attempt to conquer the road to Hana and back on the same day. If you're prone to car sickness, take Dramamine; and if you intend to picnic out of doors, be sure to take along insect repellent. You should start with a full tank of gas, as there are no stations between Paia and Hana (and gas may not be available in Hana after dark). Packing a lunch is also a wise idea, even if you choose not to picnic among the waterfalls and jungle foliage; food service on Hana Rd is limited to what's growing on the trees.

The road to Hana begins near the Kahului Airport, where you'll see the sign: "Hana 52 miles" (a gross understatement). The road to Hana seems much longer; it not only curves, it twists and curls and pirouettes—to the tune, some say, of 617 turns and 56 miniature bridges. The road is so narrow it's often impossible for two cars to pass unless one pulls over, so use caution on the hairpin curves. It took several years to build Hana Rd and several more to pave it, using convict labor. Before it was paved, the road would wash out, and drivers blocked by mud slides would swap cars. Each would continue on the road in the other's car after agreeing to meet back at the same mud slide and exchange cars again for the return trip. The Keanae Chinese Store would give free overnight beds to these stranded motorists.

The road itself—although somewhat better today—is only one reason it takes so long to drive to Hana. You have to allow time to stop to let a waterfall tickle your hands and feet, to feel the velvet touch of a rain forest fern, to

smell the flowers along the way, and to photograph a taro farm far below the road. A living catalog of Hawaiian plant life paints the side of the road. Ferns and flowers fight for space among trees hung with breadfruit, mango, and guava. Picturesque rest stops include **Waikamoi Bamboo Forest Trail and Nature Walk** (leading to a forest perfect for picnicking), **Puohokamoa Falls** (where you can swim in the natural pool), **Keanae Lookout**, and the **Miracle of Fatima Shrine.** After reaching Hana you can continue about 10 miles to the **Seven Pools** at Oheo Gulch, part of **Haleakala National Park.** For those returning to Kaanapali from the pools, the Hana Hwy is the preferred route.

The **Piilani Hwy** (off-limits to rental cars) is a dangerous and narrow road designed to

destroy cars and people. While much of the Piilani Hwy was paved years ago, it is still punctured with potholes. ♦ From Kahului Airport, 53 miles; about three hours driving time to Hana

2 Maui Swap Meet Haggle over new and used handicrafts, clothes, fresh fruits, baked goods, and knickknacks in this down-to-earth flea market much loved by residents and visitors. ♦ Admission; children under 12 free. Sa 8AM-1PM. Temporary location at the old Puunene School at the end of S. Puunene Rd, Puunene. 877.3100

3 Best of Maui Cassette Tours A worthwhile investment for anyone driving to Hana or Haleakala. This high-quality, well-researched package of audio cassette tours includes a tape, cassette player, a guidebook, bird and flower books, a detailed route map, and a Haleakala T-shirt—all for $25. The narrator has timed her information perfectly (in addition to pronouncing the Hawaiian words correctly) to describe the various landmarks as you pass them. Harp background music, professional sound quality, pertinent historical background, and tips on where to stop for a snack or picnic. ♦ 333 Dairy Rd, Kahului. 871.1555

4 Ming Yuen ★★$$ The talk of the island when it opened in 1981, this became Maui's top-rated Chinese restaurant overnight. It offers an enormous menu of Cantonese and Northern China dishes at modest prices. Despite the huge dining room, expect long lines on weekends and sometimes a two-day backup on reservations. Call ahead for a table and the Peking or stuffed duck (both require 24-hour notice). Don't miss the lemon chicken, *mu shui* pork, and chilled lychee dessert. ♦ Chinese ♦ M-Sa 11:30AM-9PM; Su 5-9PM. 162 Alamaha St, industrial section of Kahului. 871.7787

In the 1820s, the Hawaiian kingdom's greatest source of revenue was the whaling industry.

5 Sir Wilfred's Espresso Cafe ★★$ A mecca for coffee lovers, this informal coffee house offers croissants and pastries, a salad bar, sandwiches, and other deli items. ♦ M-Th 9AM-6PM; F 9AM-9PM; Sa 9AM-5:30PM; Su 10AM-3PM. Maui Mall, Kahului. 877.3711

Maui

6 Chart House ★$$ A lovely waterfront setting on East Maui serving fine steaks and fresh fish. You'll find better prices here than at many other fish houses. It was started by the same people who used to own Up-Country Maui's best, the **Makawao Steak House.** There's also a second location outside of Lahaina. ♦ Seafood ♦ Daily 5:30-10PM. 500 N. Puunene Ave, Kahului. 877.2476. Also at: 1450 Front St. 661.0937

7 Maui Palms Hotel $$ This hotel on Kahului Bay is reasonably priced and convenient, and located about two miles from the Kahului Airport. Don't expect resort glamour, though. Two stories, with a large Japanese dining room. ♦ 150 Kaahumanu Ave, Kahului. 877.0071, 800/367.5004; fax 871.5797

8 Maui Beach Hotel $$ Businesspeople from other islands frequent this hotel because of its proximity to Kahului Airport and the business hubs of Kahului and Wailuku. It features bare-bones, no-nonsense accommodations. Two stories, 154 rooms, pool. Free airport shuttle. ♦ 170 Kaahumanu Ave, Kahului. 877.0051, 800/367.5004; fax 871.5197

9 Maui's Best Maui has long been known for its arts and crafts, Kula onions, Maui potato chips, Island Princess chocolate-coated coffee beans and macadamia nuts, and up-country teas. Stop here for a wide selection of mementos and gifts such as candies, books, handmade quilted pillows, handcrafted jewelry, and Island plants (inspected and approved for travel). ♦ M-W, Sa 9AM-5:30PM; Th-F 9AM-9PM; Su 10AM-3PM. Kaahumanu Shopping Center, Kahului. 877.2665

10 Class Act Restaurant $$ The Maui Community College's advanced cooking class prepares and serves delicious, creative lunches featuring Continental, American, and Asian cuisines. ♦ W, F 11:30AM-1PM. Call W, F 8-10:30AM for reservations. Maui Community College, Kahului. 242.1210

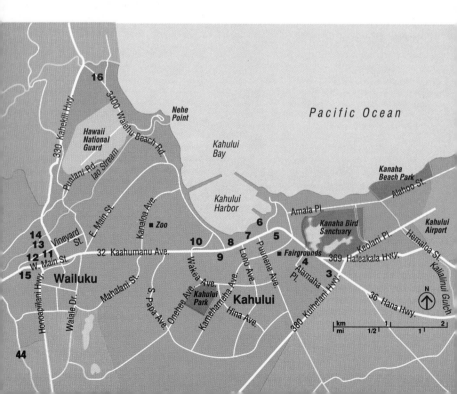

11 Chums ★$ A diner atmosphere, upgraded local food, and dishes such as saimin, Portuguese bean soup, oxtail soup, cheeseburgers, and hot turkey sandwiches make this a Wailuku institution. Early risers will like the hours (it opens between 6:30-7AM) and budget watchers the prices, which the new owners lowered when they took over in 1989. Hotcakes, omelets, and French toast round out the breakfast menu, with specials such as broiled *ono* and teriyaki chicken offered the rest of the day. The poached *mahimahi* in white wine sauce for under seven dollars is a real find. ♦ Hawaiian ♦ M-Sa 6:30AM-10:30PM; Su 7AM-10PM. 1900 Main St, Wailuku. 244.1000

12 Saeng's Thai Cuisine ★★$$ This new and favorite eatery on the block features indoor and garden seating, and a spate of fiery green, red, and yellow curries. Popular dishes are basil chicken and Masaman chicken, cooked with potatoes, peanuts, and coconut milk. ♦ Thai ♦ M-F 11AM-2:30PM, 5-9:30PM; Sa-Su 5-9:30PM. 2119 Vineyard St, Wailuku. 244.1567/1568

13 Northshore Inn $ **Chris** and **Katie Dunkel** transformed a shabby corner of Wailuku into a clean, cordial, hostel-like inn ideal for backpackers, windsurfers, and international budget travelers. The 19 low-priced rooms (single, double, and bunk) are on the upper floor of what was once the Wailuku Grand Hotel. Features include window boxes with bougainvilleas, a small TV lounge, clean shared bathrooms, and a genial atmosphere; the hosts often take their guests hiking, surfing, or to the beach for volleyball and barbecues. ♦ 2080 Vineyard St, Wailuku. 242.8999

14 Siam Thai ★★$$ Nothing fancy at this great restaurant, just spicy Thai food and friendly service. The vegetarian dishes stand out, as do the celebrity patron pictures on the walls. Owner **Mike Kachornsrichol** has kept people coming here for years. ♦ Thai ♦ M-F 11AM-2:30PM, 5-9:30PM; Sa-Su 5-9:30PM. 123 N. Market St, Old Wailuku Town. 244.3817/4132

There are about 400 passion-fruit species in existence, many of which were introduced to Hawaii and have since become so aggressively abundant they're choking the state's fragile native plants.

Restaurants/Clubs: Red　　Hotels: Blue
Shops/ 🌿 Outdoors: Green　**Sights/Culture: Black**

15 The Bailey House The Maui Historical Society operates this gallery and museum, also called **Hale Ho'ike'ike**, meaning "house of display." This former missionary home of the prominent Bailey family is a piece of history in itself. Missionaries **Edward** and **Caroline Bailey** came to Maui to run the Wailuku Female Seminary, which closed in the mid-1800s because of lack of funding. The Baileys moved to California in 1885 but left a building and legacy dedicated to the display of Hawaiian artifacts such as quilts, tapa cloth, and precontact (before Captain Cook arrived) implements and woven *lauhala* goods. A noteworthy stop, fulfilling and less tiring than other museums. ♦ Donation requested. Daily 10AM-4:30PM. 244.3326

16 Waiehu Municipal Golf Course It's hard to get a tee time on this 18-hole course because it's so reasonably priced—$25 for up to 18 holes. Local golfers, and those seeking an alternative to the expensive resort courses, where green fees are $100 or more, keep the course busy. Call at least two days in advance for reservations. Par 72, 6,330 yards. ♦ Pro shop. 243.7400

17 Maui Tropical Plantation Sugarcane, pineapples, bananas, papayas, coffee beans, macadamia nuts, exotic flowers, and other agricultural crops make this 112-acre park in Waikapu, just outside Wailuku and six miles from the Kahului Airport, a showcase for Hawaii's agricultural industry. The park was developed by **Bill** and **Lynn Taylor** of Australia on land owned by the C. Brewer Corp. More than a dozen crops are planted in the shape of a fan emanating from the restaurant and market area; the 45-minute narrated tram tours take you through 50 acres of the plantation. The *kapu* (Keep Out) signs posted on most agricultural areas in the Islands are nowhere in sight here. The tram rides take you into papaya, mango, and guava groves, coffee and macadamia nut orchards, and sugarcane and pineapple fields, with stops for walking around to take a closer look. The orchids, hibiscus, and other greenhouse plants in the nursery can be shipped home, and there's a marketplace that sells produce grown on the plantation, including a special blend of fruit that has been agriculturally inspected for shipment from the island. The **Tropical Restaurant** serves fresh fruit creations (try the *lilikoi* and ginger parfaits), and for lunch there's a tropical luncheon buffet and on Wednesday and Friday (5-8PM), a Hawaiian country barbecue, with *paniolo* (cowboy) entertainment and square dancing. Some of the offerings are steaks, chili, salad bar, and macadamia nut pie. All in all, it's touristy but enjoyable. ♦ Daily 9AM-5PM. Shuttle service available from designated pick-up points. Located on Hwy 30 at Waikapu. 244.7643

18 Kepaniwai Park and Heritage Gardens This country park beneath the Iao Needle pays tribute to Maui's various ethnic groups with exhibition pavilions and gardens reflect-

ing the cultures of the Hawaiians, Japanese, Chinese, Filipinos, and Portuguese. Kids love the park, which has a children's swimming pool and picnic pavilions. ♦ Off Iao Valley Rd, west of Wailuku. 243.7408

19 Iao Needle and Iao Valley State Park A 2,250-foot-high pillar of stone, called the Iao Needle, is the centerpiece of this lush valley where in 1790 **Kamehameha the Great** fought the decisive battle to conquer Maui in one of the bloodiest wars in Hawaiian history (the dead filled Iao Stream and the water ran red). The Iao Needle is flanked by the walls of Puu Kukui and overlooks verdant Iao Valley, where the ancients buried *alii* (royalty). Their bones, believed to contain spiritual powers, were carefully sequestered in caves to protect them against abuse or misuse. Iao's beauty is both powerful and haunting. There's a hiking trail here and many secluded spots for picnicking. ♦ Daily 7AM-6:45PM, Jan-Apr, Oct-Dec; daily 7AM-7:45PM, May-Sep. Off Iao Valley Rd, west of Wailuku

20 Fleming Beach Park This popular beach extends from Kapalua Golf Club's 16th hole to low cliffs. Use caution when swimming; the steep beach is subject to strong riptides. Picnic and public facilities. ♦ Public access off Honoapiilani Hwy north of Kapalua

21 Kapalua Golf Club Until 1991 there were only two magnificent courses at Kapalua. They received awards galore, including one from *Golf* magazine, which designated Kapalua Golf Club among the 12 best golf resorts in America. The **Village Course** and the **Bay Course** were cut into the base of a 23,000-acre pineapple plantation; with an ocean view from almost every fairway. Both courses were designed by **Arnold Palmer**, but the Village Course presents the greater test. Its deep valleys, ridges, lake, and ironwood and eucalyptus trees make it a spectacularly scenic challenge. The Bay Course is older, flatter, and more open, the longtime home of the **Isuzu Kapalua International.**

Now you can golf on a third course at Kapalua: the highly touted, brand new **Plantation Course**, designed by **Ben Crenshaw**. It's massive—240 acres—and natural, with large-scale features such as gradual slopes, deep valleys, native grasses, and long, generous fairways. It's already reaping accolades and will inherit the Isuzu tournament. A drawback is that Kapalua Golf Club is often windy, and there's a greater chance of mist and rain here than at Kaanapali or Wailea courses. Bay Course: Par 72, 6,151 yards; Village Course: Par 71, 6,001 yards; Plantation Course: Par 73, 7,100 yards. ♦ Expensive green fees; preferred starting times and fees extended to Kapalua Bay Hotel and Villas guests. Pro shop. 669.8044

22 The Grill & Bar ★★$$$ This extremely handsome bar and dining room is still commendable, and well-deserving of its long-standing reputation. Owned by **TS Enterprises**, the same reliable operators of Kimo's and Chico's Cantina in Lahaina, it overlooks the Kapalua Golf Club and parts of Napili Bay. The sophisticated menu includes fresh Island fish, steak, rack of lamb, and nightly specials. Outstanding wine list. ♦ Continental ♦ Daily 11:30AM-3PM, 5-10:30PM. Between the tennis gardens and the golf club at Kapalua Resort. 669.5653

22 Pineapple Hill ★$$$ Residents are quick to dismiss this as a touristy restaurant, and they should. It occupies a former plantation manager's home high above the pineapple fields and golf courses of Kapalua. But tourists love it because of the view and the aura it has of being a part of Hawaii's rich plantation history. Predictably, this is a restaurant whose scenery is superior to its food, which leans toward standard beef, chicken, and seafood courses, with mild attempts at Polynesian influences. If you're in the neighborhood don't miss the sunset view from here. ♦ Continental ♦ Daily 5-10PM. Kapalua. 669.6129 (call for directions)

23 Kapalua Bay Hotel and Villas $$$$ One reason Kapalua has become the venue for several world-renowned events is

its reputation as the quietest and most distinctive resort on the island. The hotel (pictured at right) has a spectacular natural setting, dominated by ocean vistas on three sides (the fourth looks toward a woodsy golf course behind the hotel), 19th-century pine trees, pineapple fields, and the West Maui Mountains. The 194 rooms feature private lanais, and the marble bathrooms all have two closets, separate shower and tub, double marble vanities, and an extra telephone. The hotel is a cocoon for guests who prefer to mix around the swimming pool over venturing off into the wilds. The Kapalua is the site of several world-class festivals, including the **Kapalua Music Festival,** which attracts a contingent of international classical musicians, and the **Kapalua Wine Symposium,** which features judging, demonstrations, and tastings of wines, champagnes, and gourmet foods by international experts. The symposium is Hawaii's most noteworthy and progressive food-and-wine event. You may also enjoy the Hawaiian program offered every Thursday morning in the mall of the Kapalua Shops, where *kumu hula* **Cliff Ahue** presents an engaging program of ancient hula, called *kahiko.* Pools, golf, tennis. ♦ One Bay Dr, Kapalua. 669.5656, 800/367.8000; fax 669.4694

Within Kapalua Bay Hotel and Villas:

The Bay Club ★★★$$$ The brief shuttle ride or walk here from the hotel is especially enjoyable at sunset or on a clear, starry night. Set on a promontory overlooking the ocean, the sophisticated Bay Club's ambience blends superbly with soft Maui evenings (it was recently cited by *The Honolulu Advertiser* newspaper as the restaurant on Maui with the best sunset view). The view is enveloping, with palm trees outside the veranda and the island of Lanai on the horizon. Fresh *mahi-mahi, opakapaka,* and *ahi* come in half a dozen preparations, and the bouillabaise is excellent. The Bay Club also has a piano

bar. ♦ Continental ♦ Daily 11:30AM-2PM, 6-9:30PM. Jacket required at dinner. 669.5656

The Garden $$ If you're tired of the beach, consider dining in this lovely setting beside a stream, looking out over lush gardens and pathways. Although it's a great place for breakfast and pleasant enough for dinner, the cuisine cannot be compared to that of The Bay Club. But you'll enjoy the fresh Kula

Maui

greens, *lilikoi* (passion fruit), fettuccine, and *ahi* carpaccio. The à la carte menu also offers veal medallions, and chicken or beef entrées. ♦ Continental ♦ M-Sa 6:30-11AM, 6-10:30PM; Su 11:30AM-2PM, 6-10:30PM. 669.5656

The Kapalua Shops Like a museum that entices without exhausting, this small, exclusive cluster of boutiques will trigger all your acquisitive instincts: jewelry, clothing, antiques, and the Indonesian and oriental artifacts of **Distant Drums,** an amalgam of collectibles from around the Pacific Rim. Fashion enthusiasts should be sure to stop at **Longhi** for designer clothing. ♦ Distant Drums M-Sa 9AM-7PM; Su 9AM-6PM. Longhi M-Sa 9AM-8PM; Su 9AM-6PM

Kapalua Bay Hotel and Villas

GEORGE MOU

24 Kapalua Resort In the mid-1970s **Colin C. Cameron** took 750 ocean-view acres of his family's 23,000-acre pineapple empire and had a team of resort experts build the consummate luxury destination. Cameron, a descendant of missionaries who presides over the family owned **Maui Land & Pineapple Company**, was not disappointed. In 1978 the Kapalua Bay Hotel opened and immediately established itself as Hawaii's landmark luxury resort, featuring West Maui's most extraordinary bays, three of the state's finest golf courses, and world-class accommodations. The 1,500-acre Kapalua Resort is set amid rolling pineapple fields and dramatic Cook pines, with a spectacular backdrop of West Maui hills. Now owned by **Tokai Kanko** and **Maui Land &**

Maui

Pineapple Company, the Bay Hotel, with its restaurants and shops, remains the centerpiece of the resort. The villas—actually multimillion-dollar homes—are owned by private landowners and rent them out short-term (except Ironwoods, which has a 30-day minimum rental). The 194-room hotel also manages and rents 130 of these villas. Luxurious and self-sufficient, but with fewer amenities, the villas appeal to families, celebrities seeking privacy, and people who like full kitchens, a lot of space, and all the features of home. The resort is still growing; additions include the Ritz-Carlton, Kapalua, scheduled to open in 1992, and the new Village Course Golf Shop and Restaurant. Access to West Maui and Kapalua has been much easier since the 1987 opening of the West Maui-Kapalua Airport on the site of a sugarcane field off Hwy 30. ♦ 500 Bay Dr, Kapalua. 669.7110, 800/527.2582

25 Kapalua Beach Along with Napili Bay, this is the safest swimming beach on West Maui and a longtime favorite among locals, who still call it **Fleming Beach.** (It was renamed when the resort was developed.) A good snorkeling and picnic spot. ♦ Public access at the Napili side of the beach, Kapalua

Happy Trails to You

For a guided walking tour of Maui's many natural splendors, contact naturalist **Ken Schmitt,** who leads groups of two to six people on hikes to Maui's waterfalls, rain forests, canyons, Haleakala Crater, and other attractions. Schmitt's well-versed on Hawaii's archaeology, mythology, and natural life, and he'll tell you all about it. Round-trip transportation, lunch, waterproof pack, raincoat, and first-aid equipment are provided for the half-day or all-day hikes. For more information, contact Ken Schmitt at: Box 330969, Kahului HI 96733, 879.5270.

26 Napili Shores Resort $$$ Choose from low-rise studios and one-bedroom condominiums with lanais and kitchens in this garden setting on the Napili Bay beachfront. Two pools and two restaurants. ♦ 5315 Honoapiilani Hwy, Lahaina. 669.8061, 800/777.1700; fax 669.5407

26 Orient Express ★$$$ The signature dishes include coconut chicken soup, spinach duck, Mandarin fish clay pot, and a hot beef and seafood dish named after the restaurant. The stuffed chicken wings and Thai noodle soup are also first-rate. ♦ Asian ♦ Daily 5:30-10PM. Napili Shores Resort, Lahaina. 669.8077

26 Napili Kai Beach Club $$$ This is the kind of seasoned, classic Hawaiian-style inn ner that is increasingly rare—and so often attempted—on the Islands. It's no wonder that up to 40 percent of its clientele are repeat guests. The tastefully landscaped grounds are bordered by a stone pathway fringed by hibiscus and *naupaka* bushes, and beyond them, is the ocean. Concrete decks, barbecue areas, outdoor bars, and complimentary coffee and mai tai parties make this is a gregarious vacation spot, a place where guests become friends, and return the following year to enjoy the fabulous sunsets together again. All 180 units are oceanfront and spread out unobtrusively over 10 acres, and nearly all of them have full kitchens; the Lahaina Wing is closest to the beach. You couldn't ask for a friendlier staff. Ask about the **Napili Foundation,** a program for the children of West Maui, who practice hula and the Hawaiian arts several times a week and perform every Friday night here. Five pools, a huge Jacuzzi, public access to Napili and Kapalua bays, excellent snorkeling, tennis, putting greens, and a restaurant. No credit cards accepted for the hotel. ♦ 5900 Honoapiilani Rd, Lahaina. 669.6271, 800/367.5030; fax 669.5740

Within Napili Kai Beach Club:

Sea House $$ This restaurant has gone through several name changes, but the menu has remained constant. Rack of lamb and surf-and-turf staples are served in a simple room overlooking Napili Bay. ♦ American ♦ Daily 8-11AM, noon-3PM, 6-9PM. Hawaiian music M-Th, Sa 6-10PM; hula dinner show F 6-8:30PM. 669.6271

26 Napili Bay This exquisite bay features a long, sandy beach between two rocky points. Excellent swimming and snorkeling; occasionally there's also good winter surfing and bodysurfing. ♦ Public access at Napili Pl, on Hui Dr

27 Kahana Keyes $$$ Seafood, steaks, and standard American fare are served in a room overlooking the condominium pool with a distant view of the ocean. Your best bet is to arrive around 7PM, when you not only snare a good table for the sunset view, but also catch the Early Bird Special, which features a complete dinner that costs substantially less than the later evening meals. ♦ American ♦ Daily 5:30-10PM. In the Kahana Villa condominiums, between the Valley Isle and Royal Kahana, on Lower Honoapiilani Hwy, Kahana. 669.8071

27 Erik's Seafood Grotto ★$$$ The tasteful, dining room offers an enormous selection of fresh Island and mainland fish plus good ocean views. You can choose from 11 different fresh fish dishes, several kinds of shell-fish, and an award-winning bouillabaise. And if it's available, try the fresh Island lobster. ♦ Seafood ♦ Daily 5-10PM. In the Kahana Villa condominiums, 4242 Lower Honoapiilani Hwy, Kahana. 669.4806

28 Kahana Beach This white, sandy beach with a shallow bottom of sand and rock is fronted by shoreline resorts. Fair for swimming. ♦ Off Honoapiilani Hwy, near Mahinahina Point

29 Mahana at Kaanapali Condominium $$$ Managed by Aston Resorts, this complex has two 12-story towers with 141 units, and a good swimming beach a hundred yards away. All studios and one- and two-bedroom units face the ocean. Your choices include rooms with refrigerators, studio suites with kitchens, and various larger units, with or without kitchens. The minimum stay is three days. Pool, tennis. ♦ 110 Kaanapali Shores Pl, Kaanapali. 661.8751, 800/922.7866

29 Aston Kaanapali Shores $$$ This four-diamond, beachfront condominium resort has all the amenities, from studios to two-bedroom, two-bath suites with luxurious kitchens and large lanais. Oceanfront views between Kaanapali and Kahana. ♦ 3445 Honoapiilani Hwy, Honoapiilani. 667.2211, 800/922.7866

"Shave ice" is a Hawaiian treat a lot like the snow cone, except the ice is shaved finer. The ice is packed into a fluffy mound and doused with tropical fruit-flavored syrups and sometimes other toppings. True aficionados ask for a dollop of sweetened *azuki* beans and vanilla ice cream at the bottom.

EMBASSY SUITES RESORT

29 Embassy Suites Resort $$$ This all-suites hotel occupies 14 oceanfront acres at the northern edge of Kaanapali Beach, with 413 one- and two-bedroom suites. You'll forgive the garish pink exterior once you enter these luxurious abodes. Amenities abound here: a typical one-bedroom suite occupies 820 square feet and includes queen-sized sofa beds, a 35-inch big-screen TV, full kitchen, oversized bath with two marble vanities, and lanais accessible from the living room and

bedroom. As if you weren't pampered enough by the views of Lanai and Molokai, there's a health club and two pools. ♦ 104 Kaanapali Shores Pl, Kaanapali. 661.2000, 800/462.6284; fax 667.5821

30 Coastline between Kaanapali and Napili West Maui's eyesore is this strip of coastline on the Honoapiilani Hwy (Hwy 30) between Kaanapali and Napili. Overgrown with condominiums, this stretch of coast is the antithesis of all that Kaanapali and Kapalua represent. Naturally, accommodations here are cheaper. Some of the older condominiums are comfortable, but the new high rises are less appealing, and units flush against the highway get a lot of traffic noise. With few exceptions, the beaches here are poor to middling. Although condominiums may advertise that they are near the water, the beach may be unsuitable for swimming. In addition, the area is far removed from some of the best restaurants, so you will have to drive to Kapalua, Kaanapali, or Lahaina for decent meals. ♦ Hwy 30

31 International Colony Club Condomninium $$$ These studios, and one- and two-bedroom cottages are grouped around landscaped grounds across the highway from Kaanapali's northern boundary. Only 44 units were built on this spacious, 10½-acre retreat. Two pools. ♦ 2750 Kalapu Dr, Kaanapali, off Hwy 30. 661.4070, 800/526.6284

32 Maui Kaanapali Villas $$$ In 1983 the east side of the Royal Lahaina hotel was converted into condos under the management of the **Hotel Corp. of the Pacific.** About 200 of the 253 studios and one-bedroom units are in the vacation rental pool, now run by Aston Hawaiiana, and various independent managers. Pool. ♦ 45 Kai Ala Dr, Lahaina. 667.7791/8687, 800/922.7866

| **Restaurants/Clubs:** Red | **Hotels:** Blue |
| Shops/ ♠ **Outdoors:** Green | **Sights/Culture:** Black |

Seashells by the Seashore

Hawaii is a mecca for shell collectors. And Maui is the hot spot, for its shores hide some of the world's rarest and most valuable shells, including the prized *checkered cowry*. Some shellseekers are ingenious and dedicated treasure hunters who check local newspapers for tide charts every day, then scavenge tide pools and study the shells' habitats and camouflages. Many also snorkel or skin-dive for the precious shells.

But the amateur sheller should bear in mind that there is much more involved here than meets the eye. Snorkeling for shells where currents are strong can be dangerous, so it's always best to follow a native guide's directions. And many shelled creatures have powerful bites or stings that can make you ill.

Maui

Most importantly, remember that a shell is not just another pretty rock; it is the home of a living sea animal better suited to its own ecological circle than to your living room bookshelves. To keep the waters from being depleted of the special specimens, shellseekers are advised to leave the shells where they found them—unless, of course, the resident has already abandoned his home.

The **Waikiki Aquarium** on Oahu features living shells, such as the spectacular Giant Clam and Chambered Nautilus, plus a well-stocked bookstore with volumes of shell information. The **Kokee Natural History Museum** on Kauai and the **Kauai Museum** also feature shell collections. For all you've ever wanted to know about mollusks, hook up with the **Hawaiian Malacological Society,** which meets the first Wednesday of every month (except in December) at the First United Methodist Church, 1020 S. Beretania St, Honolulu. For their *Hawaiian Shell News* report and more information, write to them at: Box 22130, Honolulu HI 96823-2130.

Leopard Cone (*Conus leopardus)* These fairly common cones are among the biggest in Hawaii, growing as long as 9 inches. The largest are usually found in deep water and are covered with spots.

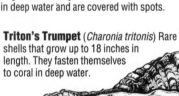

Triton's Trumpet (*Charonia tritonis*) Rare shells that grow up to 18 inches in length. They fasten themselves to coral in deep water.

Marlin Spike Auger (*Terebra maculata*) Found in depths of more than 10 feet, these grow up to 10 inches long and are the largest augers on earth.

Crenulated Auger (*Terebra crenulata*) These spiny pink or blue shells are commonly found in shallow water. They are carnivores, usually about 5 inches long. Their spiral rings distinguish them from other Island augers.

Knobby Spindle (*Latirus nodus*) This common pink shell houses a bright red sea creature.

Tile Miter (*Mitra incompta*) Miters are not generally prized by collectors, since the 4-inch-long, rough-textured shells are fairly common. They live among coral beds 30 feet to 80 feet deep.

Horned Helmet (*Cassis cornuta*) The largest of the Hawaiian shells, which may grow as long as 1 foot.

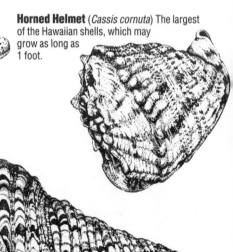

Lettered Miter (*Mitra litterata*) These viscous, tiny carnivores have a poisonous sting they use to capture worms for dinner. Only 1 inch long, they hide under loose coral at the water's surface.

Green-Mouthed Spindle (*Peristernia chlorostome*) More yellow than green, this common 1/2- to 3/4-inch shell lives in coral along the shore.

Fringed Cowry (*Cypraea fimbriata*) This orange cowry chooses orange coral as camouflage in depths of 2 to 60 feet.

Blood-Spotted Triton (*Bursa cruentata*) This is a lovely, common triton with an inner rim ranging from white to pale violet.

Pimpled Basket (*Nassarius papillosus*) This scavenger hops along on a single muscle "foot." Its shell grows 1 to 2 1/4 inches long.

Hawaiian Limpet (*Petella sandwichensis*) Growing up to 2 inches long, this shell is found in shallow water or on rocks exposed to waves. This exclusively Hawaiian animal is an important local delicacy.

Golden Yellow Cone (*Conus flavidus*) These 2 1/2-inch-long shells range from white to greenish yellow. Like other cones, they often have an outer layer of thick *periostracum,* a substance that obscures the shells' fine colors until removed.

Brilliant Drupe (*Drupa rubusidaeus*) Long spines and a pinkish mouth distinguish this 1 1/2-inch-long shell.

Snakehead Cowry (*Cypraea caputserpentis*) Hawaii's most common cowry. It's a herbivorous night feeder and grows to 1 1/2 inches in length .

Checkered Cowry (*Cypraea tessellata*) This rare and beautiful prize is a native only to Hawaii. The tiny 3/4- to 1 1/2-inch-long shell hides in about 50 feet of water.

Knobbed Drupe (*Drupa nodus*) A common shell found in shallow water. Look for its black spikes on a white background, and a lavendar mouth.

Rough Periwinkle (*Littorina scabra*) An edible animal that lives in shoreline coral.

Murex Pele (*Murex pele*) These rough, craggy carnivores use their spiky surfaces as spears to capture other mollusks. Found only in Hawaii, they hide in coral at depths of 40 feet.

Penniform Cone (*Conus pennaceua*) Habitants of these cones fire darts to stun their prey; some species are even dangerous to humans.  But the common 3-inch-long cones are safe as well as beautiful, with an intricate and varied design. They live buried in sand on the ocean floor.

Reticulated Cowry (*Cypaea maculifera*) This cowry shell is one of the most prized by world collectors. Hawaiians use the shells as jewelry and decoration. The smooth, colorful specimen is found under rocks or on coral near the shore.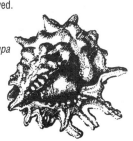

33 Royal Lahaina $$$ This hotel offers recently renovated rooms and cottages in a variety of shapes and sizes, from two-story seaside cottages to oceanfront suites in the 12-story Lahaina Kai tower. The mix of low- and high-rise buildings is enhanced by 27 acres of tropical landscaping bordered by the ocean and a golf course, and crisscrossed by meandering walkways. There is more of everything at the Royal Lahaina: four dining rooms and lounges, two swimming pools, tennis courts at the hotel's tennis ranch (plus a stadium tennis court), and two golf courses. The Royal Lahaina Luau is a pleasant outdoor dining affair, with delicious food and a program bolstered by *kumu hula* **Frank Kawaikapuokalani Hewitt,** one of Hawaii's luminaries, who commutes from Oahu to

perform at the Royal Lahaina. All rooms have private lanais and refrigerators; suite cottages have kitchen facilities. Nightly luau. ◆ 2780 Kekaha Dr. 661.3611, 800/733.7777; fax 661.6150

Within the Royal Lahaina:

Royal Ocean Terrace $$$ This dark but regal restaurant features a popular Friday seafood buffet and Sunday brunch. ◆ Continental ◆ Daily 10AM-2PM, 5:30-10PM. 661.3611

Chopsticks $$ The idea here is to pick your way through a lineup of Pacific and Asian bits and pieces (a great idea that was au courant a few years ago, but the excitement has waned). Chopsticks is perfect if you want a large sampling of exotic and ethnic dishes in one sitting. ◆ Asian ◆ W-Su 6-9:30PM. 661.3611

Moby Dick's Seafood Restaurant $$$ That ubiquitous menu item, the catch of the day, is here in full force, with a large cast of supporting seafood in a dining room with a great view. ◆ Seafood ◆ M-Tu, F-Sa 6-9:30PM. 661.3611

34 Maui Eldorado Condominium $$$ These attractive apartments sit between the highway and the beach, bordered by a golf course. More than half of the 204 units are available for vacation rentals. Pool, golf courses, and beach house for guests. ◆ 2661 Kekaa Dr, Kaanapali. 661.0021, 800/535.0085; fax 667.7039

35 Kaanapali Royal Condominiums $$$ The 105 townhouse-style, two-bedroom, two-bath suites on the 16th fairway of the Royal Kaanapali Golf Course are in 15 buildings nestled on the side of a hill. Pool and tennis courts are available. ◆ 2560 Kekaa Dr, Kaanapali. 667.7200

36 Sheraton Maui $$$ This 503-room hotel occupies the longest and broadest stretch of Kaanapali Beach—some call it the best on this side of the island—offering guests a variety of elevations for winter whale watching, and year round glorious sunsets. There are four-story guest units on top of the 80-foot-high promontory known as Black Rock; two six-story units hugging the cliff walls; and 26 Polynesian-style cottages scattered across the 23-acre site for people who like to stay close to the ground. Although an extensive renovation program added new color schemes in the guest rooms and generally upgraded the landscapes and dining facilities, this is still a Sheraton, with Sheraton-level tastes and standards. The best thing about this hotel is its location near the beach, with the best sunbathing and swimming in the area. (Although you should be prepared for an abrupt shoreline drop-off, the cove below Black Rock is excellent for beginning snorkelers.) Two pools, tennis, golf. ◆ 2605 Kaanapali Pkwy, Lahaina. 661.0031, 800/325.3535; fax 661.0458

Within the Sheraton-Maui:

Discovery Room ★$$$ The hotel's showcase dining facility is built atop Black Rock. The breakfast buffet is substantial, but the food is eclipsed by the view. The Discovery Room dinner show offers a mix of modern and ancient Hawaiian entertainment with Continental fare—fresh fish en papillote, sautéed *mahimahi*, and some Hawaiian appetizers and desserts. At sunset, in a tradition maintained since the hotel's opening, a diver plunges into the ocean from a spot near the Sundowner Bar. This daring feat follows the lighting of torches that flicker in a line leading to the summit. ◆ Continental ◆ Daily 6:30-10:30AM, 6:30-9:30PM. 661.0031

37 Kaanapali Beach Resort The first master-planned destination resort in Hawaii was created on a chunk of barren land too dry for sugar cultivation but lined with three miles of, white sand beaches too beautiful to ignore. In the early 1950s **Amfac Corp.** of Honolulu began planning a complex that would give Waikiki a run for its money. After Kaanapali Resort's unveiling in 1962, Maui became the first neighbor Island to attract a volume of business previously enjoyed only by Oahu. The resort encompasses six hotels and six condominiums, two 18-hole championship golf

---

Restaurants/Clubs: Red   **Hotels:** Blue

Shops/ 🌳 Outdoors: Green   **Sights/Culture:** Black

courses, 37 tennis courts, a whaling museum, and the **Whaler's Village** shopping complex. Each hotel has its own beach facilities and at least one pool, and a three-mile beachwalk connects the opposite ends of the resort. The resort is Hawaii's largest, occupying some 1,200 acres, 500 of which are developed. A jitney will take you around the resort, or you can travel to Lahaina, six miles away, aboard a rebuilt sugarcane train or on a shuttle bus. The planners of Kaanapali, aware that tourism was coming to Maui, designed the resort with the intention of spanning to the rest of the island. Instead of letting tourists run amok from one haphazardly placed hotel or condo to another, they would encourage people to stay in a self-contained environment. This plan has worked fairly well, although Kaanapali's proximity to Lahaina has turned the town into a Polynesian Knott's Berry Farm. ◆ 2530 Kekaa Dr, Lahaina. 661.3271

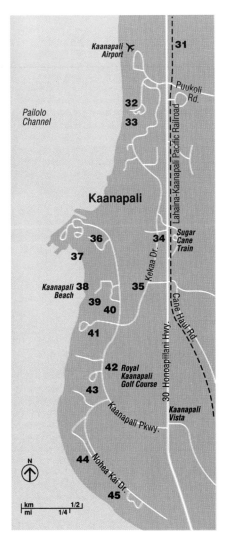

38 Kaanapali Beach Super swimming along a beautiful, sandy beach stretching for three miles. The ocean is generally calm, but hotels post red flags when it's too dangerous for swimming. The sandy bottom here drops off abruptly. ◆ Off Kaanapali Pkwy, directly in front of the hotel

39 Kaanapali Beach Hotel $$$ This 429-room hotel is built in a horseshoe shape on landscaped grounds, with the center court-

yard opening to the beach and Maui sunsets. The whale-shaped pool is only a few yards from the ocean, and the complex's immediate neighbor is Whaler's Village, where you'll find an excellent collection of shops and restaurants. Pool, golf, refrigerators, and private lanais. ◆ 2525 Kaanapali Pkwy, Lahaina. 661.0011, 800/657.7700; fax 667.5978

Within Kaanapali Beach Hotel:

Tiki Terrace $$ It's still known for its buffet and its Sunday champagne brunch, complete with a 24-foot-long pastry table and an omelet station. The dinner specialty is *kiawe*-roasted prime rib. The entrées here include fresh fish, teriyaki chicken, and standard American fare, all served with soup and salad bar. ◆ American ◆ M-Sa 7-11AM, 6-9:30PM; Su 9AM-2PM, 6-9:30PM. 661.0011

40 Whaler Condominium $$$ These twin high-rise towers, 360 units total, sit on an excellent stretch of beach adjacent to Whaler's Village. A fine facility in the heart of the Kaanapali Beach Resort with a minimum stay of three days required. Pool and tennis. ◆ 2481 Kaanapali Pkwy, Lahaina. 661.4861, 800/367.7052; fax 661.8315

41 Ricco's Old World Delicatessen $$ This classic deli is a magnet for lovers of pizza, calzone, mile-high Italian combo sandwiches, and other Italian favorites. You'll find the old-fashioned French Dip sandwich here, as well as deli dogs, cole slaw, and New York cheesecake. Informal, always busy, and a great stop for a cappuccino or a beer from West Maui's best beer list. ◆ Italian/American ◆ Daily 11AM-10PM. Whaler's Village, Kaanapali Beach Resort, Lahaina. 661.4433

Friday in Hawaii is called "Aloha Friday," and most people—even the stodgiest executives—wear colorful aloha shirts and muumuus in celebration of the end of the work week.

41 Leilani's on the Beach ★★★$$$
Three stars for atmosphere at this beach-front restaurant owned and operated by TS Restaurants of Hawaii and California, who have created a significant following on Maui with such restaurants as Kimo's, the Grill & Bar, and Chico's Cantina, also in Whaler's Village. For lighter fare, Leilani's has added a seafood bar, the Beachside

Maui

Grill, next to the cocktail lounge. The regular menu is long on fresh Hawaiian fish, broiled steaks, and smoked ribs and chicken. ♦ American ♦ Daily 11:30AM-11PM. Whaler's Village, Kaanapali Beach Resort, Lahaina. 661.4495

41 El Crab Catcher ★★$$$ The help at this well-established *in* spot is young and perfectly tanned; the clientele is young and perfectly tanned (especially at night); and the atmosphere is invigorating and festive. Large, crowded, and open to the sea, it offers the consummate West Maui scenario of poolside tables and an informal, open-air dining room. The straightforward menu features a variety of crab dishes, among them the ever-popular crab bisque. Try the crab-stuffed mushrooms with Maui onions, but leave room for the delectable hula pie, the downfall dessert. ♦ Seafood ♦ Daily 11:30AM-3PM, 5:30-10PM. Whaler's Village, Kaanapali Beach Resort, Lahaina. 661.4423

41 Chico's Cantina ★$$ This local watering hole is run by the same people who have made institutions of Kimo's on Front St, the Grill & Bar, and Leilani's. The colorful, Mexican-tile decor and open-air dining area may find you eating chips and salsa and drinking tropical concoctions and beer for the better part of the evening. The menu is good, standard fare: tacos, burritos, enchiladas, and chimichangas with rice and beans. There are also gringo selections such as burgers. ♦ Mexican ♦ Daily 11:30AM-2:30PM, 5-10PM. Whaler's Village, Kaanapali Beach Resort, Lahaina. 667.2777

41 Rusty Harpoon $$ Dieters beware! Rusty's has a waffle bar, where you can drench thick Belgian waffles with your own tropical syrups, fruit, whipped cream, and nuts. The beer 'n' burger combo and prime rib roasted in rock salt are favorite dinner selections, and they also serve pastas and fresh Island seafood. Touting its fresh fruit daiquiris, Rusty's refers to itself as the "daiquiri capital of the world." ♦ American ♦ Daily 8AM-10PM; bar until 1:30AM. Whaler's Village, Kaanapali Beach Resort, Lahaina. 661.3123

42 Royal Kaanapali Golf Course Designed in the sixties by **Robert Trent Jones Jr.**, the North Course offers spectacular views of the West Maui Mountains, the ocean, and the islands of Molokai and Lanai across the channel. It's a good golf test, with numerous water risks. The South Course, a former executive course extended to championship class, also has ocean views but is less exciting. Kaanapali can be windy, especially in late afternoons, which is why the high green fees are lowered after 2:30PM. North Course: Par 71, 6,136 yards. South Course: Par 72, 6,250 yards. ♦ Preferred starting times for guests at Kaanapali Beach Resort hotels. Kaanapali Pkwy, just north of the Westin Maui hotel. Pro shop. 661.3691

43 Westin Maui $$$$ After selling the Hyatt Regency Maui, developer **Chris Hemmeter** turned right around and went into direct competition, taking over the Maui Surf a few doors away and tuning it into the Westin Maui within the Kaanapali Beach Resort. When his $155 million resort was unveiled, it was full of Hemmeter's trademarks: a fantasy water complex consisting of five free-form, multi-level swimming pools, waterfalls, waterslides, and meandering streams; a $2.5 million collection of Pacific and Asian art; exotic wildlife, including a yellow-crested Triton cockatoo from New Zealand named Keoki; and eight restaurants and lounges. The 12-acre resort has two 11-story towers that stack up to 761 rooms and suites. The top two floors of the Beach Tower are reserved for the Royal Beach Club—37 extra-elegant rooms with a private elevator, breakfast buffet, and reserved poolside seating. ♦ 2365 Kaanapali Pkwy, Lahaina. 667.2525, 800/228.3000; fax 661.5764

Within the Westin Maui:

Sound of the Falls $$$ The hotel's main dining room features views of Lanai and Molokai, and of the resort's lagoon and exotic birds. The Continental menu leans toward French and oriental influences (from baked *onaga* to beluga Malassol caviar), but the best thing here is the Sunday champagne brunch, with its mounds of fresh Island fruit. At night you can dance under the stars to sentimental favorites in the Supper Club. ♦ Continental ♦ M-Sa 6-10PM; Su 10AM-2PM, 6-10PM. Classical pianist plays W-Th evenings; live music M-Tu, F-Su 8-11PM. 667.2525

Villa Restaurant $$$ Feast on fresh Island seafood and pastas in this dining spot surrounded by the hotel's sprawling lagoons, gardens, and waterfalls. ♦ Continental ♦ Daily 6-10PM. 667.2525

Cook's at the Beach $$ This poolside, all-day dining spot is two cuts above the typical hotel coffee shop. Island specialties, children's fare, and health-conscious entrées set this place apart. But you can forget about your waistline if you come here for the all-you-can-eat prime rib buffet in the evening. ♦ American ♦ Daily 6:30AM-11PM; also Su champagne brunch 9AM-2PM. 667.2525

Maui Marriott

44 Maui Marriott $$$
In 1981 Marriott opened its first resort hotel in Hawaii with 720 rooms in two nine-story buildings that extend seaward from a central lobby. Ninety percent of the rooms have ocean views. The design, with beautiful landscaping, cascading waterfalls, running streams, a coconut grove, and a tradewind-touched lobby, reflects the hotel chain's attempt to upgrade its image, but the architecture of the 15-acre site has been criticized as being too much like the Marriott's you find near airports. Nevertheless, the hotel's swimming pool fronts Kaanapali Beach, and each room has a private lanai. A $150 million price tag caught the attention of **Azuba USA Corp.,** a Japanese firm that bought the hotel and then, in 1990, revamped the guest rooms to the tune of $9 million. Golf and tennis. ♦ 100 Nohea Kai Dr, Lahaina. 667.1200, 800/228.9290; fax 667.0692

Within the Maui Marriott:

Moana Terrace $$$ The resort's main dining room opens to gardens and is terraced to give maximum ocean views. You can lunch either from the 25-foot-long buffet or from the menu of burgers, sandwiches, pastas, and fresh fish specials. ♦ Continental ♦ Daily 6:30AM-10PM. 667.1200

Nikko Steak House ★★$$$ Marriott's smartest move in Hawaii, the Japanese *teppanyaki* steak house has been a success since the day it opened. It filled a void in West Maui, where outstanding ethnic restaurants are still rare. After Nikko's house soup, be adventurous with the *teppanyaki* selection and the savory sauces, saving room for the fried ice cream (sponge cake filled with ice cream and then deep-fried). ♦ Japanese ♦ Daily 6-9PM. 667.1200

Lokelani Room $$$ The decor in this restaurant (named after Maui's official flow-

er) is Lahaina seafaring and the menu is American, Continental, and Polynesian, with an emphasis on fresh seafood. You can choose from five different Island fish selections daily, as well as lobster specials, beef dishes, and chowders. Best of all, it's a good value. ♦ Continental ♦ Daily 6-9PM. 667.1200

45 Hyatt Regency Maui $$$ Derring-do developer **Chris Hemmeter** built this "Disneyland for adults" in 1980 for $80 million. But in 1987 the five-star Hyatt was bought by **Kokusai Jidosha,** a Japanese company, for a cool $319 million (approximately $391,000/room), and in 1990 renovated for $12 million. The hotel consists of three connecting buildings on 18.5 oceanside acres, with 815 rooms and suites, 19 stories, and meetings facilities. The renovations included new custom-designed wall coverings, upholstery, and furniture, as well as Italian marble countertops and terracotta tile floors in every guest room. Hemmeter, however, should still be credited for the Hyatt's lavish collection of Asian and Pacific art, including John Young paintings, Hawaiian quilts, seven-foot cloisonné vases, Cambodian buddhas, Ming Dynasty wine pots, and battle shields from Papua New Guinea. Outside, a 154-foot enclosed waterslide was added to the area surrounding the half-acre swimming pool. And 14-karat gold tiles now embellish the sprawling pool's mosaic, designed by artists in Mexico, their installation was tedious. Each tile had to be numbered to ensure correct placement after being disassembled, then shipped to Maui and reassembled. If you're a water-lover you'll particularly like the swinging rope bridge and the **Grotto Bar,** which is placed in a lava cavern you swim up to between two waterfalls. Flamingos, swans, penguins, peacocks, and ducks add to the hotel's picturesque fantasyland features. The **Regency Club,** which occupies the top three floors of the Atrium Tower, is accessible only with a special elevator key. Regency Club members have access to a concierge on each floor, breakfast service, and sunset cocktails and appetizers. ♦ 200 Nohea Kai Dr, Lahaina. 661.1234, 800/233.1234; fax 667.4498

Within the Hyatt Regency Maui:

Lahaina Provision Company ★$$$ The service and the food here have not been up to their usual standards, and there's an off-putting air of exclusivity. The food—seafood, steaks, pastas, sandwiches, and salads—is served in a garden setting with nautical touches, decent but hardly memorable. The lavish Chocoholic Bar, featured nightly, still has its fans. ♦ Continental ♦ Daily 11:30AM-3PM, 6-10PM. 661.1234

Swan Court ★★★$$$ The large, elegantly appointed dining room of this award-winning restaurant overlooks its own lagoon with a flotilla of gliding swans. As the sun sets between Lanai and Molokai, you can enjoy the soft sounds of the piano from the nearby lounge and the stunning view of the waterfalls. The fresh fish and roast duckling are excellent dinner choices, or you might try the roast rack of lamb, châteaubriand, salmon, lobster in puff pastry, or the Szechuan-style, fresh catch of the day. The wine list is long and expensive. Swan Court also presents a lovely breakfast buffet with pancakes, French toast, and crepes. ♦ Continental ♦ M-Th 6-10PM; F-Sa 6:30-11:30AM, 6-10PM; Su 6:30AM-1:30PM, 6-10PM. Reservations required. 661.1234

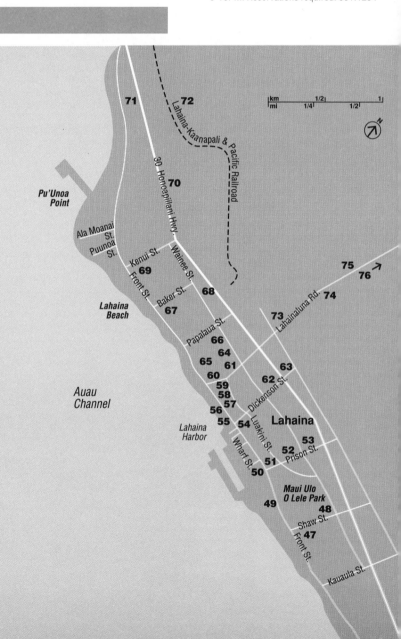

Banyan Tree

Spats II $$$ In its present incarnation, this Italian restaurant/nightclub offers an excellent selection of saucy seafood, fowl, and meat with fresh, homemade pasta. For dessert, there is homemade gelato, ambrosial mousse, and a cart of tempting pastries, so be sure to save room. Spats is as well known for its split-level nightclub, disco-dance floor, and stringent dress code. ◆ Italian ◆ Daily 6:30-9:30PM; dance club M-Th, Su 10PM-2AM, F-Sa 10PM-4AM. 661.1234

Drums of the Pacific $$$ Feel the throbbing excitement of the Pacific's sounds and colors in an extravagant South Seas show as you dig into the all-you-can-eat buffet. The main dishes include *kalua* pork, *shoyu* chicken, coconut beef, and Island fish. ◆ Dinner show M-W, F-Sa 5:30PM; cocktail show M-W, F-Sa 6:45PM. 661.1234

46 Wahikuli State Wayside Park This popular swimming and picnic site has picnic pavilions, public facilities, and nearby tennis courts. ◆ Along Rte 30 between Lahaina and Kaanapali

La Bretagne

47 La Bretagne ★★★$$$ Under the ownership of **Jacqueline Fox** and chef **Claude Gaty,** this popular French restaurant occupies a gracious little home that was built in 1923 by a former Lahaina sheriff. The mood is French country inn, but the cuisine is strictly uptown: confit of duckling in California port, Australian rack of lamb, and an array of scrumptious desserts (homemade tarts and cakes) that have earned a loyal following. The intimate ambience, friendly service, and classic French fare make this a worthy stop. ◆ French ◆ M-Sa 6-9:30PM. 562-C Front St, Lahaina (from Banyan Tree Park, follow Front St south a few blocks until you see the tennis courts and softball diamond on your left; turn left on Shaw St and go a half block) Reservations recommended. 661.8900

48 Waiola Churchyard (formerly Waine'e Cemetery) Prominent and anonymous residents of early Lahaina are buried in this first Christian cemetery in Hawaii, built in 1823. Many of the graves are those of missionaries' children (infant mortality was high then). Others who were buried here include **Queen Keopuolani,** wife of **King Kamehameha I,** mother of **Kamehameha II** and **Kame-**

hameha III, and the first Hawaiian convert to be baptized a Protestant and given a Christian burial. Her daughter, **Nahienaena;** the last king of Kauai, **King Kaumualii;** high chief **Hoapili,** Keopuolani's second husband; and **Kekauonohi,** one of the five queens of Kamehameha II are also buried here. **Waiola Church,** named Waine'e Church until 1953,

stands next to the cemetery. The original Waine'e was the first stone church on Maui. Built by Hawaiians for the missionaries in 1832, it could seat 3,000 Hawaiians (on the floor). Its history is one bad luck story after another. The church lost its roof in an 1858 whirlwind, and in 1894 it was burned down by Hawaiians opposed to the overthrow of the monarchy. The church was rebuilt in 1897 and partly destroyed by fire in 1947. It was repaired, but in 1951 another whirlwind toppled it, an easy feat since the church was not attached to its foundations and was infested with termites. Again it was rebuilt, and its name was changed, hoping to break the spell. ◆ Shaw St, Lahaina

49 Old Lahaina Luau ★★★$$$ This really is West Maui's finest luau, a smooth blend of romance, good food, and memorable entertainment. The setting—at the water's edge in Lahaina, with torches and palm trees, and an *imu* (earthen oven) roasting a 200-pound pig—is something to write home about. Far from offering the patronizing kind of program that characterizes many Hawaiian shows, this luau sparkles with ancient and modern hula dances, and breathtaking dramatic touches, such as a torch-lit canoe off-shore. The all-you-can-eat buffet of Hawaiian favorites also surpasses the norm. Open bar. ◆ Tu-Sa 5:30-8:30PM. 505 Front St, Lahaina. Reservations recommended. 667.1998

50 Banyan Tree It's hard to believe that this huge banyan tree—nearly a block in size with roots and overhang—was a mere eight feet tall when it came to Lahaina from India. Planted in 1873 by **Sheriff William Owen Smith** to commemorate the 50th anniversary of Lahaina's first Protestant Christian mission, this venerable tree is among the oldest and the largest in the Islands. It reaches up more than 50 feet and stretches outward over a 200-foot area, shading two-thirds of an acre in the town's landmark courthouse square. ◆ Corner and Front Sts, Lahaina

50 Waterfront Fort In 1831 a battle raged between the missionaries and the whalers bent on terrorizing the women of Lahaina. A law that had been passed prohibiting local women from swimming out to greet the incoming ships had prompted the rowdy whalers to fire cannons at the missionary complex. At **Queen Keopuolani's** orders, a one-acre area was enclosed by huge coral blocks hacked from the reef fronting the Lahaina shores. This fort was torn down in 1854, and the stones were used to build Lahaina's prison. When Lahaina became a historical landmark, a heap of coral blocks was put together to resemble a corner of the fort—and that's about what it looks like today. ♦ Lahaina Pl on Wharf St, Lahaina, opposite the boat harbor

Maui

50 Lahaina Courthouse This was once the palace of **King Kamehameha III** called **Hale Piula,** and was one of 20 buildings leveled in 1858 by gale-force winds blowing in from Kauaula Valley. In 1859 the stones from the destroyed building were used to build the courthouse which currently houses the **Old Jail Gallery,** the **Banyan Tree Gallery,** and the **Lahaina Arts Society.** ♦ 649 Wharf St, Lahaina, opposite the boat harbor. 661.0111

51 The Harborfront ★$$$ **Wolfgang Schumann's** previous restaurant had to close when the shopping center it occupied was turned into condominiums. Undaunted, he opened a new restaurant in another Lahaina shopping center, **The Wharf,** which until recently had consistently attracted mediocrity. The Harborfront is especially good for fresh fish. Sandwiches, salads, and hamburgers are the usual noontime fare; seafood and steaks highlight the evenings. ♦ Steak/Seafood ♦ M-Sa 11:30AM-2PM, 5-9PM; Su 5-9PM. The Wharf Shopping Center, upper level. 658 Front St, Lahaina. 667.7822

52 Hale Paahao This structure was once Lahaina's prison (the name means "the stuck-in-irons house"). Built in the 1850s by convicts, most of its inmates were mostly drunken sailors, although some were confined for desertion, working on Sunday, or dangerous horseback riding. Troublemakers were further restrained by ball and chain and wall shackles. ♦ Prison-Wainee Sts, Lahaina.

53 Maui Islander $$ Lush tropical plants distinguish this unobtrusive, 10-acre complex of two-story walk-ups. Banana trees, ancient palms, plumeria, papaya, and large torch gingers transform this otherwise plain hotel into a pleasant oasis in the middle of hectic, commercial Lahaina. The rooms are clean but unspectacular (although the upstairs rooms have high, open-beam ceilings). All the

comforts are here—TVs, telephones, air-conditioning, a pool, and lanais for the two- and three-bedroom suites— but it's modest, not luxurious. One of the Islander's best features is the knowledgeable, pleasant service of activities director **Luana Paahana,** who has great suggestions about what to do in Maui. ♦ 660 Wainee St, Lahaina. 667.9766, 800/367.5226; fax 661.3733

54 Baldwin House The **Reverend Dwight Baldwin,** a medical missionary, was transferred to Lahaina in 1835 for his own health and wound up attending to the medical needs of the Hawaiians who gathered daily on his doorstep. In 1853 the Reverand Baldwin single-handedly fought to save Maui, Molokai, and Lanai from a smallpox epidemic. He lived with his family until 1968 in this white two-story house, the oldest standing building in Lahaina, built of coral, stone, and hand-hewn timbers. He received both ship captains and royalty, providing for them a seamen's chapel and Christian reading room. The **Lahaina Restoration Foundation** operates the Baldwin House as a museum and also has its administrative offices here. ♦ Admission. M-Sa 9AM-4:30PM; Su 11AM-4:30PM. Front St, Lahaina, opposite the Pioneer Inn. 661.3262

55 Carthaginian II Built in 1972, *Carthaginian I* left Lahaina for Honolulu to be repaired, hit a reef, and sank. This 93-foot replacement—*Carthaginian II*—sailed here from Denmark and is operated by the **Lahaina Restoration Foundation.** Below deck you can see a museum of whaling history, and an informative program on the humpback whale, which migrates to Maui waters every winter. ♦ Admission. Daily 9AM-4:30PM. On the wharf opposite the Pioneer Inn, Lahaina. 661.8527

55 Pioneer Inn $$ Bawdy, run-down, and cheap, it's hard to believe that at one time this inn was the toast of Lahaina's budget travelers. When it opened in 1901 it was the only hotel in town. **George Freeland,** a member of the Royal Canadian Mounted Police, had followed a criminal to Lahaina, and falling irrevocably in love with the town, ended up building the Pioneer Inn long before the area became a hot spot for whalers and sailors. Today, whaling memorabilia and funky decor complement creaky steps and stained carpets. The rooms are bare-bones shelter for those who want the basics and don't mind the noise from the saloon downstairs. It's right next to the wharf, which accounts for some of the activity. ♦ 658 Wharf St. 661.3636; 800/457.5457; fax 667.5708

Within the Pioneer Inn:

Pioneer Inn Harpooners Lanai $$ A favorite tourist breakfast spot, this place is buzzing with wharf activity. Start the day with a cup of java and eggs or pancakes on the

Pioneer Inn

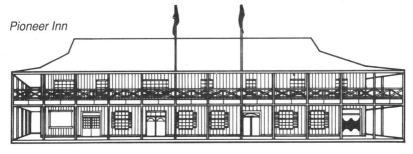

breezy lanai beside the Lahaina harbor.
♦ American ♦ Daily 7-11AM, 11:30AM-2PM, 5:30-9PM. 661.3636

Pioneer Inn Snug Harbor $$ A fun place to barbecue your own beef and fish (at a good price) in the casual South Seas-style outdoor patio with a communal grill. If you don't trust your own cooking, the kitchen delivers ribs, fresh fish, and shrimp tempura. ♦ American ♦ Daily 5:30-9PM. 661.3636

56 Lahaina Fish Co. ★★$$$ A real fish company, not only because they serve fresh fish—they also have their own fishing boat. The two-story restaurant actually hangs out over the Lahaina Harbor, with boats dotting the horizon and legendary views of Lanai and Molokai. Prices for the red snapper Caribbean, drunken shrimp, and fresh catch of the day are very reasonable. If you're not a seafood lover, there's always the _yakitori_, (skewered and broiled chicken or beef with vegetables). ♦ Seafood ♦ Daily 11AM-4PM, 5-11PM. 831 Front St, Lahaina. 661.3472

57 Avalon ★★★$$$ It's small, hip, trendy, informal, and surely one of Maui's most enjoyable restaurants. The brick-floored alfresco area offers pleasant weather, and the bamboo railings, tropical curtains, and tablecloths set the tone for the cuisine. Chef/owner **Mark Ellman** calls it "contemporary Asian"; Indonesian and Chinese preparations such as _satays_ (grilled meat) and black bean sauces enhance the fresh palette of greens, tofu, sprouts, pastas, fish, chicken, and clams. The menu, a colorful journey through exotic climes and cultures, is for the adventurous. Start with the not-to-be-missed combination platter of wok-fried sugar snap peas, chicken _satay,_ Maui onion rings with tamarind catsup, and Avalon summer rolls. Also try the shiitake mushrooms (sometimes in a salad of sautéed scallops and mixed greens), you'll find them a tasty addition to your meal. Top off your meal with the caramel Miranda, a seamless blend of fruit, ice cream, and caramel. ♦ Pacific Rim ♦ Daily noon-midnight. 844 Front St, Lahaina. 667.5559

58 Benihana ★$$$ Knife-wielding performance chefs dazzle diners with their flashing knives and cooking skills. As in the rest of the Benihana chain, the specialty here is _teppanyaki_, the Japanese technique of grilling food at your table. Meat and vegetables are sliced

in seconds, and everything is grilled tableside and served with a flourish. ♦ Japanese ♦ M-Sa 11:30AM-2PM, 5-10PM; Su 5-10PM. Wharf Cinema Center, 658 Front St, Lahaina. 667.2244

Maui

59 Sunrise Cafe ★$$ This popular cafe opens early with fresh cinnamon rolls, steaming mugs of caffè latte and cappuccino, and other aromatic breakfast specials. After parading out the croissants and pastries in the morning, the cafe offers sandwiches, quiches, homemade soups, and daily specials. Inexpensive fresh _mahimahi_ is served with pasta or rice daily. But their pastries keep the customers coming back for more: delectable raspberry-and-chocolate cheesecake, apple tarts, and nutty carrot cake. ♦ American ♦ Daily 6AM-10:30PM. 693-A Front St, Lahaina. 661.3326

59 Happy Days Cafe $$ What this trendy coffee shop serves up is somewhere between junk food and diner fare that includes burgers, sundaes, shakes, egg creams, and a daily blue plate special. Collectible fifties posters and a bubble gum machine provide the atmosphere. ♦ American ♦ Daily 7AM-3PM. Lahaina Market Pl, Lahaina. 661.3235

60 Hard Rock Cafe ★★$$ As always, the music is loud, even blaring, reverberating off the pressed-tin ceilings, and gold records, vintage surfboards, and guitars line the walls, with an old custom-woodie Cadillac suspended over the bar. In this Hard Rock, the decibel overload is manageable, largely because screened windows let out some of the indoor energy while also offering a pleasing view of the ocean. This is a great place for reasonably priced food—grilled chicken breast, Maui onion rings, grilled _ahi_, Texas-style ribs—and a leisurely afternoon. ♦ American ♦ M-Th, Su 11:30AM-10:30PM; F-Sa 11:30AM-11PM. 900 Front St, Lahaina. 667.7400

Lahaina, a town with some of the most beautiful sunsets in the world, means "cruel sun" in Hawaiian.

Restaurants/Clubs: Red	**Hotels:** Blue
Shops/ 🌴 **Outdoors:** Green	**Sights/Culture:** Black

Kimo's

61 Metropolitan Art Gallery This gallery's vast offerings include traditional and modern works, from 19th-century early wAmerican paintings to bronzes and contemporary pieces by master artists. Works by oil painter **Gil Bruvel,** designated among the top 10 living French artists by the French Ministry of Culture, and Maui visionary artist **Andrew Annenberg,** who depicts marine life and nature, are featured here. ♦ Daily 9AM-10PM. 802 Front St, Lahaina. 661.5033

62 Village Galleries The oldest gallery in Hawaii has grown bigger and better. Ninety percent of the 80 artists represented are local, with works in all media. The art of **George Allan, Lowell Mapes, Macario Pascual,** and other luminaries graces the gallery. ♦ Daily 9AM-9PM. 120 Dickenson St, Lahaina. 667.5115

63 Lahaina Coolers ★★$$ Many a bronzed surfer starts the day here with a choice of cafe au lait, fresh-squeezed orange juice, Ramos fizz, fresh fruitcakes and the surfers' special—burrito with black beans and rice. At lunch, dinner, and happy hour, when the won tons and quesadillas appear, the mood is equally upbeat. Surfboards dangling from the ceiling and some rad, bad, and truly epic surf shots add machismo to the turquoise and gray motif. ♦ Eclectic ♦ Daily 7-11AM, 11:30AM-midnight. 180 Dickenson St, Lahaina. 661.7082

64 Chris' Smokehouse ★★$$ Get ready for the best baby back pork ribs on Maui, smoked in a *kiawe* charcoal pit, smothered in Chris' Bar-B-Q sauce, and served with all the fixin's: cole slaw, fries, cornbread with macadamia nut butter, and baked beans. They supply the napkins, but bring a wheelbarrow to cart yourself home. The beef ribs, fresh-smoked Island chicken, fresh Island fish, and smoked roast beef have their followings, but it's the *kiawe*-grilled cheeseburgers that are most famous. ♦ Barbecue ♦ Daily 6-10AM, 11AM-4PM, 5-10PM. 126 Hinau Place, Lahaina, across from Pizza Hut. 667.2111

65 Wo Hing Temple In 1909 legions of Chinese laborers brought in to work in West Maui's sugarcane fields formed the local **Wo Hing Society.** It was a chapter of a 17th-century Chinese fraternal society called Chee Kung Tong. In 1912 the group built a fraternal hall in downtown Lahaina that soon became the gathering place for the local Chinese. The center was equipped with a separate cook house, Chinese utensils, fire pits fueled with *kiawe* wood for the oversize woks, and implements reflecting the Chinese culture. In 1983 the **Lahaina Restoration Foundation** turned the building into a museum, a historical remnant of one of Hawaii's significant ethnic groups. You can also see films of turn-of-the-century Hawaii taken by **Thomas Edison** here. ♦ Free. M-Sa 9AM-4:30PM; Su 11AM-4:30PM. Front St, Lahaina, across from Kimo's

66 Golden Palace $$ Chinese restaurants are about as plentiful on Maui as the dollar cocktail (meaning rare). The existing few are usually hidden, as is the Golden Palace. Don't look for a palatial building, however, it's in the Lahaina Shopping Center, which actually serves as a giant parking lot for Front St tourists. But once you find it, you'll have an overwhelming number of choices: there are more than a hundred items on the menu. Takeout is available, too. ♦ Chinese ♦ Daily 11AM-2PM, 5-9PM. Lahaina Shopping Center, Papalaua and Front Sts, Lahaina. 661.3126

67 Alex's Hole In the Wall ★★$$$ Renovations and the installation of air-conditioning have made this less a "hole-in-the-wall" than before. Owner **Alex Didio** went big time and added a new dining room upstairs, complementing the cozy intimacy of the original downstairs. Alex's has been a reliable purveyor of Italian food for nearly 20 years. Some favorites include fresh pastas, scampi, and their devastating cheesecakes. ♦ Italian ♦ Daily 5:30-9:30PM. 834 Front St (Wahie Ln) Lahaina. 661.3197

67 Kimo's ★★$$$ Two young men who made a fortune with the **Rusty Scupper** chain on the mainland used their money to build this attractive restaurant on Front St, overlooking the town's main thoroughfare, with generous views of Molokai and Lanai from the outside deck. A good, basic menu of fresh Island fish, prime rib, steaks, and Island specials such as *kalua* pork, *huli-huli* chicken, and *Koloa* pork ribs. If you're really hungry, get a side order of fried Maui onions. ♦ Steak/Seafood. ♦ Daily 11:30AM-2:30PM, 5-10:30PM. 845 Front St, Lahaina. 661.4811

Longhi's

67 Longhi's ★$$$ When this restaurant was expanded several years ago to triple its previous size, the service predictably declined (tragic for a restaurant of verbal menus). The extensive and rather complicated choices are difficult for all but the most seasoned waiters to remember while providing service that isn't spotty or hurried. Don't be afraid to ask the waiter to slow down so you can understand what he or she is saying, and by all means, be sure to ask the price of each item before ordering. Portions are rather large, so be careful about over-ordering, especially if you plan on trying one of Longhi's delectable homemade desserts—their trademark. The cuisine has an Italian flair to it, featuring pastas, seafood, and enormous sandwiches. Further eclipsed by new, high-quality restaurants down the street, Longhi's is no longer *the* Lahaina eatery. It remains a local landmark, though—a breakfast favorite and unceasingly hip choice in spite of its many flaws. ♦ Continental ♦ Daily 7:30-10PM. 888 Front St, Lahaina. 667.2288

67 Lahaina Broiler $$$ They say this is the biggest restaurant in Lahaina, but its real claim to fame is the 100-year-old monkeypod tree growing out of the roof. Portuguese bean soup, seafood chowder, and a host of steak, prime rib, seafood, and combination dishes are served in a superb setting over the water. The food is standard American fare, nothing fancy or special. The fabulous views of Molokai and Lanai are another thing altogether. ♦ American ♦ Daily 7:30-10:30AM, 11AM-2PM, 5-10PM. Front St, Lahaina, first building entering Lahaina from the north (with the huge tree growing out of it) 661.3111

68 Scaroles ★★★$$$ **Jane Donovan** and her partner/chef **Ronald Lynch** offer the island's best northern Italian cuisine, served in a tiny, stylish, unpretentious corner of Lahaina. From the piping hot, fresh-baked onion rolls to the seafood pasta and homemade sausage lasagne, the food is all you could hope for.

The pasta is not made from scratch, but it's al dente perfect. And the Italian opera on the sound system sets the stage for the dramatic desserts. ♦ Italian ♦ M-F 11AM-2:30PM, 5:30-10PM; Sa-Su 5:30-10PM. 930 Wainee St, Lahaina. 661.4466

69 Seamen's Hospital Many sailors from Lahaina's wild whaling days (during Kamehameha the Great's reign) died of "disreputable disease" here. They were dumped by American and British whaling ships seeking to lighten their loads before embarking on trading trips to Canton. (One of the hapless included a shipmate of Herman Melville's.) The care of sick sailors in Lahaina and Honolulu used up half the budget appropriated by Congress for the care of all US seamen. Ironically, the two-story, coral-block hospital

was sold to a group of nuns in 1865, and served as a Catholic school for some 20 years. Afterward, an Episcopalian minister used it as a vicarage for 30 years before it was abandoned in 1908. In 1982, through a unique arrangement between the Lahaina Restoration Foundation and architect **Uwe Schultz,** the deteriorating eyesore was completely rebuilt to historical accuracy. ♦ Not open to the public. Front-Baker Sts, Lahaina

70 Lahaina Cannery Center The center opened in 1987 with two anchor stores, Long's and Safeway, and 51 shops and food stands. You can browse through the small boutiques that sell sportswear, art, shoes, eyewear, and all manner of miscellany here. The Hobie Sports store, for one, has a display of vintage surfboards. **Compadres,** a Mexican restaurant, serves a hearty meal. ♦ Daily 9AM-9:30PM. 1221 Honoapiilani Hwy, Lahaina

71 Puamana Beach Park This is the closest beach to Lahaina. The water is fairly shallow, with rock-and-sand ocean floor. Swimming, summer surfing, and picnic facilities. ♦ Public access on Front St, two miles east of Lahaina

71 Chart House ★$$$ The restaurant's high perch only enhances its location at the northern end of Lahaina. The idea was to get a great sunset and ocean view, which it succeeds in doing. The Chart House chain's long-standing reputation for good steak and fish holds here. A cozy lanai, touches of wood and lava, and the view, combined with the signature salad bar and fresh fish dishes, add up to a pleasant dining experience. ♦ Steak/Seafood ♦ Daily 4:30-10PM. 1450 Front St, Lahaina. 661.0937

The **Great Mahele** land reform of 1848 divided Hawaii among the king, the government, and the common people, allowing Hawaiian commoners to own land for the first time.

72 Lahaina-Kaanapali & Pacific Railroad This rebuilt train from 1890, also called the sugarcane train, chugs along six miles of narrow-gauge tracks between Lahaina and the Kaanapali Beach Resort, puffing alongside much of the original railroad track used by the Pioneer Sugar Mill. The open-air passenger cars, train whistle, and steam pouring from the locomotive recall a bygone era, thrilling kids who think all trains look like Amtrak. You can buy one-way and round-trip tickets, or take your choice of combination tours that include a

glass-bottom boat ride aboard the *Golden Dragon* (formerly the *Lin Wa*). There is free bus transportation between the Lahaina depot and town, and a jitney links hotels with the Kaanapali station. If you're staying at the Kaanapali Resort, there is also a boarding platform across the footbridge at the north end of the resort. The narrated ride, which goes by cane fields, mountains, and seashore for a round-trip total of 12 miles, takes about one hour and five minutes. ◆ Six round-trips daily 8:30AM–5PM. 661.0089/0080

73 Pioneer Sugar Mill From an unlikely start in 1860 (the company mortgaged all assets for a $300 loan), the **Pioneer Mill Company**, built by **James Campbell**, thrived as others folded, and went on to become a kingpin of Maui sugar production. The mill's smokestack at Lahainaluna Rd and Hwy 30 is as familiar a part of the Lahaina landscape as the cane fields and boat harbors. ◆ Not open to tours. Lahainaluna Rd and Hwy 30

Lahaina Hotel

74 Lahaina Hotel $$$ Lahaina was the whaling mecca—a bawdy, seaside town awash in grog and land-happy sailors—when this hotel was built in the 1860s. When the whaling era ended, the old Lahaina Hotel became a gathering place for genteel travelers and local power brokers. Rumor has it that **Fanny Brice** and Swedish nightingale **Jenny Lind** often entertained here. The hotel later became a general store, then business offices (destroyed by fire in the mid-1960s), and later, the 19-room **Lahainaluna Hotel.** Today it is a small 13-room inn refurbished to new standards of splendor by its new owner, local entrepreneur, preservationist, and antiques collector **Rick Ralston.** After a three-year restoration period, the two-story inn is replete with turn-of-the-century antiques and countless details bespeaking historical luxury. You'll bask in the richness of antique armoires, leaded glass lamps, floral wall coverings, and lace curtains. No TVs, but there's Continental breakfasts, air-conditioning, and telephones. This is a place to remember. ◆ 127 Lahainaluna St, Lahaina. 661.0577, 800/669.3444; fax 667.9480

Within the Lahaina Hotel:

David Paul's Lahaina Grill ★★★$$$ Once a seedy barroom on the ground floor of the old Lahaina Hotel, this new star on the culinary scene possesses the same stylish aura that the owners worked hard to preserve in the hotel. The mood is eclectic 1890s, with pressed-tin Victorian-period ceilings, marble tables, Native American prints, black-and-white tile floors, celadon-colored wainscoting and touches of Art Deco. A 1,200-bottle wine cellar specializes in California vintages, and

Lahaina-Kaanapali & Pacific Railroad

the cuisine is new-American with Asian influences. **David Paul,** who owns the restaurant with **Rick Ralston,** is deservedly one of Maui's most notable chefs. The menu changes constantly, but here's a sample of what you might find: *ahi* (tuna) carpaccio, tequila shrimp with firecracker rice, macadamia-smoked Kona yearling tenderloin, and a wonderful Caesar salad. ♦ Eclectic ♦ M-F 11AM-2:30PM, 6-11:30PM; Sa-Su 6-11:30PM. 127 Lahainaluna Rd, Lahaina. 667.5117

75 Plantation Inn $$$ A group of private investors took over three residential lots and came up with this chic and refreshing hostelry, a plantation-style inn of 17 rooms and suites. French doors, brass and four-poster beds, verandas, stained glass, floral wallpaper and wainscoting, antique furniture, and hardwood floors with area rugs give an impression of charm in abundance. Also on the property is **Gerard's,** the best French restaurant in town, and only a block away are the shops and galleries of Lahaina's bustling Front St. Rooms range from standard to suites. Pool. ♦ 174 Lahainaluna Rd, Lahaina. 667.9225, 800/433.6815; fax 667.9293

Within the Plantation Inn:

Gerard's ★★★$$$ Gerard Reversade made his mark long ago with his tiny, charming bistro just off Lahainaluna Rd, one of Lahaina's major side streets. It had cobbled floors, greenery galore, and a chalkboard menu of innovative delights. The restaurant has since moved to the front-porch area of the two-story **Plantation Inn** just down the street, where it serves three meals a day (terrific for guests) and still attracts legions of loyal fans from all over the island. The ever-changing menu features blue crab bisque, Maui escargots in pastry shells, breast of duckling in orange sauce, and a host of seductive desserts. The classical guitarist and alfresco dining add to the pleasant ambience. ♦ French ♦ M-Th, Sa 7:30-10AM, 6-10PM; F, Su 7:30-10AM, 11AM-2PM, 6-10PM. 661.8939

76 Hale Pa'i This structure, whose name means "house of printing," is the only original school building still standing on the Lahainaluna High School campus. (Lahainaluna High School was the first school west of the Rocky Mountains.) It was established by the Protestant missionaries in 1831 to spread the Christian gospel to the Hawaiians, who had no written form of language.) In 1834 Hale Pa'i used a secondhand press to print the first newspaper, *Ka Lama Hawaii* (the *Hawaiian Luminary*). The press, which came around Cape Horn with the first missionaries, turned out translations, history texts, and even Hawaiian currency. The printing house has

been fully restored by the Lahaina Restoration Foundation. ♦ M-F 10AM-3:30PM. Lahainaluna Rd, two miles east of Lahaina. 667.7040

77 Launiupoko State Wayside Park Beach fronted by a man-made pool for children. Swimming, and picnic and public facilities. Great for whalewatching. ♦ Near Lahaina

78 Kulanaokalai Beach This unimproved roadside beach is slightly past Olowalu, if heading toward Lahaina. Swimming. ♦ Two miles east of Lahaina

78 Olowalu Historians know this seaside village as the site of the 1790 Olowalu Massacre, when **Captain Simon Metcalfe,** seeking revenge for the loss of a sailor and a boat (presumably at the hands of local thieves), invited a group of Hawaiians to visit his

American trading ship, *Eleanora,* under the pretense of trading goods. Once the natives had gathered on the starboard side of his ship, Metcalfe ordered the gunwales uncovered. He and his men fired down on the startled, defenseless Hawaiians, killing more than a hundred and seriously wounding many more. A nearby cliff face covered with petroglyphs indicate that the impervious West Maui mountains were once traversable through an ancient trail connecting Iao Valley and Olowalu. ♦ Olowalu, West Maui south coast

79 Chez Paul ★$$$ This dining landmark dates back more than a decade, when Boston Irishman **Paul Kirk** and his French wife, **Fernie,** sold their highly successful Santa Barbara restaurant and opened a tiny restaurant in the middle of nowhere. Their unusual operation was in a shabby building that had a certain cachet, especially when juxtaposed against the ultra-chic Kaanapali eateries. But today Chez Paul has lost its luster. The spate of terrific new Maui restaurants make the outdated French cuisine here seem overpriced, overrated, and simply not the find it used to be. It's still small and intimate and has good service, but don't get your hopes up on the food. ♦ French ♦ Dinner seatings 6:30, 8:30PM. Off Hwy 30, Olowalu. 661.3843

80 Olowalu General Store Another classic Hawaiian phenomenon is the old-fashioned general store. This one is a particularly nice place for a cold drink in the *V*-shaped Olowalu Valley. ♦ M-F 5:30AM-6:30PM; Sa 7AM-6:30PM; Su 8AM-6PM. 820 Olowalu Village, Olowalu. 661.3774

Restaurants/Clubs: Red   Hotels: Blue
Shops/ 🌳 Outdoors: Green   **Sights/Culture: Black**

63

Points and Parts on the Prickly Pineapple

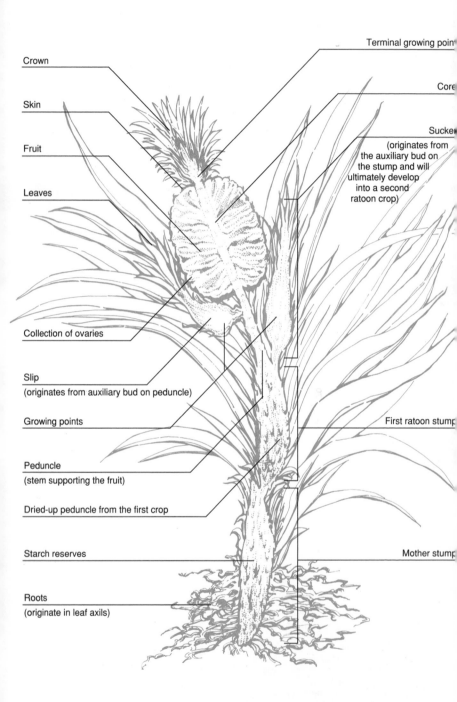

Terminal growing point

Core

Crown

Skin

Fruit

Leaves

Sucker
(originates from the auxiliary bud on the stump and will ultimately develop into a second ratoon crop)

Collection of ovaries

Slip
(originates from auxiliary bud on peduncle)

Growing points

Peduncle
(stem supporting the fruit)

Dried-up peduncle from the first crop

First ratoon stump

Starch reserves

Mother stump

Roots
(originate in leaf axils)

The pineapple is a member of the Bromeliaceae family. The plant grows about two to four feet tall, and takes about 18 to 20 months to produce a four- to five-pound fruit. The first harvest yields one pineapple per plant, and the second and third harvests yield one or two. The plants last for three years and then they're replaced. Don't be fooled by what the natives call "tourist pineapples." The pandanus (hala) tree sports large fruit that, from a distance, resembles pineapple, but is actually unrelated and is barely edible.

One of the earliest explorers to take note of the pineapple was **Marco Polo,** who was impressed enough with the fruit on his expedition in southern China in 1270 to describe it to his peers. Then along came **Columbus,** who brought the fruit (which he called *ananas,* an Indian word meaning "excellent fruit") to **Queen Isabella** after his voyage in 1493 to the West Indies. This gift to the queen launched the pineapple into stardom. The royalty and the wealthy started clamoring for more of this rare fruit, and it was soon being raised in European hothouses. Eventually the pineapple gained worldwide importance in preventing scurvy (a disease caused by vitamin C deficiency) in tropical countries. (Not a bad accomplishment for such a prickly, sticky fruit.)

It's not known when the pineapple arrived in Hawaii, but a Spaniard wrote about the fruit (then called *halakahiki*) on his first visit to Hawaii in 1813. By the end of the 19th century, pineapple pioneer **James Dole** seized on the pineapple's popularity and organized commercial production of the fruit by establishing the very successful Hawaiian Pineapple Company. In Dole's advertisement introducing pineapple to mainland America, he said, "You eat it with a spoon like a peach." The pineapple has since come a long way, although its presence in Hawaii is ebbing after a hundred years as one of the state's leading industries. Hawaii's pineapples now compete in the marketplace with those grown in the Philippines, Taiwan, Thailand, and other countries where labor costs are cheaper.

The Pineapple: How to Slice it Right

ANNIE KOOK

There are several traditional ways to carve a pineapple, but to better preserve the fruit's decorative shell and greenery, try this favorite Hawaiian method for making the perfect pineapple centerpiece.

1. Carefully cut off the bottom and the crown (the top of the shell and leaves) with a very sharp knife. Save both pieces.

2. With the knife inserted deep into the fruit as close to the shell as possible, cut an even cylinder of fruit.

3. Gently force the fruit cylinder out with your hand and cut it into long strips. Reassemble the strips and put them back into the shell, then replace the bottom and the crown of the pineapple.

81 Mai Poina Oe Iau Beach Park A good swimming beach with some rocks on the sandy ocean bottom. You can still see what's left of the old Kihei Landing at the shoreline. Picnic and public facilities. ♦ Off S. Kihei Rd, Kihei

82 Kalepolepo Beach Remains of a fish pond create a fun pool for children, but ocean swimming is trickier because of the rocky bottom. This area was once a Hawaiian village with taro, coconut, and shoreline fishponds that fed the community. There also used to be churches and a small whaling station here. ♦ Off S. Kihei Rd, Kihei

83 Kihei Condominiums Kihei is shamefully overbuilt and crowded, lacking in form, design, and cohesiveness. But the accommodations are less expensive than in

Lahaina, and the beaches along this stretch are beautiful. They are also notoriously windy; by early afternoon, you'll give up trying to keep your beach towel in place. Be sure to specify if you want a room on the beach. ♦ Condominium Rentals Hawaii, 2439 S. Kihei Rd, Suite 205-A, Kihei. 879.2778

84 Kamaole Beach Good swimming, picnic and public facilities in three beach parks. ♦ S. Kihei Rd about one mile south of Kalama Beach Park, Kihei

85 Kalama Beach Park This 36-acre park is ideal for sports enthusiasts. Soccer and baseball fields, a volleyball and basketball court, tennis courts, and a children's playground will keep you occupied for hours. ♦ Near Azeka Pl Shopping Center, Kihei

86 Surfer Joe's $ The casual indoor/outdoor tavern offers an array of local and American favorites. Entrées include burgers, chicken, and fresh Island fish. Don't miss their popular fried zucchini appetizer. The bar serves foreign and domestic beers. ◆ American ◆ Daily 11AM–2AM. 61 S. Kihei Rd, Kihei. 879.8855

87 Paradise Fruit Maui
Keep this in mind for a marvelous selection of fresh fruit and juices, late-night munchies, and last-minute picnics. The take-out

stand serves daily lunch specials including at least two vegetarian choices, and a host of smoothies, sandwiches, and baked goods. Packs of papaya, pineapple, and Kula onions are for sale here, too. ◆ 1913 S. Kihei Rd, next to Kihei Town Center, Kihei. 879.1723

87 Island Fish House ★★$$$ Excellent fresh fish, usually a choice of four—*ono, mahimahi, opakapaka, ahi,* or *uku* (when available)—is served several different ways here. Steak and chicken are also on the menu, but this is the best place in Kihei to feast on the fresh catch of the day. The excellent wine list is priced more reasonably than you might expect. ◆ Seafood ◆ Daily 5-9PM. 1945 S. Kihei Rd, Kihei. 879.7771

88 Gabel's ★★$$$ **Harry Gabel,** former executive chef at the Four Seasons Resort in neighboring Wailea, had already made a name for himself when he opened his own restaurant in Kihei. The food here melds European, Asian, and Island favorites, everything from veal schnitzel (with fresh herb mushroom sauce) to Szechuan pork, scampi fettuccine with fresh Molokai herbs, and chicken spring roll with plum sauce. Gabel's German dishes add a nice balance to the Portuguese bean soup and Pacific seafood stew on pasta. ◆ Eclectic ◆ Daily 6-10PM; live entertainment 7-9PM, 9:30PM-1AM. 2439 S. Kihei Rd, in the Rainbow Mall, Kihei. 879.5600

89 Aston Kamaole Sands This well-managed, roomy condo sits on 15 acres across the street from Kamaole Beach Park. Many of the suites look out across the ocean to the islands of Molokini and Lanai. Fully equipped kitchens include dishwasher and washer and dryer. Pool, restaurant, barbecue area, and tennis courts free to guests. ◆ 2695 S. Kihei Rd, Kihei. 874.8700, 800/922.7866

Restaurants/Clubs: Red   **Hotels:** Blue
Shops/ 🌳 Outdoors: Green   **Sights/Culture:** Black

Maui by Bike: Downhill all the Way

Coasting down the 10,023-foot-high Haleakala Crater on a bicycle is one thrilling way to get spectacular views of Maui's largest cattle ranch, protea farms, and sugarcane and pineapple fields. And the best part is you don't have to pedal *up* the hill—someone drives you up and follows you and your bicycle down the 38-mile ride (about a three-and-a-half-hour cruise). Many trips begin at sunrise with a Continental breakfast in Paia, stop for lunch in Kula, and end at sunset with a gourmet steak or fish dinner. A tour leader will provide you with a single-speed bike (specially equipped with mega-brakes), a windbreaker, gloves, helmet, and round-trip transportation. There's hardly any pedaling on this bike ride—just lots of braking. Bicycle tours are offered daily by **Cruiser Bob's Haleakala Downhill Bike Ride,** 505 Front St, Lahaina, 667.7717, 800/654.7717; **Maui Mountain Cruisers,** 250 Hana Mau St, Kahului, 871.6014; and **Maui Downhill,** 199 Dairy Rd, Kahului, 871.2155.

90 Mana Kai Ocean Terrace $$ The same folks who run the **Island Fish House** turned this restaurant into one of Kihei's most pleasant spots for oceanside dining. Half of the restaurant hugs a railing open to the sea. The *L*-shaped room's sunny ambience is perfect for casual meals: burgers, sandwiches, and salads for lunch; steaks and fresh fish for dinner. Ask about their early bird dinner specials from 5 to 6PM. ◆ Continental ◆ M-Sa 7-11AM, 11:30AM-2PM, 5-9PM. 2960 S. Kihei Rd, in the Mana Kai Maui Resort, Kihei. 879.2607

91 Keawakapu Beach This excellent swimming area has a sandy bottom and good snorkeling around the rocky areas. ◆ Access road is Alanui Dr just after the Stouffer Wailea Beach Resort. Take the walkway from the landscaped park to the beach on the right, just past Mokapu Beach

92 Wailea Resort $$$ In 1973 you could hardly have imagined that this 1,500-acre stretch of coastline dotted with patches of scraggly *kiawe* and *wili-wili* trees would become the site of this posh resort. But it had two things going for it: great weather and white sand beaches. Wailea's average yearly rainfall is 11 inches; the average temperature 75.15° (you can thank **Haleakala Crater** for those statistics). Not only is the volcano a beautiful backdrop to Wailea, it's also a natural buffer from rain and wind. Each of Wailea's five beaches has a smooth, sandy bottom separated by coral reefs, which are excellent for snorkeling. Built in 1976, the fine **Maui Inter-Continental** was the first Wailea Resort Hotel, followed two years later by the **Stouffer Wailea Beach Resort.** In 1990 the **Four Seasons Resort** opened, and a **Grand Hyatt** opened in September 1991. All of this portends well for Wailea, which is beginning to be considered a luxury resort on the level of the Big Island's Kohala Coast. Within Wailea you'll find 36 holes of golf, one of the largest tennis complexes in the Islands, the Wailea Shopping Village, and a number of first-rate restaurants. ♦ 161 Wailea Ike Pl, Wailea. 879.4465

93 **Wailea Golf Club** Golfers will find two lovely, carefully manicured courses at the bonedry Wailea Resort on the leeward slopes of Haleakala Crater. The **Blue Course** is visually pleasing but less exciting golf than the **Orange Course,** which has more hills, trees, and length, and even ancient Hawaiian stone walls. Be prepared for strong afternoon winds. Orange Course: Par 72, 6,810 yards. Blue Course: Par 72, 6,700 yards. ♦ Expensive green fees; preferred starting times to Wailea Resort hotel guests. Pro shop. 879.2966

94 **Stouffer Wailea Beach Resort** $$$$ Newly renovated to the tune of $39 million, this AAA five-diamond hotel—the only one in Hawaii to receive the recognition for 10 consecutive years—is better than ever. It's a luxury hotel for the traveler who likes to get away from it all, but never too far from room service or a world-class restaurant, and the setting is small enough to be intimate. The landscaping is as lush as a rain forest, dense with tropical foliage and sprinkled with bridges and pathways that lend themselves to romance, lingering, and weddings. Many of the 347 rooms have ocean views, and all are the same size—small but very pleasant. The renovation has added marble everywhere. The **Mokapu Beach Club,** a separate wing with 26 cottagelike suites on the beach, offers VIP perks and services: a club

host, Continental breakfast brought daily to your room, and other assorted luxuries. The beautiful, peaceful beach is ideal for swimming, sunning, snorkeling, or windsurfing. Stouffer Wailea is also the site of the **Maui Marine Art Expo,** a widely acclaimed, wildly successful event featuring hundreds of works. Pool, three new whirlpool spas in the garden, golf, and tennis. ♦ 3550 Wailea Alanui Dr, Wailea. 879.4900, 800/992.4532; fax 879.6128

Hawaii's Habitants

Hawaii is one of the most racially diverse states in the nation. The population is composed of just about every major ethnic group, making it one of America's true melting pots. For years, Hawaii was the only state where Caucasians were the minority. Now, however, whites immigrating from the West Coast have dramatically increased the Caucasian population, and it is currently the fastest-growing race on the Islands. In contrast, the pure Hawaiian population has decreased at a rate comparable to that of the American Indians. Yet in the past several years, a movement to revitalize the traditional Hawaiian culture has prompted many people to report their Hawaiian roots in population polls. Hence, as this chart of the state's major races shows, the Hawaiian population appears to have suddenly increased (although it's suspected that most of the Hawaiians reflected in the 1980 statistics are of mixed heritage).

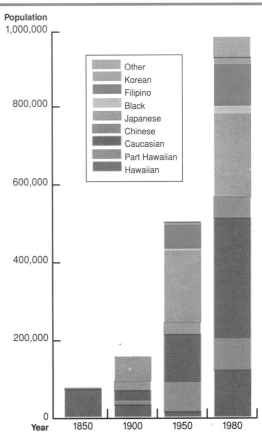

Population

Other
Korean
Filipino
Black
Japanese
Chinese
Caucasian
Part Hawaiian
Hawaiian

Year 1850 1900 1950 1980

Within the Stouffer Wailea Beach Resort:

Raffles ★★★$$$$ This spacious and beautiful room was named after **Sir Thomas Stamford Raffles,** founder of the city of Singapore, where the Raffles Hotel became legendary. The menu includes many fresh seafood specialties, rack of lamb, and renowned dessert soufflés. Piano music nightly. ♦ Continental ♦ Daily 6:30-10PM. 879.4900

Palm Court $$$ An informal, open-air terrace full of greenery. You will find the view of the blue Pacific inspirational between trips to the bountiful dinner buffet. Prime rib, seafood, and several international cuisines grace the buffet table on different nights. There's also a champagne breakfast

Maui

buffet. ♦ Eclectic ♦ Daily 6-11AM, 6-10PM; Su brunch 9AM-1PM. 879.4900

Maui Onion $$ You can lunch poolside in this gazebo decked with rare white thunbergia vines. Salads, sandwiches, hamburgers, and of course, Maui onion rings are all on the menu. ♦ M, Su 9AM-5PM; Tu-Sa 9AM-9PM. 879.4900

95 Ulua Beach This is the most popular of the Wailea beach quintet and the best for bodysurfing. On calm days, snorkeling is excellent because of the exceptionally clear water. ♦ Use the Alanui Dr access road just after the Stouffer Wailea Beach Resort and take the walkway from the landscaped park to the beach on the left

96 Maui Inter-Continental Wailea $$$ In 1991 a lengthy $37-million renovation left this hotel with a dramatic architectural appearance, a completely new porte cochere, a Hawaiian roofline based on the architecture of **C.W. Dickey,** and lounges and restaurants that had been redecorated, renamed, and revived. Flanked by a white sand, crescent beach on either side, it occupies 22 acres of oceanfront land with 525 rooms in seven low-rise buildings and one seven-story tower. Three pools, golf, tennis. ♦ 3700 Wailea Alanui, Wailea. 879.1922, 800/367.2960; fax 874.8331

Within the Maui Inter-Continental Wailea:

LA PEROUSE

La Perouse ★★★$$$$ Plans are under way to move the dining room to a new oceanfront location, which will only enhance the hotel's most beloved attraction. In addition to its brilliant à la carte menu, a prix fixe program has been introduced featuring wines and a set dinner menu selected by executive chef **Richard Reynolds** and manager **John Miller.** Vintner dinners are also offered with various vineyard owners on hand. The food, quite simply, is superb. Named after the scenic Maui Bay discovered in 1786 by the French explorer **Compte de la Perouse,** the restaurant specializes in seafood. You can start with the creamy *callaloo,* a crab and coconut soup, a La Perouse classic. Follow this with fresh Hawaiian abalone served with tomato coulis, *nori* (seaweed) pasta with bay scallops and sea vegetables, or Pacific lobster with ginger-mango sauce. Many other extraordinary items grace the menu, making the most of Hawaii's fresh seafood and exotic produce (fiddleheads, Maui mushrooms). The deep green velvets and dark koa accents, the artwork and sensitive lighting, and the service—attentive and gracious—match the cuisine. All in all, this promises to be a memorable dining experience. ♦ Continental ♦ Daily 6:30-9PM. 879.1922

Lanai Terrace $$ This dining room offers nightly specials such as Pasta Night on Wednesday nights, an Asian buffet on Saturday nights, and spectacular views of Maalaea Bay and the neighboring islands. ♦ Continental ♦ Daily 6:30-11AM, 5-11PM. 879.1922

Hula Moons ★$$ Named after one of **Don Blanding's** books, the newly unveiled poolside restaurant offers fresh seafood, meat entrées, and a generous salad bar. The new menu, new look, and new name (it used to be the Kiawe Broiler) all relate to his art and poetry. ♦ Continental ♦ Daily 6-10PM. 879.1922

Maui's Merriest Luau The oceanfront setting is hard to beat, and the food and entertainment have won awards. Hawaiian entertainment, an *imu* (earthen oven) ceremony, and a lavish buffet all contribute to the evening's enjoyment. ♦ Tu-Th 5:30PM. 879.1922

Inu Inu Lounge This popular nightclub was recently revamped with new accoutrements: drums from New Guinea, canvas and bamboo ceilings, and a large indoor space instead of the outdoor deck. A live band plays top 40 and swing nightly except Sundays, when the "Swing Is Back" program features music from Tommy Dorsey, Glenn Miller, and Benny Goodman. ♦ Daily 7PM-1AM. 879.1922

Maui on Horseback

Islanders were first introduced to horses in the early 1880s when *lio* (wild mustangs) were brought over from Mexico. These animals quickly adapted to the rough terrain and today their docile descendants can carry you on a trek through Maui's many splendors—from beaches and meadows to volcanoes and waterfalls. Here are a few of the outfitters with horses for hire:

Pony Express Tours takes riders on a unique all-day horseback trip into Haleakala Crater with a guide who can tell you all about the dormant volcano's geology and related legends. Lunch, jacket, and raincoat are provided. Other options include one- and two-hour rides on Haleakala Ranch lands, taking in the ocean view from 4,500 feet—halfway to the summit—and half-day tours, including lunch, in Haleakala Crater. For additional information, write to: Pony Express Tours, Box 535, Kula HI 96790, or call 667.2200.

Rainbow Ranch Stables operates out of Napili with one-hour horseback rides through the pineapple fields, or two-hour sunset rides. The two-and-a-half-hour Pineapple Ride leaves twice a day and includes refreshments. For additional information, write to: Rainbow Ranch Stables, Box 10066, Lahaina HI 96761, or call 669.4991/4702.

The **Adventures on Horseback** riding tour offers a five-hour odyssey into a rain forest, through waterfall country, and across the wrinkles and rolls of the verdant slopes of Haleakala Crater. A true nature extravaganza in the Makawao/Haiku area. It's free riding, not trail riding, which includes a guide, Continental breakfast, refreshments, and lunch. For additional information, write to: Adventures on Horseback, Box 1771, Makawao HI 96768, or call 242.7445, 572.6211.

97 Polo Beach A walkway from a landscaped park leads to the beach, where you'll enjoy good swimming and bodysurfing. ♦ Public access clearly marked to this Wailea Resort beach

98 Grand Hyatt Wailea Opened in 1991 this 40-acre, $500 million hotel has the usual Hyatt trademarks: swim-in caves, lots of fountains, several restaurants, large reflecting pools, and a health spa. ♦ 3850 Wailea Alanui Dr, Wailea. 875.1234, 800/233.1234; fax 879.4077

99 Polo Beach Club $$$ These well-appointed two-bedroom, two-bathroom condos are set on a white sand beach with ocean views. The club includes a pool, spa, and sundeck. ♦ 20 Makena Rd, Makena. 879.5266

Hawaii, the southernmost state in the US, is the only island state in the country, and is larger than Rhode Island, Delaware, and Connecticut combined.

100 Four Seasons Resort $$$$ This eight-story, 380-room hotel offers comfortable, sensitively planned rooms on 15 acres at Wailea Beach, and super-deluxe, mansionlike suites that may leave you speechless with their splendor. The large, specially commissioned works of art in the public areas are scaled to the architecture—understated yet grand. The rooms feature teak interior on the lanais, potted orchids, and thick-cushioned rattan furniture. The enormous bathrooms are all marble and mirrors, with a deep bathtub, separate glass shower, and an eight-foot marble counter with double vanities. Most if not all of the rooms have ocean views, with whale watching during winter. The service is excellent; on the large pool terrace attendants will even bring you towels and chilled Evian

spritzes. Although very little is ostensibly Hawaiian about this resort, the views, tradewinds, and cuisine embrace the most desirable Island influences. ♦ 3900 Wailea Alanui Ave, Kihei. 874.8000, 800/332.3442

Within the Four Seasons Resort:

The Seasons ★★★★$$$$ The open-air, no-smoking dining room has a piano, a small dance floor, and an unforgettable menu. You can't help but notice the effort made to use fresh Island ingredients in innovative ways. There's a spinach salad with mountain apple, the Big Island pink abalone ceviche, *lilikoi* (passion fruit) risotto, and, of course, fresh Island fish or chicken embellished with mango, watercress, seaweed, and papaya. The extraordinary dining experience is enhanced by the crisp, cordial service. Don't miss their desserts (ask about the chocolate marjolaine) and vintage port, then end the evening with dancing the night away. ♦ Continental ♦ Daily 6-10PM. Jacket required. 874.8000

Pacific Grill ★★★★$$$ If the weather's nice, as it generally is, you should ask to sit at one of the tables on the lanai overlooking the pool, courtyard, and ocean. Although healthy "alternative cuisine" is served here, who can resist the lobster omelet, the macadamia nut rice, or the Molokai sweet bread French toast? And that's just breakfast. Lunch is similarly staggering. There's a lobster club sandwich, and grilled swordfish with mango-lime coulis. Sizzling *onaga* fish is the dinner specialty, but the tempura sashimi (tuna wrapped in seaweed and crisply fried) and the Vietnamese shrimp soup should not be missed. You'll enjoy this creative menu, complemented by ocean breeze. ♦ Eclectic ♦ Daily 6AM-10PM. 874.8000

Restaurants/Clubs: Red   **Hotels:** Blue
Shops/ ♣ Outdoors: Green   **Sights/Culture:** Black

Catch of the Day

Whether you're looking through a diving mask or gazing at your dinner plate, you will encounter many types of fish in Hawaii—even some you've never heard of before. And since Island menus often identify seafood by Hawaiian names, it helps to know some of the terms you'll come across. Fish you eat are often completely different from the fish you see while snorkeling or scuba diving, and you may want to know which is which. Here's a brief guide to edible fish, followed by descriptions of fish you'll just want to marvel at.

Fish to Eat

The fish most often served in Hawaiian restaurants include *aku* (skipjack or striped tuna), *a'u* (broadbill swordfish), *ono* (a game fish also known as the *wahoo*), *opakapaka* (pink snapper and a favorite Island food), *uku* (gray snapper), *onaga* (red

snapper), and *ulua* (a deep-sea fish also known as *pompano*).

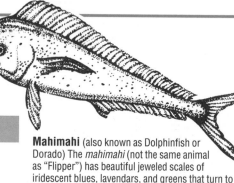

Opakapaka (or Pink Snapper) Hawaii's premium table snapper is usually caught in deep water. It's a versatile fish that appears abundantly on Island menus year-round, although availability peaks from October through February. For nearly a century, it's been Hawaii's most important bottomfish for its value and weight, which averages 18 pounds.

Onaga (or Red Snapper) A popular bottomfish served in upscale restaurants that ranges from one to 18 pounds in Hawaiian waters. Harvested mainly during the fall and winter months, *onaga* is most available in restaurants in December.

Opah (or Moonfish) One of the most colorful commercial fish species in Hawaii, with crimson fins and large, gold-encircled eyes. *Opah* ranges from 60 to 200 pounds and is an up-and-coming gourmet fish that's well-liked for its soft, moist, extremely flaky texture.

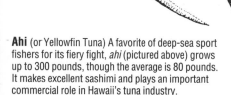

Ahi (or Yellowfin Tuna) A favorite of deep-sea sport fishers for its fiery fight, *ahi* (pictured above) grows up to 300 pounds, though the average is 80 pounds. It makes excellent sashimi and plays an important commercial role in Hawaii's tuna industry.

Mahimahi (also known as Dolphinfish or Dorado) The *mahimahi* (not the same animal as "Flipper") has beautiful jeweled scales of iridescent blues, lavendars, and greens that turn to dull gray as the fish (pictured above) dies. A playful swimmer, it is commonly seen chasing flying fish through the waves. Weighing up to 25 pounds, *mahimahi* is a favorite local food available most of the year, although availability peaks from March through May, and September through November. Large fillets of frozen *mahimahi* from Taiwan and Japan have made this fish available to budget-conscious diners, while fresh *mahimahi* can be a coveted item on pricey Continental menus.

Ahipalaha/Tombo Ahi (or Albacore) The world's premium tuna (pictured above), usually destined for US canneries, is a small predator that averages 40 to 80 pounds. It migrates extensively throughout the north Pacific, far away from Hawaii, and is occasionally substituted for *ahi* and *aku* (other types of tuna) in raw fish preparations.

Ono (or Wahoo) *Ono* is Hawaiian for "good to eat," and this fish is aptly named. Its flaky white meat is served in everything from grilled fish sandwiches to sophisticated Continental preparations. Among Hawaii's less abundant fish, the best time for *ono* is during the summer and fall months. In Hawaii, it typically weighs eight to 30 pounds, but it can grow up to a hundred pounds.

Uku (or Gray Snapper) One of Hawaii's three most popular deep-water snappers, usually weighing four to 18 pounds. *Uku* is most abundant from May through July.

Fish to Meet

Exotic Island fish are among the south Pacific's most spectacular sights. The adventurous can snorkel or scuba dive for panoramic or even close-up views of these native beauties. Landlovers will enjoy the informative tours at such spots as the **Waikiki Aquarium** (see page 114) in **Kapio-lani Park** and at **Sea Life Park** (see page 135) on Oahu. Whichever view you choose, don't miss these underwater jewels. Here's an illustrated guide to some of the popular fish you can swim with in Hawaii's waters.

Kihikihi (or Moorish Idol) The breathtaking beauty and fragility of the *kihikihi* places it in a class by itself. It is usually found in small schools using its long snout to probe for food in the crevices of reefs.

Lauwiliwili (or Crochet or Lemon Butterfly) Found in abundance throughout the Hawaiian Islands, but so far the *lauwiliwili* has been seen nowhere else. You can identify this butterfly fish, which grows up to six inches long, by the 11 vertical rows of spots on either side of its body.

Oiliuwiuwi (or Fan-tailed Filefish) Yellow with black dots, the fan-tailed filefish is named for the grunting and squealing noises it makes when removed from the water (*oiliuwiuwi* means "squealing oili"). Too scrawny to be used as food, the early Hawaiians used it as fuel to cook tastier fish.

Uhu (or Parrotfish) A fascinating fish often found in the waters of Hanauma Bay off Oahu. By day, *uhu* confidently flash their one- to four-foot-long gaudy

Maui

bodies covered with blue-green, gray, and rust-colored scales. You'll also see them scraping algae off the coral with their jagged beaks. By night, they sleep by surrounding themselves in a secretion that forms a protective bubble. Remarkably, *uhu* can change their sex; those that were born as males eventually turn into females. The omnivores also create sand: they eat coral, crustaceans, and mollusks, which are excreted as grains of sand.

Humuhumunukunukuapua'a (or Triggerfish) The fame of this fairly common fish, which was briefly Hawaii's state fish, comes from its long name. *Humuhumu* means "to fit pieces together," and *nukunukuapua'a* is Hawaiian for "nose like a pig." The triggerfish is equipped with two protective devices: when frightened, it dives for its nest and locks itself in place with its dorsal fin, and its eyes can rotate independently, enabling it to see in two directions at once.

Snorkel Maui

If you want to snorkel off Maui's coast with someone who knows the best spots, contact marine biologist **Ann Fielding,** who's an expert on Maui's reefs and underwater life. She leads small groups on wonderful snorkeling adventures. In the summer, snorkel tours are usually held in the north, where the waters are calmer; winter trips are held at a marine preserve on the South Shore. Fielding provides masks, fins, snorkels, and vests. For more information, contact Ann Fielding at: Box 1107, Makawao HI 96768, 572.8437.

Up-Country Cruising

The cattle and farming land on the fertile slopes of Haleakala is Maui's up-country; it extends from the 10,000-foot summit to the island's isthmus and the foot of the West Maui mountains. A drive to these parts offers unlimited opportunities to explore another side of Maui—beyond the beaches and the high-rise resorts—that's well worth your time.

There's no precise route to the up-country—just start near the Kahului Airport as you travel down Haleakala Hwy toward *Pukalani* (hole in the heavens), and keep heading up to the crest of Haleakala Crater. The gently ascending road is bordered by elegant eucalyptus trees, cactus plants, brightly flowering jacarandas, and green hillsides where

Maui

cattle graze among brilliant wildflowers. The air grows much cooler as you reach the top, so bring a jacket. If you have time, there are worthy side trips in several directions: Makawao, a dusty little *paniolo* (cowboy) town with funky storefronts and a down-home flavor; Tedeschi Vineyards, once a whaler's mountain estate and now Hawaii's pioneer winery; Kula Botanical Gardens; and Hawaii Protea Corporation, home of Hawaii's proud floral industry. And don't miss the rich volcanic soil's tasty products—namely onions, lettuce, tomatoes, cabbage, persimmons, and grapes—sold in roadside stores.

101 Makena Beach More than 3,000 feet long and 100 feet wide, Makena Beach is much loved by Maui locals, who have been coming here with their families and coolers for generations. Makena (also called Oneloa Beach) is a glorious golden stretch still fondly remembered as "Big Beach" (over a hill to the right is Little Beach). Both are excellent swimming beaches but must be approached with caution because of occasional steep shorebreaks and riptides. Though popularly thought of as a nude beach, visitors who have been arrested here for sunbathing in the buff have found out the hard way that nude sunbathing is prohibited by Hawaii state law. ♦ Off Makena Rd, about two miles south of Makena

102 Maui Prince Hotel $$$$ This hotel was controversial when it opened in 1986, so spare and Japanese were its architecture and rooms. But the Maui Prince has matured into a beautiful resort that many former critics have grown to appreciate. Its 300 rooms are in an arrowhead-shaped design that maximizes views of Molokini and Kahoolawe on the ocean horizon. The central courtyard, with waterfalls, rock gardens, fish ponds, and footpaths, is a lush, pleasing centerpiece where musicians perform for passersby. The hotel will greet you with hot, almond-scented towels (the t-raditional *oshibori* service) for freshening up after the journey to this rather isolated spot at the western end of the island. The road fronting the hotel—a sticking point in past battles between the hotel and Maui activists—will soon be made into a wide walkway to the public beach. Golf, tennis, two pools at Makena Resort. ♦ 5400 Makena Alanui, Makena. 874.1111, 800/321.6284; fax 879.0082

Within the Maui Prince Hotel:

Hakone ★★★$$$ The Japanese owners of the Maui Prince may have had something to do with the fact that this restaurant is top of the line. Hakone is built of wood imported from Japan, slate floors, and a clean, refined aesthetic that pervades in the food, service, and atmosphere. The multicourse *kaiseki* dinners consist of dainty samplings of soup, salad, appetizers, and fish—raw, boiled, grilled, fried. The sushi is fresh, the *chawanmushi* (a light steamed custard) otherworldly, and ordinary dishes such as tempura and noodles are cooked to perfection. ♦ Japanese ♦ Daily 6-9:30PM. 874.1111

Prince Court ★★★★$$$$ Chef **Roger Dikon** catapulted this restaurant into Maui's culinary heights with his exuberant menu. Simple pleasures such as corn bread (called corn cakes here) and carpaccio, black bean chili, and soft-shell crab (with black bean sauce) become dining adventures here. You'll find American cuisine elevated to a higher level by the natural riches of Hawaii: seared tuna with Maui ginger marmalade, fresh catch of the day in avocado and roasted shrimp cream, and Hawaiian slipper lobster in caviar sauce, to name a few. The Sunday brunch, with free-flowing champagne and hundreds of international dishes, will start your week off right. ♦ Continental ♦ Daily 6-9:30PM; Su brunch 10:30AM-2PM. 874.1111

Cafe Kiowai $$ Prince's main dining restaurant is in a lovely outdoor garden setting beside ponds filled with Japanese carp. The breakfast and lunch menus are fairly broad, with slightly more elevated fare for dinner. Also, poolside snacks and drinks. ♦ Continental ♦ Daily 6:30AM-9:30PM. 874.1111

103 Makena Golf Course **Robert Trent Jones Jr.** designed this course at the Makena Resort, which has mountain and ocean views, tight fairways, huge greens, and enough sand to cover a generous portion of beach. It was named one of the top 10 courses in Hawaii by *Golf Digest*, and there are plans for another

18 holes. The 15th and 16th holes skirt the ocean, and throughout the course you can spot glimpses of quail, panini plants, hibiscus, and the rolling hills of Ulupalakua. Par 72, 6739 yards. ♦ 5415 Makena Alaniu, Makena. Pro shop. 879.3344

104 Tedeschi Vineyards The rich volcanic soil of **Ulupalakua** proved fertile ground for Hawaii's first and only commercial vineyard. Today the vineyards produces four wines—Maui Brut Champagne, Blanc de Noirs, the Rose Ranch Cuvee, the Maui Blush, and Maui Nouveau—on 22 acres. It all began in 1974, when vintner **Emil Tedeschi** (*Te-des-ke*) and **Pardee Erdman,** owner of the surrounding 20,000-acre Ulupalakua Ranch, experimented with numerous varieties of grapes to determine which would best adapt to the 2,000-foot elevation. They eventually decided that the Carnelian grape, a cross developed at the University of California at Davis, held the best prospects. You can tour the winery, which makes use of an old white-washed structure that was once the jailhouse on the ranch, where Hawaiian royalty and other visiting dignitaries used to gather for lavish parties. You'll find this an interesting outing if you're a wine connoisseur or simply looking for an extraordinary sightseeing experience. ♦ Free guided tours daily 10AM-2PM, tasting room daily 9AM-5PM. Take Hwy 37 from Kahului toward Haleakala to the Hwy 37 and Hwy 377 junction, then continue uphill on Hwy 37 until you reach **Grandma's Maui Coffee** (on your right), continue another five miles to the winery. 878.6058

105 Bloom Cottage $$ **Herb** and **Lynne Horner's** B&B is filled with the fragrance of herbs picked from their garden and displayed as potpourri in the rooms. Polished hardwood floors and area rugs, a precious Hawaiian quilt, four-poster bamboo bed, full kitchen, and fireplace are some of the nice touches in their cozy two-bedroom, one-bath cottage. ♦ Rural Route 2, Box 229 (Kula Hwy, 1.8 mile from where Hwys 377 and 37 intersect for the second time) Kula. 878.1425

106 Halemanu $$ The lack of hotels and resorts in Kula, and its growing popularity has inspired some terrific bed-and-breakfast operations in the area. Because these retreats are small, few, and far between, they don't threaten the rural experience. *Halemanu,* meaning "perch" or "birdhouse," is just that—an elevated aerie with a spectacular view and a hostess with impeccable taste who loves to cook. Maui native **Carol Austin's** two-story B&B is filled with collectibles from all over the world. Complete attention to detail is evident in the design; as a result, you can enjoy such pleasures as facing the ocean while soaking in the bathtub. ♦ 221 Kawehi Pl, Kula. 878.2729

107 Haleakala Crater Haleakala (which means house of the sun), is the showpiece of the 27,284-acre **Haleakala National Park.** The vastness of the world's largest dormant volcano is overwhelming. Vital statistics are a 21-mile circumference, 10,023-foot elevation (Maui's highest), and 30 miles of winding interior trails. Hawaiian legends flourish around this giant landmark, and modern-day spiritualists come here for inner soul renewal. But if you're just looking for a gorgeous sunrise, this is Hawaii's best. The drive takes about 90 minutes from Kahului to the summit (open 24 hours daily). Wear something warm (it's at least 30 degrees cooler than down on the flatlands). A flashlight will also help in making your way from the parking lot up to the unattended observatory at the

summit lookout. Be sure to call park information (572.7749) the night before for sunrise time and viewing conditions. If you aren't much of an early bird, stop at the headquarter near the entrance to the park for maps, information, or camping and hiking permits (daily 7:30AM-4PM). En route to the summit 11 miles from the entrance are two overlooks and a visitors center (daily 8:30AM-3PM). Park rangers conduct tours on a scheduled basis. Haleakala cabins are reserved by monthly lottery; cabin requests must be made 90 days in advance. Send requests with preferred and alternate days to Haleakala National Park, Box 369, Makawao HI 96768. ♦ Admission charge per car. Visitors center open summer only. For additional information, call 572.9177/9306. From Kahului Airport, take Hwys 37 to 377 to 378 to Haleakala (37 miles)

108 Seven Pools Tour guides years ago hustled these as the Seven Sacred Pools, and they're still misidentified as such more times than not. Although these seven pools are inspiring and beautiful, "sacred" is not in their official title. Seven Pools (sometimes referred to as **Oheo Pools**) is a series of pools cascading down to the sea, a perfect setting for swimming, picnicking, and camping. The road bridge passes between the fourth and fifth pools, where you can park and take the trail down to the lower pools near the ocean or hike up to the higher pools. If you choose to venture upslope, you'll be rewarded by the Makahiku and Waimoku waterfalls. (If you have any doubts about trekking uphill, ask the park ranger there about the weather conditions.) The pools are part of the **Haleakela National Park.** ♦ Off Hwy 31, 10 miles south of Hana

---

Hawaii has the greatest number of threatened, endangered, and extinct indigenous species of flora in the nation.

109 Hana Plantation Houses $$$ There are only three rentals on this lush five-acre property on the outskirts of Hana. You'll find the surroundings splendidly thick with banana trees, palms, and other tropical plants that flourish in Hana's moist environment. Choose from a charming studio with its own deck and Jacuzzi, and a two-bedroom, one-bathroom house with a color TV, covered lanai, and rear deck lanai for private sunbathing. Other

homes for rent are **Hale Kipa,** a two-story plantation house with levels that can be rented separately, and a one-bedroom cedar home surrounded by coconut palms. There are all the amenities and conveniences, and the hosts will give you directions to their favorite secret spots, including a natural ocean pool that's a five-minute walk across the meadow. ◆ Just past the 48-mile marker coming from Hana on the Hana Rd. 248.8240, 800/657.7723; fax 248.8240

110 Hasegawa General Store This Hana landmark burned down tragically in 1990, but it's being rebuilt on the same spot. Ordinary towns and cities have boring community centers and convention halls, but Hana's Hasegawa General Store was once *the* town attraction, a gathering place for passersby and residents, and purveyor of everything from appliances to food and fishing supplies. There has even been a song written about it. The Hasegawa family created an institution by piling their store from floor to ceiling with goods. Chances are, if you wanted it, they had it—it was just a matter of finding it. ◆ Off Hana Hwy, south of Hana

111 Aloha Nui Loa Tours They'll pick you up at your hotel anywhere on the island, take you to Hana (in an air-conditioned van that carries up to 10 passengers), and saddle you up for horseback rides that lead into ranch land, rain forest, and down to a private beach for a picnic and swim. The rides are coordinated with **Hana Ranch Stables.** ◆ 1995-A Main St, Wailuku. 242.8790

The first flight from the West Coast to Hawaii was made in 1925 (although it wasn't exactly a nonstop flight). A two-engine PN-9 Navy seaplane left San Francisco on 31 August and ran out of gas 300 miles short of Maui. The pilots improvised sails and sailed the seaplane into Kauai on 10 September. Two years later, an army Fokker C-2-3 Wright 220 Trimeter made the first successful, nonstop flight from Oakland, California, to Wheeler Field in Wahiawa, Oahu.

112 Hotel Hana-Maui $$$$ This hotel is synonymous with seclusion, luxury, and the ultimate in pampering. For more than 40 years, it has attracted celebrities and world travelers seeking a respite from their hectic schedules (no TVs in the rooms). In 1984 the powerful **Rosewood Corp.** of Dallas announced its purchase of the hotel and the Hana Ranch Inc., Hana's two largest employers. Under the direction of then-general manager **Carl Lindquist** and the Rosewood Corp., the Hotel Hana-Maui kept its warmth and charm (and its mostly Hana-native staff) while attaining higher levels of service and accommodations. But following the hotel's $24 million renovation, Rosewood sold the property to present owners **Keola Hana Maui Inc.,** a group of Hawaiian, Japanese, and British investors. **Sheraton Corp.** took over management in 1990 (to the distress of some), but so far there's no visible evidence of decline. The 66-acre site houses 97 rooms and suites in various one-story cottages and large, luxurious suites that are both spread out and private. The **Sea Ranch Cottages** skirt the shoreline with stone pillars, pitched corrugated iron roofs, and borders of lava rock and their dark-green stained exteriors look like old plantation homes. The decor is elegant Hawaiian beach cottage, with bleached hardwood floors, Hawaiian quilts, tiled baths that open onto private gardens, and lots of rattan, bamboo, fresh orchids, and baskets of greenery. Another extra-nice touch: every room comes stocked with fresh Kona coffee beans and a coffeemaker. But the greatest luxury is the artwork, the four-poster bamboo beds, and the huge decks with Jacuzzi tubs and ocean views. The leisurely pace and various recreational activities—hiking, picnics, horseback riding—will give you ample opportunity to enjoy the natural surroundings. As you can imagine, the rates are astronomically high. The restored **Plantation House,** formerly the plantation manager's home, sits on a hill away from the beach. It's an ideal facility for families, meetings, and groups of up to 20. The new **Hana Health and Fitness Retreat** offers ongoing programs in nature walks and hikes, aerobics, yoga, exercise, and diet. The hotel offers cookouts, bicycle riding, and planned outings to the historic **Piilanihale Heiau,** a nearby stone temple, and the adjacent **Kahanu Botanical Garden.** And don't miss the hotel's luau, put on every Friday night by employees who are mostly related and longtime Hana residents, is among the best in all of Hawaii. The Hana Airport is serviced daily by Aloha IslandAir from Kahului and airports throughout the Islands. ◆ Off Hana Hwy. 248.8211, 800/325.3535; fax 661.0458

Within Hotel Hana-Maui:

Hotel Hana-Maui Dining Room
★★★$$$$ Executive chef **Amy Ferguson-Ota** has made a name for herself in Hawaii's culinary realms. Her inventiveness with local ingredients (she's married to a local champion spear fisher) is showcased through the menu of Polynesian, Asian, and Pacific delights. Try the fresh fern shoots with Maui onions and Kula tomatoes, Vietnamese curry chicken, prime rib smoked in guava wood, and fresh fish that might be grilled with *kiawe* wood and spiced-rum marinade, wok-seared with banana curry, or bamboo steamed with three caviars. The *ahi* (yellowfin tuna) cakes served with breadfruit, cilantro, and lime mayonnaise are also exceptional. The room is old Hawaii elegant, with polished wood floors and views of the lush courtyard. Although the meals are expensive, they incorporate wonderful local touches which are evident even at breakfast, where you can sample taro hash browns and banana-macadamia nut waffles with guava, *lilikoi* (passion fruit), and coconut syrups. The dining room also prepares fabulous picnic baskets. ◆ Pacific Rim/Polynesian ◆ Daily 7:30-10AM, 11AM-2PM, 6-9PM. Reservations required of nonguests. 248.8211

Hana Coast Gallery Thirty percent of the artists whose work is displayed here are from Hawaii, and all of the art is original (no reproductions), ranging from a 17th-century Rembrandt etching to Island artist **Herb Kane's** Pele bronzes and rare paintings, **Cal Hashimoto's** wood and metal sculptures, and a stone lithograph by **Claude Renoir,** Auguste Renoir's son. The owners are **Gary Koeppel,** producer of the annual **Maui Marine Art Expo,** and **Carl Lindquist,** prominent in the community as a longtime Hana resident, writer and publisher, and former manager of the Hotel Hana-Maui. ◆ Daily 9AM-5PM. 248.8636

Hana Ranch Restaurant ★$$ This downhome, ranch-style restaurant has been a runaway success since reopening in 1986 after renovations. The take-out counter at one end serves up eggs, ham, French toast, and bacon for breakfast, and burgers, hot dogs, and teriyaki sandwiches (a local favorite) for lunch, while the dining room doesn't swing into operation until the midday lunch buffet. But it's the pizza on Thursday and the huge Friday and Saturday night dinners that bring in the crowds. The dinner menu features grilled meats, a salad bar, seafood, and lots of local color. ◆ American ◆ Daily, takeout 6:30AM-4PM, buffet 11AM-3PM; pizza Th 6-9PM; sit-down dinner F-Sa 6-8PM. 248.8255

Restaurants/Clubs: Red   **Hotels:** Blue
Shops/ 🌳 Outdoors: Green   **Sights/Culture:** Black

112 Hana Ranch Stables You can choose from two types of trail rides here—down along the coastline or up into the hills. The guides take you on Hana Ranch land, rolling hills on the velvet flanks of Haleakala Crater. A two-hour luau ride on Tuesday goes up into the hills and back down to Hamoa Beach, and there are breakfast and lunch rides Monday through Wednesday and Friday. Although the rides are arranged through Hotel Hana-Maui, they are open to both guests and nonguests. ◆ Off Hana Hwy. 248.8211

113 Hana Cultural Center This building houses **Babes Hanchett's** Hawaiian artifacts collection. Also called **Hale Waiwai,** the center's more than 200 members collect and display

photographs, shells, quilts, and other objects and artifacts found in the Hana area. ◆ Daily 10AM-4PM. On Uakea Rd, next to the old courthouse, Hana. 248.8622

114 Hana Beach Park This is the safest swimming area in Hana, so it's great for children. The beach is 700 feet long and 100 feet wide, with a pier to one side and an island, **Puu Kii,** beyond it. Picnic and public facilities. ◆ Off Hwy 360. Hana

114 Tutu's at Hana Bay $ This small take-out stand on Hana Bay is known for its Maui-made *haupia* (coconut pudding) ice cream. You can also get sandwiches, plate lunches, hamburgers, and soft drinks here. ◆ In Hana Beach Park, Hana. 248.8224

115 Hana Kai-Maui Resort Apartments $$$ These studios and one-bedroom apartments overlooking Hana Bay are simple but glorious, in two 2-story walk-ups surrounded by lush, tropical plants. All 18 units have full kitchens. ◆ Contact the following for additional rental information: Hana Kai-Maui Resort Apartments, 1533 Uakea Rd, Hana HI 96713. 248.8426/7346, 800/346.2772; and Hana Kai Holidays, Box 536, Hana HI 96713. 248.7742

116 Waianapanapa State Park Try not to leave Hana without exploring the rugged volcanic shoreline of **Waianapanapa** (which means "glistening water" and refers to the cold pool in a cave in the park). You can hike along an ancient three-mile trail to Hana, sunbathe at the black sand cove (although swimming here can be treacherous), and look for turtles and seabirds from the elevated trail over the lava rock outcroppings. There are also sea caves and lava tubes. Cabins, picnic facilities. ◆ Three miles northwest of Hana

117 Bicycle Tours A 38-mile bracing coast down the 10,023-foot-high Haleakala Crater is only one of a number of bicycle tours offered on Maui. (See page 66).

Tropical Treasures

Chances are, one of your first impressions of Hawaii centers around beautiful flowers, since most guests to the Islands are greeted with leis either at the airport or their hotel. The Islanders take pride in their flowers, and will appreciate a visitor who is familiar with the exotic varieties found in Hawaii. Here's a guide to some of Hawaii's finest flora.

Bird-of-paradise (*Strelitzia reginae*) An ostentatious flower that's easy to pick out—just look for sharp orange and blue petals (plumage) topping a long gray-green stalk. This colorful showpiece hails from South Africa. Each flower blooms in six stages, a new one every couple of days.

Night blooming cereus (*Hylocereus undatus*) A nocturnal beauty, this flower blooms for about two weeks from June through October. The yellow blossoms open at dusk and close with the morning sun.

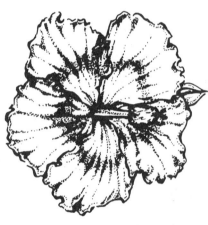

Anthurium (*Anthurium andraenum*) This heart-shaped flower grows in many colors—white, greenish white, pink, red, lavendar, and pink-streaked. The surface of the bloom has a waxy shine that looks almost artificial, and when it's cut, it will stay fresh-looking for weeks.

Hibiscus (*Hibuscus rosa-sinensis; Hibiscus koki'o*) Hibiscus shrubs grow easily on all the Islands and come in several colors and shapes. They're rarely used in lei making, because the large showy flowers are very fragile.

Vanda orchid (*Vanda hookeriana x V. teres*) If you're lucky, you may see a rare and exquisite lei made from the lavendar pads of these popular orchids.

Lobster claw heliconia (*Heliconia humilis*) A member of the same family as the bird-of-paradise, this plant has leaves the color and shape of cooked lobster claws. Cradled within these leaves are small green flowers.

Silversword
(*Argyroxiphium sandwicense*) This plant grows in Maui's Haleakala National Park and on the Big Island in rock or volcanic earth at altitudes of 6,000 to 12,000 feet. You'll recognize its silver spike leaves growing on a six-foot-tall stalk, which is capped in August by blooming tufts of flowers.

Maui

Plumeria (*Meli; Frangipani*) This fragrant, durable flower is a favorite of lei makers. The name *frangipani* (French for thick milk) refers to its poisonous milky sap.

118 Kula Lodge ★$$ This up-country lodge offers a few rustic, charming cabins with lanais that look out at the sloping flanks of Haleakala, the West Maui Mountains, and the flower fields of Kula. Service and food are forgettable, but the views are not. Dinner is served by an intimate roaring fire. ♦ Off Rural Route 1, Kula Hwy 378. 878.1535

119 Makawao Steak House ★★★$$$ Things have been looking up since **Dickie** and **Judy Furtado** bought this place. It was always a popular steak house, but it's gotten even better. There are three fireplaces, lots of artwork, and a diverse menu: *kiawe*-broiled duck and rack of lamb, prime rib, fresh catch of the day cooked four ways, a seafood sampler, pastas, chicken, and at least five salads. ♦ Steak ♦ M-Th, Su 5-9:30PM; F-Sa 5-10PM. 3612 Baldwin Ave, Makawao. 572.8711

119 McKay Country Cottage $$ You can rent a room in **Stewart** and **Shaun McKay's** home or your own cottage at the other end of the 12½-acre property, some 4,000 feet above Makawao. It's like an English retreat, with protea gardens and genial hosts. The cottage is large, with open-beam ceilings, window seats, antique furniture, and special touches such as a Bombay chest in the foyer and a number of windows to let in the light and the view. This is one of the more remote B&Bs, so be prepared for a winding drive. ♦ 536 Olinda Rd, Makawao. 572.1453

120 Makawao Rodeo If it's summer and you're a rodeo fan, you're in luck; the annual Makawao Rodeo is a real down-and-dirty experience, with the best *paniolos* (cowboys) from around the Islands. There's also plenty of wild cattle, bronco and bull riding, beer, junk food, and country music. ♦ Held around the Fourth of July. Oskie Rice Rodeo Arena, Olinda Rd, Makawao

121 Bullocks of Hawaii ★$ Home of the moonburger—two all-sirloin patties, special "moon" sauce, and the works on a buttered-grilled bun. Ask **Hazel Bullocks** to whip up a pure fruit-nectar shake. A great place to stop near Haleakala Crater. ♦ American ♦ Daily 7:30AM-3PM. 3494 Haleakala Hwy, Pukalani. 572.7220

122 Pukalani Terrace Country Club $$ This is a convenient choice on the way up to or down from Haleakala Crater. You'll appreciate the inexpensive menu specializing in down-home cooking with everything from pan-fried Island fish to tripe stews, and homemade pies. ♦ Hawaiian/American ♦ M-F 7AM-2PM, 5-9PM; Sa-Su 6:30AM-2PM, 5-9PM. 360 Pukalani Rd, Pukalani. 572.1325

123 Up-Country Maui Drive There is no allotted time or precise route for this drive, only unlimited opportunities for you to explore another side of Maui, beyond the beaches and high-rise resorts. (See page 72).

124 Casanova Italian Restaurant ★★★$$ It started as a deli that wholesaled black squid-ink pasta to Maui's upscale hotels (before it became vogue) and *gnocchi* and cappuccino to growing Makawao clientele. Its popularity spawned a restaurant, and then a nightclub/disco that commands an entire corner of Makawao. You can either pack a picnic of lasagna, ravioli, pasta salads, cheeses, and desserts from the petite but bountiful deli, or you can go next door and dine on Italian cuisine. Carpaccio, a vegetarian *fritto misto*, and linguine with clams are only a few of the items on the lengthy menu. From fresh fish to Big Island beef and seafood risotto, the choices are bound to satisfy. Monday is reggae night at the disco. ♦ Italian ♦ Restaurant: M-Sa 5:30PM-1AM. Deli: M-Sa 8:30AM-7:30PM; Su 8:30AM-6:30PM. 1188 Makawao Ave, Makawao. 572.0220

125 Polli's Mexican Restaurant $$ Traditional Mexican food (try finishing their Haleakala-sized *chimichanga*) with all the trimmings, including live music Thursday through Saturday nights. Order take-out food if you're hurrying up-country. ♦ Mexican ♦ Daily 11:30AM-11PM. 1202 Makawao Ave, Makawao. 572.7808

126 Komoda's This adorable bakery is half a century old, a combination old-fashioned general store and bakery (famous throughout the Islands for its monumental cream puffs). The *azuki* bean pie is also popular. ♦ M-Sa 6:30AM-5PM. 3674 Baldwin Ave, Makawao. 572.7261

127 Viewpoint Galleries New and earnest, Viewpoint is devoted to Maui artists (and

rightfully so). Maui is Hawaii's art center and ripe for this kind of artists' collective. All media are represented here. ♦ Daily 11AM-9PM. 3620 Baldwin Ave, next to Makawao Steak House, Makawao.. 572.5979

128 Haliimaile General Store ★★★★$$$ **Bev** and **Joe Gannon** converted an old plantation store in the middle of the pineapple fields into an oasis of fine dining. High ceilings, hardwood floors, two dining rooms, and works by prominent Maui artists provide great ambience. The air is crisp—at 1,200-foot altitude—and the food consistently good. Diners come from miles away for the brie-and-grape quesadilla, Bev's boboli (a pizza-like crust) with crab dip, the blackened sashimi, and the Hunan-style rack of lamb. Save room for dessert—the chocolate-macadamia nut pie is unforgettable. The owners' show-biz background (Joe currently produces concerts for Julio Iglesias, Alice Cooper, and Ringo Starr; Bev was once the road manager for Liza Minelli and Joey Heatherton) makes this a celebrity haunt, too. You never know who might just show up. ♦ Eclectic ♦ Tu-Su 11AM-3PM, 6-10PM; also Su brunch 10AM-3PM. 900 Haliimaile Rd, Haliimaile. 572.2666

Restaurants/Clubs: Red   **Hotels:** Blue

Shops/ 🌴 Outdoors: Green   **Sights/Culture:** Black

129 Hui No'eau Visual Arts Center Noted architect **C.W. Dickey** designed this 1917 stucco mansion in its manorial five-acre setting in Makawao. Vestiges of one of the island's first sugar mills mark the tree-lined entrance. Originally built for prominent Maui *kamaaina* **Harry** and **Ethel Baldwin,** the estate was given over to the arts by their grandson, **Colin Cameron,** in the late seventies. Today Hui No'eau offers ongoing exhibits, regular classes in line drawing, printmaking, and other arts, and a beautiful environment to visit the gift shop features earrings, paintings, ceramics, and handmade paper. ♦ Daily 10AM-4PM. 2841 Baldwin Ave, Makawao. 572.6560

130 The Vegan Restaurant ★★$$ This restaurant is persuading more and more people that pure vegetarian cuisine is not only wholesome, but entirely appetizing, even delicious. There's the tofucci, a lasagne without meat or dairy products, the potato Wellington, and the banini, a banana shake without milk or sugar. A favorite is the vegan burger, made of cleverly combined wheat gluten, tempeh, and grains. ♦ Vegetarian ♦ 115 Baldwin Ave, Paia. 579.9144

131 Picnics ★★$ Everyone loves Picnics, which is basically a take-out counter (and what food) with a few bright orange plastic tables and benches for the contented loiterers. The newsprint menu is reason enough to stop: it has a guide to Hana on one side, with a map of Maui, a list of the state and county parks, and a time chart for distances on the road to Hana. It even lists Hana's 54 bridges. The food is no less engaging—picnic favorites, of course—with a hefty selection of robust vegetarian goodies (the fabled spinach-nut burger and tofu burger). Lots of salads, and box lunches for road trips, with everything from a broiled half chicken to the Executive Picnic, a sizable selection of cut meats, *kiawe*-broiled chicken and salad. A tablecloth, ice chest, and ice are provided for a fee. Espresso and cappuccino are also available, a godsend for weary drivers. ♦ Daily 7:30AM-7PM. 30 Baldwin Ave, a half block from Hana Hwy, Paia. 579.8021

132 Charley's Restaurant and Saloon ★★$$ Charley's manages to please everyone with its pizza, other Italian foods, and Mexican fare, as well as pancakes that are 10 inches in diameter. Light eaters can choose from the omelets, salads, and plenty of other healthy foods and good vibes. ♦ American ♦ Daily 7AM-2PM, 4-10PM. 142 Hana Hwy, Paia. 579.9453

MAMA'S FISH HOUSE

133 Mama's Fish House ★★$$$ Despite its remote location on the northeast coast, this has been Maui's best-known fish house for years. This tropical restaurant is fully blessed with ocean views, soft sea breezes, and romantic sunsets. You'll also enjoy the fresh fish, especially the house specialty stuffed with herbs, bay shrimp, mushroom sauce, and honey wheat bread topped off with a Hookipa sundae: ice cream, Frangelico, amaretto, cocoa, cream, and nuts. You may want to stop here on your way to or from Kuau Cove, an idyllic piece of shoreline near Hookipa, and an incredible windsurfing spot. ♦ Continental ♦ Daily 11AM-9:30PM. 799 Poho Pl, Hana Hwy, just one mile past Paia. 579.9672

134 The Hana Drive The Hana Hwy is a challenge and a pleasure (to most), and certainly an unorthodox way to enter Hana. A full description of the drive is on page 43.

A full description of the drive is on page 43.

Maui's Highlights

Watching the sunrise (only when the weather is perfect) at **Haleakala Crater.**

Driving the crooked road from Honokahua to Hana (provided you're not prone to car sickness).

A take-out lunch from **Picnics** in Paia for a picnic in Ulupalakua, a beautiful spot off Honoapiilani Hwy, south of Wailea.

A snorkeling tour led by marine biologist **Ann Fielding** of **Snorkel Maui.**

Whale watching from **Papawai Point Lookout.**

Breakfast or dessert at **Longhi's.**

Leisurely driving tours through up-country Maui.

All the festivals at **Kapalua Bay Hotel.**

Coconut ice cream at **Tutu's** on Hana Bay.

A picnic around **Seven Pools** in Kipahulu.

Lingering at **Hui Noeau Center for Visual Arts** in Makawao.

Sunday brunch at the **Prince Court,** the bastion of haute cuisine, located in the **Maui Prince Hotel.**

Many Hawaiians—especially those of Japanese ancestry—believe the bird-of-paradise flower is a sign of good luck. They often plant this exotic flower in their front yards in hope of bringing good fortune to the household. The bird-of-paradises with orange blossoms grow up to five feet tall, while those with white flowers can reach heights of 20 feet.

Hawaii's Best

Carl Lindquist
Publisher/Writer, Maui

Maui's **Hana Coast** at sunrise provides the mystical light and innate sense of power that accompanies the beginning of each Hana day.

Pi'ianihale Heiau, on Maui, is the largest of the ancient stone temples left standing. A place revered for its antiquity and its *mana* (spiritual power).

Ulupalakua on Maui at sunset. Sipping wine high on the slopes of Haleakala (the world's largest dormant volcano) as the sun fades, then leisurely driving through Kaupo to Hana.

Haleakala Crater on Maui has the kind of grandeur and silence that puts one's life back in perspective.

Maui

Blackie's Bar in Lahaina, Maui, has good, live jazz and the kind of meatloaf sandwiches that Mom never made.

Ann Fielding
Marine Biologist/Tour Director, Snorkel Maui

Reef's End at Molokini Island near Maui. This shallow, coral-covered ridge rises hundreds of feet off the ocean floor to within only a few feet of the surface. The colors are vibrant; the water very clear.

Jody Baldwin
Owner, Kilohana Bed & Breakfast, Maui

Driving to **Tedeschi Vineyards** at Ulupalakua and stopping for cappuccino at **Grandma's Coffee House** in Keokea, Maui.

A windy day at **Hookipa Beach** (outside of Paia on Maui) watching the pro windsurfers.

Gala art openings at the **Hui No'eao** on Baldwin Ave, Makawao, Maui.

Moonlight concerts at the **Maui Prince Hotel's** outdoor theater in Makena, Maui.

Hiking **Haleakala Crater** on Maui—from Sliding Sands to Kaupo Gap—and spending the night at **Paliko Cabin.**

CHRIS MIDDOUR

Kahoolawe

Of Hawaii's eight major islands, Kahoolawe (kaw-*hoe*-law-wee) is the smallest and the only one that is uninhabited. The island has gone through several incarnations, from a fishing colony, to a penal colony, to grazing land for sheep, and, finally, to a site used for extensive bombing practice by the US Navy. It is a tragic irony that although Kahoolawe is on the **National Register of Historic Places**, it was controlled by the US Navy and used as a federal target area since 1941. The nighttime bombing exercises eerily resembled a Fourth of July celebration, and reverberations could be felt even on Maui.

Hawaiian activists and environmentalists, pointing to archaeological remains, believe the island is sacred and historical and should be returned to the public, or at least to native Hawaiians. Members of the group **Protect Kahoolawe Ohana** (*ohana* means family) have sailed the seven miles from Maui to Kahoolawe several times throughout the years to try to occupy the island. They have always been removed by authorities and charged with trespassing on federal property. But their efforts—which have always received strong support from Hawaii residents and government officials—have finally paid off. In 1990, **President George Bush** stopped the bombing of the island. His decision prompted celebrations all over Hawaii. And now, a federal commission has been appointed to recommend the conditions for returning Kahoolawe to the state.

Kahoolawe

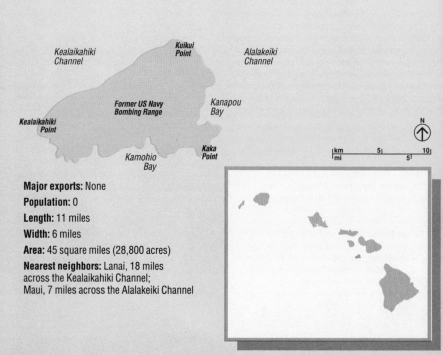

Major exports: None
Population: 0
Length: 11 miles
Width: 6 miles
Area: 45 square miles (28,800 acres)
Nearest neighbors: Lanai, 18 miles across the Kealaikahiki Channel; Maui, 7 miles across the Alalakeiki Channel

The Sound of Music

People either love it or hate it. Unfortunately, most who say they hate Hawaiian music have never heard "authentic" Hawaiian music. They always describe the *Sweet Leilani* type of music, probably written in Chicago for some *Bird of Paradise*-type movie.

Prior to Captain James Cook's discovery of the Islands, chanting was the music of Hawaii. The missionaries brought their hymns in the 1820s, and when the *paniolos* (Hawaiian cowboys) came to the Islands from Mexico and Spain in the 1830s, they brought the guitar. These contributions helped form the varied sounds that make up the fabric of traditional Hawaiian music.

The Hawaiian word for song is *mele*, which means "chanted poetry." A *mele inoa* is a "name song," one written about a person or sometimes a home. A *hapa haole*, translated as "half caucasian," is a song that usually originated from the ragtime era and always uses both Hawaiian and English words; this music is often played in a style the Hawaiians call *cha-lang-a-lang*, a sort of fast ragtime beat. A *himeni* song is a score that is only sung and is never accompanied by dancing. It comes from the English word "hymn," and originated when the missionaries introduced their music to the Islands.

Not too long ago, all you had to do was go to a club like Honolulu's old Aloha Grill to hear down-home Hawaiian music. Musicians gathered there after performing in Waikiki and played for locals until the wee morning hours. Many such clubs are closed now, so it is harder to find that kind of entertainment. But it still can be done. If you really want to hear what the *kamaaina* (old-timers) listen to, just ask the musicians playing in any Waikiki hotel where you can go to hear a Hawaiian jam session. If that doesn't work, the Parks and Recreation Department occasionally sponsors concerts in the parks on Oahu. Don't miss the **Slack Key Guitar Concert,** held every August on Oahu, a runaway success featuring the best performers and attracting slack-key lovers from all over the world. (Slack key is a guitar-tuning technique unique to Hawaii; musicians loosen their guitar strings to create various tones that are very mellow and quite different from normal guitar sounds.)

For Hawaiian music of all types, tune into the Honolulu-based radio station, KCCN. It is the only all-Hawaiian music station in the Islands. For more than 40 years, KCCN used to broadcast the weekly live radio show "Hawaii Calls" to hundreds of stations around the world. The program first aired in 1935 and was devoted to preserving authentic Island music until the show's final broadcast in

1978. A number of good "Hawaii Calls" records are available today at shops such as the House of Music in the Ala Moana Shopping Mall on Oahu. This record store has one of the largest selections of Hawaiian music on the Islands. Favorite traditional Hawaiian musicians include old-timers Genoa Keawe, the late Gabby Pahinui and his son Bla Pahinui, Benny Kalama, Kekua Fernandez, Sonny Chillingworth, Myra English, Auntie Edith Kanakaole, and Auntie Alice Namakelua. Other performers who play traditional music include Keola and Kapono Beamer, Peter Moon, the Brothers Cazimero, Hookena, Haunani Apoliona (who sings with Jerry Santos in a group called Olomana), Sandwich Island Band, Makaha Sons of Niihau, Lim Family, Sons of Hawaii, Hui Ohana, Diana Aki, Halona, Na Leo Kani o Punahele, and the Ho'aikanes.

Kahoolawe

Article and drawing by graphic designer **James Cross** of Los Angeles, who has been collecting and singing Hawaiian music since 1948.

"No alien land in all the world has any deep, strong charm for me but [Hawaii]; no other land could so longingly and so beseechingly haunt me sleeping and waking, through half a lifetime, as that one has done. Other things leave me, but it abides; others change, but it remains the same. For me its balmy airs are always blowing, its summer seas flashing in the sun, the pulsing of its surf-beat is in my ear; I can see its sugarlanded crags, its leaping cascades, its plumy palms drowsing by the shore, its remote summits floating like islands above the cloud rack; I can feel the spirit of its woodland solitudes, I can hear the splash of its brooks; in my nostrils still lives the breath of flowers that perished 20 years ago."

Mark Twain, 1889

Molokai

Residents of Molokai (mall-ah-*kai* or mo-loh-*ka*-ee) are proud that their island has never had an elevator or a traffic light. In fact, there are many things Molokai does without: discotheques, movie theaters, a hamburger emporium's familiar golden arches, and most of the other trappings of urban development and commercialism.

This is a unique island, full of what appears to be strange contradictions. It has evidenced little appetite for tourism developments, and yet has a major resort, **Colony's Kaluakoi Hotel and Golf Club**, on its western shores. It has beautiful

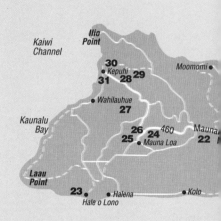

beaches, lush valleys, and a rugged, arid interior. However, since 1866, one of the most beautiful parts of Molokai has been known to the rest of the world as a colony for people with Hansen's disease, also known as leprosy. It was the stigma of Hansen's disease that led the island to attempt to change its image with the adoption of Molokai's slogan "the Friendly Island."

Kalaupapa, a green and scenic peninsula on the north side of Molokai, is the area where people with leprosy were sequestered. It's a section of Molokai that's cut off from normal access by steep cliffs and treacherous waters. This section of Molokai is also a National Historical Park known as the **Kalaupapa Settlement,** which is managed by the state Department of Health's Hansen's Disease Institutional Services Branch. Fewer than 90 leprosy patients still live on this peninsula, but they have been fully cured and are free to come and go as they please. Ever since the need to use Kalaupapa as a leprosy treatment center was eliminated, Molokai has experienced some noticeable changes. Today many Molokai residents commute to and from their jobs on Maui aboard the **Maui Princess,** a 118-foot yacht that also transports visitors from Maui to Molokai for day tours and recreational activities. Colony's Kaluakoi Hotel and Golf Club offers the only resort life on Molokai, with its low-rise hotel, complete with an 18-hole golf course that runs along a beautiful beach on the western rim of the island. The rest of Molokai is made for the active outdoor person ready for some self-guided exploration.

The rectangular island is 38 miles long, 10 miles wide, and about 52,000 acres are owned by the **Molokai Ranch.** There are wide variations of terrain, from sandy beaches and verdant valleys to almost desert-like, windblown landscapes. Like **Lanai,** its neighbor to the south, this is an island best suited for the traveler who enjoys and respects the natural attractions of the

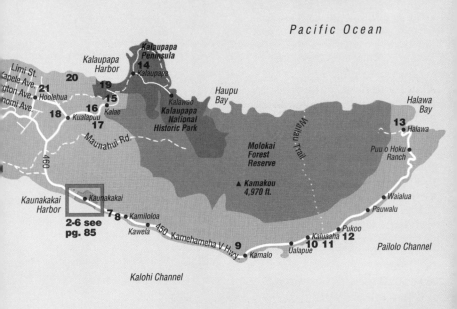

Pacific Ocean

Limi St.
Kapele Ave.
gton Ave.
nomi Ave.

21
• Hoolehua

20

Kalaupapa
Harbor

**Kalaupapa
Peninsula**

14
• Kalaupapa

19

15

16
• Kalae

18
• Kualapuu

17

Maunahui Rd.

460

Kalawao

**Kalaupapa
National
Historic Park**

Haupu
Bay

Halawa
Bay

13
• Halawa

Puu o Hoku
Ranch

**Molokai
Forest
Reserve**

Waiau Trail

▲ **Kamakou**
4,970 ft.

• Waialua

• Pauwalu

Kaunakakai
Harbor

• Kaunakakai

**2-6 see
pg. 85**

7 8
• Kamiloloa

Kawela

450

Kamehameha V Hwy.

9

• Kamalo

• Ualapue

10 11

• Kaluaaha **12**

• Pukoo

Pailolo Channel

Kalohi Channel

N

| km | 5 | 10 |
| mi | 5 |

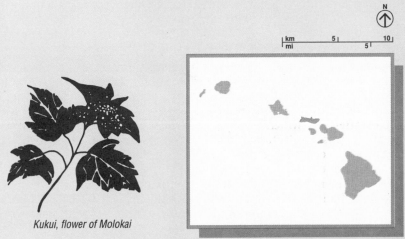

Kukui, flower of Molokai

unspoiled outdoors. Respect, in fact, is an important consideration for any visitor to Molokai. Beyond the Kaluakoi resort, this is not an island that is set up to accommodate tourists, and visitors who are overly demanding or disrespectful of the natural values of Molokai will not receive a hospitable welcome. If, however, you go there to enjoy the land without unduly disturbing it, you will indeed find it to be "the Friendly Island."

1 Kapuaiwa Grove King Kamehameha V
planted 1,000 palm trees here in the 1860s
and several hundred of them remain in this
extensive grove. A shoreside park nearby is
enjoyed by picnickers. ◆ Hwy 460, near
Kaunakakai

2 Molokai Drive Inn ★$ A take-out counter
with fresh fish-plate lunches is a rarity, even
in Hawaii. If the fishin's good, try the fresh
mahimahi or *opakapaka*, a perfect comple-
ment to the great French fries. The hamburgers are also popular. ◆ Seafood ◆ M-Th
6:30AM-10PM; F-Sa 7AM-10:30PM; Su
7AM-10PM. Kaunakakai. 553.5655

2 Kaunakakai This is the town that inspired
the song, "The Cock-eyed Mayor of Kaunakakai," although, truth be told, Kaunakakai
has no official mayor because the island of
Molokai is technically a part of Maui County,
and therefore is under the jurisdiction of
Maui's mayor. The town's two biggest attractions are its main street, Ala Malama, which
looks like it did in the 1920s, and the wharf,
which extends a half mile out into the ocean
(and is a popular spot for the local teens who
drive their cars on the wharf over the ocean).

Molokai

3 Molokai Fish & Dive
As the only sporting goods
store on an island big on
the outdoors, this is a
major attraction.
Here you can rent
snorkeling gear,
boogie boards, fishing
poles, or pick up an original Molokai-
designed T-shirt and cap. ◆ M-Sa 8:30AM-
6PM; Su 9AM-2PM. Kaunakakai. 553.5926

4 Rabang's $ Filipino food and hamburgers
are the main items on the menu. Located in
the middle of Kaunakakai, it has a take-out
counter and only a few tables, which fill up
quickly with local families. ◆ Filipino/Ameri-
can ◆ Daily 10AM-9PM. Kaunakakai.
553.5841

4 Outpost Natural Food ★★$ The juice bar
is known for its Mexican food, smoothies,
and sandwiches. The produce is mostly fresh
from Molokai. Great stop for a healthy take-
out snack, hot or cold. ◆ Health Food ◆ M-F,
Su 9AM-6PM. Kaunakakai. 553.3377

5 Kanemitsu Bakery ★$ Whether you pick
up the famous Molokai raisin-nut, onion-
cheese, or wheat bread, or fresh donuts, or
cinnamon crisps, you won't regret stopping
at this popular Kaunakakai bakery. Open
since 1925, it's a Molokai legend, with bread
that appears on menus all over the island. It's
small, but don't miss it. ◆ M, W-Su 5:30AM-
8PM. Kaunakakai. 553.5855

5 Molokai Island Creations
Swimwear, T-shirts, fra-
grances, soaps, Hawaiian
note cards, and other
Molokai miscellany are
offered at this pleasant
country boutique, right
next door to Molokai
Fish & Dive. ◆ M-Sa 8:30AM-6PM; Su 9AM-
2PM. Kaunakakai. 553.5926

6 Mid Nite Inn ★★★$$ Many Islanders
wouldn't dream of coming to Molokai with-
out stopping at this modest, no-nonsense
local institution that began as a noodle shop
back in the days when steamers and passen-
ger ships anchored in Kaunakakai Harbor. It
famous for its grilled *akule* (scad) and oxtail
soup, and pizza was recently added to the
menu. ◆ Japanese/American ◆ M-Sa 6AM-
1:30PM, 5:30-9PM. Kaunakakai. 553.5302

7 Pau Hana Inn $$ A cottage-style inn on the
fringe of Kaunakakai that overlooks the ocea
and has lots of down-home charm. The bud-
get-priced accommodations include poolsid
studios with kitchenettes. *Pau Hana* means
"after work" and, indeed, the terrace is a
gathering place for locals who come to appre
ciate the beauty of the Bengalese banyan tre
conveniently located near the bar. Lunch in
the **Pau Hana Dining Room** is good (★$$)
and the **Friendly Isle Band Rhythmic Experi-
ence (FIBRE)** plays on Friday and Saturday
nights. Pool, restaurant. ◆ Off Hwy 450,
Kaunakakai. 553.5342

8 Hotel Molokai $$ Rustic, low-rise buildings on a narrow strip of
beach. There are 56
units in shingled A-
frame bungalows
with lanais contain-
ing swinging love-
seats. Settle into one
and you'll hear the palm
fronds rustling in the breeze. There are no
TVs, radios, or telephones in the rooms, but
that's consistent with Molokai style. The larg
er rooms have lofts with twin-sized beds. Lik
the island, this is a friendly place to stay,
although the change in management of the
hotel's restaurant, **Holo Holo Kai,** has sad-
dened many habitués; it's simply not as good
as the old favorite. ◆ Off Hwy 450, Kamiloloa
two miles east of Kaunakakai. 553.5347,
800/423.MOLO; fax 531.4004

9 St. Joseph Church A wood-frame church
built in 1876 by Father Damien (see the syn-
opsis on this Belgian priest in the "Kalaupapa" entry on page 87).

10 Our Lady of Sorrows Church Father
Damien built this church, too, in 1874. There
is a statue of him in the pavilion. ◆ Off Hwy
450, Kaluaaha

11 Kaluaaha Church Built in 1832, this is the
oldest standing church in Hawaii. ◆ Off Hwy
450, Kaluaaha

Restaurants/Clubs: Red   Hotels: Blue

Shops/ 🌴 Outdoors: Green   **Sights/Culture:** Black

12 Molokai Wagon and Horse Ride A stellar island experience for anyone, visitor or resident. The jovial, guitar-playing **Larry Heil** will serenade you with Hawaiian songs as you depart from the beachside hut into a 50-acre mango patch and straight up the mountain, where a turn-of-the-century stone temple awaits in quiet splendor. You'll cross a stream on this wagon ride, smell the wild guavas and flowers, and return to the beach, where you'll be greeted with a laid-back, Hawaiian-style barbecue. ♦ M-Sa noon. From the Mapulehu Mango Grove, take Hwy 450. 567.6773

13 Halawa Valley The major adventure on Molokai is driving to Halawa Valley and hiking through its lush, green-carpeted jungle, which is marked by a pair of beautiful waterfalls, a lovely lagoon, and a beach. The valley begins where Hwy 450 ends at the northeastern tip of the island. Hundreds of families once occupied the valley, but a tidal wave in 1946 prompted their evacuation. Only a few families returned. Remains of the once-thriving taro patches and old irrigation ditches can still be seen. The two-hour hike to the falls is well worth the time, but it is more than a little outing. Come prepared with clothing that can get wet (you'll be wading across streams), a thick shield of insect repellent, and an adventurous spirit (for persevering along trails with few signs). Beware the giant *mo'o* (lizard); this is Hawaii's own version of the Loch Ness monster and legend has it that it's only safe to swim in the pool at the bottom of the falls if a ti leaf thrown into the water floats. ♦ Take Hwy 450 around the east side of the island until you can't drive any farther, about 37 miles from the airport and 48 miles from the Kaluakoi Hotel. The highway offers beautiful views of neighboring Lanai and Maui.

Wild and Crazy Shirts

Harry Truman wore them. So did Bing Crosby, Frank Sinatra, Burt Lancaster, and Montgomery Clift (though they were paid to do it in the movie *From Here to Eternity*). Tom Selleck wore them prominently, and before him, Arthur Godfrey of *Hawaii Calls* fame, and Hawaiian Olympic surfer Duke Kahanamoku, one of the world's greatest watermen. They all wore classic Hawaiian shirts—those loud, blinding bursts of flowers, birds, palm trees, and pineapples (the real reason sunglasses were invented, some say).

The history of the Hawaiian shirt dates back to the 19th century, when missionaries gave the natives plain-colored shirts to cover their bare chests. They, in turn, painted them by hand with colorful Hawaiian

Molokai

motifs, and the shirts have been copied ever since. Visitors have been buying Hawaiian shirts as souvenirs for decades, and with the "here-I-come" attitude of the 1990s, they're all the craze.

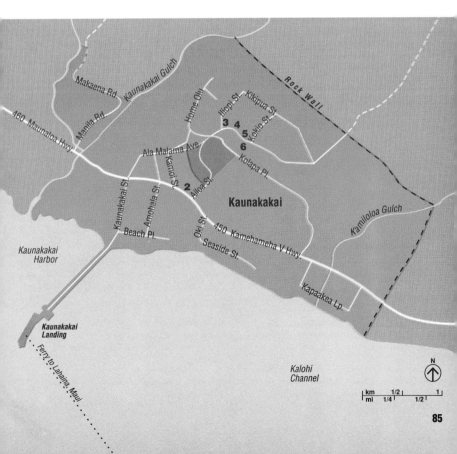

Tongue Tied

In keeping with its cultural diversity, Hawaii has three languages—two official (English and Hawaiian) and one unofficial (Pidgin Hawaiian). Most of the Islanders speak English, but Hawaiian is regaining popularity as more natives rediscover their roots.

Hawaiian is an oral tradition first put into written form by *haole* (Caucasian) missionaries in 1823. The language is a Polynesian dialect that combines the five vowels with only seven consonants (*h, k, l, m, n, p,* and *w*) to give it a soft, lyrical cadence.

Pronounce these consonants the same as in English, except when a *w* follows an *i* or *e*, in which case you may pronounce the *w* as a *v*. Pronounce *a* as in palm, *e* as in they, *i* as in ring, *o* as in go, and *u* as in truth.

English	Hawaiian
At once	Koke (*koh*-keh)
Beach	Kahakai (*kah*-hah-kye)
Breakfast	Aina kakahiaka (*eye*-nuh kah-kah-*he*-ah-kah)
Coffee	Kope (*koh*-peh)

Molokai

Forbidden	Kapu (kah-*puh*)
Glad to meet you	Hauoli (hah-oo-*oh*-lee)
Hello, Greetings, Love	Aloha (ah-*loh*-hah)
Hotel	Hokele (*hoe*-keh-leh)
How about it?	Pehea la (pah-*heh*-ah lah)
How are you?	Pehea oe (peh-hay-ah *oh*-ee)
I want to go	Makemake hele au (*mah*-keh-*mah*-keh *heh*-leh ow)
Left/Right	Hema/Akau (*heh*-ma/ah-*cow*)
Market	Makeke (mah-*keh*-keh)
Restroom	Lua (*loo*-ah)
Thank you	Mahalo (mah-*hah*-low)
The road to	Ala (*ah*-lah)
Today	Keia la (*kay*-ee-ah la)
Tomorrow	Apopo (*ah*-poh-poh)
Tonight	Kela po (*keh*-lah poh)

Local Lingo

Keep your ears open for Islanders speaking among themselves in **pidgin,** a fun but sloppy dialect that combines Hawaiian with English, Polynesian, Samoan, Filipino, Japanese, and other languages originally brought to the Islands by traders and plantation workers. In fact, pidgin originally developed as a device to help traders communicate. Islanders are very possessive of their pidgin, so you probably shouldn't try to speak it until you've spent some time on the Islands. But if you'd like to try, here's a tourist's guide to Island slang.

Pidgin Hawaiian	English
An'den	And then?; So what, I'm bored.
Any kine	Anything
Ass why hard	Life's tough, isn't it?
Bag	To leave
Brah	Brother; pal
Buggah	Pal; pest
Da	The
Da kine	It; Thing; Stuff (a general noun); The best
FOB	Fresh off the boat; Newcomer
Fo' days	Lots of; Long
Fo' real	Really?; You can say that again!; I mean it!
Fo' what	Why?
Garans	Guaranteed
Geev'em	Go for it; Give it all you've got
Grinds	Food
Haole	Caucasian
Hawaiian time	Late
Hele on	Take off; Get going
Innahs	Great!; Cool!; The *in* thing
JOJ	Just off the jet; Newcomer
Kay den	OK then!; Alright already!
Laydahs	Later; Good-bye
Lesgo	Let's go
Like?	Would you like to?
Lolo	Crazy
Max	To do something all the way (variations: max out, to the max, da max)
Momona	Fat
No ack	Be cool; Quit cutting up
No can	Cannot
No ka oi	You can't beat this
No shame	Don't be shy; You have no class!
Ono	Delicious
O'wot?	Or what? (This is commonly added to the end of sentences.)
Radical	To the extreme
Spahk	Look at; Check it out; See
Wahine	Woman or girl

Boys Will Be Boys: A Classic Pidgin-Hawaiian Conversation

Charlie: Eh, why you bag it, man? Dis party no ovah.

Bob: An'den? Dat Clyde one lolo buggah man. Hees mouth go on fo' days. Laydahs fo' me!

Charlie: Fo' real, brah. Main ting cool head. Time we hele on. Catch some grinds. Lesgo.

Bob: I can dig some grinds, too, man, but dis Hawaiian time, no mo' nahtin' open dis late.

Charlie: We go Maui side, all dem joints got some plenty eats.

Bob: Innahs, man! Dem wahines are da max, garans.

Charile: No ack, man. You fo' real like them JOJ chicks o'wot?

Bob: Brah, for me—any kine wahine.

Charlie: Fo'real, man, fo'real.

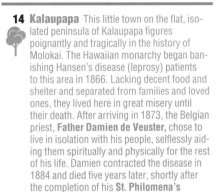

14 Kalaupapa This little town on the flat, isolated peninsula of Kalaupapa figures poignantly and tragically in the history of Molokai. The Hawaiian monarchy began banishing Hansen's disease (leprosy) patients to this area in 1866. Lacking decent food and shelter and separated from families and loved ones, they lived here in great misery until their death. After arriving in 1873, the Belgian priest, **Father Damien de Veuster,** chose to live in isolation with his people, selflessly aiding them spiritually and physically for the rest of his life. Damien contracted the disease in 1884 and died five years later, shortly after the completion of his **St. Philomena's Church** in Kalawao.

Father Damien was a living legend, and after his death became known as the "martyr of Molokai" for his heroic dedication to the leprosy victims. Sulfa drugs brought leprosy under control in the 1940s, and the fewer than a hundred patients still living at Kalaupapa were cured and free to go. However, since Kalaupapa was their home since childhood, they chose to stay. Today, fewer than 90 still live here. The steep, zigzag **Jack London Trail,** a foot trail, leads down the 1,600-foot slopes overlooking the settlement. ♦ Air taxi service is available from the Molokai Airport

15 Molokai Mule Ride Start at the top of a 1,600-foot cliff and wander down a switchback for three miles while you enjoy a panoramic view of the Pacific. The surefooted mules know the trail and do all the work. The tour takes you down to the beach at Kalaupapa where you board a bus to view the settlement and visit St. Philomena, one of Father Damien's churches, and stop for a picnic lunch near the crashing surf. ♦ Reservations required. For information, contact: Rare

Adventures, Box 200, Kualapuu HI 96757. 567.6088, 800/843.5978

16 Ironwood Hills Golf Course The 1,500-foot elevation and majestic eucalyptus and ironwood trees make this a distinctive course —not well-known, but scenic and enjoyable. The 9-hole championship course in the rolling hills of Kalae can be played twice for an 18-hole round. For 18 holes, Par 68, 6,176 yards. ♦ Daily 7AM-6PM. North on Kalae Hwy, turn left at .8 mile after the four-mile marker. 567.6000

16 Kualapuu Cook House ★$$$ A petite, box-size plantation house was converted into a quaint restaurant that feels like an old-fashioned diner, complete with Formica tables and intimidating omelets. Tropical chili, pizza, hot dogs, teriyaki chicken, and quarter-pound burgers are the offerings, but the real specialties are the plate lunches and pies. ♦ American/Eclectic ♦ M-F 7AM-8PM; Sa 7AM-3PM. Kualapuu. 567.6185

17 Purdy's Nut Farm You can learn everything you've ever wanted to know about macadamia nuts on this five-acre plot of

land, thanks to **Tuddie Purdy** and his mother, **Theo.** They'll teach you how to crack the hard inner shell of the nut without breaking your fingers, how long it takes for a nut to mature (nine months), how to open a coconut and use its flesh to dip into honey, and how long macadamia nuts have been in Hawaii (100 years). They'll also give you the reassuring news that macadamia nuts roasted without oil have very few calories and no saturated fats or cholesterol. Great macadamia nuts are sold here, too. ♦ M-Sa 9AM-1PM; Su 10AM-1PM. Kualapuu. 567.6601, 567.6495

18 Kualapuu Reservoir The rubber-lined reservoir is the world's largest, containing 1.4 billion gallons of water. Molokai residents are very proud of it. ♦ Off Hwy 470, near Kualapuu

19 Palaau State Park A forested mountain area of 234 acres that forms part of the Molokai Forest Reserve on the north side of the island. At the end of Hwy 470 is a 1,500-foot lookout over Kalaupapa Peninsula. ♦ Off Hwy 470, north of Kualapuu

20 Phallic Rock This large stone has given rise to various legends, including the tale that childless women who spend the night at the base of the stone will go home and soon become pregnant. ♦ Palaau State Park

21 Hoolehua An agricultural area known for its cockfights, quilted patches of farmland, and budding taro industry. ♦ Off Hwy 480

22 Puu Nana Translates as "viewing hill," and from its 1,381-foot elevation, Oahu is visible 30 miles away, clouds willing. ♦ Off Hwy 460, near Maunaloa

23 Hale-o-Lono Harbor If you want to experience the real excitement, skill, and competition
of ancient Polynesian canoeing, visit during
Hawaii's annual **Aloha Week** (which actually
lasts several weeks) in September. The world's
fastest male and female Polynesian outriggers
participate in this grueling, 42-mile-long,
Molokai-to-Oahu canoe race. Founded in 1952
by Oahu canoeing enthusiast **Albert Edward
"Toots" Minvielle,** the race is celebrated as
the world's first and foremost long-distance,
open-ocean canoeing competition. It begins
with a great ceremony at southwest Molokai's
little Hale-o-Lono Harbor, crosses the treacherous Molokai Channel, and ends in a flourish
of flowers and shouts at the Duke Kahanamoku Beach fronting the Hilton Hawaiian
Village in Waikiki. The women race first, and
the men compete two weeks later. ♦ One mile
west of Halena

24 Maunaloa General Store It's the only
store within miles of this old plantation town,
and its merchandise is appropriately diverse.
Everything from coolers and picnic supplies to
fishing equipment and groceries is carried in

this chockablock store. ♦ F-Sa 9AM-8PM; Su
10AM-7PM. Maunaloa. 552.2868

**25 Big Wind Kite Factory
and Plantation Gallery**
It took a windy town like
Maunaloa to spawn Hawaii's
only kite factory. **Jonathan
Socher** and his wife, **Daphne,**
design and make kites with images
of Diamond Head, tropical fish, and
other colorful Hawaiian motifs. Adjoining the
kite shop is their gallery of local and Indonesian crafts—clothing, handbags, T-shirts,
native wood bowls, Balinese carvings, and the
like. ♦ M-Sa 8:30AM-5PM; Su 10AM-2PM.
Maunaloa. 552.2364

26 JoJo's Cafe $ The specialty here is fish,
along with Portuguese bean soup, Korean
short ribs, teriyaki steak, and chicken. Locals
love JoJo's fish and ribs in ethnic preparations. ♦ American/Oriental ♦ M, Th-Sa
11:45AM-2:45PM, 5-7:45PM. Maunaloa.
552.2803

27 Molokai Ranch Wildlife Park A venture of
the cattle-raising and hay-growing Molokai
Ranch, this African safari-like wildlife park has
hundreds of exotic animals, including antelope,
Indian black buck, eland, giraffe, zebra, and
Barbary sheep. They're all raised on some
1,000 acres of fenced-in pastureland. Groups
of up to 14 can have a picnic lunch in the
wildlife park, an affair that inevitably attracts the
gregarious giraffe, who may lean over the fence
to say hello. The narrated tour of the wildlife
park takes about two hours. ♦ Admission. Daily
8AM, 10AM, 1PM, 3PM. Molokai Ranch.
552.2767

28 Kaluakoi Golf Courses
There is a joke within
Hawaii's hotel circles that
people here lower their golf
handicap by 10 strokes—
meaning there is not much else
to do on Molokai. The Kaluakoi course is
windy but otherwise appealing, with five of
its holes bordering the ocean. Many inveter-
ate golfers from Oahu consider this their
getaway course, a place to enjoy the game
while taking in views of the ocean and, if
they're lucky, the quail, deer, pheasant, wild
turkey, and partridge that may be roaming
the 160 acres. Nice putting green and driving range. ♦ Par 72, 6,618 yards. Moderate
green fees. Ask about money-saving golf
specials. Pro shop. 522.2739

29 Paniolo Hale Condominiums $$ There
are 36 rentals on this 77-unit, 6 1/3-acre
property on Kepuhi Beach, some featuring a
private hot tub on the lanai. Included are a
telephone, full kitchen, washer, and dryer—
all the conveniences. The studios and one-
and two-bedroom suites all have wood
floors. There's also a pool and golf at the
nearby Kaluakoi course. ♦ Off Kakaako Rd,
Maunaloa. 552.2731, 800/367.2984; fax
552.2289

The Mighty Mongoose

Made famous as **Rikki-Tikki-Tavi** in Rudyard Kip-
ling's *The Jungle Book,* the mongoose is a small,
ferocious carnivore. Legend has it that this ferret-
sized mammal is immune to poisonous snake
venom, and it is celebrated throughout Africa,
southern Europe, and India as an effective control
for snakes and rats. In the 1880s the mongoose
was imported to Hawaii to help fight an explosion
of the Islands' crop-destroying rodent populations.
But the effort quickly became an ecological disas-
ter when the mongoose began attacking harmless
small mammals, reptiles, and ground-nesting
birds. The agile creature is responsible for the
extinction and near-extinction of several of the
Islands' native ground-nesters.

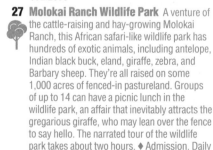

The first horses arrived in Hawaii in 1803, when two
American merchant seamen tried to court favor with
King Kamehameha I by presenting him with a stal-
lion and two mares. Kamehameha was unimpressed.
He said it was better for a man to run to his destina-
tion than to bear the expense of feeding a horse so
he could ride.

30 Colony's Kaluakoi Hotel and Golf Club

$$ Molokai's top—and only—destination resort is a serene oasis for the traveler who truly wants to get away from the crowds. Managed by Colony Resorts, the two-story redwood and ohia wood structures are strung along the oceanfront overlooking a wide stretch of white sand Kepuhi Beach. In this neck of the woods, sports are the only recreation. A championship golf course, 15-kilometer jogging path, horseback riding, four tennis courts, a pool, and a volleyball court are available to guests. For the less athletically inclined, the hotel gives lessons in hula dancing, lei making, and coconut frond weaving. There are 290 guest rooms with lanais, high-beamed ceilings, and fans to augment the ocean breezes. ◆ Off Kamehameha Hwy, Maunaloa. 552.2555, 800/777.1700; fax 552.2821

Within Colony's Kaluakoi Hotel and Golf Club:

Ohia Lodge ★★$$$ This is as fancy as you can get on Molokai: a high-ceilinged dining room built in tiers, giving every table a panoramic view overlooking the beach and a distant view of Oahu. Molokai bread becomes memorable French toast at breakfast, and to build up reserve energy, order the paniolo beef stew for lunch. Dinner menus are rotated nightly; the Continental fare includes fresh island fish, Hunan duck, Indonesian herbal chicken, rack of lamb, and a few pasta dishes. The bountiful salad bar is something to look forward to. Live music nightly at the adjoining bar. ◆ Continental ◆ Daily 6:30-10:30AM, noon-2PM, 6-9PM. 552.2555

Paniolo Broiler ★$$ Steaks broiled over *kiawe* charcoal, accompanied by the best salad bar on Molokai. ◆ Steak ◆ Open when the hotel is 60 to 65 percent occupied. 552.2555

31 Ke Nani Kai $$$ Adjoining Colony's Kaluakoi Hotel and Golf Club, this hotel offers large one- and two-bedroom suites that are well managed, clean, and spread out in clusters of brown two-story wooden buildings. Not deluxe, but comfortable, with ocean and mountain views, large kitchens, and lanais. ◆ Off Kamehameha Hwy, Maunaloa. 552.2761, 800/552.2761 (HI), 800/888.2791 (US); fax 552.0045

Molokai's Highlights

Halawa Valley and waterfalls (when you're slathered with insect repellent).

The view from **Puu Nana,** at more than a thousand feet elevation.

Our Lady of Sorrows Church (Father Damien's Church), in Kaluaaha, when the doors are open.

A safari picnic in **Molokai Ranch Wildlife Park.**

Molokai Wagon and Horse Ride.

Phallic Rock in Palaau State Park.

Molokai mango chutney from the **Mapulehu Mango Grove.**

Pau hana (after work) time at the **Pau Hana Inn.**

Grilled *akule* (scad) at **Mid Nite Inn.**

A fresh fish-plate lunch at **Molokai Drive Inn.**

Hawaii's Best

Bonnie Friedman
Co-Owner, Grapevine Productions, Maui

A *dim sum* and *manapua* breakfast in Honolulu's **Chinatown.**

A full-moon picnic at Maui's **Keawakapu Beach.**

A drive through up-country Maui's **Kula district** on a May morning when the jacaranda trees are in full bloom. Best place to end is at **Grandma's Coffee House** in Keokea for a cup of java.

Sharing a salad and pizza at **Casanova** in Makawao, Maui.

Dessert and cappuccino at **Hali'imaile General Store** on Maui.

Dinner at **Merriman's** on the Big Island.

Sunday brunch at the **Maui Prince Hotel.**

Molokai

Renting a cabin at **Waianapanapa State Park** in Hana on Maui, and walking the beach trail at sunrise.

Watching an authentic hula.

Flower leis—for me, the giving (and receiving) of leis is the most beautiful of Hawaiian traditions. So stop at any supermarket or flower shop and buy one for yourself. Guaranteed to make you feel fantastic!

Sitting outside on a clear, starlit night watching for moonbows, shooting stars, and *pueos* (Hawaiian owls that symbolize good luck).

Pardee Erdman
Rancher/Owner, Tedeschi Winery, Maui

Lanai's **Lodge at Koele** for a weekend getaway.

Prince Court Restaurant on Maui.

Roy's Restaurant in Honolulu.

Kahala Hilton in Honolulu.

Mauna Lani Suites in Kawaihae on the Big Island.

Joyce Matsumoto
Director of Public Relations, Halekulani Hotel, Honolulu

Whale watching off **Wailea,** Maui.

May Day Twilight Celebration with the **Cazimero Brothers** at Waikiki Shell on Oahu (don't miss the lei exhibition, either).

Sunset cocktails and traditional Hawaiian entertainment at **Halekulani's House Without A Key** in Waikiki, Oahu.

A rainbow-colored shave ice at **Matsumoto's** on Oahu's North Shore.

Christmas celebration with the **Honolulu Boys Choir.**

Lanai

In ancient Hawaiian legends, **Lanai** (la-*nye* or la-*naw*-ee) was portrayed as an island occupied solely by evil spirits. Then along came **Kaululaau**, the exiled nephew of a Maui king, who is credited with banishing the evil spirits from the island, thus making it finally habitable. Centuries later, **Jim Dole** was responsible for bringing pineapple to the island. Attempts to grow sugarcane on Lanai, starting as early as 1802, had been unsuccessful. The Mormons' effort to establish a colony in 1855 was also a failure. So the 140-square-mile island was used principally for fishing and cattle-grazing until 1922, when Dole bought it from the Baldwin family of Maui for $1.1 million. Although Lanai eventually became the home of the world's largest pineapple plantation, the 15,000-acre Dole plantation covered only a fraction of Lanai's total land area of 90,000 acres.

In 1990, **Castle & Cooke Inc.**, the parent company of the Dole Company and owner of 98 percent of Lanai, announced that within two and a half years it would phase out pineapple production on the island, which until then had provided 90 percent of the jobs on Lanai. The company said it would keep only about a hundred acres of its pineapple farms for the local people and the resorts. During that same year, the luxurious and distinctive **Lodge at Koele** opened to rave reviews, signaling the beginning of a new era of tourism for the tiny pineapple island. In the spring of 1991, the **Manele Bay Hotel** opened, the second luxury hotel to open on the island within a year.

Although these new hotels bring many more visitors to the island than ever before—not to mention all the construction workers hired for the development activities—there's still a lot of uncultivated ground for exploring, much

of it among the stately Norfolk Island pine trees that are second only to the pineapple as a Lanai trademark. The wonderful beaches ringing the island are virtually unpopulated—partly because many of them are not easily accessible and because there are only 2,400 residents on the island.

The island's humped shape is responsible for its name. In the old Hawaiian language, the word lanai was pronounced la-*naw*-ee, which means "hump" or "swell." With today's more popular pronunciation of la-*nye,* the word means "a veranda." From its sandy shorelines, Lanai rises quickly to the 1,700-foot elevation of Lanai City and ultimately to 3,370 feet at Lanaihale, where, on a clear day, you can see five of Lanai's sister islands: Maui, Molokai, Kahoolawe, the Big Island, and Oahu.

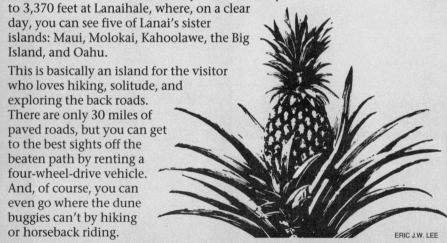

This is basically an island for the visitor who loves hiking, solitude, and exploring the back roads. There are only 30 miles of paved roads, but you can get to the best sights off the beaten path by renting a four-wheel-drive vehicle. And, of course, you can even go where the dune buggies can't by hiking or horseback riding.

ERIC J.W. LEE

Kalohi
Channel

Shipwreck
7 Beach

Auau
Channel

8 Garden of
the Gods

Kanepuu Hwy

Keomuku Hwy

6 *Keomuku*

*Pacific
Ocean*

4

• *Koele*

Munro Trail

• *Lanai
City*

5

**1-4 see
pg. 92**

▲ *Lanaihale
3,370 ft.*

Kaumalapau Hwy

Miki Rd.

Manele Rd.

Awehi Rd.

9 44

• *Kaumalapau*

✈ **Lanai
Airport**

Kaupili Rd.

441

*Kamaiki
Point*

*Palaoa
Point* **10**

*Hulopo'e
Beach Park* **11**

*Manele
Beach Park*

12 *Manele
Bay*

*Hulopo'e
Bay*

Ferry to Lahaina, Maui • • • • • •

*Kealaikahiki
Channel*

Kaunaoa, flower of Lanai

N

km   5
mi   2

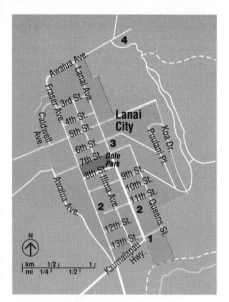

1 Lanai City Lanai's commercial hub; most of the island's 2,400 residents live here. Surrounded by silvery fields of pineapple (and now flanked by residential developments on the southern edge of the populated area), it is still a picturesque and rustic village nestled

Lanai

among Norfolk Island pine trees planted in the 1920s. ♦ Off Hwy 44, about four miles northeast of Lanai Airport

1 Hotel Lanai $$ Longtime visitors to Lanai remember when this was the only hotel on the island. It still has a fireplace, simple, clean rooms, good food, and a homey atmosphere. From the veranda that doubles as a bar to the rustic dining room with a fireplace and the 11 plainly decorated rooms, this is a charming establishment that has been accommodating visitors since 1927, when the **Dole Pineapple Company** built it for out-of-town guests. A lot of hunters still stay here—when they can get a room. ♦ 828 Lanai Ave, Lanai City. 565.7211, 800/624.8849

Within the Hotel Lanai:

Hotel Lanai Dining Room ★★$$ When the fire is going and the fresh fish, prepared differently every night, is brought from the kitchen on steaming platters, it's a hearty, cozy, casual atmosphere. Pasta is served nightly, and if the fresh seafood marinara is one of the evening's specials, don't miss it. In the mornings, Lanai residents love to warm up here

with a steaming cup of coffee. ♦ Continental ♦ M-Sa 7:30-9AM, 11:30AM-1:30PM, 6:30-8:30PM; Su 7:30AM-noon, 6:30-8:30PM. 565.7211

2 Jeep and Car Rentals There are two gas stations in Lanai City and both rent Jeeps and cars. ♦ Oshiro Service and U-Drive: 850 Fraser Ave, 565.6952. Lanai City Service: 1036 Lanai Ave, 565.6780

3 S&T Properties $ Lanai City's version of a short-order operation. Hamburgers and shakes are served from a soda fountain that ranks as one of Lanai's favorite attractions. ♦ American ♦ M-T, Th-Su 6:30AM-1PM. 419 Seventh St. 565.6537

4 The Lodge at Koele $$$$ This is a 102-room Rockresorts hotel that cuts a distinctive profile in Koele, a pine-lined section of the island at a 1,700-foot elevation. Purple jacarandas and elaborate formal plantings give you the feeling you're entering an old, elegant English estate. The nontropical mood of Koele is a welcome change from the sea-level tropicana that envelops Hawaii visitors, and the chilly upland air is equally invigorating. The **Great Hall,** with 35-foot-high ceilings and immense stone fireplaces, is a place for lingering with a book, a friend, or a glass of port.

There is a dining room where only organic produce is used, a library, tea room, game room, and the full range of activities, from horseback riding to tennis, boating, hiking, and croquet. The common areas are uncommonly gorgeous, with eucalyptus floors and the works of a community of artists that express the spirit of Lanai. An 18-hole championship golf course, designed by **Ted Robinson,** opened in August of 1991. ♦ Off Keomuku Hwy, just outside of Lanai City. 565.7300/7231, 800/321.4666; fax 565.4561

Within the Lodge at Koele:

The Dining Room at the Lodge at Koele ★★★★$$$$ The octagonal-shaped dining room looks out over the English gardens and pools while waiters and waitresses quietly ensure that your glass of pineapple cider (it is ambrosial) is full; you can also dine on the terrace. When the gazebos are lit up at night, the effect is stunnng. Favorite entrées include *ahi,* snapper, roasted *uku,* marlin pastrami (smoked marlin), local Axis deer, veal with shiitake mushrooms, and seafood caught that day and served steamed, poached, smoked, raw, or however you like. The vegetables are picked fresh from an organic farm a few miles away. ♦ Pacific Rim ♦ Dining room: daily 6AM-9:30PM. Terrace: daily 6-10AM, noon-9:30PM. Jackets required in the dining room. 565.7300

5 Munro Trail The winding dirt road known as the Munro Trail extends the length (about one and a half miles) of Lanaihale Mountain, which rises behind Lanai City. New Zealander **George C. Munro,** Lanai's answer to Johnny Appleseed, scattered seeds and plants from his homeland along this ridgeline in the early 1900s. His Norfolk Island pine trees were so successful on the 3,370-foot mountain that more were planted in Lanai City, helping, they say, to make it cooler. This is a popular hiking trail for the hardy. ♦ From Hwy 44, turn onto the dirt road at Koele

6 Keomuku An extreme example of what happens to a town when a nearby sugar plantation fails. Keomuku was abandoned at the turn of the century when a commercial sugar venture collapsed. The buildings vanished, but the six miles of shoreline did not. The **Ka Lanakila o Ka Malamalama Church,** built in 1903, still stands in the deserted village. ♦ From Hwy 44, turn at Poaiwa Rd

7 Shipwreck Beach An old ship's hull lends credence to the name; it was wrecked during WWII. Timbers from other unlucky vessels have disintegrated or been used in building squatters' shacks nearby. Hawaiian petroglyphs dot the neighborhood. A good beach for wading and beachcombing. ♦ From Hwy 44, turn at Poaiwa Rd

8 Garden of the Gods A scattered assemblage of huge rocks and unusual lava formations give every indication of having dropped in from nowhere. The eerie, moonlike shapes are in every shade of purple, pink, and sienna. ♦ Off Awalua Hwy, seven miles northwest of Lanai City across a bumpy road

9 Kaumalapau Harbor The harbor was built to ship pineapples from Lanai to the Dole Cannery in Honolulu. When pineapple operations were in high gear during the summer months from 1968 to the mid-1970s, more than a million pineapples a day were transferred from trucks to barges for the journey. Nowadays, you can enjoy good shore fishing here. ♦ Hwy 44, Kaumalapau

10 Kaunolu The fishing grounds of this ancient Hawaiian village were **Kamehameha the Great's** favorite. This is also one of the best preserved Hawaiian ruins in the Islands, where archaeologists have counted 86 house sites, 35 stone shelters, and numerous grave markings. A visit to this southernmost tip of Lanai is a bumpy, dusty ride or hike, but worth the journey. Don't swim here—the current is too strong. ♦ Seven miles south of Lanai City, near Palaoa Point

11 Manele Bay Hotel $$$$ In May 1991, this two-story hotel opened on the hills of Hulopoe Bay, the island's most beautiful white sand beach. There are 250 luxury villas and suites with private verandas, all with ocean views. Very expensive and posh, with Mediterranean-style architecture, formal gardens, fountains, courtyards, ponds, and lots and lots of bromeliads. ♦ Off Manele Rd, on the south shore. 565.7700, 800/321.4666; fax 565.2483

12 Hulopoe and Manele Bays These two lovely bays with white sand beaches fringed by palm trees sit side by side. Ideal for picnics and swimming, with picture-perfect sunset views. Public facilities. ♦ From Hwy 441, turn at Manele Rd

Lanai's Highlights

Kaunolu, site of an ancient Hawaiian village.

Garden of the Gods.

The view from atop **Lanaihale.**

Hulopoe and **Manele** bays and beaches.

The **Munro Trail.**

Hawaii's Best

George Mavrothalassitis
Executive Chef, La Mer, Halekulani Hotel, Honolulu

My favorite restaurant (after La Mer at the Halekulani, of course) is **Uraku** on Kapiolani Blvd in Honolulu. The young and talented Japanese chef with European training creates exciting contemporary French cuisine with local ingredients. New and still undiscovered.

Lanai

Strolling down the best ocean sidewalk, which was recently built along Oahu's south shore between Kaimana Beach Hotel and Kapahulu Ave. Try it at sunset.

My favorite hotel (after the Halekulani, of course) is **The Lodge at Koele,** on the isle of Lanai. Go with the love of your life. It is the most romantic place in the world and the food is great.

The Contemporary Museum, Makiki Heights, Honolulu. Visit the Pavilion displaying a set from Mozart's opera *L'Enfant et les Sortilèges.* Good lunch spot; bring your own wine.

Do not miss **The Brothers Cazimeros'** annual outdoor concert on 1 May at Oahu's Waikiki Shell. It's a glimpse of *real* Hawaii on the stage and in the audience.

Sheila Donnelly
Public Relations Counselor, Sheila Donnelly & Associates, Honolulu

Mauna Lani Bay Hotel on the Big Island—stay in a bungalow.

Dining at **La Mer** in Honolulu and **A Pacific Cafe** on Kauai.

Staying at the **Lodge at Koele** on Lanai, and at the **Stouffer Wailea Beach Resort** on Maui.

Restaurants/Clubs: Red   Hotels: Blue
Shops/ 🌳 Outdoors: Green   **Sights/Culture:** Black

Oahu

The focal point of Oahu (uh-*wa*-who) is **Waikiki,** and the secret to Waikiki is to ignore it—unless, of course, you don't mind its overcommercialization or the throngs of tourists that bask in the sun on this strip of the island. Waikiki is glamorous, and you'll find the most obvious forms of food and drink, shopping, and entertainment here. But lately, with the swelling numbers of return visitors demanding more than a surface look at Hawaii, the rest of this island has taken on a greater allure and importance.

Oahu packs more into a relatively small package than any other island. It's virtually ringed by perfect white sand beaches, many pleasant for swimming, others offering vigorous bodysurfing, and still others with surfing waves of all sizes, beginner to expert levels. (Contrary to published reports, there *are* uncrowded beaches on Oahu beyond the commonly photographed, elbow-to-elbow and rump-to-rump scenes on Waikiki Beach.) And within this circle of beaches is

Oahu

an interior covered with gentle mountains and lush valleys.

Aside from Waikiki Beach, Oahu's other world-famous attractions include Pearl Harbor and, as exhausting and contrived as it may be, the Polynesian Cultural Center. Less noted are the simple pleasures of walking a quiet beach lined with ironwood trees on the North Shore, or sitting on a bench eating "shave ice" (the tropical form of a snow cone) on a hot day in Haleiwa. Better yet, eat your way completely around the island courtesy of wooden shacks selling fresh fruit and roadside vans selling *manapua* (steamed or baked Chinese dumplings with meat or sweet fillings) and local-style plate lunches.

It may be more than a concession to Oahu's odd configuration that when you ask how to get somewhere beyond Waikiki, you won't be told to head north, south, east, or west. The standard points on the compass are not applied to directions on Oahu. Instead, the four points are the volcanic crater Diamond Head, which is obvious unless you're farther east than Diamond Head, in which

Kawela
Bay

163 Kawela

Kamehameha
Hwy.

162

161 Kahuku

• Paumalu
• Sunset
4 Beach

65
imea •
166
Pupukea

8
167

ley Rd.

vailoa Rd.

Laie
Bay

159 **160**

• Laie

158

• Hauula

n Bridge Rd.

171

mehameha Hwy.

California Ave.

Wahiawa

eeler
Force
Base

Waipio
Acres
Mililani
Town

176

Koolau
Mountain
Range

Sacred
Falls

• Punaluu

157

Kahana
Bay

• Kahana

Kahana
Valley
State Park

• Kaaawa

• Waikane

• Waiahole

Kaneohe
Bay

• Kahaluu

156

Ahuimanu

155

• Heeia

Kailua
Bay

Schofield
Barracks Military
Reservation

H2

180

179 • Pearl City
181

1

177 • Waipahu
178

Koolau
Mountain
Range

Kealwa
Helau

154

Kaneohe

Kailua

148

151 **150** **147**

Olomana •

149 **146**

184

Pearl
Harbor

183
182

US
Naval
Reservation

185

186

152 **153**
▲ Puu
Konahuanui
3,105 ft.

Bellows
Air Force
Base

72

Waimanalo
Bay

• Ewa

Hickam
Air Force
Base

H1

187

• Waimanalo

145
• Waimanalo
Beach **144**

er's
al Air
ion

Ewa
Beach

Honolulu
International
Airport

Lunalilo Hwy.

61 - Pali Hwy.

• Honolulu

Mamala Bay

• Waikiki

**1-68 see
pg. 98**

■ Diamond
Head

**69-135 see
pg. 116**

Kalanianaole Hwy

137

138

Maunalua
Bay

143
142
Makapuu
Point
139 **141**
140
Koko
Head

136 Hanauma
Bay

Kaiwi Channel

km   1/2   1
mi   1/4   1/2

N

case it would be the volcano Koko
Head; *ewa,* the opposite direction
from Diamond Head; *makai,* toward
the sea; and *mauka,* toward the mountains. This is the key to navigating on
Oahu; things are simply oriented
toward the mountains, the sea, or on
either side of Honolulu proper.

Llima, flower of Oahu

Around-the-Island Drive Traffic on the Honolulu-Waikiki side of Oahu can be as brutal as that of any large city. But Oahu is also the only Hawaiian island that can easily be circled by car, bringing all the island's coastlines into close view, except the Waianae Coast on the leeward (in this case, western) shoreline. The drive that best reveals Oahu's beauty is the circular tour east from Waikiki, around Diamond Head to Koko Head and Makapuu Point, along the windward coast to the famous North Shore beaches, and then along the H-1 Fwy to Pearl Harbor, downtown Honolulu, and back to Waikiki. A caveat: Construction began in April 1991 on a three-year road-widening project along Kalanianaole Hwy (Rte 72) on the way to Koko Head and Makapuu Point, causing enormous traffic slowdowns. Keep this in mind if you attempt the drive. Construction hours are 9AM-3PM, but tremendous patience is required at all times, especially during rush hour, because this is a major commuter corridor.

If you decide to brave the traffic, start early in the morning so you'll be heading against the commuters. Begin by following Kalakaua Ave out of Waikiki, past Kapiolani Park and around Diamond Head, onto Kahala Ave. This leads you through the Kahala residential area, formerly one of Honolulu's most prestigious neighborhoods, and now a sad caricature of what foreign investment can bring. Once the bastion of quaint beach cottages and *kamaaina* (old-timer) homes, Kahala is now

overcome with nouveau riche Mediterranean-style stucco villas.

The Kahala Hilton, one of Oahu's finer hotels, and the exclusive Waialae Country Club, site of the annual Hawaiian Open golf tournament, are optional stops for viewing points at the end of Kahala Ave. From Kahala Ave, about two blocks before it dead ends at the Kahala Hilton, turn left on Kealaolu Ave and follow it past the Kahala Mall Shopping Center (on your left) to the freeway on-ramp to Kalanianaole Hwy.

Kalanianaole Hwy takes you past the residential areas of Aina Haina, Niu Valley, and the sprawling mainland-like suburban development of Hawaii Kai, which **Henry J. Kaiser** built in the 1960s around the ancient Hawaiian fishing lagoon, Kuapa Pond. After Hawaii Kai, pass between Koko Head (on the right) and 1,206-foot Koko Crater, formed 10,000 years ago. Crowded as it is, Hanauma Bay, a marine preserve, is the first picture-perfect stop. From here on, the roadside view is one brilliant vista after another, from the thunderous bodysurfing waves of Sandy Beach and Makapuu Beach to the sheer cliffs of Makapuu where hang gliders soar above Sea Life Park. The offshore view is marked by the rocky profiles of Rabbit Island and Kaohi-

kaipu Island just off Makapuu and, in the distance, the Mokulua Islands offshore from Lanikai Beach.

After passing the drowsy seaside community of Waimanalo and Bellows Air Force Station, skirt the windward-side bedroom community of Kailua and turn right onto Kamehameha Hwy toward Kaneohe. A few miles after Kaneohe you will parallel the windward coastline, with the pounding surf and the Koolau Mountains raising a misty green curtain. Sleepy villages nestled between the craggy cliffs and the ocean line this part of the island; truly a time warp.

Passing roadside stands that beckon with fresh fruit and vegetables near the tiny communities of Kahaluu, Kaawa, Punaluu, and Hauula, you reach Laie, home of the Mormon Temple and the Polynesian Cultural Center. You've arrived at the northern tip of the island, also the site of Turtle Bay Hilton and Country Club, and a stone's throw from some of the most fabled surf in the world at Sunset Beach, the Banzai Pipeline, and Waimea Beach. Land lovers will enjoy tranquil Waimea Falls Park and the friendly little town of Haleiwa, where a Tropical Dreams ice cream cone or a shave ice at the S. Matsumoto Store offers the consummate tropical refreshment. From Haleiwa, drive through the pineapple fields and across the plains of Wahiawa, cutting between the Koolau and Waianae mountain ranges until you're on the H-2 Fwy and then the H-1 Fwy, passing Pearl Harbor and eventually winding back to Waikiki. ♦ Round-trip, approximately 115 miles (three and a half hours driving time)

The Short Circle-Island Drive Follow the same route out of Waikiki as the Around-the-Island Drive, circling Koko Head and Makapuu Point, but instead of turning onto Kamehameha Hwy toward Kaneohe, continue toward Honolulu on the Pali Hwy, passing through the Pali Tunnel, perhaps stopping at the Pali Lookout, and returning to Waikiki. The old Nuuanu Pali Drive (the exit is 8.7 miles north of Waikiki) is a beautiful detour. ♦ Round-trip, approximately 40 miles (90 minutes driving time)

Waianae Coast Drive For a view of leeward Oahu, take Ala Moana Blvd and Nimitz Hwy out of Waikiki toward Honolulu International Airport. Pass the airport and take the Pearl Harbor turnoff, passing Pearl Harbor on the Farrington Hwy, continuing toward Makaha. (You can also take the H-1 Fwy, following the signs that say "west.") Eventually you will pass the small seaside towns of Nanakuli and Maili; continue past Pokai Bay to Makaha and the beautiful Makaha Valley, site of the Sheraton Makaha Resort and Country Club. (The road ends a few miles from here, just before Kaena Point.) Some of the best beaches on the island can be found along the Waianae Coast between Nanakuli and Makaha, but this area has also suffered from a high incidence of crime and vandalism and is recommended more for a driving view of the leeward coast than for a recreational day on the Waianae Coast beaches. ♦ Round-trip, approximately 80 miles (three hours driving time)

1 Ilikai On the outer fringe of Waikiki, overlooking the Ala Wai Yacht Harbor, this 800-room high rise offers a compromise for people who want to be near the action but not consumed by it. It has been dramatically eclipsed, however, by the new Hawaii Prince hotel next door. A placid beachfront lagoon and full-fledged beaches are nearby, including **Ala Moana Beach Park,** beloved by locals as an alternative to Waikiki Beach. Shoppers should also note that the Ilikai is a five-minute walk from the **Ala Moana Shopping Mall.** Waikiki's only complete tennis center is found within this eight-acre property, along with two pools and kitchens (including refrigerator) and minibars in all rooms. Five executive-meeting suites and a new fitness center were recently added in the **Yacht Harbor Tower,** and all guest rooms as well as the 15,340-square-foot **Pacific Ballroom** were renovated. Extensive meeting and convention facilities. ♦ 1777 Ala Moana Blvd, Waikiki. 949.3811, 800/367.8434; fax 947.5523

Within the Ilikai:

Champeaux's ★$$$ Sunday brunch at the top of the 30-story Ilikai (reached via an outdoor glass elevator) centers around the view. A handful of tables along the windows look out at the boats packed into the Ala Wai Yacht Harbor and out on the ocean. Champeaux's shares the floor with Annabelle's discothèque, which comes to life when the sun sets and the lights of Honolulu flicker through the night. ♦ Champeaux's: Su 10AM-2PM; Annabelle's: daily 5PM-2AM. 949.3811

Yacht Club Restaurant and Bar $$$ Great view of the harbor while dining on the terrace and in the split-level dining room. Watch the rare, exotic tropical fish swimming in the surrounding aquariums. Seafood appears in about two dozen different preparations, served with everything from black bean sauce to caviar butter. Fresh Island seafood is the specialty here. Live entertainment nightly. ♦ Seafood ♦ Daily 4PM-midnight. 949.3811

Vanda Court Cafe $$ Formerly the Pier 7 coffee shop, Vanda Court has picture windows with marina views on all sides. Look for theme nights when they offer special values on prime rib, seafood, and barbecue ribs. Renowned for its breakfast bar and sandwich bar at lunch, and good clam chowder; otherwise it's standard American fare. ♦ American ♦ Daily 6:30AM-9PM. 949.3811

The Comedy Club Local and national comedians perform here, many of them straight from The Tonight Show and other mainland talk shows. Everything from budding hypnotists to big-name acts—the bright new stars of the comedy scene. New location on upper parking level, near security station. ♦ Shows Tu-Su 7, 10PM. 922.5998

2 Bon Appetit ★★$$$ Tucked away and too often lost inside the mammoth **Discovery Bay** condominium towers, this charming little French restaurant is the kind you would expect to find in Beverly Hills or Carmel. Owner/chef **Guy Banal** has cooked in some of the world's best kitchens. The menu changes weekly and prix-fixe dinners are exceptional. Guy does wonderful things to fresh Island fish, duckling, chicken, and lamb. ♦ French ♦ M-Sa 5:30-10:30PM. Discovery Bay, 1778 Ala Moana Blvd, Waikiki. Across from the Ilikai hotel. 942.3837

3 El Crab Catcher ★$$$ Here's another fresh seafood restaurant competing for a share of Honolulu's market. But this one's already got a good track record on Maui (where it originated), on Kauai, and on the West Coast. The airy, natural interior is filled with plants and lots of bamboo, wood, and natural fixtures. Crab-stuffed fish, shrimp scampi, and the catch of the day—especially the *opah,* or moonfish—are big favorites. A lighter menu is served at the **Seaside Cafe**—great for moviegoers. ♦ Seafood ♦ Daily 11:30AM-10PM, until 11PM in the Seaside Cafe. 1765 Ala Moana Blvd, Waikiki. 955.4911

Parade on the Pacific

The Transpacific Yacht Race, the world's oldest, long-distance sailing competition, was first staged during the summer of 1906 by famed Honolulu yachtsman **Clarence Macfarlane.** During Macfarlane's first organized race between San Pedro, California, and Honolulu, three yachts survived what many thought was the ultimate yachting test. If you are in Hawaii during June or July of an odd-numbered year (such as 1993, '95, or '97), head for Waikiki and watch the pros sail down Oahu's south coast with spinnakers and spirits soaring. It's an unforgettable sight. On even-numbered years, this is the site of the **Kenwood Cup,** another popular yachting tournament. Activities are centered around the Ala Wai Yacht Harbor and Waikiki Yacht Club. For more information, write to: Stanley Thornton, 735 Bishop St, Honolulu HI 96813, or call 538.3632.

4 Hawaii Prince $$$ One of Waikiki's newest luxury hotels, the Prince is a bonanza of marble, brass, glass, and soaring proportions—likable to many, but commonly criticized for having too much pink marble and air-conditioning for tropical Hawaii. It's designed so all rooms face the ocean and is within walking distance of **Ala Moana Beach Park** and **Ala Moana Shopping Mall.** Two 32-floor towers house 521 rooms with floor-to-ceiling glass windows that capture the view of the yacht harbor, nearby Magic Island, and even the distant Waianae Mountains. Five floors of public areas, including five restaurants and lounges (three of them exceptional) and a lobby lounge with high ceilings, infused with light through glass made in Spain and laminated in Belgium. ♦ 100 Holomoana St, Honolulu. 956.1111, 800/321.6284; fax 946.0811

Within the Hawaii Prince:

Prince Court ★★★$$$$ Although they call this American-regional cuisine, the extensive menu has so many Pacific and local elements it almost seems like a misnomer. Never mind, the food is fantastic—slipper lobster and Kahuku shrimps on grilled corn bread, Hawaiian salmon and corn cakes, seafood and taro-leaf minestrone, seared and smoked *ahi* with radish salsa and ginger-lime vinaigrette. The American favorites are also featured—

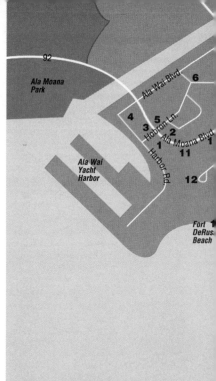

92
Ala Moana Park
Ala Wai Blvd
6
4 3 5 Hobron Ln.
Ala Moana Blvd
1 2 1
Ala Wai Yacht Harbor
Harbor Rd.
11
12
Fort DeRus. Beach

Oahu

kiawe-grilled capon with corn-bread pudding, pan-seared duckling breast, and a wide selection of beef, lamb, and veal in all sorts of exotic dishes. The view of the boat harbor from the large, glass-fringed room is cheerful by day and romantic at night—like the desserts, a bonus. A handsome choice for Sunday brunch, too. ♦ American/Pacific ♦ M-Sa 6:30-10:30AM, 11:30AM-2PM, 5:30-10PM; Su 9AM-2PM, 5:30-10PM. 956.1111

箱根

Hakone ★★★$$$$ Japanese food at its best, served in a quietly elegant room of polished blond woods from Japan with garden and harbor views. The cuisine is traditional and exquisite: *kaiseki* dinners of soup, pickles, sashimi, broiled fish, and other samples of Japanese favorites; grilled clam and salmon roe appetizers; and noodles, tempura, and assorted sashimi. When in season, the fresh Kona crab is incredible, done to prefection. ♦ Japanese ♦ Daily 6-10AM, 11:30AM-2PM, 5:30-10PM. 956.1111

Takanawa ★★$$$ The more informal of the two Japanese restaurants, slightly less expensive but with an appealing menu: sushi, sukiyaki, *kaiseki* dinners (up to 12 small courses), and various cold and hot appetizers. Like Hakone, it serves Japanese food of the highest quality. ♦ Japanese ♦ Daily 6-10PM. 956.1111

THE CAPTAIN'S ROOM

The Captain's Room This cozy after-hours jazz spot in Honolulu is always filled with fans and friends of **Azure McCall,** the hottest jazz singer in town. Decorated in marble and black glass. McCall's talented friends often share the stage impromptu, making for some excellent spontaneous, down-home entertainment. ♦ Hawaiian entertainment M-Tu, Su 6-11PM; jazz W-Th 8PM-midnight, F-Sa 8PM-2AM. 956.1111

Restaurants/Clubs: Red   Hotels: Blue
Shops/ 🌴 Outdoors: Green   **Sights/Culture: Black**

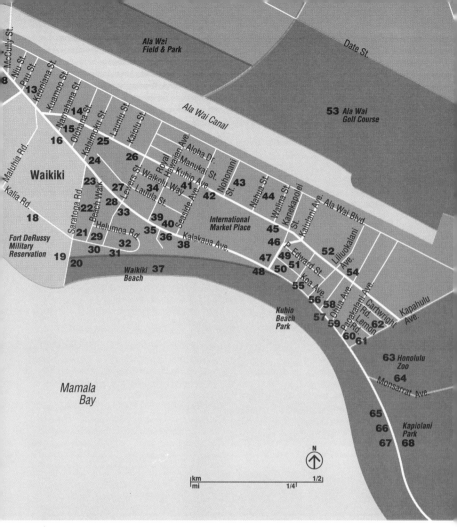

Ala Wai
Field & Park

Date St.

McCully St.
Niu St.
Pau St.
Keoniana St.
Kuamoo St.
Namahana St.
Olohana St.
Kalaimoku St.
Launiu St.
Kaiolu St.

Ala Wai Canal

53 Ala Wai
Golf Course

8
13
14
15
16
24
25
26
23
22
21
27
28
33
29
30
31
32
34
35
39
40
36
38
37
41
42
43
44
45
46
47
48
49
50
51
52
54
55
56
57
58
59
60
61
62
63
64
65
66
67
68

Aloha Dr.
Royal Hawaiian Ave.
Manukai St.
Kuhio Ave.
Nohonani St.
Nahua St.
Walina St.
Kanekapolei St.
Kaiulani Ave.
Ala Wai Blvd.
Liliuokalani Ave.
P. Edward St.
Koa Ave.
Ohua Ave.
Kapakahi Rd.
Lemon Rd.
Cartwright Rd.
Kapahulu Ave.

Waikiki

Matulia Rd.
Kalia Rd.
Saratoga Rd.
Beach Walk
Lewers St.
Waikolu Way
Lauula St.
Helumoa Rd.
Seaside Ave.
Kalakaua Ave.

18

Fort DeRussy
Military
Reservation 19
20

Waikiki
Beach

International
Market Place

Mamala
Bay

Kuhio
Beach
Park

63 Honolulu
Zoo

64

Monsarrat Ave.

Kapiolani
Park

N

km
mi   1/4   1/2

Promenade Deck $$

This casual poolside bar features live Hawaiian entertainment at sunset, and a view of the ocean—very pleasing. The menu includes light salads, sandwiches, and grilled specials at night. ♦ American ♦ M-Sa 11AM-8PM; Su 6:30-10:30AM. Hawaiian music Th-Sa 5-8PM. 956.1111

Marina Front $$ The spot for late-afternoon tea and casual cocktails. The English-style tea includes scones, finger sandwiches, and French pastries served in a high-ceilinged room of marble and glass. ♦ Complimentary coffee daily 6-11:30AM, cocktail and tea service daily 2:30-6PM. 956.1111

5 Wailana Coffee House $$ A Honolulu classic, the spot for sweet-bread French toast filled with guava jelly, hearty breakfasts, and the full range of coffee shop favorites. Standard fare, but very popular among long-time residents and Waikiki tourists. ♦ 24 hours. 1860 Ala Moana Blvd, Waikiki. Across from Hilton Hawaiian Village. 955.1764

6 Chez Michel $$$ No ocean view, no Hawaiian music, and no gimmicky themes. Just classic French cuisine at a long-standing Honolulu favorite. The restaurant had some shaky times after original owner **Michel Martin** sold it, so fans were heartened to see him return in 1991. The old-style cuisine is still a bit heavy-handed, and service could be improved. (Be careful not to confuse this with Michel's at the Colony Surf, originally opened by Martin years ago.) ♦ French ♦ M-Sa 11AM-2PM, 5:30-10PM; Su 5:30-10PM. Eaton Sq, 444 Hobron Ln, Waikiki. 955.7866

7 Wave Waikiki Getting rough around the edges—frankly, seedy—but still the hottest hip dance spot for the younger, post-punk crowd. Great live entertainment, with performances by visiting and local bands. ♦ Admission. 9PM-4AM (But the real edgy action doesn't get going until about 11:30PM.) 1877 Kalakaua Ave, Waikiki. 941.0424

8 Eggs 'n Things ★★$$ A late-night haunt for night owls and workers getting off the graveyard shift. For a midnight snack or early breakfast, try their popular fresh spinach, bacon, and cheese omelet, lemon crepes, or pancakes with macadamia nuts, chocolate chips, pecans, raisins, or bananas. Fresh *mahimahi*, swordfish, and *ono* are favorites, too. A Honolulu institution, even among neighbor islanders. ♦ Daily 11PM-2PM. 1911 Kalakaua Ave, Waikiki. Validated parking at Hawaiian Monarch Hotel. 949.0820

9 California Pizza Kitchen ★★$$ The immensely popular pizza-and-pasta chain serves its pizzas piping hot from the wood-burning brick oven, topped with fresh herbs, vegetables, garlic shrimp, Peking duck, Thai chicken, and a host of other exotic toppings. Ingredients are fresh, and the crust is the real thing; even the pasta dishes are pleasing. ♦ Pizza ♦ M-Th 11:30AM-10PM; F-Sa 11:30AM-11PM; Su noon-10PM. 1910 Ala Moana Blvd (Ena Rd), Waikiki. Validated parking for two hours. 955.5161

Oahu

9 Inn on the Park $$ Condominiums and hotel units near the giant Ala Moana Shopping Mall, less than a block from Fort DeRussy Park and Waikiki Beach. A varying number of condominium units, plus 170 hotel rooms, all with refrigerator, wet bar, toaster, and coffeemaker, and some with kitchenettes and/or ocean views. Operated by **Pacific Hospitality, Inc.** ♦ 1920 Ala Moana Blvd, Waikiki. 946.8355, 800/922.7866; fax 922.3368

10 Kobe Steak House ★$$$ Chefs perform at the *teppanyaki* grills, adding a festive, flamboyant atmosphere, but they're still serving formula Japanese food. Sushi bar, late-night happy hour, and colorful dinners in a cozy, country-inn atmosphere. ♦ Japanese ♦ M-Th, Su 5:30-10PM; F-Sa 5:30-10:30PM. Sushi bar daily 10PM-1:30AM. 1841 Ala Moana Blvd, Waikiki. Valet parking. 941.4444

11 Aston Waikikian Hotel $$ There are no more low-rise hotels actually on Waikiki Beach, but the Waikikian comes very close. The original buildings are no higher than two floors, with a separate seven-story tower that was built later. It's an easy stroll from the hotel's **Duke Kahanamoku Lagoon,** which has its own little beach, to the sands of Waikiki Beach. This hotel's enduring charm is that it's everything the rest of Waikiki isn't—small (132 rooms), friendly, and Polynesian in both appearance and mood. The spacious, ground-level lanai rooms open onto jungle growth thriving throughout the interior courtyard. Planted in 1956, the gardens are luxuriantly overgrown. Second-level rooms have lanais and partial views of the ocean, the mountains, or at least the Waikikian's own lush gardens. (The 88 garden-wing units have no TVs.) Guests who come to enjoy the Waikikian's low elevation should specify a room in the original **Banyan Wing** building. Sadly, an enormous high rise is slated to replace the present complex as soon as permits are obtained. ♦ 1811 Ala Moana Blvd, Waikiki. 949.5331, 800/922.7866; fax 946.2843

Within the Aston Waikikian Hotel:

TAHITIAN LANAI

Tahitian Lanai ★★$$$ Old-timers love this balmy poolside setting, with its casual Polynesian ambience, superb breakfasts, and popular sing-along piano bar. Sit at an outdoor table within sight of the beach or under the roof, either way you can feel the warm breeze. Romantic dining is available in little thatched huts. Breakfast is recommended, especially the famous eggs Benedict. Backups include banana muffins, popovers, coconut waffles, and the Hawaiian breakfast of papaya, eggs, Portuguese sausage, pineapple fritters, and pan-fried taro. Lunch and dinner specialties include "Moa Ta Hari" (Tahitian-style chicken cooked in coconut milk), shrimp curry, shrimp Papeete (butterflied, stuffed with crabmeat, and topped with hollandaise sauce), fish Tahitian, and *haupia* (a coconut custard dessert). Seafood is the specialty, everything from Louisiana catfish to live Maine lobster and fresh local catch. The convivial tropical bar is open until 2AM. ♦ Polynesian ♦ Daily 7AM-10PM. 946.6541

The mile-and-a-half-long strip of beach called Waikiki, which means "spouting water," was once a swampland fed by mountain streams and springwaters. Waikiki's boggy inland area was filled with rice paddies, taro patches, and fish ponds until it was capped and drained in 1922 by the Waikiki Reclamation Project. The addition of sand and seawalls to the shoreline made it the beach you see today.

12 Hilton Hawaiian Village $$$ Well worth the $100 million forked out for architectural renovations in the 1980s, the palatial Hilton has a grand "new" face. Several small buildings were torn down and replaced by beautifully landscaped gardens and a two-tier swimming pool. The Ocean Tower was gutted and reborn as the upscale **Ali'i Tower,** an exclusive hotel within the hotel with its own separate guest reception area, concierge, private pool, and exercise room. Some of the original architecture remains especially eye-catching, such as the brilliant, 16,000-tile rainbow mural on the **Rainbow Tower's** exterior. With a total room count of 2,523, it is the largest hotel in Hawaii—and just about anywhere else. It is more like a self-contained village, with more than a hundred shops, 22 restaurants and lounges, three pools, banquet and convention facilities for up to 5,000 people, a six-story parking garage, its own boat dock, the **Hilton Lagoon Apartments,** and one of Waikiki's largest showrooms, the **Hilton Dome,** home of the **Don Ho** show. The hotel has a choice location on Waikiki Beach, with lots of fun activities, including catamaran sailing and Pearl Harbor cruises. The Hilton is noticeably better than it was and deservedly moves up the list of places to stay in Waikiki. The Hilton's weekly fireworks show, a spectacular tribute to **King David Kalakaua,** is set off from a barge offshore. It's free, at 7:15PM in the spring and summer and 6:45PM in the winter. (Don't confuse this giant with the exclusive Kahala Hilton on the other side of Diamond Head.) ♦ 2005 Kalia Rd, Waikiki. 949.4321, 800/HILTONS; fax 955.3027

Within the Hilton Hawaiian Village:

Benihana of Tokyo $$$ Part of the far-reaching mainland chain and the favorite of Americans scared of Japanese food and the thought of eating raw fish. Not only is everything cooked here; cooking is the main attraction. Performing chefs at *teppanyaki* grills twirl their knives and slash away—samurai-style—at beef, shrimp, and vegetables with blinding speed and precision. ♦ Japanese ♦ Daily 11:30AM-2PM, 5-10:30PM. 955.5955

Golden Dragon ★$$ Famous chef **Dai Hoy Chang** has retired, leaving his stellar menu and many doubtful fans hoping that his suc-

cessor, **Steve Chiang,** can continue the legacy. A large festive atmosphere still prevails, as well as the Peking duck and Beggar's chicken, the signature dishes of this very expensive Chinese restaurant. The extensive menu still includes traditional Cantonese dishes such as lemon chicken, smoked duck, and lobster in curry sauce. ♦ Chinese ♦ Tu-Su 6-9:30PM. Rainbow Tower. 949.4321

Bali by the Sea ★★$$$ This casual restaurant lives up to its name, with spectacular views of Waikiki Beach and Diamond Head. Chef **Yves Menoret** has a knack for fresh Island seafood and imaginative sauces—*opakapaka* with fresh basil sauce, venison medallions with cranberry and *poivrade* sauce, roast rack of lamb with black fig-and-peanut sauce, *coquille* of shrimp and scallops in ginger sauce. The shrimp-and-lobster bisque is not to be missed. ♦ French ♦ Daily 6-10PM. Rainbow Tower. 949.4321

Rainbow Lanai $$ Hilton's version of a coffee shop, with breakfast and dinner buffets, hamburgers, salads, and sandwiches for lunch. Special children's menu. ♦ American ♦ Daily 6AM-10:30PM. Rainbow Tower. 949.4321

13 Tony Roma's $$ Bargain shopping for barbecue-rib lovers. Hefty portions of ribs, chicken, and onion rings at decent prices. ♦ American ♦ Daily 10AM-11PM. 1972 Kalakaua Ave, Waikiki. 942.2121

14 Outrigger Maile Court $$ A tall, narrow tower with 596 rooms two blocks from Waikiki Beach, in the seedy part of Kuhio Ave. Reasonable rates, no-nonsense rooms. ♦ 2058 Kuhio Ave, Waikiki. 947.2828, 800/733.7777; fax 943.0554

15 Nick's Fishmarket ★★$$$ **Nick Nickolas** opened the first of his seafood palaces here, then moved on to greater fame and glory with other "Fishmarkets" in Los Angeles, Chicago, and Houston. The name's the same, as are the luxurious black booths, the elegant decor (complemented by young handsome waiters in tuxedos), and trendy bar crowds. And the classic seafood selections still have their following. ♦ Seafood ♦ M-Th, Su 6-11:30PM; F-Sa 6PM-midnight. Waikiki Gateway Hotel, 2070 Kalakaua Ave, Waikiki. Valet parking. 955.6333

16 Kyo-ya ★★★$$$$ The best Japanese food in town, served in a shocking environment that will eventually win you over. The landmark neon pagoda of the old Kyo-ya has been transformed into an ultracontemporary but very Japanese structure: marble, glass, slate, and concrete—a statement in minimalist elegance. A corner of the restaurant is devoted to *soba* (noodles) and the main dining room is downstairs. The breathtaking, private tatami rooms are upstairs amid tasteful Zen gardens. Much has changed (including prices, which have gone up), but the food is still first rate. The sashimi is always fresh, and the fish *misoyaki* (a savory soybean by-product soaked in miso) is the best on the island. ♦ Japanese ♦ M-Sa 11AM-2PM, 5:30-10PM; Su 5:30-10PM. 2057 Kalakaua Ave, Waikiki. 947.3911

17 Fort DeRussy Beach Part of Waikiki, this Army-owned oasis of green open space is a favorite of residents and military. ♦ Opposite Kalia Rd, Waikiki

18 Hale Koa Hotel $$ Don't do cartwheels over the low rates; this is a military-owned hotel. The 419-unit high rise is the kingpin of the Army's Fort DeRussy reservation, consisting of 72 acres—quite a large chunk of Waikiki. This hotel is a sweet deal for military personnel and retired officers with a pool, tennis, and one of the best beaches in Waikiki. ♦ 2055 Kalia Rd, Waikiki. 955.0555, 800/367.6027

19 Fort DeRussy Army Museum Wartime artifacts and memorabilia are displayed inside a 1911 bunker with 22-feet-thick walls built so solidly that the Army turned it into a museum to avoid tearing it down. Ancient Hawaiian weapons, as well as memorabilia from the Korean and Vietnam wars, WWII, and even the Spanish-American War. Uniforms and tanks, coastal defense artillery, and articles galore relating to the Army in

Hawaii have been preserved. ♦ Tu-Su 10AM-4:30PM. Guided tours must be booked in advance. Bdg 32, Kalia Rd, Fort DeRussy, Waikiki. 438.2821

20 Outrigger Reef Lanais $$ This small new addition to the Outrigger chain near DeRussy Beach has 110 rooms. ♦ 225 Saratoga Rd, Waikiki. 923.3881, 800/733.7777; fax 923.3881

20 Buzz's Steak & Lobster $$ The usual steak-and-salad-bar menu, in the heart of Waikiki. ♦ Steak/Seafood ♦ Daily noon-midnight. 225 Saratoga Rd, Waikiki. 923.6762

21 Royal Islander Hotel $$ Small, budget-minded hotel within walking distance of Waikiki Beach, with a hundred nicely decorated rooms. ♦ 2164 Kalia Rd, Waikiki. 926.0679, 800/733.7777; fax 922.1961

21 Trattoria ★★$$$ A longtime Honolulu favorite, with a large variety of pasta dishes, veal (very popular), lasagna, fettuccine Alfredo, and other northern Italian classics. One of Waikiki's perennial, reliable eateries, popular among local folks and the visitors who stumble onto its lively corner. ♦ Italian ♦ Daily 5:30-10:30PM. Entertainment M-Sa. 2168 Kalia Rd, Waikiki. Valet parking. 923.8415

22 The Breakers $$ For guests who want to be close to the beach without paying the price of a big-name hotel, this shady two-story lodge is hidden among the high rises between Kalakaua Ave and Waikiki Beach. Reasonably priced, with 64 rooms and lush tropical surroundings. Pool. ♦ 250 Beach Walk, Waikiki. 923.3181, 800/426.0494

23 The Hawaiiana Hotel $$ A refreshingly unpretentious low rise toward the *ewa* (west) side of Waikiki, half a block from Waikiki Beach and close to the Fort DeRussy Beach. Ninety-five small and simple rooms with kitchenettes, and connecting rooms for families. Two pools. ♦ 260 Beach Walk, Waikiki. 923.3811, 800/367.5122; fax 926.5728

24 Popo's $$ What began as a strange architectural hodgepodge—containing even stranger restaurants—built by Japanese investors folded quickly, was bought out by the omnipresent **Spencecliff** chain, and is now a popular Japanese-owned Mexican restaurant serving the motley crowd that frequents Kalakaua Ave. Authentic Mexican dishes in addition to the mandatory tacos, burritos, enchiladas, and a cheerful open-air atmosphere. Good selection of Mexican beers. ♦ Mexican ♦ Daily 11:30AM-2:30PM; 5-9:30PM. 2112 Kalakaua Ave, Waikiki. 923.7355

24 South Seas Village $$ Here's your chance to try some Hawaiian food on Kalakaua Ave. For daytime snacks sample *pipikaula* (Hawaiian beef jerky) and poi (pudding made of taro), Hawaiian platter of *kalua* pork, *lomi lomi* salmon, rice, and *haupia*. The dinner menu also has Japanese *shabu-shabu*, American dishes, and even curry. ♦ Polynesian ♦ M-Th 6-9PM; F-Su 5:30-9PM. 2112 Kalakaua Ave, Waikiki. 923.8484

25 Hamburger Mary's Organic Grill and Bar ★$$ Delicious and imaginative sandwich combinations, including a meaty mushroom burger (sautéed mushrooms, raw-milk cheddar, and ground beef on 10-grain wheat bread). Fresh fish, chicken hollandaise, a Greek salad, nachos, and more—all tasty, nutritious, and in generous portions—round out the menu. Great vegetarian eggs Benedict, soups, and steamed vegetables for health-conscious eaters. Casual tropical atmosphere in an open-air setting, right in the middle of Waikiki's gay quarter. ♦ American ♦ Daily 10AM-11PM. 2109 Kuhio Ave, Waikiki. 922.6722

The Charlie Chan mysteries of the twenties and thirties, written by **Earl Derr Biggers,** were inspired by Honolulu detective **Chang Apana,** who used to spend time under the ancient *kiawe* tree at **Halekulani's House Without A Key** restaurant in Waikiki, Oahu.

Restaurants/Clubs: Red	Hotels: Blue
Shops/ 🌴 Outdoors: Green	Sights/Culture: Black

26 Waikiki Joy Hotel $$$ A boutique hotel—petite, catering to business travelers, and big on things like bathrooms with Jacuzzi tubs and state-of-the-art stereo speakers. Some of the nicer touches include the Corporate Suite program, which guarantees special rates; "59-second" check-in; complimentary newspaper, breakfast, and local calls; and many business services. Off the beach and on a small, noisy side street, the Joy Hotel has a curious charm despite the absence of views. Two towers, one with 11 floors and the other with eight, totaling 52 rooms and 49 suites. Pool, restaurant. ♦ 320 Lewers St, Waikiki. 923.2300, 800/733.5569; fax 923.2285

27 Moose McGillicuddy's Pub and Cafe $$ Hefty, cheap breakfasts—21 different omelets, Belgian waffles, French toast—and an array of inexpensive dishes for any time of day make this a popular place among students and the budget-minded. They also have fresh fish and a reasonably priced steak-and-lobster meal—all in all, a deal. ♦ American ♦ Daily 6:30AM-2:30AM. 310 Lewers St, Waikiki. 923.0751

28 House of Hong $$$ This restaurant has dropped on the popularity charts, but for many years it was the leading choice for Chinese dining in Waikiki—big, glittering dining rooms decorated with ancient art objects and serviced by a huge Cantonese menu. ♦ Chinese ♦ M-Sa 11AM-3:30PM, 4-10:30PM; Su 4-10:30PM. 260-A Lewers St (Kalakaua Ave) Waikiki. 923.0202

28 Perry's Smorgy $$ Still big with the all-you-can-eat-cheap buffet crowd. ♦ American ♦ Daily 7-10:30AM, 11AM-2:30PM, 5-9PM. 250 Lewers St, Waikiki. 922.8814

29 Outrigger Waikiki Tower $$ Less than a block from the beach in one of the most congested, noisy sections of Waikiki. Some 439 rooms, many with kitchenettes. Pool. ♦ 200 Lewers St, Waikiki. Across from the Reef Towers. 922.6424, 800/733.7777; fax 924.6042

29 Outrigger Edgewater Hotel $$ One of the smaller Outrigger hotels, with 185 rooms near the beach, some with kitchenettes. Pool. ♦ 2168 Kalia Rd, Waikiki. 922.6424, 800/733.7777; fax 923.7437

29 The Patisserie $ Croissants, European pastries, and sandwiches. Ask them to pack up a picnic box special. ♦ M-Sa 6AM-10PM; Su 6AM-8PM. Lobby of the Outrigger Edgewater Hotel, 2168 Kalia Rd (Beach Walk) Waikiki. 922.4974. Also at: Outrigger West Hotel, 2330 Kuhio Ave, Waikiki. 922.9752

Condo City

Condominiums abound in Waikiki, and many of them are available to short-term visitors who want to avoid Oahu's ritzy resort scene. Prices range from the reasonable to the ridiculous and minimum stays vary from one day to several weeks. Amenities usually match the price tag, although kitchens are standard features—a plus for families and large groups who want to cut costs on food. Discounts are often given for long stays, too. For assistance in finding a condo, contact one of these rental agencies:

Aston Hotels and Resorts 2255 Kuhio Ave, Honolulu HI 96815. 923.0745, 800/922.7866

Colony Hotels and Resorts 841 Bishop St, Honolulu HI 96815. 523.0411, 800/367.6046

Resort Marketing Services 1833 Kalakaua Ave, Suite 409, Honolulu HI 96815. 943.8889, 800/800.3242

30 Outrigger Reef Hotel $$$ Located on Waikiki Beach with 885 rooms, some with kitchenettes, in a wide price range. Great views from the oceanfront rooms; fabulous Fort DeRussy Beach nearby with its volleyball games, singles, and lots of recreational activities. Rates have gone up because of recent renovations, but are still more reasonable than most beachfront hotels. Pool. ♦ 2169 Kalia Rd, Waikiki. 923.3111, 800/733.7777

Halekulani

31 Halekulani Hotel $$$$ The only five-diamond hotel on Oahu, a sparkling oasis tucked in the jam of vacationers and high-rise hotels in Waikiki. The Halekulani successfully combines the impeccable standards of a modern, first-class establishment with the gracious atmosphere of old pre-glitz Hawaii. The original Halekulani (which means "the house befitting heaven") was opened in 1907 by **Robert Lewers**. When the hotel was sold to the Halekulani Corp. in 1981, its quaint cottages with overhanging eaves, nestled in a coconut grove, represented Waikiki's last vestiges of traditional Hawaiian resort life. The new owners razed the aging cottages to make way for the existing medium-rise resort. They also restored the **Main Building** and the **House Without a Key** lounge, leaving untouched an impressive beachside *kiawe* tree. Almost all of the 456 rooms look out at the beach and Diamond Head, and the views grow more magnificent the higher up you go.

Each guest room is tasteful down to the smallest detail—bathrobes, complimentary morning papers, freshly cut flowers, and views of Diamond Head from some of the bathrooms. Order room service at breakfast, and the waiter will set up a personal tableside toaster; dine at any of the three restaurants and you will be pampered with gracious service and exemplary cuisine. If you have to be in Waikiki, this is *the* place to stay. ♦ 2199 Kalia Rd, Waikiki. 923.2311, 800/367.2343; fax 926.8004

Within the Halekulani Hotel:

Orchids ★★★$$$ For breakfast, lunch, or dinner, Orchids stands out as one of Hawaii's most pleasant settings. The open-air dining room sparkles with white linens and attentive service. And the regularly changed, innovative menu meets up to the casually elegant surroundings. Entrées include fresh Island seafood such as smoked and broiled *mahimahi*, fresh local produce, and an occasional Asian specialty, such as green papaya salad. The desserts are outstanding. ♦ Continental ♦ M-Sa 7:30-11AM, 11:30AM-2PM, 6-10PM; Su 9:30AM-2PM, 5:30-10PM. 923.2311

Oahu

La Mer ★★★★$$$$ The dining room of your dreams looks out over Diamond Head and the ocean, with palm trees silhouetted against the darkening ocean at sunset. It's a picture-perfect setting, and chef **George Mavrothalassitis** makes sure the menu matches it. The signature here is fresh seafood, prepared in a number of imaginative, marvelous ways—*onaga* (red snapper) poached with three-caviar sauce; *kumu* (goatfish) en papillote, with seaweed and shiitake mushrooms; and a carefully gleaned selection of meat and fowl. Whatever you do, leave room for dessert; the fruit tulip with passion fruit coulis is a dazzler. Very expensive. ♦ Continental ♦ Daily 6-10PM. Jacket required. 923.2311

House Without a Key ★★$$ An open-air restaurant and cocktail bar with a view of the ocean and Diamond Head. Full breakfast buffet, light meals, and cocktails are served here. Excellent whole-wheat sandwiches and hamburgers, as well as local favorites such as sashimi and saimin (noodles in broth). At sunset, a romantic hula show under the old *kiawe* tree may inspire you to dance under stars—many do. The best mai tai in town. ♦ Continental ♦ Daily 7-10:30AM, 11AM-9PM. 923.2311

Lewers Lounge Plush with lots of leather and teak, this nightspot is quiet except for the tinkling of ivory at the piano bar or the voices of fine jazz singers who regularly perform here. Perfect cocktail spot for couples and conferring businesspeople. Quiet, comfortable, intimate setting. The enclosed veranda serves tea and is ideal for a game of backgammon. ♦ Daily 8:30PM-1AM. Tea served from 2-6PM. 923.2311

32 **Waikiki Parc** $$$ The **Halekulani Corp.** built this 22-story, 298-room hotel in 1987 as a less expensive alternative for those who like an elegant setting close to, but not on the beach. "Affordable luxury" are the buzzwords here, with ocean views around and over the rooftops of the classy Halekulani Hotel, the Parc's sister property located across the street on Waikiki Beach. The Waikiki Parc is an attractive alternative to the Halekulani, with two fine restaurants, charming rooms, and an unobtrusive, nearly hidden entrance. All rooms have private lanais or balconies, fully stocked refrigerators and minibars, and the beach is just a hundred yards away. Ask for restaurant-signing privileges at the Halekulani. Pool. ♦ 2233 Helumoa Rd, Waikiki. 921.7272, 800/422.0450; fax 923.1336

Within the Waikiki Parc:

Parc Cafe ★★★$$$ In terms of price and selection, this is among the most appealing buffets in town—certainly not as big as those at the larger, fancier hotels, but with a tasteful, carefully prepared selection. The dinner buffet is one of Honolulu's best values, a variety of fresh catch of the day, stir-fried vegetables, duck, leg of lamb or chicken carved to order, and a fabulous salad bar (everything from Peking duck salad to Kula tomatoes and charbroiled eggplant). A good choice any time of day. ♦ Eclectic ♦ M-Sa 7-10AM, 11:30AM-2PM, 5:30-10PM; Su 11AM-2PM, 5:30-10PM. 921.7272

Kacho ★★$$$ A stunning, contemporary room highlighted by a long granite sushi bar and very authentic Japanese cuisine. Sushi is the specialty, but the more adventurous might try the *kaiseki* dinner (a set-menu affair) or the 11-course traditional Japanese breakfast, which includes miso soup, grilled fish, steamed rice, raw egg, and more. ♦ Japanese ♦ Daily 6-9:30AM, 11:30AM-2PM, 5:30-10PM. 921.7272

Catch a Wave

Surfing was formally introduced to the Islands by Polynesians, who brought the ancient sport with them when they migrated from the South Seas around AD 500. You can visit the Banzai Pipeline on Oahu's northwest shore and view the petroglyphs on lava that show Polynesian surfers from ancient days. Hawaiian chants dating back to the 15th century also refer to surfing exploits and contests. And when **Captain James Cook** arrived on Oahu in 1778, he found Hawaiian men and women riding waves on long and short wooden planks or canoe fragments. At that time, surfing was the sport of Hawaiian royalty. They not only got the best surfboards (made of choice lighter woods), they had exclusive rights to the best surfing beaches. In fact, if commoners were caught using the prime surfing spots, they faced the death penalty.

The sport all but disappeared during the missionary era and wasn't officially reestablished until the early 1900s, when **Duke Kahanamoku,** a champion Hawaiian swimmer and surfer, formed Waikiki's first surfing club. Kahanamoku was a major force in popularizing surfing throughout the world, demonstrating his prowess in competitions from Atlantic City to Australia.

As new surfboard materials were developed in later decades, the boards became lighter and easier to ride. The first "modern" board was made in the mid-1940s from balsa wood covered with fiberglass. Today, boards are made of lighter synthetic foam. Professional boards are cut, shaved, and sanded by hand, and are of the highest-quality fiberglass and resin, offering the ultimate in speed and control. Visual designs on the boards have become almost as important as their shape and polish, since some believe boards reflect a surfer's personality.

Skateboarding moves such as the "floater" and "aerial" are often borrowed by surfers, who try to imitate motions invented for "riding" concrete. The floater (when a skateboarder glides up the side of a curved wall, makes a quick U-turn, and then rolls back down to the starting point) is duplicated by advanced surfers.

Hawaii's professional surfing events established the foundation for the world circuit, in which the Island surfers still reign supreme. In the 1950s the **Makaha International** was the only major international surfing event. Some of the best surfing conditions in Hawaii are still found at Makaha Beach, where **Buffalo Keaulana** holds his annual **Big Board Classic** in February or March, depending on when the surf is good. But most of the attention is focused on the giant North Shore waves, which professional surfers discovered in the sixties. Every December the North Shore hosts the **Marui Pipeline Masters,** the **Hard Rock Cafe World Cup of Surfing,** and the **Hawaiian Professional Surfing Classic**—collectively known as the Triple Crown—to determine who will reign as the next surfing champion (see "Hang Ten" on page 138). In 1990, one event in the Triple Crown offered $250,000 in prize money.

Surfer music, movies such as *Endless Summer* and *North Shore,* and even the *Gidget* TV series in the 1960s helped promote the sport's mystique. Now surfing is popular enough to support several publications dedicated to the sport, dozens of instructional videotapes and taped competitions, and even nationally aired cable television programs.

If you're curious about your sense of balance, a great way to test the waves and some of the thrill is

Oahu

by boogie boarding—a combination of bodysurfing and surfing. The boogie-boarder lays down on a three-foot-long board and rides with the waves. Boogie boarding is much easier than surfing and a lot less dangerous. If you're ready for *real* surfing, the widest, longest boards are best for beginners; they can catch waves earlier, allowing time for the novice to get a good feel for the wave and get situated before the wave grows too steep. Most hotels offer surfing classes and supply the boards, too.

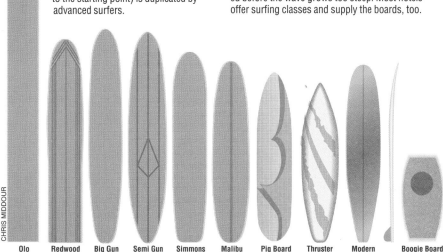

CHRIS MIDDOUR

| Olo | Redwood Balsa | Big Gun | Semi Gun | Simmons | Malibu | Pig Board | Thruster | Modern | Boogie Board |

33 Outrigger Reef Towers $$ On congested Lewers St, about a half block from the beach, this hotel is noisy but popular among budget-conscious singles and students. There are 466 rooms, some with kitchenettes. Pool. ♦ 227 Lewers St, Waikiki. 924.8844, 800/733.7777; fax 924.4957

34 Duty Free Shops If you've got an airline ticket for a destination outside the US, you can enter a duty free shop at the Honolulu International Airport. It's popular with Japanese tourists because the merchandise is generally less expensive than in Japan, but there are very few bargains for Americans. ♦ Hours vary according to flight schedules. Honolulu International Airport, near Gates 12 and 24. 837.3172. Waikiki Duty Free Shop daily 9AM-11PM. 330 Royal Hawaiian Ave, Waikiki. 926.2364

35 Royal Hawaiian Shopping Center A three-block-long, 150-store complex with the big names in international fashion: **Chanel, Louis Vuitton, Hermès, Lancel, Gianni Versace,** and a liberal selection of restaurants. ♦ On Kalakaua Ave (Lewers St and the Outrigger Hotel) Waikiki. 922.0588

Within the Royal Hawaiian Shopping Center:

Restaurant Suntory ★★★$$$ Suntory Ltd., the big Japanese liquor producer who has built showcase restaurants in the major capitals of the world, reportedly spent more

than $2 million on this gem. Quiet elegance abounds from the beautiful cocktail lounge to the separate dining rooms, each tastefully devoted to a special style of Japanese cuisine: *shabu-shabu, teppanyaki,* sushi, and a traditional Japanese room with tatami seating (sunken areas to accommodate extended legs). Top of the line in Japanese dining. ♦ Japanese ♦ M-Sa 11:30AM-1:45PM, 6-9:45PM; Su 6-9:45PM. Bldg B, third floor. 922.5511

Seafood Emporium ★$$$ Locally owned and a star among Waikiki's better seafood choices. Certainly the largest seafood menu on Kalakaua Ave, served in a large, brightly decorated dining room. ♦ Seafood ♦ M-Th, Su 11AM-10PM; F-Sa 11AM-11PM. Bldg A, second floor. 922.5547

Cafe Princess $$ Nicely decorated coffee shop with an American menu embellished with several Island favorites. Outdoor tables for beverages. ♦ American ♦ Daily 7AM-10PM. Bldg B, ground floor. 926.2000

Beijing Chinese Seafood Restaurant ★★$$$ You get the full range of Chinese food here, from Cantonese to Shanghai to Szechuan. Dim sum at lunch, and seafood dishes galore. ♦ Chinese ♦ Daily 11:30AM-2PM, 5-11PM. Bldg C, third floor. 971.8833

36 Sheraton-Waikiki $$$ A giant of a hotel with 1,852 rooms, a 31-story tower, and more than 39,000 square feet of meeting space. Even after the much touted millions spent in improvements in the eighties, the lofty ocean views remain the best feature of this monstrosity, the largest resort in the world when it opened in 1971 (Hilton Hawaiian Village has since surpassed it). Although advertisements promote it as a hotel on the beach (which it is in a structural sense) don't blink or you'll miss the actual beachfront, which, especially compared to the size of the hotel, seems as tiny as a postage stamp. Two pools. ♦ 2255 Kalakaua Ave, Waikiki. 922.4422, 800/325.3535; fax 923.8785

Within the Sheraton-Waikiki:

Hanohano Room ★$$$$ Take the glass elevator 30 floors to the highest viewing area on Waikiki Beach for some panoramas of Diamond Head and the beaches. Best spot for breakfast or sunset cocktails, but there's also a large dining room with music for dancing after dinner; also a scenic place to watch fairy terns (birds) circling outside the window as the sun peeps up over Diamond Head. Entertainment nightly. ♦ Continental ♦ M-F 6:30-10:30AM, 6-9PM; Su 8:30AM-2PM, 6-9PM. 922.4422

Esprit Nightclub $$ Drop in for drinks beside Waikiki Beach, sunset views, and live (and lively) entertainment from cocktail hour to closing. ♦ M-Sa 6:30PM-midnight; Su 2:30PM-midnight. 922.4422

Ocean Terrace $$ Ocean-view breakfast, lunch, and dinner buffets served in a large open-air room. Ethnic buffets, from Chinese to Hawaiian and all-American, are featured throughout the week. Lots of local delicacies for the adventurous. ♦ Eclectic ♦ Daily 6AM-3PM, 5:30-9:30PM. 922.4422

Ciao! $$$ The African big-game theme of the Safari Steak House restaurant (formerly located here) has been transformed into an Italian trattoria, dishing up pasta and pizza. ♦ Italian ♦ Daily 6-10PM. 922.4422

36 Royal Hawaiian Hotel $$$$ Despite being surrounded by overbearing high rises, the Royal Hawaiian clings to its nostalgic glory as the "Pink Palace of the Pacific." The original $4 million building is of Spanish-Moorish design by **Warren & Wetmore. Matson Navigation Company** opened the hotel in 1927, primarily to provide world-class accommodations for passengers sailing on Matson's luxury liners. Before WWII, the hotel was the exclusive playground of the wealthy and famous. Hollywood celebrities such as **Mary Pickford** and **Douglas Fairbanks** vacationed here; **Nelson Rockefeller** and **Henry Ford II** honeymooned here with their brides. Guests brought steamer trunks, servants, and sometimes Rolls-Royce cars. Sheraton bought the hotel in 1959 and added the 16-story **Royal**

Tower. They later sold it, along with several other Waikiki properties, to Japanese industrialist **Kenji Osano**; however, Sheraton continues to run operations. Arrival at the lovely porte cochere is impressive; the walkways leading from the spacious lobby are wide and richly carpeted under crystal chandeliers; the famous Flower Tree at the entrance to the **Monarch Room** retains its brilliance with hundreds of tropical blossoms. A wide, green lawn leads to Waikiki Beach, where Royal Hawaiian guests enjoy a private chained-off stretch of sand, and the grounds remain lush with tropical foliage and banyan trees. Visit the expansive **Coconut Grove,** where as many as 3,000 people can gather under the stars for luaus and private parties. Though the Royal Tower offers modern levels of comfort, the nostalgic will prefer the ocean- or garden-view rooms and suites in the original stucco structure, still faithfully and regularly repainted to its traditional pink color. There are 556 rooms on the 10-acre property. ♦ 2259 Kalakaua Ave, Waikiki. 923.7311, 800/325.3535; fax 924.7098

Within the Royal Hawaiian Hotel:

Mai Tai Bar An open-air, surfside bar where you can watch Waikiki Beach action and catch the sunset. True to its name, the bar makes excellent mai tai drinks. Hawaiian entertainment by **Keith** and **Carmen Haugen** is tops. ♦ Daily 10:30AM-1AM. 923.7311

Monarch Room This large, ornate room overlooking the beach has been the premier Waikiki showroom since it opened in 1927 as the Persian Room. For many years black tie was the required dress (aloha attire is now accepted). Most of Hawaii's great entertainers have performed here, along with stars from all over the world. For years, the immensely talented **Brothers Cazimero** have put on a show encompassing the best in traditional and modern Hawaiian dance, contemporary Hawaiian music, and their unique brand of humorous, nostalgic "talk-story" routines. ♦ Shows Tu-Sa 6:30-10PM. 923.7311

Surf Room $$$ Indoor-outdoor dining overlooking Waikiki Beach. Large buffet and à la carte choices throughout the day, Sunday brunch buffet, and a seafood buffet (pricey) on Friday. ♦ Continental ♦ Daily 6:30AM-10PM. 923.7311

Royal Hawaiian Luau $$$ Standard hotel-style luau offered on the ocean lawn beside Waikiki Beach. ♦ M 6PM. 924.5196

37 Outrigger Waikiki $$$ Right on Waikiki Beach, with 530 rooms, some with spectacular views. One of the Outrigger chain's largest and most expensive hotels, but with a wide range of rates. Nothing below $120 a night, though. ♦ 2335 Kalakaua Ave, Waikiki. 923.0711, 800/733.7777; fax 921.9749

Within the Outrigger Waikiki:

Monterey Bay Canners $$$ A mainland seafood chain in the Outrigger Waikiki's main lobby level, with partial ocean views. Includes *kiawe*-broiled items such as fresh fish, steak and lobster, and an oyster bar. ♦ Seafood ♦ Daily 7AM-2PM, 5-10PM. 922.5761

37 Waikiki Beach This "Mother Superior" of all Hawaii's beaches, extends from Ala Wai Canal to Diamond Head. Excellent swimming spot for beginners. Although many hotels front it, the beach is public property up to the high-

water mark. Good news: Parts of the beach were widened in the mid-1980s to help rein in congestion problems. Surfboards, boogie boards, umbrellas, beach mats, and more can be rented from concessions along the beach. ♦ Off Kalakaua Ave, Waikiki.

Royal Hawaiian Hotel

37 Wizard Stones When you see these boulders at Kuhio Beach, think of the four Tahitian priests, or *kahuna*, said to have transferred their powers to the rocks. Hawaiian lore has it that **Kapaemahu, Kahaloa, Kinohi,** and **Kapuni** journeyed here from Tahiti in the 16th century, transferred their *mana* (healing powers) to the stones and vanished. Modestly cropping out of the sand, near the bronze statue of champion Hawaiian surfer/swimmer **Duke Kahanamoku,** the Wizard Stones look like ordinary rocks, but like Kahanamoku's statue, add a quiet majesty to the spot. ♦ Off Kalakaua Ave, Waikiki

38 Chuck's Steak House $$$ What can you say about Chuck's except that it's another Chuck's? This one does have a good ocean view from the second floor. ♦ Steak ♦ Daily 6-10PM. Outrigger Hotel, 2335 Kalakaua Ave, Waikiki. 923.1228

39 Ray's Seafood Restaurant $$$ Seafood, seafood, and more seafood. Like most of the restaurants that originally opened in the Waikiki Shopping Plaza (most of them long gone), Ray's went through a troubled

period and was sold by the Seattle seafood specialists who started it. Still, with its mix of locals and tourists, it managed to survive. ♦ Seafood ♦ Daily 11AM-2PM, 5-10:30PM. Fourth floor, Waikiki Shopping Plaza, Waikiki. 922.4702

39 Tanaka of Tokyo $$$ The Waikiki Shopping Plaza entry in the Benihana-of-Tokyo imitation sweepstakes. One of the nicest restaurants in the plaza. ♦ Japanese ♦ M-F 11:30AM-2:30PM, 5:30-10:30PM; Sa 5:30-10:30PM; Su 5:30-10PM. Fourth floor, Waikiki Shopping Plaza, Waikiki. 922.4702

39 Lau Yee Chai $$$ This once-famous Chinese restaurant on Oahu dates back to 1929. Closed and then reopened by the Waikiki Shopping Plaza owners in a cavernous, garish room on the fifth floor. The menu carries standard Cantonese and Szechuan dishes. The most interesting items are two murals: the 1929 Chinese landscape, 18 feet long and covering an entire wall, and the 1946 mural on the opposite wall. These beautiful works of art and many other Chinese pieces were kept in storage for nearly 15 years after the original restaurant closed in 1965. ♦ Chinese ♦ Daily 11AM-2PM, 5-10PM. Fifth floor, Waikiki Shopping Plaza, Waikiki. 923.1112

40 Waikiki Beachcomber $$ Set in the very heart of Waikiki, which means heavy congestion. Pluses include easy access to shopping; Waikiki Beach (just across the street) and almost 500 rooms. Another Waikiki hotel in the hands of **Azabu USA Corp.,** along with the Hyatt Regency Waikiki. Hawaiian entertainment nightly in the **Surfboard Lounge** and dining in the **Beachcomber Restaurant.** ♦ 2300 Kalakaua Ave, Waikiki. 922.4646, 800/622.4646; fax 923.4889

41 Matteo's ★★$$$ Owner **Fred Livingston,** well-known restaurateur, also owns **Trattoria** and the **Tahitian Lanai.** Matteo's has a masculine, rich decor—intimate booths, soft lighting, amber tones—wonderful Italian food, and very professional service. Popular with lawyers, yuppies, and show-biz types. The osso buco, chicken Florentine, and steaks are all popular. ♦ Italian ♦ Daily 6PM-midnight. 364 Seaside Ave, Waikiki. Valet parking. 922.5551

42 Maharaja Though it fancies itself Honolulu's hottest nightclub, Maharaja is really quite uppity and self-conscious. It's a Japanese-owned restaurant and disco with a dress code, a VIP room where members are ushered in for $500 a year in dues, and a varied menu for late-night diners and snackers. All marble and brass, with the full gamut of eccentricities on the dance floor. ♦ Daily 8PM-4AM. Waikiki Trade Center, 2255 Kuhio Ave, Waikiki. 922.3030

43 Sergio's ★★★$$$ A gourmet northern Italian restaurant frequented mostly by local patrons, many of them loyal and longtime habitués. **Sergio Battistetti,** former owner of the Trattoria for 13 years, has applied his seasoned culinary wizardry to the more than 50 different dishes on the menu. Osso buco, fresh fish, lamb, and everything with shiitake mushrooms is recommended. ♦ Italian ♦ M-W, Sa-Su 5:30-11PM; Th-F 11:30AM-2PM, 5:30-11PM. Ilima Hotel, 445 Nohonani St, Waikiki. 926.3388

44 Country Life Vegetarian Buffet ★$ The international chain has come to Hawaii, with more than 50 vegetarian entrées: lasagna, pecan loaf with cashew gravy, pizza, chow mein, and a host of dishes made without cholesterol, animal fat, dairy products, or eggs. Soy sour cream livens up baked potatoes, while greens galore and whole-grain breads and spreads make for a bountiful salad bar. No sugar in the desserts, only lots of bran, fruit, carob, dates, and fruit concentrates. Validated parking at any Outrigger hotel. ♦ M-Th, Su 11AM-2:30PM, 5-8PM; F 11AM-2:30PM. 421 Nahua St, in the Honolulu Prince Hotel (not to be confused with the high-profile Hawaii Prince) Waikiki. 922.5010

The first automobile in Hawaii was a Wood Electric, delivered on 8 October 1899 to **H.A. Baldwin** of Honolulu.

Good Reads on Hawaii

Beaches of the Big Island, Beaches of Kaua'i and Ni'ihau, Beaches of Maui County, Beaches of O'ahu by John R.K. Clark (1985, 1990, 1980, and 1977, respectively; University of Hawaii Press) The most authoritative, exhaustively researched, and interesting volumes on these prodigious beaches. Also enormously helpful in navigating Hawaii's great outdoors.

Fragments of Hawaiian History by John Papa Ii (1959; Bishop Museum Press) An invaluable record of the lifestyles, customs, and history of the Islands as seen and told by one of the most prominent citizens of the Hawaiian kingdom in the 1800s.

Hawaii by James Michener (1959; Random House) Michener gives his epic treatment to the Islands in this entertaining novel.

Hawaii, The Islands of Life by Gavan Daws (1988; Signature Publishing) This coffee-table hardcover, sponsored by the Nature Conservancy and beautifully written and photographed, covers the fragile volcanoes, rainforests, dryland forests, and flora and fauna of Hawaii.

Hawaii Pono by Lawrence H. Fuchs (1961; Harcourt Brace Jovanovich) A social history of Hawaii from the late 1800s, when the Hawaiian monarchy was overthrown by westerners, to the 1960s, the years following statehood.

Nana I Ke Kumu (Volume 1) by Mary Kawena Pukui, E.W. Haertig, M.D., and Catherine A. Lee (1972; Queen Lili'uokalani Children's Center, Lili'uokalani Trust) Required reading for anyone who wants to know more about Hawaiian customs and family traditions. Legends, oral histories, and information on everything from family healing practices to Hawaiian spiritual beliefs make this a well-documented and extensively researched Hawaiian classic.

The People of Old by Samuel Kamekau (1964; Bishop Museum) These writings from the 1860s document the daily activities of Hawaiian life, focusing on spiritual and religious aspects.

Ronck's Hawaii Almanac by Ronn Ronck (1984; University of Hawaii Press) Statistics galore on anything and everything, from geography to economics.

Shoal of Time by Gavan Daws (1968; Macmillan) One of the best histories of Hawaii.

Tales from the Night Rainbow by Pali Lee and Koko Willis (1986; Lee and Willis) This fascinating history of a Hawaiian family on Molokai encompasses many aspects of Hawaiian life, from spiritual and healing practices to planting, genealogy, and local legend. You can learn a lot about Hawaiian cosmology and customs from this account of a single family.

Waikiki Beachboy by Grady Timmons (1989; Editions Ltd.) A book for anyone who loves Hawaii. Original research and one-of-a-kind stories capture the romance of Waikiki in its heyday, the mind-boggling feats of the beachboys, and the romance, glamour, and joie de vivre of Hawaii's legendary watermen. Largely an oral history as told by the beachboys, this book establishes once and for all that these men occupied a specific time in Honolulu history.

Oahu

45 Hotel Miramar $$ You'll know you've found it by its gaudy and ornate appearance. Right in the middle of the Kuhio Ave action, a block from Waikiki Beach, with 270 rooms and a pool. Same owners as the Miramar Hotel of Hong Kong. ◆ 2345 Kuhio Ave, Waikiki. 922.2077, 800/367.2303

46 Chuck's Cellar $$$ A member of the Chuck's Steak House family. ◆ Steak ◆ Daily 5:30-10:30PM. Outrigger East Hotel, 150 Kaiulani Ave, Waikiki. 923.4488

47 Princess Kaiulani Hotel $$$ This Sheraton hotel has expanded since 1955, when the 11-story main building opened. A 28-story tower built in 1970 and three wings bring the present total to 1,152 rooms. On Kaiulani Ave across from the King's Village shopping center, with easy access across Kalakaua to Waikiki Beach. Several categories of rooms, with prices dictated by ocean, city, or mountain views, although keep in mind this is not an oceanfront hotel. Pool, several restaurants and bars. ◆ 120 Kaiulani Ave, Waikiki. 922.5811, 800/325.3535; fax 923.9912

48 Sheraton Moana Surfrider $$$ A stately oceanside landmark that first opened in 1901— the first hotel on Waikiki Beach. In the old days, the Hawaiian beachboys hung out at the 300-foot  Moana pier, playing music as the sun set. There was a dance floor, saloon, billiard room, roof-garden observatory, and the area's first electric-powered elevator. Subsequent expansions, changes in ownership, and, most recently, a 20-month, $50-million historic restoration project resulted in today's truly impressive Moana Surfrider. Restored to its original architecture, the hotel is listed in the National Register of Historic Places. It gleams with indigenous woods, brass poster beds, marble-top tables, a grand staircase, Victorian-style lamps, colonial verandas and millwork, and all manner of memorabilia. **Robert Louis Stevenson** penned some of his famous prose under the famous banyan tree in the courtyard. Planted in 1885, it now towers more than 75 feet high, with a 150-foot limb span. The **Banyan Court** and **Banyan Veranda** feature some of

---

Restaurants/Clubs: Red   Hotels: Blue

Shops/ 🌴 Outdoors: Green   Sights/Culture: Black

the best Hawaiian music on the Islands. When the sun is setting offshore and **Hookena, Olomana, Mahi Beamer,** or **Emma Veary** and **Charles K.L. Davis** are performing in the historic courtyard, the effect is, as they say, "goose bumps." Three towers, 793 rooms. ♦ 2365 Kalakaua Ave, Waikiki. 922.3111, 800/325.3535; fax 923.0308

Within the Sheraton Moana Surfrider:

Captain's Galley $$$ Tranquil setting with an open-air dining room that overlooks the wide lawn leading to the beach. *Kiawe*-charbroiled steaks and seafood are the specialty. There's a salad bar, too. ♦ Steak/Seafood ♦ Daily 5-10:30PM. 922.3111

Banyan Veranda ★★★$$ Since they instituted a Hawaiian music program, this has become Waikiki's best beach attraction. Sunday with Emma Veary and Charles K.L. Davis get rave reviews, and Mahi Beamer's weekend shows bring out the regal *kamaaina* from all over the island. The ambience is unbeatable: rattan chairs, polished wood floors, open to the Banyan Court below and beyond to the Pacific. Close enough to Waikiki Beach to count seashells on the shore, and distinguished by the venerable banyan tree. A colorful mix of locals and tourists—all characters—makes this a lively location for taking in Waikiki Beach life. Drinks, be forewarned, are hideously expensive. ♦ Daily 7AM-11PM. 922.3111

Oahu

Ship's Tavern ★★$$$$ Fine oceanfront dining, more formal than the Captain's Galley. Seafood specialties include fresh Maine lobster, poached *onaga,* sautéed scallops, Kahuku prawns, and other classical delicacies. Romantic. ♦ Continental ♦ Daily 5:30-10PM. 922.3111

49 **The Rose and Crown** ★★$$ This is one of the hottest bars in Waikiki, your neighborhood pub away from home. Mainly for uninhibited, boys-meet-girls socializing with lusty sing-alongs and Island-style pub grub. Very popular with the Aussies, Brits, and New Zealanders, with a dart board and brews from all over the world. ♦ Daily 11:30AM-2AM. King's Village, 131 Kaiulani Ave, ground level (directly behind the Hyatt Regency Waikiki) Waikiki. 923.5833

50 **Hyatt Regency Waikiki** $$$$ Designed by **Wimberly, Whisenand, Tong & Goo** in association with **Lawton & Taylor,** the Hyatt was built in 1976 for $100 million, and sold in 1987 for $300 million. Twin 39-story towers rise on either side of a 10-story, elaborately landscaped atrium, designated as the **Great Hall.** There are 1,230 rooms, restaurants and bars, and hip, glitzy guests who like being in the middle of the action and don't mind the impersonality of a very large hotel. Regency Club guests receive choice rooms with special perks, including a chilled bottle of champagne left nightly in their rooms. ♦ 2424 Kalakaua Ave, Waikiki. 923.1234, 800/228.9000; fax 923.7839

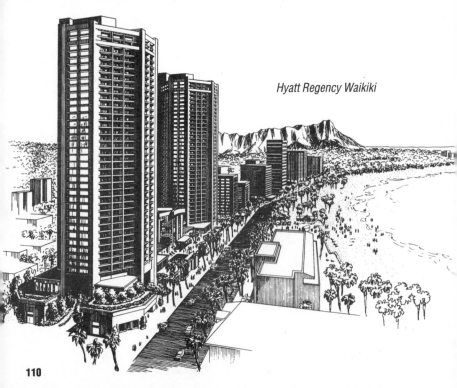

Hyatt Regency Waikiki

Within the Hyatt Regency Waikiki:

Musashi ★$$$ As much attention is paid to drama and theater as to food in this Japanese restaurant, named after a famous samurai **Miyamoto Musashi.** (His classic study of the warrior code, *A Book of Five Rings,* is the bible of Japanese business schools.) Waitresses are dressed in kimonos, chefs in samurai garb, and busboys in traditional street-acrobat wear. For breakfast, try the traditional Japanese breakfasts. For dinner, order the duckling glazed with herb sauce and dessert of five sherbets, called the "jewel box." Sushi bar, teppan grills, or table dining. ♦ Japanese ♦ Daily 5:30-10:30AM, 6-10:30PM. 923.1234

The Colony Seafood and Steak House ★$$$ Fresh seafood entrées include Hawaiian prawns, lobster, scallops, and the catch of the day. Of course, steak, chops, prime rib, and chicken broiled over *kiawe* wood are also available. Leave room for the elaborate dessert bar. A special treat in the lounge is the music of Hawaii's No. 1 ukulele virtuoso, **Herb Ohta.** ♦ Steak/Seafood ♦ Daily 6-10PM. 923.1234

Trappers ★★$$$ A beyond-midnight hangout for visiting celebrities, musicians, and other Waikiki night owls. Just about every jazz great who visits Hawaii has stopped in at Trappers. Versatile and popular, with bands playing contemporary hits and brassy sounds from the forties, fifties, and sixties. The Art Deco motif includes lots of mirrors and etched glass, couches, and cozy booths. Late-night happy hour starts at 1AM, with half-price drinks and free *pupus.* Live entertainment nightly. ♦ Daily 8PM-1AM, private club daily 1-4AM. 923.1234

Terrace Grille $$ Hyatt's upscale version of the hotel coffee shop, a cheerful poolside restaurant with indoor and outdoor seating, a breakfast buffet, and extensive lunch and dinner selections. Be sure to see the collection of beautifully framed authentic aloha shirts and Hawaiian quilts. ♦ American ♦ Daily 6AM-11PM. 923.1234

Harry's Bar $$ Cheerful umbrellas shade the tables of this sidewalk cafe next to the Hyatt's raging artificial waterfall. A popular cocktail spot for people-watching. Nightly Hawaiian entertainment. ♦ Daily 2:30-11PM. 923.1234

Spats $$$ Those who get past the strict dress code might enjoy the Italian restaurant and disco. After trying out the dance floor, go to the luxurious private **Boss' Office** for intimate dining and specially prepared courses. Voyeurs love the one-way mirrors. Notorious for its snobby atmosphere, though. ♦ Restaurant: daily 6-10PM, pasta bar until 2AM; nightclub: daily 8PM-4AM. 923.1234

Furusato ★★★$$$ This is the only restaurant within the Hyatt Regency that is independently owned and operated. It actually predates the hotel, having been a popular restaurant in the old Biltmore Hotel, razed to make room for the Hyatt. An excellent choice in every respect and among Waikiki's best sushi bars. ♦ Japanese ♦ Daily 6AM-2PM, 5:30-10:30PM. 922.4991

51 Odoriko ★$$$ Tanks of lobsters, prawns, crabs, and oysters add living color to this authentically furnished Japanese seafood and steak house. There's a list of Japanese specialties, plus a sushi bar. For something out of the ordinary, try the Japanese-style breakfast. ♦ Japanese ♦ Daily 6AM-2AM. King's Village Shopping Center, 2400 Koa Ave (just off Kalakaua Ave, behind the Hyatt Regency Waikiki) Waikiki. 923.7368

52 Hy's Steak House ★★$$$ If this plush bar and dining room give you the feeling of being inside the rich, wood-paneled walls in some baron's library, that's because the interior of Hy's actually came from a private estate in the eastern US. The dining room also features a stunning brass-broiler gazebo. Steak is the best choice. ♦ Continental ♦ Daily 6-10PM; entertainment W-Sa 7PM-midnight. 2440 Kuhio Ave, Waikiki. Valet parking. 922.5555

53 Ala Wai Golf Course A flat, moderately interesting course bordering the murky Ala Wai Canal in the heart of Waikiki. Inexpensive green fees mean that it's crowded with local players. Getting a tee-off time is difficult. Par 71, 6,065 yards. ♦ 404 Kapahulu Ave, Waikiki. Starting times 732.7741

54 Outrigger Prince Kuhio $$$ Somewhat removed from the heart of the action in Waikiki, this 626-room hotel is only a short walk from the beach and Kapiolani Park. Pool. ♦ 2500 Kuhio Ave, Waikiki. 922.0811, 800/733.7777; fax 923.0330

Within the Outrigger Prince Kuhio:

Trellises $$$ Island cuisine served in a garden setting—the latest reincarnation of the hotel's main restaurant. ♦ Hawaiian ♦ Daily 6AM-10PM. 922.0811

55 Aston Waikiki Beachside Hotel $$$$ This new hotel is impressive if you like marble and don't mind the ultra-European, non-Hawaiian decor. It's *tiny,* with 79 rooms (also tiny, but well-appointed) in a narrow 10-floor tower drenched in travertine marble. **Andre** and **Jane Tatibouet** of Aston made this their dream project, decorating it lavishly, with careful attention to details. The entrance looks like Tiffany's, with moldings galore, oriental art and furnishings, and expensive wall coverings. Three of the eight rooms on each floor have fabulous ocean views over bustling Kalakaua Ave; all feature Chinese lacquered furniture, oriental screens, and black chrome-and-gold shower heads that cost more than a room for the night. ♦ 2452 Kalakaua Ave, Waikiki. 931.2100, 800/922.7866; fax 922.8785

56 Pacific Beach Hotel $$$ The 38-story Ocean Tower and 17-story Beach Tower, across from Kuhio Beach, hold 850 rooms, with ocean, city, and mountain views, and refrigerators or full kitchens. Guests can enjoy the pool, two tennis courts, and Jacuzzi. ♦ 2490 Kalakaua Ave, Waikiki. 922.1233, 800/367.6060; fax 922.0129

Within the Pacific Beach Hotel:

Oceanarium Restaurant ★$$$ The big attraction is dining alongside what they claim is Hawaii's largest indoor oceanarium—three stories of glass holding 250,000 gallons of water. Otherwise, it's steaks and seafood (also served buffet-style) featured on a basic,

unexciting American menu. ♦ American ♦ Daily 6AM-10PM. 922.1233

Neptune Restaurant $$$ The hotel's fine dining room specializes in seafood, including a seafood luncheon buffet, with rack of lamb and scampi featured on the dinner menu. You can see the famous three-story oceanarium from the second floor. ♦ Daily 6-10PM. 922.1233

Shogun $$ A good-value Japanese restaurant that's especially popular among seafood lovers. The trade-off is its pedestrian environment. Seafood buffet. ♦ Japanese ♦ Daily 6AM-10PM. 922.1233

57 Kuhio Beach Swarming with hundreds of people, this section of Waikiki opposite the Hyatt Regency doesn't boast the clearest water in the world, but it's still great for strolling and wading. Use caution while swimming—large invisible holes pose an underwater danger. ♦ Off Kalakaua Ave, Waikiki.

58 Damien Museum Interesting displays of pictures, artifacts, and other possessions of **Father Damien,** the martyr of Molokai who dedicated his life to the physical and spiritual needs of patients with Hansen's disease (leprosy). ♦ Free. M-F 9AM-3PM; Sa 9AM-noon. 130 Ohua Ave, Waikiki. 923.2690

ʀ
hawaiian regent

59 Hawaiian Regent Hotel $$$ A decent but not dazzling hotel, except for the architecturally impressive lobby and courtyard. The Hawaiian Regent is managed by **Otaka Hotels and Resorts** and is a sister property to the nearby Hawaiian Waikiki Beach Hotel. There are 1,346 rooms, many with ocean views, in two towers on 5.3 acres. It's worth it to request one of these rooms; the view is spectacular. And if you like historical trivia, **Queen Liliuokalani,** Hawaii's last reigning monarch, had her last seaside cottage here. Six restaurants, two pools, tennis court, shopping arcade. ♦ 2552 Kalakaua Ave, Waikiki. 922.6611, 800/367.5370; fax 921.5255

Hawaiian Regent Hotel

Within the Hawaiian Regent Hotel:

The Secret ★★★$$$$ Formerly The Third Floor, which was among Honolulu's most highly acclaimed restaurants, The Secret is recognized for extraordinary cuisine and its stunning dining room. Lavish displays of fruits and vegetables mark the entrance to a brilliantly designed dining area, done in rattan, wood, copper, crystal, and bright overhanging banners. The effect is of intimate, understated luxury. You'll sit in high-backed rattan chairs at parquet tables. The lamb and venison dishes are unforgettable, and nightly specials, especially the fresh Island fish, are reliably good. All dinners begin with complimentary *naan* bread, a legendary house ritual, delivered warm from clay ovens, and served with goose liver pâté. Relish the first-rate service and outstanding wines. ◆ Continental ◆ Daily 6:30PM-1AM. 922.6611

Regent Hatsuhana $$$ A quiet, refined room tastefully done with rich woods and soft lighting, offering fine Japanese cuisine served by lovely ladies in traditional kimonos. ◆ Japanese ◆ Daily 8AM-10PM. 922.6611

Tiffany Steak House $$$ Steaks and seafood in a restaurant that cantilevers over the tropical gardens in the main lobby. Salad and seafood bar. ◆ Steak/Seafood ◆ Daily 6-9:30PM. 922.6611

The Point After Videos and DJs provide musical entertainment in the Regent's mirrored dance club. There is a good size dance floor surrounded by a few booths and cocktail tables. ◆ Daily 7PM-4AM. 922.6611

60 Hawaiian Waikiki Beach Hotel $$$ This former Holiday Inn Waikiki Beach has 715 rooms in two towers just across Kalakaua Ave from Kuhio Beach, at the Diamond Head end of Waikiki. The Honolulu Zoo, Kapiolani Park, and Waikiki Aquarium are within easy walking distance. Pool. ◆ 2570 Kalakaua Ave, Waikiki. 922.2511, 800/877.7666; fax 923.3656

Within the Hawaiian Waikiki Beach Hotel:

Captain's Table $$$ Continental cuisine with Eastern and Polynesian touches, served in a room with ocean views and a nautical theme. ◆ Continental ◆ M-Sa 6:30-9:30AM, 6:30-9:30PM; Su 10AM-2PM, 6:30-9:30PM. 922.2511

60 Park Shore Hotel $$ Smack dab on the busy corner of Kalakaua and Kapahulu Aves, with Kuhio Beach and the beginnings of Waikiki Beach across one street, and Kapiolani Park across the other. The 227 large guest rooms feature private lanais and Diamond Head, park, or ocean views; some have kitchenettes. Pool. ◆ 2586 Kalakaua Ave, Waikiki. 923.0411, 800/367.2377; fax 923.0311

61 Waikiki Grand Hotel $$ Across the street from Kapiolani Park and the Honolulu Zoo (you can hear the animals at night), and a short walk across Kalakaua Ave to the Diamond Head end of Waikiki Beach. The Waikiki Grand is relatively small (170 rooms), with a rooftop sun deck and pool. ◆ 134 Kapahulu Ave, Waikiki. 923.1511

62 Queen Kapiolani Hotel $$ A Waikiki veteran across the street from Kapiolani Park and the Honolulu Zoo, a block from Kuhio Beach. Views of the park, Diamond Head, and the ocean. A total of 315 rooms and a pool for guests. ◆ 150 Kapahulu Ave, Waikiki. 922.1941, 800/367.5004; fax 922.2694

63 Honolulu Zoo Typical zoo animals peering out through vegetation-covered cages for a tropical jungle effect. The **Children's Zoo** lets

kids pet the lemurs, ponies, goats, chickens, and other animals. Kids also have a chance to feed **Mari**, the zoo's only elephant, under the supervision of zookeepers. The **Education Pavilion** is yet another experience, featuring puppet shows on Saturday and hands-on demonstrations in weaving, basketry, and other crafts. The main attraction during summer months is the *Wildest Show in Town,* held weekly and featuring the best local entertainment, from **Hookena** to **Gabe Baltazar** and the **Pandanus Club.** It's immensely popular, and it's free. ◆ Daily 8:30AM-4PM, summer shows W at 6PM. 151 Kapahulu Ave, Waikiki. 971.7171

64 Weekend Art Mart One of the more offbeat sights unfolds every weekend outside the Honolulu Zoo. Local artists of varying degrees of expertise set up card tables and prop their wares against the zoo fence, hoping to make a sale. The proverbial ocean sunsets and palm-fringed beaches cover most canvasses, although snowy New England scenes occasionally find their way to the mart. A pleasant outing with souvenir potential and the opportunity to mix with the local artists. ◆ Free. Tu 9AM-1PM; Sa-Su 10AM-4PM. Kapiolani Park, along Monsarrat Ave, Waikiki

65 Queen's Surf Beach Park Toward the Diamond Head end of Waikiki, Queen's Surf parallels Kapiolani Park. The beach is popular among local families who love the park for picnicking. ♦ Off Kalakaua Ave, just north of Kapiolani Park

66 Waikiki Aquarium The newest addition is a *mahimahi* (dolphinfish or dorado) hatchery, a working aquaculture research center where you can observe *mahimahi* bred on site, not caught in the wild. Other tanks display sharks, stingrays, butterfly fish, turtles, monk seals, octopi, live coral, lionfish, a seahorse, and a giant clam, a total of 280 marine species. In 1990 the aquarium became the first in the US (and second in the world) to successfully hatch a chambered nautilus. The Nautilus Nursery tank opened that year and furthered the aquarium's renown as a national resource on the rare mollusk. Children's programs, summer reef explorations, music festivals, field trips, workshops, travel programs, guided tours, and many other types of programs make this a lively experience for adults and children. ♦ Donation. Daily 9AM-5PM. 2777 Kalakaua Ave, Waikiki. 923.9741

Oahu

66 Waikiki War Memorial Natatorium Located on the oceanside of Kapiolani Park, this deteriorating structure has seen better days since it was built in 1927. Once the site of gala swimming meets and kiddie swim programs, the saltwater pool became a living laboratory of refuse, algae, and grime. Nostalgia, not to mention its dedication as a war memorial, saved it from destruction. ♦ Closed to public, but can be viewed at the Diamond Head end of Kalakaua Ave, Waikiki

Honolulu Marathon

Honolulu must be one of the jogging capitals of the world, and a chief source of inspiration may be the Honolulu Marathon, which annually attracts about 10,000 runners on a Sunday in early December. The tradition began in 1973, when 85 runners set Oahu's marathon course. Today the event is open to anyone, regardless of age, sex, handicap, or ability. The 26.2-mile race begins with a cannon boom just before dawn at **Aloha Tower** (see page 131) in downtown Honolulu. The route winds through Waikiki to suburban Hawaii Kai and around the volcanic crater Diamond Head to Waikiki's Kapiolani Park. Unlike most races, this one's not officially over until the last runner stumbles across the finish line. For additional information, write to: Honolulu Marathon Association, 3435 Waialae Ave, Honolulu HI 96816, or call 734.7200.

67 New Otani Kaimana Beach Hotel $$ A favorite among many visitors, this modest high rise is found in the best part of Waikiki —on historic Sans Souci Beach, where **Robert Louis Stevenson** sunned himself in the 1890s. The small white sand beach is popular among locals and visitors as a good alternative to Waikiki congestion. Hikers and joggers have easy access to Kapiolani Park and to the winding road around the base of Diamond Head, where a lookout offers sweeping views of the surfers and windsurfers below. In fact, Kaimana manager **Steve Boyle** formed the very popular **Diamond Head Climbers Hui**, a club for hikers who've made it to the top of Diamond Head. Following a lengthy, $10-million renovation, the hotel was reintroduced in 1989 with a slightly more upscale feel. There are 125 guest rooms (and beautiful suites) on the third to the ninth floors, in a small atrium design. Some rooms are quite small, but they all have refrigerators; corner suites have the best views. ♦ 2863 Kalakaua Ave, Waikiki. 923.1555, 800/733.7949; fax 922.9404

Within the New Otani Kaimana Beach Hotel:

Hau Tree Lanai ★★$$ A million-dollar ocean view—about as close as you can get to the water and still be at a table in the restaurant. A giant *hau* tree serves as a canopy for the open-air dining room. Local treats worth trying on the vastly improved menu include poi pancakes and fresh Island fish. Great for breakfast, lunch, or dinner, especially at sunset. ♦ Polynesian ♦ Daily 6:30-11AM, 11:30AM-2:30PM, 5:30-10PM. 923.1555

Miyako $$$ Fine food in an oceanfront setting, with family-style seating on tatami mats at low tables. The menu includes *shabu shabu* (cook-it-yourself soup), good tempura, *teppanyaki* items grilled at the table, and a wide variety of other Japanese delights. ♦ Japanese ♦ Daily 6-9:30PM. 923.1555

Colony Surf

67 Colony Surf Hotel $$$$ The 21-story hotel looks unimpressive from the outside, but its choice location and first-rate accommodations have convinced many discriminating travelers to adopt it as their exclusive Hawaiian hideaway. Not exactly hidden, but far enough removed from Waikiki to afford some feeling of elegance. The Colony Surf offers views of Kapiolani Park on one side, with views of Diamond Head rising in the background. Of more importance to most guests, however, is the almost private beach in front of the hotel. The large and elegantly appointed one- and two-bedroom suites are equipped with full kitchens, and the one bedrooms feature floor-to-ceiling windows with spectacular views. The adjacent **Colony East** tower has kitchenettes and substantially lower rates, but anyone preferring the hotel's true luxury should request a room in the main building on the beach, not in the Colony East that's set back from the beach. ♦ 2895 Kalakaua Ave, Waikiki. 923.5751, 800/252.7873 (US), 800/423.7781 (Canada); fax 922.8433

Within the Colony Surf Hotel:

Michel's ★★★$$$$ Few restaurants can match this setting. Literally on the beach, the oceanside half of the three large dining rooms is kept completely open except during storms. Diners fortunate enough to secure the best tables are within a linen napkin's toss of the beach. The interior decor is every bit as lavish as a French restaurant on top of Nob Hill in San Francisco. Sitting in the chandeliered splendor, with close-up views of canoeists, swimmers, sparkling surf, and distant horizons during the day, and Waikiki's glittering lights by night, can prove mesmerizing—the food, less so. Although Michel's has traditionally billed itself as "Hawaii's Very French Restaurant," the menu is more silk-purse Continental, with veal and seafood specialties and rack of lamb. Because of crowded dinner conditions, you might enjoy Michel's more at lunch, and it's unquestionably the most elegant location for breakfast in Hawaii. Old-timers complain, however, that it's not the same Michel's with the recent, extensive changes in staff. (Not to be confused with Chez Michel, also founded by Michel Martin.) ♦ Continental ♦ M-Sa 7-11AM, 11:30AM-2PM, 5:30-10PM; Su 7-10AM, 11:30AM-2PM, 5:30-10PM. Jacket required. 923.6552

Bobby McGee's Conglomeration $$$ A theme restaurant with waiters in cartoon character costumes, salad bars in bathtubs, and generally corny, crazy decor. Everyone, celebrities included, seems to love it. Comedians **Don Rickles** and **Bob Newhart** once got so caught up in the spirit of Bobby McGee's they did table-hopping insults of guests, gratis. A mainland chain that's been extremely successful. It's located on the ground floor of the Colony East tower. ♦ American ♦ M-Th 5:30-10PM; F-Sa 5:30-11PM; Su 5-10PM; disco daily until 2AM. 922.1282

68 **Kapiolani Park** Hawaii's first public park (named for **Queen Kapiolani**, King Kalakaua's wife) has been a popular sports, recreation, and picnic hub since it first opened in 1877. These 220 acres sprawl in the shadow of Diamond Head where the sun never sets when someone isn't walking through the rose garden, wrapping up a softball game, or polishing off a barbecued hamburger somewhere in the park. The park's one-time racetrack and

polo field were sacrificed to provide space for soccer and rugby games. **Waikiki Aquarium** and the **Honolulu Zoo** are both in the park. Musical events at the **Waikiki Shell Amphitheater** and traditional dancing at the **Kodak Hula Show** attract a few crowds, and there's always a steady stream of joggers and fitness enthusiasts. If you're in town for the annual **Honolulu Marathon,** one of the world's largest, stop by the park to watch runners cross the finish line. ♦ Kalakaua Ave (Monsarrat Ave) Waikiki. 971.2500

In Kapiolani Park:

Kodak Hula Show This Waikiki institution, which premiered in 1937, proves that low-cost camp still prevails. For one hour, three mornings a week, people plop themselves down on bleachers to watch a parade of wiggling Hawaiians in authentic native garb. Plunky ukulele music played by *tutus* (grandmothers) in bright muumuus and floppy hats accompanies the choreographed hula of energetic flower-bedecked dancers in *ti*-leaf skirts. Spectators who volunteer to dance with the performers provide more entertainment. ♦ Admission. Tu-Th 10-11:15AM. Bleacher area next to Waikiki Shell Amphitheater, opposite Monsarrat Ave, Waikiki

69 **Diamond Head Beach Park** A dangerous beach for swimming, and surfing should be for experts only. Check out the sight-seeing overlook and the trail leading to a great beach for walking and exploring tide pools.

♦ Diamond Head Rd, Waikiki. Below the lighthouse

70 **Diamond Head** The first glimpse airborne visitors have of Hawaii, at least those sitting on the plane's right-hand side, is of this landmark. The volcanic crater has been dormant for an estimated 150,000 years. Early Hawaiians gave it the name *Leahi* (meaning the forehead of an *ahi* tuna) because its lines resemble the profile of a fish. When 19th-century sailors found diamond-like crystals there (they were calcite), the nickname "Diamond Head" was invented, and it stuck. The crater's walls are 760 feet high; you can hike up the inside slopes to the top, a perfect picnic spot with an extensive view. ♦ Diamond Head Rd, Waikiki.

Touring the Town

Walk the island of Oahu on a tour sponsored by the **Kapiolani Community College.** You'll visit everything from historic cemeteries to the territory once frequented by Charlie Chan. Contact the Kapiolani Community College Office of Community Services for a schedule and rates by writing to: 4303 Diamond Head Rd, Honolulu HI 96816, or call 734.9211.

Restaurants/Clubs: Red   Hotels: Blue
Shops/ ♥ Outdoors: Green   **Sights/Culture:** Black

115

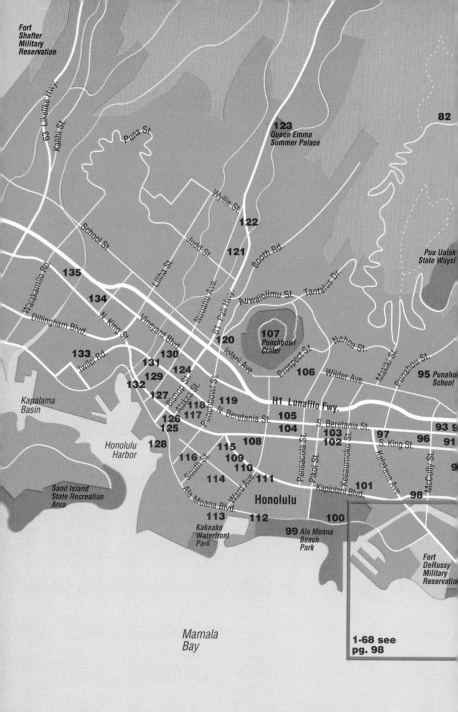
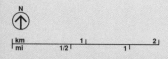

81

80

Monoa
Valley
Park

E. Manoa Rd.

noa Rd.

Waahila
State Park

79

83

Bertram St.

84
University
Of Hawaii

ole St.

Chaminade
University

85

Palolo Ave.

10th Ave.

Wilhelmina Rise

16th Ave.

Kilauea Ave.

Ainakoa Ave.

Halekoa Dr.

Laukahi St.

86

Waialae Ave.

8

74

H1 Lunalilo Frwy.

75

76

Keatsolu Ave.

Date St.

6th Ave.

Pahoa Ave.

Hunakai St.

Waialae
Beach Park

a Wai Canal

73

Kilauea Ave.

Alohea Ave.

78

77

aikiki
ach

Honolulu
Zoo

72

Monsarrat Ave.

18th Ave.

Elepaio St.

Maunalua
Bay

Kapiolani
Park

70
Diamond Head
State Monument

Kahala Ave.

Kupikipkio
Point

Sans Souci
Beach

71

Diamond Head Rd.

69

71 Diamond Head Beach Hotel $$$ A small European-style hotel with just 56 rooms and suites, including studios and one bedrooms with kitchens. This charming hotel occupies a minuscule wedge of white sand on Diamond Head beach, removed from the Waikiki frenzy. Guests can jog, play tennis and soccer, or fly kites in Kapiolani Park, which is just across the street. A Colony Resorts hotel. ♦ 2947 Kalakaua Ave, Waikiki. 922.1928, 800/777.1700; fax 924.8980

72 Queen Kapiolani Rose Garden Pathways meander around dozens of varieties of fragrant roses free for the looking, but not for picking. Many are named after public figures such as Princess Grace of Monaco and Lady Bird Johnson. This showcase garden thrives on conscientious care from its curator and manure from the nearby Honolulu Zoo. ♦ Free. Paki and Monsarrat Aves, Waikiki

73 Keo's ★★★$$$ The owners of **Mekong** on Beretania St in Honolulu created such a following for their little dining room that they converted this former strip joint into a larger, orchid-drenched establishment. Keo's is the

best-known name for Thai food in Hawaii, a magnet for celebrities and the otherwise chic. The menu is enormous, but the usually fabulous food can be inconsistent. Highlights include Evil Jungle Prince (a blend of chicken, lemon grass, coconut milk, Chinese cabbage, and red chilies), green papaya salad, shrimp with a sweet peanut sauce, and delicious spring rolls. Owner **Keo Sananikone** grows his own herbs, bananas, and produce on the North Shore, and, using great imagination, decorates the ornate room with fresh orchids and stalks of jungle greens. Keo's is a star in the island's ethnic dining scene and deserving of its fame. ♦ Thai ♦ Daily 5:30-10:30PM. 625 Kapahulu Ave, Kapahulu. 737.8240

74 Che Pasta ★★$$$ From the simplest *pomodoro* to the fancier seafood pastas, you can find memorable Italian food here. Paintings by local artists liven up the walls. ♦ Italian ♦ M-Th, Su 5:30-9:30PM; F-Sa 5:30-10PM. 3571 Waialae Ave, Kaimuki. 735.1777

74 Azteca Mexican Restaurant ★★$$ The best salsa in town, with hefty meat or vegetarian burritos and the full range of Mexican favorites served in a colorful, kitschy environment. ♦ Mexican ♦ M-Sa 11AM-9:45PM; Su 5-9:45PM. 3569 Waialae Ave, Kaimuki. 735.2492

74 Hale Vietnam ★★$$ The specialty here is *pho*, the steamy Vietnamese soup that's cooked for hours and prepared in nearly two dozen versions. *Pho* lovers come here from all over the island to linger over the hot bowls of soup or light, piquant spring rolls. Hearty Vietnamese fare in a modest environment. ♦ Vietnamese ♦ 1141 Twelfth Ave, Kaimuki. 735.7581

75 California Pizza Kitchen ★★$$ Be prepared to feast on piping hot pizzas served hand over fist out of the wood-burning brick oven. Shrimp Caribbean, roasted garlic chicken, shrimp pesto; pick your toppings. Creative good food, including pastas, prepared with everything from black bean sauce to Thai chicken. ♦ Pizza ♦ M-Th 11:30AM-10PM; F-Sa 11:30AM-11PM; Su noon-10PM. Kahala Mall, 4211 Waialae Ave, Honolulu. 737.9446

75 Yen King ★★$$ Small, reliable, and a longtime favorite of locals with Chinese food cravings. Their specialty is northern China cooking, with nearly a hundred items on the menu, most of which are reasonably priced. If you like spicy dishes, try the garlic chicken, lemon beef, or sizzling rice shrimp. ♦ Chinese ♦ Daily 11AM-2:30PM, 5-9:30PM. Kahala Mall, 4211 Waialae Ave, Honolulu. 732.5505

75 Yum Yum Tree ★$$ Convenient place to stop for burgers, salads, and omelets while shopping at Kahala Mall. ♦ American ♦ M-Th, Su 7AM-11PM; F-Sa 7AM-midnight. Kahala Mall, 4211 Waialae Ave. 737.7938

76 Hajji Baba's ★★$$$ Moroccan food served by caftanned waiters and waitresses. The food is moderate, but the seating is awkward (with some people sitting on chairs and others on the floor, and waiters reaching around and hopping over them). Belly dancers liven up the evening. ♦ Moroccan ♦ Daily 6-10PM. 4614 Kilauea Ave, Kahala. 735.5522

77 Waialae Country Club This is one of Hawaii's most exclusive and private country clubs, and home to the **Hawaiian Open** golf tournament. Built in 1927 in a then-remote part of Oahu, the flat course borders the ocean and offers vicious doglegs, deep bunkers, and nearly 2,000 palm trees—many of them two centuries old—prove challenging obstacles to the best golfers. Par 72, 6,651 yards. ♦ Members and guests only. Adjacent to the Kahala Hilton (but hotel guests do not have playing privileges) 4997 Kahala Ave, Kahala. Pro shop 732.1457

78 Kahala Hilton Hotel $$$$ One of Oahu's finer hotels, the Kahala Hilton commands an exclusive setting—six and a half acres of quiet oceanside luxury well removed from the congestion of Waikiki. Guests enjoy a private beach—wide and sandy with excellent swimming—surrounded on three sides by the greenery of the Waialae Country Club. Designed by **Edward Killingsworth,** the 10-story hotel opened in 1964, with 369 rooms and suites, some of them right at the edge of a lagoon filled with large sea turtles, tropical fish, and cavorting dolphins (lagoon units are booked far in advance). **Hoku,** born in the lagoon on 30 March 1991, has become the new dolphin star, swimming beside its mother in front of adoring fans. The Kahala is 27 years old, so you can imagine the lush landscaping: quiet pathways winding among tropical foliage, tiny streams, miniature waterfalls, and flowering gardens. Guests, many of them Hollywood stars, producers, agents, and writers, appreciate the privacy here. The hotel keeps a record of repeat guests' preferences in rooms, views, and other partialities. ♦ Deluxe ♦ 5000 Kahala Ave, Kahala. 734.2211, 800/367.2525; fax 737.2478

Within the Kahala Hilton Hotel:

Hala Terrace ★★$$ This pleasant open-air room with ocean views, excellent service, and fine food is a wonderful choice for a leisurely breakfast or Sunday brunch. The eggs Benedict and the pancakes with coconut syrup are both divine. There's also a large breakfast buffet. The lunch menu includes fresh Island fish, pastas, salads, and sandwiches. ♦ American ♦ M-Sa 6:30-11AM, 11:30AM-2PM, dinner show M-Sa from 7PM. Su 7-10AM, 11:30AM-2PM, seafood buffet 6-9PM. 734.2211

Maile Restaurant ★★★$$$$ Excellent in every way, from the soothing, garden-like atmosphere, complete with fountains and pools, to the memorable cuisine. Fresh orchids everywhere, gracious service by ladies in kimonos, and a table d'hôte menu noted for roast duckling Waialae, a signature dish embellished with bananas, lichees, mandarin oranges, spiced peaches, and Grand Marnier. Another house specialty is the Hawaiian trio: *opakapaka* (pink snapper) with a mushroom sauce, *mahimahi* (golden dolphinfish) with spinach sauce, and *onaga* (red snapper) with chardonnay sauce. Indulge yourself, but save room for the Grand Marnier soufflé. Extensive, pricey wine list. ♦ Continental ♦ Daily 6:30-9PM. Live music and dancing 8PM-12:30AM in the adjoining Maile Lounge. 734.2211

Plumeria Cafe ★★$$ A courtyard cafe with a tropical mood, serving morning pastries, delightful lunches, afternoon tea, early evening snacks, and supper. Special menus featured monthly. ♦ Continental ♦ Daily 11:30AM-10:30PM. 734.2211

Danny Kaleikini Show Danny Kaleikini, one of Hawaii's most visible entertainers, has been the Kahala's resident star since 1967. He and his lovely cast of dancers and Hawaiian entertainers perform inside the Hala Terrace, a romantic setting, with the nearby surf glowing in the moonlight. ♦ M-Sa 9PM. 734.2211

79 Waahila State Park A cool, elevated retreat at the top of residential St. Louis Heights, a 15-minute walk from Waikiki Beach. Barbecue and other picnic facilities available among the ironwood trees and Norfolk pines. Splendid view of Manoa Valley and the Koolau ridgeline from the hiking trail. ♦ Top of St. Louis Dr, Kahala

80 Lyon Arboretum Lush botanical gardens, with waterfalls in the distance. You'll find taro, orchids, bromeliads, ferns, cinnamon, coco, native koa and kava, palms, coffee, yams, bananas, and hundreds of different species on these 124 acres at the end of Manoa Valley. The arboretum is closely associated with **Beatrice Krauss,** an ethnobotanist who has taught here for decades. Crafts and cooking workshops, plant sales, special outings, hikes, and may other educational activities are offered here. Bring along mosquito repellent. ♦ M-F 9AM-3PM; Sa 9AM-noon for self-guided tours. One-hour guided tours at 1PM every first F and third W of each month, and 10AM every third Sa. 3860 Manoa Rd, Honolulu. Reservations required. 988.3177

81 Manoa Falls The perfect place for a long picnic followed by a swim in the fresh-water pool underneath the falls. To get here, take the trail that begins at the end of Manoa Rd behind Paradise Park; it's about a 30-minute hike (one mile) to the falls. Ginger and tropical blooms enhance the path. ♦ Exit west off of Manoa Rd

82 Tantalus Wealthy *kamaaina* families liked the cool high slopes of this volcanic peak overlooking Honolulu so much they built their homes here, hidden from view by lush vegetation. You can see these enclaves from the winding Round Top Dr as well as from various lookout points, particularly Puu Ualakaa State Park on Tantalus. ♦ Daily until dusk. Round Top Dr, off E. Manoa Rd

82 Contemporary Museum This former Spalding estate is gorgeously landscaped on the slopes of Mount Tantalus, with a view to match the art collection. A world-class collection with a **David Hockney** pavilion and regular exhibits of the finest contemporary artists from Hawaii and across the country. Visit the gift shop and the **Contemporary Cafe,** with indoor and outdoor dining and a light menu of salads, pastas, and soups. ♦ Tu-Sa 10AM-4PM; Su noon-4PM. 2411 Makiki Heights Dr, Mount Tantalus. 526.0232

The Island's Representatives

State Bird The rare and fascinating Nene (pronounced *nay*-nay) is the state's largest bird, a species of goose that is able to survive in the rugged terrain of old lava beds. The Nene has claw-like digits instead of webbed feet.

State Flower The hibiscus, a large showy flower, is commonly known as the Mallow Marvel (it belongs to the Malvaceae or Mallow family). This edible flower is sometimes used in salads.

State Mammal
The humpback whale, which visits Hawaiian waters during its annual winter migration, was named the official state mammal in 1979.

State Motto *Ua mau ke ea o ka aina i ka pono,* which means "The life of the land is perpetuated in righteousness." It was written by **King Kamehameha III** in 1843, when Great Britain restored Hawaiian sovereignty, and became the official

Oahu

state motto in 1959.

State Song *Hawaii Pono'i,* which means "Great" or "Mighty Hawaii," was composed by **King Kalakaua** in 1874, with music by royal bandmaster **Henri Berger.** The song was written as a tribute to **Kamehameha I,** Hawaii's great ruler and warrior.

State Tree The *kukui* (or candlenut tree), whose

83 Coffee Manoa ★★$$ A popular local gathering place for a diverse crowd, mainly coffee lovers who live in the valley. The store sells dozens of different coffee beans, or you can take home a bag of your favorite gourmet blend ground on the premises. Oat cakes are the latest fad along with muffins, breads, scones, and assorted pastries. ♦ M-F 8AM-9PM; Sa 8AM-5PM; Su 8AM-4PM. Manoa Marketplace, Woodlawn Dr, Manoa. 988.5113

84 University of Hawaii Probably the ugliest collection of unrelated architectural styles in Hawaii can be found on the university's 300-acre campus in Manoa Valley, but extensive landscaping provides some relief. The center for higher education began in 1908 with 12 teachers and five full-time students. Now nearly 19,000 full-time students attend the flagship Manoa campus, with another 26,000 enrolled at the Hilo campus and in the university's statewide community college system. Because of its South Pacific location, the university has continually strived to strengthen its reputation in international studies. The university is also in the forefront of astronomy research and a leader in the world search for alternative energy sources. And naturally, it supports a long-time interest in marine programs. ♦ M-F 8AM-4:30PM. University Ave, Manoa Valley. 956.8111

85 East-West Center In 1906 the center began promoting cultural and technical interchanges among people of Asia, the Pacific, and the US. Many of the students trained here pursue careers in the Orient. The center is federally funded, and after decades of direct affiliation with the university, has attained independent corporate status. The center contains several artistic treasures from the Far East, and the grounds around Jefferson Hall are quite beautiful. ♦ M-F 8AM-4:30PM. 1777 East-West Rd, University of Hawaii, Honolulu. 944.7111

86 India House $$ Owner/chef **Ram Arora** introduced the *naan* bread that helped build The Secret's (formerly The Third Floor restaurant) lofty reputation. His own restaurant is less glamorous, but the dishes baked in his tandoor (clay) oven have their own following. ♦ Indian ♦ Daily 5-9:30PM. 2632 S. King St, Honolulu. 955.7552

87 Buzz's Original Steak House ★$$$ An extension of the always reliable Buzz's steak house empire in the old Moiliili neighborhood, conveniently located across the street from the Varsity Theater. ♦ Steak/Seafood ♦ M-Th, Su 5-10PM; F-Sa 5-10:30PM. 2535 Coyne St, Honolulu. 944.9781

the Willows

88 The Willows $$$ This is exactly the kind of restaurant experience many tourists hope to find in Hawaii but rarely do. Founded in 1944 as a neighborhood family restaurant in the old McCully-Moiliili district, the Willows grew into both a *kamaaina* (old-timers) and tourist favorite. Everyone loves the tropical mood created by long, thatched-roof dining pavilions overlooking lagoons filled with colorful carp, and the outdoor **Garden Court,** with its intimate thatched-top tables. The food, if unremarkable, is at least highlighted by Willows traditions—Hawaiian curries and sky-high coconut cream pie. You may not remember the

food, but you'll enjoy the restaurant's distinctively Hawaiian ambience, and poi suppers where the more courageous can try *lomi* salmon, *lau lau,* and other Hawaiian dishes. A strolling trio sings traditional Hawaiian songs during dinner hours, and **Puamana, Genoa Keawe,** and other beloved Hawaiian entertainers stroll among the ohia log pillars during the delightful "Poi Thursday" luncheons. Inevitably, their friends and relatives in the audience will join in and you'll be treated to family-style Hawaiian entertainment. Upstairs in its own separate corner of the restaurant, the Kamaaina Suite offers more upscale fare—a seven-course prix-fixe meal—with reservations. ♦ Polynesian ♦ M-Sa 11:30AM-1:30PM, 5-8:30PM; Su 10AM-1PM, 5-8:30PM. 901 Hausten St (S. King-Date Sts) Honolulu. 946.4808

89 Down to Earth Natural Foods Store
This well-stocked, natural foods store carries everything from fresh organic produce and Tom's of Maine Natural Spearmint Toothpaste to a fine selection of vegetarian vitamins, pastas, Indian chutneys, grains and nuts, greeting cards, health-conscious cosmetics, cheeses, and many things inexpensively sold in bulk. Adjoining the store is the **Natural Deli,** a vegetarian mecca with salads, chili, tabouleh, pastries, pastas, and hearty vegetarian plate lunches. Be sure to bring your own bag for groceries—it's de rigueur these days. ♦ Daily 8AM-10PM. 2525 S. King St, a block west of University Ave, Honolulu. 955.2479

Restaurants/Clubs: Red   Hotels: Blue
Shops/ 🍴 **Outdoors:** Green   **Sights/Culture:** Black

90 Maple Garden ★★$$$ This longtime favorite for spicy Mandarin and Szechuan cuisine is usually crowded and noisy with chatter and platter-clatter, but the food is worth it all. Specialties include eggplant with a hot spicy sauce, smoked Szechuan duck, and squid, chicken, and shrimp in a white sauce. ♦ Chinese ♦ M-Sa 11AM-2PM, 5:30-10PM; Su 5:30-10PM. 909 Isenberg St, three blocks west of University Ave, Honolulu. 941.6641

91 India Bazaar Madras Cafe ★★$ Great Indian food from a tiny take-out counter with a few tables. Make your own plate lunches of *dal* (lentil soup), curried vegetables, shrimp, or chicken, and an assortment of simple, savory dishes. ♦ Indian ♦ M-Sa 11AM-8:30PM. 2320 S. King St, Honolulu. 949.4840

92 Greek Island Taverna ★★$$$ A real sit-down Greek restaurant in busy little Moiliili. Opened in October 1983 by **Dimitrios** and **Georgia Nikolaou** (she's from Olympia, he's from Arta), this family-run inn comes complete with belly dancing, Greek folk dancing,

and fisher's hats on the walls. Feast on the *ami psito* (spring lamb baked with herbs and spices), the *souvlaki* (charcoal-broiled lamb kebabs), or *arneki nikos* (lamb, feta cheese, and vegetables baked within a filo pastry). At lunch, try a beef and lamb gyro or *mahimahi souvlaki* sandwich. Imported Greek beer, wines, and spirits available from the bar. ♦ Greek ♦ Tu-F 11AM-1:30PM, 7:30-10PM; Sa-Su 7:30-10PM. 2570 Beretania St (University Ave) Honolulu. 943.0052

93 Anna Bannana's ★$ In the sixties and seventies, this was a hangout for beer-guzzling students from the nearby university campus. You'll still see the occasional Harley-Davidson motorcycles parked out front of this unpretentious social pub that hosts serious dartboard tournaments and serves substantial Mexican food. Live reggae, blues, and rock music Wednesday through Sunday evenings upstairs (cover fee). Music by the **Pagan Babies,** Friday and Saturday nights. ♦ Mexican ♦ Daily 11:30AM-2AM, upstairs 9:15PM-2AM. 2440 S. Beretania St (University Ave) Honolulu. 946.5190

94 Manoa Valley Inn $$ This antique-furnished 1920s mansion and cottage is just a few miles outside of high-rise Waikiki in quiet Manoa Valley. Under the direction of preservationist **Rick Ralston,** the former owner, the two-story structure was designated an historical home and survived impending destruction. Ralston furnished the inn from his extensive collection of antiques and period furnishings. The present innkeepers, the **Nakamichi Corp.** (who purchased it in 1989), continue to offer patrons brass beds and Continental breakfasts, afternoon cheese and fruit, and other pleasant amenities. Choose one of seven bedrooms or the detached cottage. ♦ 2001 Vancouver Dr, Honolulu. 947.6019, 800/634.5115; fax 946.6168

95 Punahou School Hawaii's most famous private school opened in 1841 for the education of children whose parents were Congregationalist missionaries and Hawaiian *alii* (royalty). The grounds were donated by **Queen Kaahumanu,** King Kamehameha I's favorite wife and one of the mission's noteworthy converts. Punahou's alumni list reads like a Who's Who of Hawaii, and new generations of missionary descendants, joined by Honolulu's nouveau riche, perpetuate the exclusivity of the kindergarten through high school enrollment. ♦ 1601 Punahou St, Honolulu. 944.5711

96 King Tsin ★★$$ The **Joseph Wang** family oversees the marvelously creative kitchen specializing in spicy Szechuan dishes, particularly the beggar's chicken baked in clay pots. ♦ Chinese ♦ Daily 11AM-2PM, 5-9:30PM. 110 McCully St, Honolulu. 946.3273

97 King's Bakery and Coffee Shop ★$ Generally crowded because the food is good and affordable and it's cooked the way Islanders like it. Try their famous Portuguese bean soup, French toast, and baked goodies. Owner **Bob Taira** started with a tiny bakery in Hilo, became famous for his Portuguese sweet bread, expanded to this site in Honolulu, and now owns a big plant in Southern California where his famous King's Hawaiian Sweet Bread is baked and sold throughout the US. ♦ Hawaiian ♦ M-Th, Su 5AM-midnight; F-Sa 24 hours. 1936 S. King St, Honolulu. 941.5211

98 Hard Rock Cafe ★★$$ Like all the other Hard Rock Cafes, this is noisy and teeming with T-shirt buyers. It's all here, with an added twist; surfboards mixed in with the rock 'n' roll memorabilia (including John Lennon's Starfire 12 guitar). The carhop-style waitresses wear name tags, and the loud music never stops. A solid, all-American menu with Texas-style ribs, barbecued chicken, chili, sandwiches, apple pie, and strawberry shortcake. ♦ American ♦ M-Th, Su 11:30AM-11PM; F-Sa 11:30AM-11:30PM. 1837 Kapiolani Blvd, Honolulu. 955.7383

99 Ala Moana Beach Park Protected from rough water by an offshore reef, this beach is safe for swimming year-round. Picnic and public facilities, snack stand, and tennis courts. Lifeguards on duty during peak hours. ♦ Opposite the Ala Moana Shopping Mall, Honolulu

100 Ala Moana Shopping Mall The largest shopping center in the state, with more than 150 stores and restaurants on four levels, open-air malls, and carp-filled streams. When it opened in 1959, it was the largest shopping center in the world. Palm Boulevard is its snobby subsection, a mini-version of LA's Rodeo Drive, with **Chanel, Gucci, Escada, Dior, Cartier,** and **Emporio Armani.** Other stores include **The Nature Company, Sharper Image, Ralph Lauren, Laura Ashley, Adrienne Vittadini, Benetton,** and **Crazy Shirts,** a locally owned chain of T-shirt shops. **Liberty House,** the major local department store, anchors one end. Nearby is **Shirokiya,** a Japanese department store. ♦ M-Sa 9AM-9PM; Su 10AM-5PM. Bounded by Ala Moana and Kapiolani Blvds, Piikoi St, and Atkinson Dr, Honolulu

Within the Ala Moana Shopping Mall:

Makai Market $$ This carnival of fast-food eateries includes Sbarro's, for outstanding pizza; Yummy's, for Korean plate lunches; Patti's Chinese Kitchen, for Cantonese; and Panda's, for Szechuan fare. And there's much more. Japanese and Thai food takeout, Mexican, hot dogs, hamburgers, deli items, and baked potatoes and salads. ♦ Street level

Bryon II Steak House $$$ Steaks are the best items on the menu at this business-lunch hangout. It's the only true restaurant at the shopping center, and stays open after the stores have closed. ♦ Steak ♦ M-Th 11AM-10PM; F-Sa 11AM-11PM. 949.8855

Asian Palate $$ At lunch, waitresses walk through with selections of dim sum in little steamer baskets; take your pick, or select from the menu. ♦ Chinese ♦ Daily 10AM-9PM. 957.0088/0089

100 China House $$$ A fine place for lunch, dinner, or a banquet, this restaurant also has outstanding dim sum. You'll see local residents picking up white cake boxes of dim sum as takeout around lunchtime. ♦ Chinese ♦ M-F 10AM-9PM; Sa-Su 9AM-9PM. 1349 Kapiolani Blvd, Honolulu. 949.6622

100 Ala Moana Hotel $$$ The Ala Moana Hotel is 36 stories high, the tallest building in the state, linked by a footbridge to the Ala Moana Shopping Mall. Ala Moana Beach Park is across the street. Refrigerators upon request. ♦ 410 Atkinson Dr, Honolulu. 955.4811, 800/367.6025; fax 944.2974

Within the Ala Moana Hotel:

Royal Garden $$$ Waitresses serve dim sum from carts as you make your lunch choice. A popular place for dinner parties thrown by local Chinese-Americans. ♦ Chinese ♦ Daily 11AM-2PM, 5:30PM-5AM. Third floor. 942.7788

Nicholas Nickolas $$$$ Treat yourself to fabulous views of Waikiki while dining on steaks and an array of Island seafood (the fresh catch is always delicious). Among the hippest places in town, especially for dancing. ♦ Steak/Seafood ♦ M-F 5:30PM-2AM; Sa-Su 5:30PM-3AM. 36th floor. 955.4466

101 Cafe Cambio $$$ The creative menu focuses on pasta and antipasto, and the dining room is full of people enjoying good food and conversation in bright surroundings. A wall of scribbles and great thoughts spans the length of the restaurant and its handsome black marble bar. ♦ Italian ♦ Tu-F 11AM-2PM, 5:30-10:30PM; Sa-Su 5:30-10:30PM. 1680 Kapiolani Blvd, Honolulu. 942.0740

102 Sada Restaurant $$$ You can order off the menu, but most folks come for the sushi, prepared with the freshest fish and seafood. Several sushi bars and tatami rooms. ♦ Japanese ♦ M-Sa 11AM-2PM, 5PM-midnight; Su 5-11PM. 1473 S. King St, Honolulu. 949.0646

Oahu

103 Wisteria ★$$ A longtime local favorite; nothing fancy, just plenty of good Japanese (and some American) cooking at reasonable prices. Here's an opportunity to sample Japanese dishes without breaking the bank. Great for families, but don't try to get in on a Friday night without reservations. ♦ Japanese ♦ M-Th, Su 6AM-10:15PM; F-Sa 6AM-11:15PM. 1206 S. King St, Honolulu. 531.5276

103 Mekong I ★★★$$ This tiny restaurant, the first of a now well-established chain, offers a huge list of Thai specialties from the well-known family of **Keo Sananikone.** Mekong I is enormously successful, and known for the consistently good food. People who like glamour go to sister restaurant **Keo's** in Kapahulu; those who come here are strictly interested in the food. Curries, spring rolls, *satays,* Evil Jungle Prince—the choices are numerous. No alcohol, but you are welcome to bring beer or wine. ♦ Thai ♦ M-F 11AM-2PM, 5-9:30PM; Sa-Su 5-9:30PM. 1295 S. Beretania St, Honolulu. 521.2025

King Kalakaua was Hawaii's last king, the first monarch to sail around the world, and a man who unsuccessfully offered the hand of his niece, **Princess Kaiulani,** to the prince of Japan in 1881.

104 Auntie Pasto's $$ People don't seem to mind standing in line outside (and there is always a long line) for the inexpensive Italian food here. Country-style cuisine includes pasta seafood, eggplant parmesan, and veal marsala, the most expensive item on the menu. Red neon lights reflecting on orange walls, paddle fans, and the friendly kitchen clatter add to the casual atmosphere of this incredibly busy cafe. ◆ Italian ◆ M-Th 11AM-10:30PM; F 11AM-11PM; Sa 4-11PM; Su 4-10:30PM. 1099 S. Beretania St, Honolulu. 523.8855

105 Thomas Square Canopies of trees shade this inviting oasis between two busy streets, and the fountain provides a cooling respite for aching feet. Named for British **Admiral Richard Thomas,** who in 1843 returned Hawaii to King Kamehameha III on this exact site. (Several months earlier, an over-eager British officer had seized the Honolulu fort by force and raised Britannia's flag over it, declaring Hawaii under the empire's control. His superiors did not approve.) ◆ Between Beretania and King Sts, bounded by Ward Ave, Honolulu

106 Honolulu Academy of Arts This prestigious art center contains 30 galleries displaying world-renowned European and American masterpieces, the best of Hawaiian art, and a

permanent collection of oriental works. Landscaped courtyards filled with plants and sculptures are housed in the handsome, tile-roofed structure, which opened as a museum in 1927. The academy was founded by avid art collector **Mrs. Charles Montague Cooke,** whose family home had been on this site. New York architect **Bertram Goodhue** designed the structure, a blend of Hawaiian, oriental, and western styles. ◆ Donation requested. Tu-Sa 10AM-4:30PM; Su 1-5PM. 900 S. Beretania St, Honolulu. 538.3693

Within the Honolulu Academy of Arts:

Garden Cafe ★$$ A bright courtyard where you can lunch on tasty soups, salads, and sandwiches. The cafe is a fundraising venture for the academy, operated entirely by volunteers who often share favorite family recipes with the cafe. ◆ Tu-W, F seatings at 11:30AM and 1PM; Th 11:30AM, 1PM and 6:15PM (one menu item that corresponds with the movie at the academy that evening) 531.8865

Kinau Cafe ★$$ A coffee counter with sweets and light snacks, serving before and after the Friday and Saturday evening films. Volunteer-staffed, with outdoor tables for lingering moviegoers. ◆ F-Sa 7-7:30PM, after the movie until 10PM. 538.3693

107 Punchbowl Crater This dormant volcano's Hawaiian name is **Puowaina** or "Hill of Sacrifice." Centuries ago, human lives were sacrificed here to appease the gods. Now the crater's 114-acre floor—officially known as the **National Memorial Cemetery of the Pacific**—is the final resting place for veterans of WWI and WWII, the Korean and Vietnam wars, and the recent Persian Gulf War and their dependents. Some 34,000 white pillars line the velvet expanse in neat rows. The effect is powerful when the first rays of sun begin probing the rim of the crater at dawn, especially on Easter Sunday during the traditional sunrise service. **Ernie Pyle,** the WWII journalist, is buried here among the soldiers he so fondly immortalized. Also buried at Punchbowl is **Ellison Onizuka,** the astronaut from Hawaii who was killed in the Challenger Space Shuttle disaster in 1986. ◆ Free. Daily 8AM-6:30PM, 2 Mar-29 Sep; 8AM-5:30PM 30 Sep-1 Mar. 2177 Puowaina Dr, Honolulu. 541.1430

108 Neal S. Blaisdell Center Formerly the HIC (Honolulu International Center) and now known as the NBC, this $12.5 million complex for concerts, sports events, and conventions was renamed in the seventies for a popular Honolulu mayor, **Neal S. Blaisdell,** who served from 1955 to 1968. The 8,000-capacity arena plays host to basketball, boxing, and sumo wrestling events, as well as rock concerts, circus, and the Ice Capades. Blaisdell's 2,158-capacity concert hall is home of the Honolulu Symphony Orchestra. Ballet and major theatrical productions are also performed here. ◆ 777 Ward Ave, Honolulu. 538.7331

108 TGI Friday's $$ Directly across the street from the Blaisdell Center, Friday's is part of the mainland chain designed for adults who want to act like teenyboppers. A contrived circus atmosphere, assembly-line American food, and lots of single men and women. ◆ American ◆ Daily 11AM-midnight. In the Honolulu Club building, 950 Ward Ave, Honolulu. 523.5841

109 Hawaiian Bagel $ This modest bagel factory blends in with the rest of the small businesses in the Kakaako District, most of which are auto shops and warehouses. Bagels baked here are delivered to delis and restaurants all over the island. Sandwiches, quiches, and a limited selection of deli items are also available. ◆ M-Th 6:30AM-3:30PM; F 6AM-5:30PM; Sa 6AM-3PM. 753-B Halekauwila St, Honolulu. 523.8638

110 Columbia Inn ★$$ Every city has a media bar and this is Honolulu's. Located next door to the News Building, which houses both of the state's daily newspapers, the bar is filled with journalists and flacks and cluttered with sports memorabilia. The original Columbia Inn opened the day the Japanese bombed Pearl Harbor, and survived to become a popular spot in spite of subsequent changes in ownership. The menu is mixed, from basic American to Japanese plus assorted local favorites such as peach Bavarian cake, sizzling steak platter, and teriyaki dishes. ♦ Japanese/American ♦ M-Sa 6AM-12:30AM; Su 6AM-11:30PM. 645 Kapiolani Blvd, Honolulu. 531.3747

111 Ward Centre This trendy shopping mall on the Diamond Head side of Ward Warehouse has restaurants and fast-food eateries upstairs and shops downstairs. ♦ M-F 10AM-9PM; Sa 10AM-5PM; Su 11AM-4PM. 1200 Ala Moana Blvd, Honolulu

Within the Ward Centre:

Keo's Thai Cuisine $$$ An offshoot of **Keo Sananikone's** restaurant dynasty in Honolulu. You can dine in air-conditioning or in the open-air courtyard amid orchids and Thai art. The menu offers a limited selection compared to his popular Kapahulu establishment, but it's still a pleasant place to enjoy Evil Jungle Prince (a popular selection), spring rolls, or spicy curries. ♦ Thai ♦ M-Sa 11AM-10:30PM; Su 5-10PM. 533.0533/0534

Honolulu Chocolate Company For chocoholics and sweets lovers or anyone looking for whimsical food gifts. The owners, who have stores in several other locations, have filled their largest shop with toys, boxes for giftgiving, holiday gifts, preserves and teas, as well as sinful chocolates such as apricots or ginger dipped in white, dark, or milk chocolate, truffles, liqueur-flavored cordials, macadamia or pecan turtles, and much more. ♦ M-Sa 10AM-10PM; Su 10AM-6PM. 531.2997

Il Fresco ★$$$ The original owners had a reputation for very good California-style dining, but the quality doesn't seem to be holding under new ownership. Specialties include *ahi* pasta and grilled eggplant with chili peppers and goat cheese. The pizzas are popular, and among the outstanding desserts is a decadent chocolate cake with raspberry coulis. ♦ California ♦ M-F 11:30AM-2PM, 6-10PM; Sa-Su 6-10PM. First level. 523.5191

Big Ed's Deli $$ Hefty Dagwood-style sandwiches are Big Ed's specialty. This is really a restaurant with a take-out counter. ♦ Deli ♦ M-Th, Su 7AM-10PM; F-Sa 7AM-11PM. First level. 536.4591

Mary Catherine's Bakery One of Honolulu's finest bakeries, whether you're looking for a chocolate cake, heart-shaped cookies (try the Ishler Hearts, two cookies with raspberry preserves between them, dipped in chocolate), or breakfast pastries (the scones and croissants are exceptional). You can enjoy a cup of coffee or cappuccino with dessert at one of the patio tables. ♦ M-Th 7AM-9PM; F-Sa 7AM-10PM; Su 7AM-5PM. 521.3525

Andrew's ★$$$ Local residents come here for the Italian food and generous servings. The best buy is the complete dinner, which includes a respectable minestrone soup, salad, and dessert. The traditional Italian menu offers a wide selection of seafood, veal, and chicken. Part of the **Orson's** family of restaurants. ♦ Italian ♦ M-Tu, Su 11AM-10PM; W-Sa 11AM-11PM. Second level. 523.8677

Compadres Mexican Bar and Grill $$ A good place to enjoy a pitcher of margaritas with complimentary tortilla chips and salsa. A few Island fish dishes have been slipped onto the basically Mexican menu, and you can't go wrong ordering items such as the all-American burger and the *pollo* burger (broiled chicken sandwich), which come with a huge pile of Maui chips. ♦ Mexican ♦ Daily 11AM-midnight. Second level. 523.3914

Ryan's Parkplace Bar & Grill $$ A fun singles bar, with a wide beer selection and fresh oyster shooters. Extremely popular for the affordable menu, which includes fish,

salads, and pastas as well as appetizers. ♦ M-Th, Su 11AM-10PM; F-Sa 11AM-11PM. Reservations recommended. Second level. 523.9132

Hail to the Chiefs

In 1796, after years of civil war, the Hawaiian Islands were united under Kamehameha the Great. His ascension to the throne gave birth to a dynasty that would last nearly a century and forever change the way of life of his subjects. After his death in 1819 he was succeeded by seven monarchs, the last of which was Queen Liliuokalani, the first female ruler of Hawaii, who was overthrown in 1893. For more on the Hawaiian monarchy, see "History" on page 168.

Kamehameha I (1796-1819)
Kamehameha II (1819-24)
Kamehameha III (1825-54)
Kamehameha IV (1855-63)
Kamehameha V (1863-72)
William C. Lunalilo (1873-74)
David Kalakaua (1874-91)
Liliuokalani (1891-93)

Kamehameha the Great

112 Ward Warehouse This two-story wooden-style mall includes family restaurants (everything from pizza, sandwiches, seafood, and fish), and boutiques and specialty stores. ♦ M-F 10AM-9PM; Sa 10AM-5PM; Su 11AM-4PM. Ala Moana Blvd and Ward Ave, Honolulu. 531.6411

Within the Ward Warehouse:

Orson's $$$ A popular business-lunch restaurant that serves hot sourdough bread with its seafood dishes. ♦ Seafood ♦ Daily 11AM-10PM. Reservations recommended. 521.5681

Chowder House ★$$ Owned by the same family that operates Orson's, this quick casual eatery offers chowder, salads, and sandwiches. Great fresh fish sandwiches. ♦ Seafood ♦ M-Th, Su 11AM-9:30PM; F-Sa 11AM-10:30PM. 521.5681

Horatio's $$ A good selection of fresh fish at very affordable prices. You can also order soup, salad, or pasta. Don't pass up the Burnt Creme (their special crème brûlée) or the pies. ♦ American ♦ M-Th 11AM-9:30PM; F-Sa 11AM-10PM; Su 5-9:30PM. 521.5002

Dynasty II Restaurant $$$ Fabulous food in an elegant setting with rosewood furniture and pink tablecloths. There are two Dynasty restaurants, the other a smaller and simpler establishment, so don't confuse these when making reservations. ♦ Chinese ♦ Daily 11AM-2PM, 5:30-10PM. 531.0208. Also at: 1830 Ala Moana Blvd. 947.3771

Oahu

Nohea Gallery An eclectic gallery filled with crafts by Island artists. You'll find Japanese-influenced woodblocks by Hiroki Morinoue, watercolors by Barbara Britts, and woodwork by Ron Kent. Also ceramics, sculpture, glasswork, prints, wearable art, and jewelry. ♦ M-F 9AM-9PM; Sa 9AM-6PM; Su 10:30AM-5PM. 599.7927

Pomegranates in the Sun Innovative Island clothing and jewelry designs, as well as a small selection of children's clothing. ♦ M-Sa 10AM-6PM; Su 11AM-4PM. 531.1899

112 Pearl Harbor Tours The three-hour cruises from Kewalo Basin, the hub of the Honolulu fishing fleet, follow the coastline, sailing slowly through Pearl Harbor. The cruises include narrations on the details of Japanese bombing raids on 7 December 1941, but you won't be able to tour the **Arizona Memorial** unless you take the Navy tour (see page 142). ♦ Admission. Pearl Harbor cruise daily 9:30AM and 12:30PM. 536.3641

According to *The New York Times,* Hawaii is America's leading consumer of Spam, a canned meat.

Restaurants/Clubs: Red   **Hotels:** Blue
Shops/ ☂ Outdoors: Green   **Sights/Culture:** Black

113 John Dominis ★★$$$$
Spectacularly located on a point in Kewalo Basin, the floor-to-ceiling windows showcase an exceptional view of the sea and the sunset. A fabulous, albeit high-priced place for Sunday brunch, with chefs preparing omelets, pastas, or waffles to order at different bars. Loyal customers return for the selection of fish and seafood. ♦ Seafood ♦ M-Sa 5:30-10PM; Su 9AM-1PM, 5:30-10PM. 43 Ahui St, off Ala Moana Blvd, Honolulu. 523.0955

114 Royal Brewery People have been trying to tear down this old (circa 1900) redbrick building for years; others are equally determined to keep it up. The local Primo beer was once brewed here, but the building is now unoccupied. ♦ 533 S. Queen St, Honolulu

115 News Building Home of the two daily papers in the state, this green three-story stone building with a red-tile roof is also a museum and gallery. Contemporary art is displayed throughout the building. The **Twigg-Smith** family runs *The Honolulu Advertiser*, the morning newspaper, and **Gannett Corp.** owns the *Honolulu Star-Bulletin,* the afternoon paper. ♦ 605 Kapiolani Blvd, Honolulu. 525.8000

115 Yanagi Sushi ★★★$$$ Yanagi serves some of the freshest sashimi and best sushi in Hawaii. This shoji-screened restaurant packs in locals as well as American and Japanese tourists. Photos and autographs of celebs who've eaten here cover the walls. ♦ Japanese ♦ Daily 11AM-2PM, 5:30PM-2AM; Su 11AM-2PM, 5-10PM. 762 Kapiolani Blvd, Honolulu. 537.1525

116 Restaurant Row One of the *in* places for discriminating singles and yuppies, thanks to its selection of trendy restaurants and bars near the Honolulu waterfront. ♦ Between South St and Ala Moana Blvd, Honolulu

Within Restaurant Row:

Sunset Grill $$$ This high-ceilinged, airy restaurant can get noisy, but it's extremely popular, especially for lunch. The menus offer a pleasant selection of pastas, salads, grilled fish, and meat. Appetizers are hard to resist, especially the mozzarella cakes, Anaheim peppers, and roasted garlic and goat cheese. And if you've room for dessert, try the deep-dish fruit pie or an ice cream concoction. Sunday brunch is bright and cheery with egg selections, waffles, pancakes, and pastas. ♦ California ♦ M-Th 11:30AM-10PM; F-Sa 11:30AM-midnight; Su 10AM-3PM, 3-10PM. Reservations recommended. 521.4409

Black Orchid $$$$ Some are overwhelmed by the stylish Art Deco interiors, but the space has been nicely divided so that diners eat in different rooms. The food can be inconsistent, although fish is generally a good choice. The black-and-blue *ahi,* pan-seared rare and Cajun style, is spicy and tasty. Sinful dessert choices for sweets lovers. The lounge serves a late-night menu. ◆ California ◆ M-Th 11AM-2PM, 6-10PM; F 11AM-2PM, 6PM-midnight; Sa 6PM-midnight; Su 6-10PM. 521.3111

Rose City Diner $$ The decor, jukebox, and framed photos of fifties heartthrobs are lots of fun, but don't expect more from the malt-shop menu than hamburgers and milk shakes. ◆ American ◆ M-Th, Su 7AM-midnight; F-Sa 7AM-2AM. 524.7673

Ruth's Chris Steak House $$$ If you're happiest eating steak, this place won't let you down. The steaks are tender, succulent, and sizzling when they arrive at your table. Everything is à la carte, so dinner can get pricey. ◆ Steak ◆ M-Th 11AM-3PM, 5-10PM; F-Sa 11AM-3PM, 5-10:30PM; Su 5-10PM. 599.3860

117 Honolulu Hale *Hale* means "house" in Hawaiian; Honolulu Hale, built in 1929, simply means Honolulu City Hall. The building's gracious California Spanish-style design (pictured above and below) stands out next to Iolani Palace, the State Capitol, and neighbor-

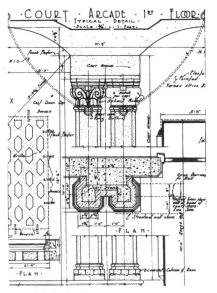

Honolulu Hale, Court Arcade

ing state buildings. The terra-cotta tile, open-ceiling courtyard is patterned after the 13th-century Bargello Palace in Florence, Italy. Italian sculptor **Mario Valdastri** designed the bronze-sheeted front doors weighing 1,500 pounds each, the 4,500-pound chandeliers in the courtyard, and the columns and balconies made of coral and crushed Hawaiian sandstone. Two three-story wings in the original style were added to Honolulu Hale in the early 1950s. A belt of green space links it to the colonial-style **Mission Memorial** buildings and the gray concrete **Honolulu Municipal Building.** ◆ M-F 7:45AM-4:30PM. 530 S. King St, Honolulu. 523.4385

117 Skygate **Isamu Noguchi's** sculpture was unveiled in 1977 as a public work of art for the green belt between Honolulu Hale and the municipal building. Then, people moaned and chuckled; it was hardly a popular piece. Now, however, the 15-ton, 24-foot-high black steel abstract form has been assimilated, if not accepted. Families picnic under its arches, and on special occasions, concerts are held nearby. ◆ Off S. King St

117 Kawaiahao Church and King Lunalilo's Tomb This church is to Honolulu what the Old North Church is to Boston. Completed in 1842, some 22 years after the first New England missionaries arrived aboard the ship *Thaddeus.* The handsome structure took five years to build, using 14,000 coral blocks that the congregation cut from ocean reefs. The

walls of *Kawaiahao,* which means "freshwater pool of Hao" (the ancient spring), have witnessed royal marriages, coronations, and funerals. The 10:30AM Sunday service is noted for its stirring sermons, first-rate choir, and organ music. **King Lunalilo's Tomb** is near the entrance to the church. He is the only Hawaiian monarch who refused to be interred in the Royal Mausoleum in Nuuanu Valley, requesting on his deathbed to be buried closer to his people at Kawaiahao. The churchyard is the cemetery for several missionaries and converts. ◆ Sunday services conducted in English and Hawaiian. Visitors usually welcome to tour the church following the 10:30AM Sunday service. 957 Punchbowl St (S. King St) Honolulu. 538.6267

117 Mission Houses Museum The first frame house in the Islands, built in 1821 for the newly arrived Congregationalist missionaries suffering from culture shock. Soon after, two coral-block buildings were added to the prim, white-frame structure. One, the **Coral House,** is where printer **Elisha Loomis,** had Hawaii's first press. The other, the **Chamberlain House,** was for the mission's purchasing agent. Now operated as a museum by the **Hawaiian Mission Children's Society** (descendants of the missionaries), Mission

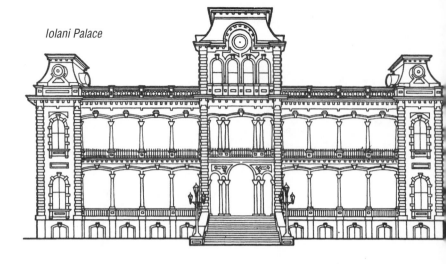

Iolani Palace

Houses is a repository of mementos from the state's early history. ♦ Admission includes guided tour. Tu-Sa 9AM-4PM; Su noon-4PM. 953 S. King St, Honolulu. 531.0481

118 Iolani Palace America's only royal palace will give you booties to cover your shoes to upkeep highly polished Douglas fir floors scuff-free. The palace epitomizes **King Kalakaua's** preoccupation with emulating the royal courts of Europe. Aptly called "The Merry Monarch," his penchant for surround-

ing himself with material goods was unsurpassed by Hawaiian kings and queens. Iolani, which means "the hawk of heaven," was completed in 1882, eight years after Kalakaua was crowned king, for $360,000. The Florentine design, the work of architects **Thomas J. Baker, Isaac Moore,** and **C.J. Wall,** was the perfect backdrop for Kalakaua's elaborate court life. The palace was filled with period furniture shipped around Cape Horn or painstakingly copied by local craftsmen. Royal guards were outfitted in dazzling uniforms that weighed entirely too much for the tropics, and he and his wife, **Queen Kapiolani,** entertained on a grand scale. Following Kalakaua's death in 1891 and the coup that toppled **Queen Liliuokalani** and the monarchy in 1893, the palace became Hawaii's seat of government. Until 1969, when the new State Capitol was built, the Senate met in the palace's royal dining room and the House of Representatives in the throne room. Since then, some $6 million has been spent restoring the palace to its former glory. The nonprofit **Friends of Iolani Palace** conducts 45-minute tours. ♦ Admission. Tours W-Sa 9AM-2:15 PM every 15 minutes. Reservations recommended. King and Richards Sts, Honolulu. 522.0822

118 Iolani Banyan This massive tree is really two banyans that have been intertwined for a century. Said to have been planted by **Queen Kapiolani,** the banyan's arched branches provide a shady canopy for passersby. ♦ Located in the parking lot between Iolani Palace and the State Archives Building

118 King Kamehameha I Statue King Kamehameha I, who conquered and then united the Islands into one kingdom, is regarded as Hawaii's greatest warrior. This statue of him is outside **Aliiolani Hale** (the State Judiciary Building) on S. King St across from Iolani Palace. The gold-and-black monument of the spear-carrying chief wearing a feather cloak and helmet is often photographed, and during the annual **King Kamehameha Day** celebration in June, dozens of 30-foot leis are layered over his outstretched arms. This statue is a replica; however, the original stands in front of the **Kapaau Courthouse** in Kohala on the Big Island, where Kamehameha was born, raised, and first came to power. ♦ 417 S. King St, Honolulu

118 Queen Liliuokalani Statue Hawaii's last monarch is memorialized in a bronze sculpture unveiled in 1982 at the entrance to the State Capitol near Iolani Palace, where she was imprisoned following her overthrow. The eight-foot statue by Boston artist **Marianne Pineda** shows the queen standing erect, her left hand holding the proposed constitution of 1893 that cost her the throne, and a page of the composition to "Aloha Oe," the Islands' traditional song of farewell. Her right hand is extended in friendship. ♦ S. Beretania, between Punchbowl and Richards Sts, Honolulu

---

Oahu's **Iolani Palace** was the first building in Hawaii to have an electric light system and an in-house telephone, and it was the first palace in the world to have flush toilets.

119 Coronation Bandstand King Kalakaua wanted a fitting site for his coronation, so in 1883 he built this gazebo and crowned himself and **Queen Kapiolani** in a lavish ceremony. The copper dome of the wedding cake-like pavilion is the original, but termites weakened the rest of the structure and it was rebuilt of concrete. Eight pillars symbolizing Hawaii's eight major islands support the dome. While Kalakaua was the only king crowned here, the bandstand occasionally serves as a stage for gubernatorial inaugurations, and also for weddings. Each Friday the **Royal Hawaiian Band,** established in 1836 by King Kamehameha II and now part of the local governments, gives free concerts at noon. ♦ On the grounds of Iolani Palace, between S. King and Richards Sts, Honolulu

119 State Capitol The capitol was designed to take advantage of the views of the ocean, city, and mountains, including an atrium that rises four floors so that the sky's natural light fills the center of the structure. Some Hawaiian touches include the koa wood used for interior trim, paneling, and furnishings; the Molokai sand used in paving the courtyard; and the sign on the governor's double doors that says *E komo mai* (Please come in). The state legislature and the governor moved into the dramatic $24.5 million building in 1969, after being headquartered in Iolani Palace. Visitors are free to sit in on regular sessions of the Senate and the House of Representatives from January through April. While the laws of parliamentary procedure are followed, proper English crumbles in favor of local pidgin (Hawaiian slang) during heated arguments on the floor. The capitol's most festive occasion is the traditional opening of the legislature the third Wednesday of every January. On that day the capitol overflows with flowers and leis on the legislators and their desks. Morning festivities include hula, song, and even comedy, by leading Island entertainers. At noon, everyone adjourns to lavish buffets. ♦ Courtyard: 24 hours. Elevators: M-F 8AM-4:30PM. Bounded by S. Beretania, Punchbowl, and Richards Sts, Honolulu. 548.2211

119 Father Damien Statue Belgian priest **Damien Joseph de Veuster,** who lived and worked among the lepers of Molokai for 16 years before dying of the disease in 1889, is memorialized in this bronze statue by **Marisol Escobar.** When the statue was selected and unveiled, it ignited a great deal of public unhappiness because of its unusual treatment of the priest, who has since been nominated for sainthood. The statue captures Father Damien in his last days, when he was a victim of leprosy. It depicts a short, squat man with a cape and brimmed clerical hat, his features deformed and bloated. ♦ State Capitol courtyard, Honolulu

119 Washington Place The state governor lives in this stately white mansion, named after George Washington by a US commissioner who once rented rooms here. An American sea captain built the home in 1846 and soon after was lost at sea. His son, **John Dominis,** then moved into the mansion with his wife, **Lydia Kapaakea,** the future **Queen Liliuokalani.** After Dominis' death and the overthrow of the monarchy in 1893 (see "History", page 168), Liliuokalani returned to Washington Place, where she lived until her death in 1917. Most of the first floor of the two-story residence has been restored to look as it did then, and is often used for hosting state receptions. Past governors have hosted dinners here for visiting dignitaries, including **Queen Elizabeth,** the late emperor of Japan, and US presidents. The upstairs rooms are private quarters for the governor and his family. ♦ Not open to the public. S. Beretania St, across from the State Capitol, Honolulu

119 St. Andrew's Cathedral King Kamehameha IV converted to the Church of England shortly after the traumatic death of his four-year-old son, **Albert,** and founded St. Andrew's in 1862. The king died a year later at age 29. Construction on this Episcopalian headquarters in Hawaii began in 1867 under the direction of his widow, **Queen Emma.** The uniformed students on the premises go to St. Andrew's Priory, at the back of the cathedral. ♦ Daily 6:30AM-6PM. Queen Emma Sq, between S. Beretania and Alakea Sts, Honolulu. 524.2822

King Kamehameha V and Prince Lunalilo were both bachelors when they died.

State Capitol

120 Honpa Hongwanji This pristine, white temple at the entrance to Nuuanu Valley is the headquarters for the Islands' Buddhist congregations. In summer, beginning in June, *obon* dance festivals are held at the various Buddhist temples throughout the state. These ceremonies to honor the dead welcome people of all ages, and even visitors dance to the beat of the Japanese drums and folk songs. The temple grounds assume a carnival atmosphere during the festivals, with food and crafts for sale. Each year, Honpa Hongwanji hosts one of the larger *obon* dances on Friday and Saturday evenings in June. ♦ 1727 Pali Hwy, Honolulu. 536.7044

121 Alexander Cartwright Tomb The man who invented baseball died in Honolulu on 12 July 1892. His pink granite tomb is in **Oahu Cemetery.** Cartwright didn't play in the first baseball game (held 19 June 1846, between the New York Knickerbockers and the New York Nine in Hoboken, New Jersey) but he was the umpire. Later, during a trip, Cartwright became so enamored of Honolulu, he moved here. He taught baseball and founded the city's first volunteer fire department. **Cartwright Playground** in Makiki, where it is said he laid out Hawaii's first baseball diamond, is named after him. ♦ Oahu Cemetery, 2162 Nuuanu Ave, Honolulu

122 Royal Mausoleum The most important burial place in the Islands, containing the remains of **King Kamehamehas II** through **V,**

King Kalakaua, Queen Liliuokalani, and other royalty and favored friends of their courts. King Kamehameha I's bones are the only ones missing from his dynasty. The warrior chief's remains have never been

Royal Mausoleum

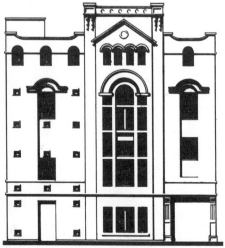

discovered, though historians presume they're hidden in secret burial caves on the Big Island, where he died in 1891. The other Hawaiian monarch who was not buried here is **King Lunalilo,** who requested a private tomb on the grounds of Kawaiahao Church (see page 127). King Kamehameha V selected the mausoleum's three-acre site in 1865, and royal remains were transferred from an old, overcrowded tomb on the Iolani Palace grounds. The cross-shaped chapel was designed by Hawaii's first professional architect, **Theodore Heuck.** ♦ Free. M-F 8AM-4:30PM. 2261 Nuuanu Ave, Honolulu. 536.7602

123 Queen Emma Summer Palace This cool summer retreat in Nuuanu Valley was owned by **Queen Emma** and her husband, **King Kamehameha IV.** When the **Duke of Edinburgh** visited Hawaii in 1869, Emma had the elegant Edinburgh Room built to accommodate a lavish gala for him (unfortunately, he missed the party). The palace was purchased by the Hawaiian government in 1890, after Emma's death, and has been maintained as a museum by the Daughters of Hawaii since 1915. The grand rooms contain many personal belongings of the royal family, including the koa wood cradle of Emma and Kamehameha's son, **Albert,** heir to the throne and Queen Victoria's godson, who died at the age of four. The palace is easily visible from the Nuuanu Pali Hwy. ♦ Admission. Daily 9AM-4PM. 2913 Pali Hwy, Honolulu. 595.3167

124 Cathedral of Our Lady of Peace New England missionaries dominated the Christian enlightenment of the Hawaiians for several decades, leaving little room for competition. The first Catholic priests arrived in 1827 from France, but it was not until 1843 that opposition to Catholicism had died down and this cathedral could be dedicated. It was here, three years later, that the first pipe organ on the Islands was played. ♦ Daily 5:30AM-6:30PM. Located on the *mauka* (mountain) end of Fort St Mall, next to Beretania St, Honolulu. 536.7036

125 Yong Sing $$ Lunch conversations bounce off the high ceiling of this popular and crowded Chinese restaurant. The extensive menu includes outstanding dim sum (Chinese dumplings of beef, pork, and seafood). ♦ Chinese ♦ Daily 9AM-9PM. 1055 Alakea St, Honolulu. 531.1366

126 Croissanterie $$ For a quick croissant sandwich or quiche and salad, try this open-air cafe in downtown Honolulu's business district. They also serve espresso, cappuccino, and other coffee drinks. ♦ M-Th 6AM-8PM; F 6AM-11PM; Sa. 7AM-4PM. 222 Merchant St, Honolulu. 533.3443

Restaurants/Clubs: Red   Hotels: Blue
Shops/🌳 Outdoors: Green   Sights/Culture: Black

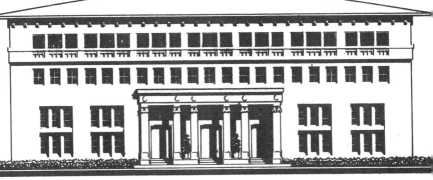

Alexander & Baldwin Building

126 Alexander & Baldwin Building This distinctive headquarters opened in 1929, a memorial to **Samuel T. Alexander** and **Henry P. Baldwin,** founders of the youngest of the Big Five companies. (Until Hawaii became a state, the Islands were ruled economically by a group of corporations known as the Big Five: Alexander & Baldwin, C. Brewer & Company, Theo. H. Davis & Company, Amfac Inc., and Castle & Cooke Inc.) Architects **C.W. Dickey** and **Hart Wood** designed the structure with Dickey's trademark Hawaiian roof (a double-pitched roof with a high peak and low, widespread eaves); the subtle Chinese influence was Wood's signature. At the time, it was one of only two Honolulu buildings made completely of concrete and steel. Critics praised its excellent workmanship and unique details, including the murals, terracotta ornamentation, and black Belgian marble in the first-floor reception area. A second-floor floating mezzanine has since been added, but many of the original details remain. ♦ 822 Bishop St, Honolulu

127 Tamarind Park This green, open space fronts the Pauahi Tower at Bishop Square, with a reflecting pool that's a popular place to brown bag and listen to the music performed at frequent noontime concerts. **Henry Moore's** *Upright Motive No. 9*, an 11-foot bronze statue in the reflecting pool, was executed in 1979 and cast in six editions. Loosely derived from the human figure, it draws its inspiration from the prehistoric monoliths at Stonehenge, North American Indian totem poles, and Polynesian sculpture pieces. ♦ Bishop St (between Hotel and King Sts) Honolulu

127 C. Brewer Building
Constructed in 1930, this last and smallest of the Big Five offices built in downtown Honolulu, looks more like a mansion than a corporate office. Chief architect **Hardie Phillips** gave

the two-story structure a Mediterranean flavor with Hawaiian motifs, most notably the double-pitched tile roof with a wide overhang, commonly referred as the "Dickey," or Hawaiian roof. Modest details include wrought-iron railings and grillwork that represent sugarcane, and light fixtures designed to recall the form of sugar cubes. ♦ 827 Fort St, Honolulu

128 Aloha Tower Passengers who sailed Matson steamships to Hawaii decades ago will remember this as an imposing architectural landmark, probably because it was the tallest building on the waterfront. But the 10-story, 184-foot tower, designed in 1921

by **Arthur Reynolds,** has long since been dwarfed by the high-rise, steel-and-glass structures in downtown Honolulu. ♦ Pier 9, adjacent to Irwin Park and Nimitz Hwy, Honolulu. 537.9260

128 Hawaii Maritime Center This museum traces the role of the sea in Island life, from Polynesian migration by canoe to the Islands, to the whaling and commercial fishing days and the era of Matson steamships. The ship docked outside, *Falls of Clyde,* is part of the tour. ♦ Admission. Daily 9AM-8PM. Honolulu Harbor, Pier 7, Honolulu. 536.6373

C. Brewer Building

At the Hawaii Maritime Center:

Falls of Clyde This full-rigged, four-masted ship, the last of its kind in the world, used to sail into Honolulu Harbor more than a century ago, when the docks were lined with similar square-rigged wooden vessels, and sailors could virtually step from one ship to another. Built in Scotland, it was purchased in 1898 by the Matson cruise line and used on the route between San Francisco and Hawaii. Now the *Falls of Clyde* is a restored museum and a popular site for private parties.

129 Chinatown Galleries Art came to Chinatown hand in hand with the gentrification of the neighborhood. Low rents and interesting storefronts and spaces attracted gallery owners, and there are a number of art galleries clustered within several blocks of Nuuanu Ave. Some favorites include:

Waterfall Gallery Folk art from Bali and Thailand, with puppets, sculpture, masks, and paintings that photographer **William Waterfall** has gathered on his travels through Asia. The collection features cases of Thai silver jewelry and hand-tinted photographs of turn-of-the-century Hawaii. Prices range from a few dollars into the thousands. ♦ M-F 10AM-5PM; Sa 11AM-4PM. 1160-A Nuuanu Ave, Honolulu. 521.6863

Pegge Hopper Gallery One of Hawaii's best-known artist, Hopper's trademark is huge Hawaiian women painted in Paul Gauguin colors. Their various poses create a feel-

ing of calm serenity. You can also buy novelty items of her work, including greeting cards, calendars, and T-shirts. A small, koa-framed print might sell for about $75. ♦ M-F 10AM-5PM; Sa 11AM-3PM. 1164 Nuuanu Ave, Honolulu. 524.1160

Lai Fong Inc. This isn't really a gallery, but a bit of nostalgia in the heart of gallery row. You could easily mistake Lai Fong's for a musty thrift shop, with the Chinese bric-a-brac from who knows when. But real treasures lurk in the store's shadows: carved jade buttons, cheongsams (fitted Chinese dresses), funky ivory jewelry from pre-statehood days, and garish Chinese statues of folk gods. ♦ M-Sa 10AM-4:30PM. 1118 Nuuanu Ave, Honolulu. 537.3497

Gateway Gallery This whimsical, colorful gallery features contemporary artists, many of them from Hawaii. Among the art that's most fun is co-owner **Shirley Reo Beene's** furniture. You'll also find wearable art, jewelry, paintings, and sculpture. ♦ M-Sa 11AM-5:30PM. 1050 Nuuanu Ave, Honolulu. 599.1559

Honolulu's **Great Chinatown Fire** of 20 January 1900 was started by the Board of Health to control bubonic plague. The fire whipped out of control, destroying 38 acres and leaving 4,000 people homeless.

129 Hotel Street Although gentrification is fast on its heels, Hawaii's version of skid row still occupies a few seedy blocks of this downtown street. Hotel Street's reputation, however, isn't what it was during WWII, as is documented in James Jones' novel *From Here to Eternity*, when servicemen frequented the area's red-light establishments. You can still buy a cold beer at any of the Hotel Street bars and there are still ladies of the night on the street corners, but the city is making an effort to clean up the area (as is indicated by a police station on one of the side streets). Restaurants and groceries operated namely by new immigrants from Southeast Asia are replacing the bars and X-rated businesses. ♦ Hotel St (between Bishop and River Sts) Honolulu

130 Foster Botanic Gardens This fertile, 20-acre domain of greenery is a tranquil setting at the edge of downtown Honolulu. Feel free to picnic and wander the grounds, enjoying the orchid gallery and other plant pleasures (4,000 species of tropical flora are represented here). ♦ Admission. Daily 9AM-4PM. Tours W 1PM. Call for reservations. 180 N. Vineyard Blvd, Honolulu. 522.7060

131 Chinatown In 1900 a fire was intentionally started to stop the spread of bubonic plague from a group of shacks in Chinatown. Instead, the wind-whipped blaze razed most of the area. From its ashes rose a new Chinatown of two-story wooden buildings with Chinese-operated laundries, grocery stores, bakeries, and tailor and herb shops on the first floors (the families lived upstairs). The first Chinese arrived in Hawaii around 1850 as contract laborers for sugar plantations. Those who stayed saved their money and started their own businesses. Within 10 years, 60 percent of the stores in downtown Honolulu were owned by *pakes* (pah-KAYS), as Hawaiians called the Chinese. Some of the wealthiest people in Hawaii today are among their descendants. Chinatown's population has never been pure Chinese, however. Its multiracial complexion includes Filipinos, Hawaiians, and a recent influx of Vietnamese and Laotian refugees. Urban renewal has recently given the area—bounded by Nuuanu Ave, Beretania and River Sts, and the Nimitz Hwy—a face-lift, although the lived-in look is far from gone. Seedy bars, pool halls, and rooming houses aren't as plentiful as the noodle factories, open-air markets, herb shops, bakeries, clothing and jewelry stores, and restaurants. Rather than randomly exploring the streets of Chinatown, you might want to take a walking tour, an entertaining and informative way to absorb the ethnic flavor.
♦ A few groups that give tours are: **Hawaii Heritage Center** (fee) F 9:30AM; 12:30PM from 1128 Smith St, 521.2749; **Chinatown Historic Society,** M-F 10AM; 1PM, 521.3045; and **Chinese Chamber of Commerce** (fee) Tu 9:30AM, 42 N. King St. Reservations required. 533.3181

131 Ba-le Sandwich Shop 1 ★★$ Some of the best French baguettes in the Islands (and great French coffee, too) are made and sold by the Vietnamese owners of the Ba-le concessions around Honolulu. This little coffee shop is its headquarters, which serves Vietnamese dim sum, spring rolls, noodle dishes, and sandwiches that hint of the flavors of Saigon. ♦ Daily 5AM-7PM. 150 N. King St, Honolulu. 521.3973

131 Maunakea Street Lei Stands Along a few short blocks on Maunakea St you'll find little storefronts selling leis, with workrooms behind the large refrigerated flower cases. The scent of carnation, maile, ginger, pikake, and tuberose fill the air as women string the leis with long, thin needles. Leis are sold all over the Islands, but these are some of the best prices and selections. **Cindy's Lei Shoppe,** 1034 Maunakea St, is a landmark (Cindy has been here for a couple of generations). Other recommended shops on Oahu are **Lita's Leis,** 59 N. Beretania St; **Aloha Leis and Flowers,** 1145 Maunakea St; and **Janet's** and **Sweetheart's,** on Beretania St near Maunakea St

131 Wo Fat $$ This architectural landmark in Chinatown is Hawaii's oldest restaurant, established in 1882. It used to be the choice restaurant for banquets and celebrations among the Chinese community, but its heyday has passed. It's still worth a try for lunch or dinner, especially if you're an experienced expert at ordering from a Cantonese menu. ♦ Chinese ♦ Daily 10:30AM-9PM. 115 N. Hotel St, Honolulu. 533.6393

131 Wong and Wong Restaurant ★★$$ Some wonderful down-home cooking comes from this small and modest restaurant. The trick is to order from signs on the walls touting the specials. The steamed fish, especially the mullet, is deliciously prepared Chinese-style with a soy sauce, ginger, and green onion sauce. You may be able to walk right in at lunchtime, but dinner reservations are a good idea. ♦ Chinese ♦ Daily 10AM-2AM. 1023 Maunakea St, Honolulu. 521.4492

131 Doong Kong Lau-Hakka Restaurant ★★$$ The food's as superb as the surroundings are simple. *Hakka* cuisine isn't as spicy as Szechuan but it's just as tasty. Some of the more popular selections are served on sizzling platters. ♦ Chinese ♦ Daily 8AM-9:30PM. 100 N. Beretania St, Suite 111. Chinese Cultural Plaza, Honolulu. 531.8833

In the early 1930s, tourists asked tailors in Honolulu's Chinatown to make colorful shirts for them like the ones worn by Waikiki beachboys. **Ellery J. Chun** was the first to make and sell the shirts at his Chinatown shop. He coined the brand name **Aloha Sportswear** in 1936, and the garments were known forever after as aloha shirts.

---

132 Oahu Market Every morning except Sunday this large bustling market shows how busy Chinatown was, before supermarkets came into existence. A number of regular customers obviously prefer to select their fresh fish and roast pork from butchers who know their names. You'll hear Cantonese, Vietnamese, and other Asian dialects as prices are agreed on. When in season, mangoes and lychee are on sale, but you'll have the most fun buying *char siu* (barbecue pork). The butcher will chop the meat into bite-sized pieces so you can nibble as you browse through the stalls. If you're still hungry, you'll find restaurants with more ethnic foods down the street and around the corner. ♦ M-Sa 6:30AM-4PM; Su 6:30AM-noon. 145 N. King St, Honolulu. 528.2879

133 Dole Pineapple Cannery Back in the old days, the cloying smell of pineapple filled the air as you neared the pineapple cannery in the Iwilei district. Dole's landmark is a kitschy pineapple-topped water tank on stilts. There was a time when two million pineapples a day were processed in the cannery, each one inspected by women in white aprons, gloves, and caps. Now the machines and workers are only there seasonally. At the end of the cannery tour, you get to taste the fruit and juice. ♦ Admission. Tours daily 9AM-4PM, every 15 minutes. 650 Iwilei Rd, Honolulu. 548.6600

133 Hawaii Children's Museum Only a couple of years old, this museum features a range of

hands-on exhibits for children who like arts, crafts, and science. ♦ Admission. Tu-F 9AM-1PM; Sa-Su 10AM-4PM. 650 Iwilei Rd at Dole Cannery Square, Honolulu. 522.0040

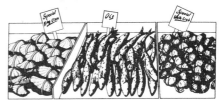

134 Tamashiro Market Look for a hot-pink, two-story building and the landmark sign (a bright orange crab), and hope there's a parking space. Worth a visit, especially if you can never get enough seafood; the market has a wide selection of fresh Island fish as well as favorites from the mainland and other parts of the world. The kids will keep busy looking at the live crabs, frogs, and lobsters crawling around in tanks. A huge board hanging over one of the fish counters lists the Hawaiian and mainland names for fish (see page 70 for some examples). If you're not squeamish, Tamashiro's has one of the best selections of *poke* (raw fish and seafood appetizers). ♦ M-F 9AM-6PM; Sa 8AM-6PM; Su 8AM-4PM. 802 N. King St, Honolulu. 841.8047

135 Helena's Hawaiian Food $ The customer seated next to you may have driven miles to this down-home restaurant just to order Helena's specialties: *pipikaula* (spicy smoked beef), *lau lau (imu-*roasted pig),*opihi* (shellfish) and *poke* (raw fish). This simple diner has been a longtime favorite among the Islanders; paintings on the walls are gifts to the owner from leading Hawaiian artists who are also appreciative regular customers. **Helena Chock** radiates aloha; customers adore her and the prices are reasonable. It's impossible to spend more than $10 here. ♦ Hawaiian ♦ Tu-F 11:30AM-7:30PM. 1364 N. King St, Honolulu. 845.8044

136 Hanauma Bay The perfect escape, and one of the most beautiful spots anywhere for snorkeling. Fish in this underwater state park are protected by law from scuba divers and fishers. Snorkelers often find themselves nose-to-nose with curious, brightly colored reef fish that, accustomed to being stared at, boldly go about their business. The bay sits protected by the walls of a volcanic crater that lost a chunk of one side. **Elvis Presley** came here to film *Blue Hawaii*, as did *From Here to Eternity* for beach scenes (the **Burt Lancaster-Deborah Kerr** clincher, however, was shot near Makapuu Beach for the surging waves). The waves are so gentle that even nonswimmers feel safe. And so you'll know, fish food cannot be brought in but must be purchased at the concession stands, where snorkel gear can

Oahu

also be rented. ♦ M-Tu, Th-Su 6AM-7PM; W noon-7PM. Off Kalanianaole Hwy, at the Hanauma Bay turnoff, Honolulu

137 Swiss Inn ★★$$$ Fans of **Martin Wyss'** cooking love the Swiss Inn for its affordable good food. The veal dishes (Wiener schnitzel, veal medallions, Holstein schnitzel) are very popular, but there's also pasta, chicken, seafood, and fondue. Friendly people and reasonably priced. ♦ Continental ♦ W-Sa 6-10PM; Su 10:30AM-1PM, 6-9PM. Niu Valley Shopping Center, 5730 Kalanianaole Hwy, Honolulu. 377.5447

137 Al Dente ★★$$$ French and Italian fare orchestrated by the seasoned hands of **Jean Pierre Germaine.** A small, excellent wine list accompanies a menu featuring linguine with clams, osso buco, fresh salmon steamed in lettuce leaves, and many other delicacies. An intimate, pleasing restaurant. ♦ French/Italian ♦ Tu-Su 5:30-10:30PM. Niu Valley Shopping Center, 5730 Kalanianaole Hwy, Honolulu. 373.8855

It wasn't until 1931 that **Sandy Beach** and the east **Halona Blowhole** area in Oahu were accessible by car. Before then, you had to take a foot trail.

138 Roy's Restaurant ★★★★$$$ **Roy Yamaguchi** was a leader in establishing a regional Hawaiian/California cuisine, and his innovative creations keeps it interesting. He calls his version "Euro-Asian" cuisine. Specialties include seafood potstickers; ravioli of lamb, goat cheese, and pesto; lobster in macadamia nut butter sauce; rack of Niihau lamb; and grilled Lanai venison in fresh basil port sauce. The hundreds of other selections change regularly, depending on the produce and seafood in season. Although Roy's is for the adventurous palate, even tried-and-true conservatives will walk away satisfied. The noise level in the dining room can prove distracting to conversationalists and it's in an odd location on the outskirts of suburban Hawaii Kai, but Roy's is wildly successful nevertheless. ♦ M-Th 5:30-9:45PM; F-Sa 5:30-11PM; Su 10AM-2PM, 5:30-9:45PM. 6600 Kalanianaole Hwy, Hawaii Kai. 396.7697

139 Koko Marina Shopping Center Oahu's only waterfront shopping complex, convenient to snorkelers at Hanauma Bay. Stop here for a quick bite to eat at **Zippy's,** the proverbial fast-food chain with good burgers, sushi, and great donuts. ♦ Off Kalanianaole Hwy, near Hanauma Bay

140 Halona Blowhole Ocean waves shoot through a lava tube and, as pressure builds, a powerful gush of water spews into the air. You may also hear an occasional honking sound. A lookout over the geyser is a popular stopping place to get a perspective of this spectacular section of the east Oahu coastline. (The city council is pushing to turn this shoreline area into a national park.) On clear days, the islands of Molokai and Lanai are visible on the horizon, and on those rare, exceptionally clear days, you may see Maui between them. ♦ Off Kalanianaole Hwy, east of Hanauma Bay, at the Hawaii Visitors Bureau marker

141 Sandy Beach Despite the people you'll see frolicking in the surf, this shorebreak is extremely dangerous for swimming and bodysurfing because the waves break in shallow water. Many swimmers have suffered broken necks here throughout the years. Also known as **Koko Head Beach Park,** this beach is popular for kite-flying, unbeatable for watching bodysurfing, and offers the best tubes for bodysurfing—but only for the experts. Picnic and public facilities. A lifeguard is on duty. ♦ Off Kalanianaole Hwy, northeast of Hanauma Bay

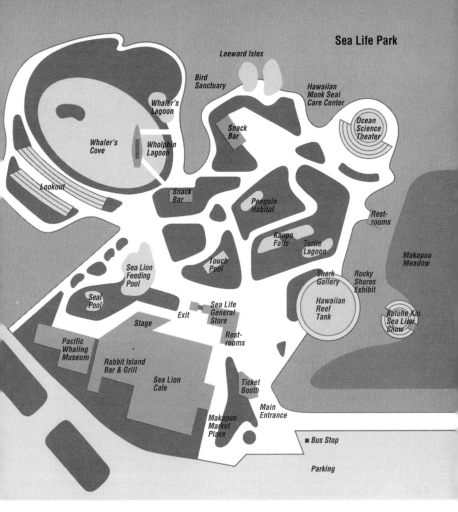

Sea Life Park

Leeward Isles

Bird Sanctuary

Whaler's Lagoon

Hawaiian Monk Seal Care Center

Ocean Science Theater

Snack Bar

Whaler's Cove

Wholphin Lagoon

Lookout

Snack Bar

Penguin Habitat

Rest-rooms

Kaupo Falls

Turtle Lagoon

Makapuu Meadow

Touch Pool

Sea Lion Feeding Pool

Shark Gallery

Rocky Shores Exhibit

Hawaiian Reef Tank

Seal Pool

Exit

Sea Life General Store

Kalohe Kai Sea Lion Show

Stage

Rest-rooms

Pacific Whaling Museum

Rabbit Island Bar & Grill

Sea Lion Cafe

Ticket Booth

Makapuu Market Place

Main Entrance

■ Bus Stop

Parking

142 Makapuu Beach Park A dangerous swimming spot, but excellent bodysurfing for experts. The point above Makapuu, as you turn the corner from east Oahu, offers a breathtaking view of the windward coastline, outlying islands, and bodysurfers in the waves below. Public facilities and lifeguards. ◆ Off Kalanianaole Hwy, east of Sea Life Park

143 Sea Life Park Paying to see fish and sea mammals in land-based tanks and pools seems ridiculous in Hawaii, surrounded as it is by waters full of these saltwater denizens. But Sea Life Park, similar to San Diego's Sea World, is well worth the price of admission for budding oceanographers and anyone else who likes to watch dolphins soar through hoops, not to mention tropical fish galore, monk seals, penguins, and all manner of marine life. The **Touch Pool** is a favorite among children, who can reach into a shallow pool and touch sea cucumbers, starfish, shells, giant worms, and other slippery and spineless creatures. Be sure to visit the **Rocky Shores Exhibit,** which re-creates the surf-swept intertidal zone of Hawaii's shoreline; the **Hawaiian Reef Tank,** a simulated offshore reef three fathoms below sea level with live sharks, eels, sea turtles, and fish; and the **Ocean Science Theater,** home to a boogie board-riding Pacific bottlenose dolphin. You can also meet **Kekaimalu,** the world's only "wolphin"—yes, a cross between a whale and dolphin. The park's setting, in beautiful Makapuu, is great for swimming, sunbathing, and picnicking. Great Hawaiian entertainment on "Kamaaina Friday Nights," when local bands liven up the **Sea Lion Cafe** and **Rabbit Island Bar and Grill.** ◆ M-Th, Sa 9:30AM-5PM; F 9:30AM-10PM. Off Kalanianaole Hwy, southeast of Waimanalo Bay, Honolulu. 259.7933

143 Pacific Whaling Museum This privately owned museum near Sea Life Park houses the largest collection of whaling artifacts and scrimshaw in the Pacific. The 36-foot-long skeleton suspended from the ceiling is from a sperm whale that became stranded and died off Barber's Point on Oahu in 1980. ♦ Free. M-Th, Sa 9:30AM-5PM; F 9:30AM-10PM. Outside the turnstiles of Sea Life Park. 259.7933

144 Bueno Nalo ★$$ Honolulu's no mecca for Mexican food, but the fare at Bueno Nalo is among the best in town, so don't be surprised to find a line outside this humble establishment in Waimanalo. If you don't mind eating early, however, you can escape the wait. Otherwise, join the party outside the restaurant while waiting your turn for seats (they can only seat 20 or so at a time). Specials include the Baja chowder and chicken chimichangas. Bueno Nalo has no liquor license, so BYOB. ♦ Mexican ♦ Tu-F 5-9PM; Sa-Su 3-9PM. 41-865 Kalanianaole Hwy, Waimanalo. No credit cards. 259.7186

145 Dave's Ice Cream Forty flavors, including such tropical palate pleasers as tangy mango and lychee. There are 10 branches of Dave's on the island. ♦ Daily 10AM-9PM. 41-1537 Kalanianaole Hwy, Waimanalo. 259.8576

145 Olomana Golf Links A short, relatively easy course in Waimanalo on Oahu's northeast shore. Par 72, 6,081 yards. Inexpensive

green fees. ♦ 41-1801 Kalanianaole Hwy, Waimanalo. Pro shop. 259.7926

146 Bellows Field Beach Park Ride the gentle bodysurfing waves at this rural beach (part of the Bellows Air Force Station). ♦ Open to the public F noon-Su 6PM. Kalanianaole Hwy, Waimanalo

Slurpin' Saimin

Kalihi, a community in Honolulu, is home to dozens of mom 'n' pop saimin (pronounced *sigh*-min) stands, little hole-in-the-wall restaurants where you can find the noodle soup entrée that's an island favorite. Just drive along N. King St and settle in for some saimin at diners such as **Hall Saimin** (927 N. King St) or **Palace Saimin Stand** (1256 N. King St); both of these saimin spots are no-nonsense, formica-topped wonders. Order a bowl of the soup flavored with seafood, thin noodles, *char siu* (barbecue pork), green onions, and fishcake. Most local residents also order grilled meat on a stick or sushi to round out the meal.

The *'ie'ie* is a rare, sacred Hawaiian plant that was dedicated to the forest god, Ku. Its roots and fibers were once used in homes, canoes, fish traps, helmets, and sandals, as well as for decoration. Now it is reserved for offerings in ancient hula ceremonies.

147 Buzz's Original Steak House ★$$ One of Oahu's original surf 'n' turf restaurants, Buzz's has the feel of old Hawaii. At lunch, you order off the menu. For dinner, there's a selection of specials, including fresh fish and steaks, and a salad bar that's better than most. ♦ Steak/Seafood ♦ Daily 11AM-2PM, 5-10PM. 413 Kawailoa St, Lanikai. 261.4661

148 Kailua Beach Park Popular windward-side family beach, this spot is safe for swimming and bodysurfing. But look out for the windsurfers zipping by. Picnic, public facilities, and lifeguard. ♦ Off Kalaheo Ave, Kailua

149 Mid-Pacific Country Club The club offers long, tight, challenging course on the windward side of the island. Par 72, 6,848 yards. ♦ Walk-ons allowed M-Tu in the afternoon; W-F before 11AM. 266 Kaelepulu Dr, Kailua. Pro shop. 261.9765

150 L'Auberge Swiss Restaurant ★$$$ **Alfred Mueller** runs this cozy 48-seat restaurant that serves Swiss cuisine—a combination of German, French, and Italian. His desserts are sublime, especially the apple fritters à la mode and the Swiss meringue with ice cream and raspberry sauce. ♦ Swiss ♦ Tu-Sa 5-10PM; Su 5:30-9PM. 117 Hekili St, Kailua. 263.4663

150 Los Arcos ★★$$$ This tiny restaurant serves high-class Mexican dishes. Recommendations include the stuffed squid, the not-very-Mexican but superb *lilikoi* (passion fruit) pie, and the black forest torte. ♦ Mexican ♦ M-W, F 11:30AM-2PM, 5:30-10PM; Sa 5:30-10PM; Su 5:30-9PM. 19 Hoolai St, Kailua. 262.8196

150 Harry's Cafe and Deli ★★$$$ You'll be charmed by the decor in this cafe: framed Hawaiian sheet music from the thirties and forties, and Hawaiian quilts hang from the walls. The fare is Italian, with such innovative dishes as pasta Lugano—*mostaccioli* pasta with sautéed chicken and sweet peppers in a tomato-and-cream sauce, topped with fresh basil. ♦ Italian ♦ M-Sa 11AM-9PM. 629 Kailua Rd, Kailua. 261.2120

151 Koolau Farmers Stop at this nursery just outside of Kailua for freshly cut flowers and potted plants. Colorful hibiscus, bougainvillea, heliconia, anthuriums, and orchids add to the fragrant air. Longtime customers rave about the personal service: If you love cut gardenias, the nursery will call you when a delivery is made. They ship to the mainland daily. ♦ M-Sa 8AM-5PM; Su 8AM-4PM. 1127 Kailua Rd, Kailua. 263.4414

152 Nuuanu Pali Lookout Follow the signs along the Pali Hwy to this lookout, and hold onto your hat as you step out of your car. This 1,000-foot-high point is one of the windiest spots in Hawaii, a place where gentle trade winds turn into formidable gusts. Marvel at the view of windward Oahu: green carpets of banana farms, pastures, and golf courses at the foot of the cliffs, with miniature subdivisions and the ocean beyond. Legend has it that the **Battle of Nuuanu Valley** was fought here in the spring of 1795, with **King Kamehameha the Great** and his forces pushing the opposing army over the palisades to their deaths. ♦ From Pali Hwy, take the Nuuanu Pali Lookout turnoff, Kaneohe

153 Pali Golf Course Beautifully lush course at the foot of the Koolau Mountains. Par 72, 6,493 yards. Inexpensive green fees for both residents and visitors. Call a week ahead for reservations. ♦ 45-050 Kamehameha Hwy, Kaneohe. 261.9784

Haiku Gardens

154 Haiku Gardens A luxuriant spot, rife with tropical growth, beneath the misty, green Koolau Mountains. Pathways wind through the landscaped grounds and around a pond for pleasant after-dinner walks. The **Chart House** restaurant here offers steak, seafood, prime rib, and chicken. ♦ Daily 5-10PM. 46-336 Haiku Rd, Kaneohe. 247.6671

155 Byodo-In Temple This replica of a 900-year-old Buddhist temple in Japan is found in the **Valley of the Temples Memorial Park,** a cemetery in Kaneohe at the foot of the Koolau Mountains It was built in 1968 to honor Hawaii's first Japanese immigrants. A Buddha statue near a pond filled with swans and carp adds to the serenity of the grounds, where peacocks roam and visitors can ring the three-ton bronze bell. ♦ Admission. Daily 8:30AM-4PM. 47-200 Kahekili Hwy, Kaneohe. 239.8811

156 Senator Fong's Plantation and Gardens Former US Senator **Hiram Fong** retired to devote more time to cultivating this botanic garden, which opened to the public a few years ago. There are 75 kinds of fruits and flowers, and sweeping ocean views from certain sections of the garden. The gift shop offers a discriminating selection of Hawaiian-made items. ♦ Admission. Daily 10AM-4PM. Last tour 3PM. 47-285 Pulama Rd, Kahaluu. 239.6775

157 Paniolo Cafe $$ If you're driving around the island, this little cafe will have something to quench your thirst or to nibble on. It's a modest wooden shack with a bar and restaurant area that serve up 16-ounce margaritas in mason jars, and a Texas-style menu with rattlesnake chili when in season. ♦ American ♦ M-F 11AM-4PM, 5:30-9PM; F-Su 5:30-10PM. 53-146 Kamehameha Hwy, Punaluu. 237.8521

Restaurants/Clubs: Red   Hotels: Blue
Shops/ Outdoors: Green   **Sights/Culture:** Black

158 Polynesian Cultural Center If you haven't been to the South Seas, this is a good introduction to the cultures of Polynesia: Hawaii, Fiji, Tonga, Samoa, Tahiti, and the Marquesas. A kind of Disney-goes-Pacific, with village replicas and traditions demonstrated by students at the nearby **Brigham Young University at Hawaii,** many of them natives of Polynesia. The center has been one of the leading visitor attractions in Hawaii since the Church of Jesus Christ of Latter-day Saints opened it in 1964. Set aside an entire day to make the round-trip drive from Waikiki, tour the various villages, and take in all the demonstrations. You may be exhausted and overwhelmed, but the narration is as entertaining as it is corny. Watch as they pound poi, make leis, husk coconuts, and make tapa cloth from mulberry bark. Each half hour there's a song-and-dance revue, and in the evening a buffet dinner show. You can purchase a general admission ticket, which includes daytime activities, and the buffet dinner show (exhausting), or an admissions-only ticket, which does not include evening buffet. ♦ Admission. M-Sa

12:30-9PM. Kamehameha Hwy, Laie. 293.3333, 923.1861

159 Mormon Temple Since 1864, the Mormon Temple headquarters has occupied 6,000 acres in the community of Laie, where 95 percent of the population is Mormon. The Church of Jesus Christ of Latter-day Saints built the temple here in 1919, a handsome white edifice on impeccably landscaped grounds. Visitors are not allowed to enter the temple but you're welcome to tour the surroundings, which feature reflecting pools. ♦ Grounds open to visitors daily 9AM-8PM. 55-600 Naniloa Loop, off Kamehameha Hwy, Laie. Visitor's Center 293.9297

160 Malaekahana State Recreation Area Just past Laie, right before you reach the former plantation town of Kahuku, sits postcard-perfect Malaekahana. On weekdays the arc-shaped beach is usually empty, except for a fisher or two waiting to cast a net. There's good swimming and bodysurfing, but no lifeguard on duty. Remember to lock your car and keep valuables out of sight. That done, take your time strolling down the wide, white sand beach or picnicking on the Laie-end, under the ironwood trees. There's a bathhouse with cold-water showers. ♦ Off Kamehameha Hwy, three miles from Laie

Hang Ten

Many surfers have declared the **Banzai Pipeline,** a turbulent ocean strip off Oahu's North Shore, as the home of the perfect wave. Banzai (a Japanese war cry) refers to the courage required to surf the waves here (a courage reserved for expert surfers only), and the name Pipeline comes from the tube-shaped form a wave creates as it breaks. There are larger and other tube-shaped waves, but none as ferocious as the pipeline wave during the winter months.

Surfers trying to tackle a pipeline wave have about 15 seconds to soar from one end of the tube to the other before they're buried under swirling sand or caught by the "guillotine"—the name for the wave's falling edge (which is also known for breaking some surfers' necks). The only thing surfers can see as they race to get through the pipeline is a trickle of light gleaming at the other end. If a surfer fails to get through the tube and manages to survive the fall, the next 10 seconds of being hurled through the water can be even more terrifying, and once the water starts to pull back, the coral bottom can be a worse enemy than the tube. The surfer then has to wait until his or her head clears the foamy surf to breathe again.

Petroglyphs on lava near the Banzai Pipeline show Polynesian surfers from ancient days, suggesting that perhaps they were the first to ride a pipeline wave. However, the first known person to ride a pipeline was **Phil Edwards** in 1961, and the filmed event, called *String Hollow Days,* was a forerunner of the movie *Endless Summer.* Edwards used a

Oahu

10-foot board, although today the most commonly used boards measure seven feet and shorter.

Formation of a Pipeline Wave

1. Off shore (deep water)
Light winds cause ripples in the water

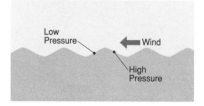

2. Wind increases
Water molecules travel in stationary circles as the wave travels over

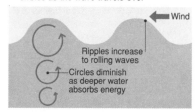

3. 500 yards from shore
Wave hits a coral reef, increasing the wave's speed and height

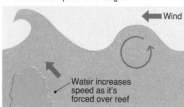

4. 100 yards from shore
Wave hits a second coral reef, further increasing speed and height

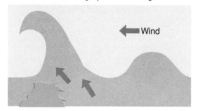

5. Beach
Water becomes too shallow to absorb energy, forcing the wave to break

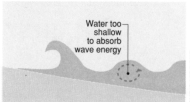

CHRIS MIDDOUR

161 Huevos Restaurant $ As you enter Kahuku from the southeast on Kamehameha Hwy, watch for a sign by the roadside indicating where to turn off the main road onto a dirt road to get to Huevos. Housed in a former mom 'n' pop grocery, this little country restaurant serves breakfast only: down-home cooking that includes generous portions of omelets with fresh veggies, short stacks, and French toast. It's worth starting off the morning here if you're planning a day at the Polynesian Cultural Center or at a beach on this side of the island. ♦ Breakfast only. M-W, F-Su 7AM-noon. Kahuku. 293.1016

162 Royal Hawaiian Seafood $ If it weren't for the cars and folks queued at the side of the road, you'd drive right by this small roadside stall. The attraction is fresh prawns and shrimp prepared any number of ways, including steamed and tempura style. Behind the stall is the aquaculture farm where they were raised, which is about as fresh as you can get. ♦ Seafood ♦ Daily 10:30AM-5:30PM. Off Kamehameha Hwy west of Kahuku

163 Turtle Bay Hilton and Country Club $$$ More than an hour's drive from Waikiki, this is for people who really want to get away. There's not much to do but golf (on the 18-hole **Arnold Palmer Championship Golf Course**), sunbathe by the two pools, or hit the beach. It can get pretty windy on Kuilima Point, where the hotel's 486 guest rooms and cottages are located. But that's one of the reasons the beach next door is popular with surfers. You can sit back and watch the surfers hang ten, or play tennis, ride horses, try dune cycling, or windsurf. If you rent a car, Waimea Bay, Sunset Beach, or the town of Haleiwa are nice day trips. ♦ 57-091 Kamehameha Hwy, Kahuku. 293.8811, 800/445.8667; fax 293.9147

Within the Turtle Bay Hilton and Country Club:

Sea Tide Room $$ The Sunday brunch buffet draws the local residents for the bountiful selection of foods, including sashimi and sushi, and the fine beach view. ♦ Su brunch only. 9AM-2PM. 293.8811

Turtle Bay Hilton Golf Course This oceanside course is known for its ferocious winds, but that doesn't keep folks away. Legend has it that Mickey Mantle, with the wind at his back, drove a ball over the 357-yard fourth hole—using a No. 4 wood. But George Fazio supposedly designed the course to compensate for the wind. Par 70, 6,411 yards, with a 70 championship rating. In 1992, a second course will open. Preferred starting times and rates for Turtle Bay Hilton guests. ♦ Starting times 293.8811

164 Sunset Beach A world-famous North Shore site for winter surfing contests, but high surf and strong currents make it dangerous for swimmers year-round. Good beach for strolling and sunbathing during spring and summer. In winter, don't ever turn your back on the waves. ♦ Off Kamehameha Hwy, seven miles north of Haleiwa

165 Ke Iki Hale $$$ This is the Hawaii everyone dreams of—palm trees silhouetted against the sunset, shells glistening on the sand, whales cavorting in the winter, and cottages with large picture windows to take it all in. Ke Iki Hale is one of Oahu's best beaches, a broad expanse of white sand except during the winter, when thundering, 10-foot waves crash on the reefy shoreline. Rinse off under a shower that's been fastened to a palm tree, lay in a hammock, or picnic at tables near the sand: the place is glorious. Only a dozen cottages occupy this acre and a half of oceanfront property, from one-bedrooms on the street side to one- and two-bedroom adjoining units facing the

ocean. Everything is modest; no Jacuzzi, room service, or even a restaurant, but the cottages are immaculate and the amenities of Haleiwa are only minutes away. Clean linens, full kitchens and bathrooms, and public pay phones. You can easily stay in your swimsuit all day. Owner **Alice Tracy** is a treat, too; hardworking and big-hearted. ♦ 59-579 Ke Iki Rd, Haleiwa. 638.8229

166 Puu-o-Mahuka Heiau For an incredible view of the North Shore and Waimea Bay, drive up Pupukea Rd to this *heiau* (ancient temple), where humans were once sacrificed as part of the Hawaiian religion. This is a sacred place, where offerings of *ti* leaves and stones are still made. ♦ Take Pupukea Rd east to the Hawaii Visitor's Bureau marker

---

Sans Souci Beach (French for "without a care"), located near the volcanic crater Diamond Head on Oahu, was the favorite haunt of author **Robert Louis Stevenson.** He also penned some of his famous prose under the Moana Hotel's old banyan tree on Waikiki Beach.

Restaurants/Clubs: Red	**Hotels:** Blue
Shops/ 🌳 Outdoors: Green	**Sights/Culture:** Black

167 Waimea Falls Park In 1990 a tropical storm devastated the 1,800-acre park, across the street from Waimea Beach Park. Remodeled, it opened to the public in May 1991. The lush grounds include an arboretum and botanical gardens, with thousands of tropical and subtropical species. You can ride through the grounds on an open-air minibus or take a guided walking tour. Be sure to see the cliff divers jumping from the 45-foot falls that give the park its name, and **Halau O Waimea,** the park's resident hula troupe, which performs the *kahiko* (ancient) hula in the upper meadow several times a day. The **Proud Peacock Restaurant** ($$$) features nightly entertainment. There's also a snack bar, and visitors are invited to picnic on the grounds. ♦ Admission. Daily 10AM-5:30PM. Off Hwy 83, seven miles north of Haleiwa, a 90-minute drive from Waikiki. 638.8511

168 Waimea Beach Park Waters are calm during the summer, when you'll see local kids playing king of the mountain on the huge rock in the bay. But you'd never recognize this beach during the winter, when enor-

mous waves pound the shores and make the bay hazardous even for the best surfers. One of the world's premier surfing spots, great for spectators in the winter when the experts are out. Lifeguards and public facilities. ♦ Off Kamehameha Hwy, just north of Haleiwa

169 Haleiwa Beach Park Good swimming and snorkeling during the spring and summer, but surfing should be left to the experienced. ♦ 62-449 Kamehameha Hwy, Haleiwa

170 S. Matsumoto Store For generations, Haleiwa has been the home of a local treat—shave ice—which is finely shaved ice flavored with fruit syrups, served modestly in a cone-shaped paper cup. Snow cones simply don't compare. The best establishments, like Matsumoto's, make their own syrups and offer variations with vanilla ice cream and Japanese sweet *azuki* beans. ♦ Tu-Su 8AM-5PM. 66-087 Kamehameha Hwy, Haleiwa. 637.4827

170 Kua Aina Sandwich Shop ★★$ Kua Aina hamburgers are so juicy they'll drip down your elbows. The French fries are thin and stringy and really taste like potatoes. Outstanding sandwiches, especially those with creamy avocados. ♦ American ♦ Daily 11AM-8PM. 66-214 Kamehameha Hwy, Haleiwa. 637.6067

170 Jameson's by the Sea ★★$$$ A roadside stop for seafood and pasta, with a sunset view worth your while. Scampi, fresh *opakapaka*, and other Jameson's traditions are served for dinner in the upstairs dining room. Downstairs, in an informal open-air lanai, *pupus* (appetizers) and drinks flow all day. ♦ Seafood ♦ M 11AM-5PM; Tu-Sa 11AM-9:30PM; Su 10AM-9:30PM. 62-540 Kamehameha Hwy, Haleiwa. 637.4336

170 Chart House at Haleiwa ★★$$$ The popular seafood-and-steak chain opened its North Shore eatery on the site of the old Seaview Inn and immediately became the local hotspot. Pleasant indoor and outdoor dining, right next to Haleiwa Harbor. Service may be spotty, but the salad bar is always good (including the Caesar salad) and the fresh fish menu is commendable. Opah or moonfish, either one is a terrific choice. ♦ Steak/Seafood ♦ Daily 11AM-10PM. 66-011 Kamehameha Hwy, Haleiwa. 637.8005

170 Pizza Bob's $$ Beer and pizza worthy of a college town, served at small booths in a bustling surfer atmosphere. Make your own combination of pizza toppings. ♦ Pizza ♦ M-Th, Su 11AM-10PM; F-Sa 11AM-11PM. Haleiwa Shopping Plaza, Haleiwa. 637.5095

170 Rosie's Cantina $$ Good margaritas, standard Mexican cuisine, and a pleasant environment. Hefty breakfasts for the sunrise surfers. ♦ Mexican ♦ M-F 7AM-10PM; F-Sa 7AM-11PM. Haleiwa Shopping Plaza, Haleiwa. 637.3538

170 Kaala Art Buy your for T-shirts, *pareus* (Polynesian cloth wrap-arounds), local art, and scads of imported casual wear from Thailand and Bali. Artist/owner **John Costello** has his Gauguin dreams gracing the canvases, and brother **Kevin** keeps the racks stocked with tropical wear and the walls lined with flapping sheets of colorful, wonderful *pareus*, the perfect gift. ♦ Daily 9AM-6PM. 66-456 Kamehameha Hwy, Haleiwa. 637.7065

170 Raising Cane Great stop for beachwear, Island crafts, and *pareus* designed by local artists. Everything from hand-painted children's wear to the Tutuvi line of T-shirts and Polynesian wraps. ♦ M-F 10AM-6PM; Su-Su 10AM-5PM. 66-521 Kamehameha Hwy, Haleiwa. 637.3337

171 H. Miura Store & Tailor Shop Stepping into the H. Miura Store is like stepping back in time to the days when Haleiwa was a plantation town. The Miuras can tell you about that era because they were settled here even then. They're a friendly family, and the secret to their success is selling shorts. They make swim trunks and walking shorts for the surfers who frequent the North Shore without fail every winter. The names and measurements of their regular customers are kept in a ledger, but the Miuras never forget a face. ♦ M-Sa 8AM-5PM. 66-057 Kamehameha Hwy, Haleiwa. 637.4845

71 Dole Pineapple Pavilion Try a piece of the fruit, or at least a glass of juice at this roadside stop in the heart of Hawaii's pineapple country. Note the neatly trimmed pineapple fields and the rich red soil that'll stain your white sneakers. A pictorial display tells the pineapple's history. Stop in at the gift shop. ♦ Daily 9AM-5:30PM. Off Hwy 99, north of Wahiawa. 621.8408

72 Schofield Barracks The US Army's 25th Infantry Division headquarters are here, right by the sugarcane and pineapple fields Japanese bombers flew over during the 7 December 1941 raid on Pearl Harbor. It is named for **Major General John M. Schofield,** the US Army's Pacific military division commander, who came to Hawaii in the 1870s on the pretext of vacationing, but spent more time around the Pearl River Lagoon—as Pearl Harbor was then called—investigating its suitability as an American military enclave. ♦ Off Hwy 99, Wahiawa

73 Makaha Beach Park Home of the annual **Buffalo Keaulana Big Board Classic,** a championship tournament for surfers who use the long, elegant boards that first put the sport on the map. The competition is held every February or March, depending on when the surfing conditions are best. This is where professional surfing originated before the sport shifted to the giant North Shore waves. As with many other beaches along the Waianae Coast, these aren't the most hospitable places for tourists. ♦ Off Farrington Hwy, Makaha

74 Sheraton Makaha West Course This 18-hole championship course is set against the green cliffs of the Waianae range, with great views of the Pacific coastline, especially at sunset. Expensive green fees but uncrowded play. Par 72, 7,091 yards. Shuttle service from Sheraton hotels in Waikiki also available. ♦ Sheraton Makaha Resort. Starting times 695.9544

75 Sheraton Makaha Resort & Country Club $$$ Not everyone will want to be this far from the action; a 90-minute drive from Waikiki, with nothing much to do here except play tennis or golf, cool off in the Olympic-sized pool, or explore Makaha Beach. Golfers will likely enjoy this for an overnight stay; the **West Course** features an 18-hole championship course. Guest rooms and suites are in low-rise cottage clusters, with lanais and views of the Pacific or the golf course. ♦ 84-626 Makaha Valley Rd, Makaha. 695.9511

Honolulu means "sheltered bay" in Hawaiian.

175 Pokai Bay Beach Park The only fully sheltered beach along the Waianae Coast. Unfortunately, this part of the island isn't the most hospitable for tourists. To avoid vandalism, be sure to lock your car. Picnic and public facilities. ♦ Off Farrington Hwy, south of Waianae

176 Mililani Golf Club In the Mililani suburbs of leeward Oahu, this golf course is shaded by trees on former sugarcane fields. Par 72, 6,800 yards, 70 rating. Moderate green fees. ♦ Mililani is about a 40-minute drive north from Waikiki. Starting times 623.2254

177 Arakawa's Watch for the sugar-mill smokestack once you get to the town of Waipahu, and nearby you'll find a little plantation store called Arakawa's. More fun than the International Market Place, with home appliances, Japanese dishes for sashimi and soup, *palaka* (plaid) aloha shirts that have more cachet among the local residents than the garish prints you'll find in Waikiki, coconut husk lamps, jade pendants, and more. Take home a souvenir baseball cap; the store has one of the best athletic departments in town. ♦ M-Sa 9:30AM-5:30PM; Su 11AM-4PM. 94-333 Waipahu Depot Rd, Waipahu. 677.3131

178 Pearl Harbor Naval Ship Tours On the first Saturday of every month, the US Navy opens one of its ships in Pearl Harbor to the public from noon to 4PM. ♦ Free. Enter through the Nimitz Gate. Pearl Harbor. 474.6156

179 Pearl City Tavern $$$ Don't miss the tavern's **Monkey Bar** or rooftop bonsai tree garden. The house specialty is Maine lobster. ♦ Japanese/American ♦ M-Th 11:30AM-2PM, 5:30-9PM; F-Su 5-9PM. 905 Kamehameha Hwy, Pearl City. 455.1045

180 Pearl Country Club A country club in name only, this public golf course overlooks Pearl Harbor; a small forest of trees waits eagerly for the hooks and slices that bring stray balls. Par 72, 6,230 yards. Expensive green fees. ♦ 98-535 Kaonohi St, Aiea. Starting times 487.3802

181 Pearlridge Center The two sections of this air-conditioned mall are connected by monorail. **Liberty House, J.C. Penney,** and **Sears** anchor the boutiques and specialty shops, movie theaters, and fast-food restaurants. Some places to eat at the **International Food Court** include **Bravo,** for pizza; and **Monterey Bay Canners,** for grilled fish and other seafood selections at affordable prices. On the corner of the busy intersection leading to Pearlridge is **Anna Miller's,** a coffee shop with winning pies. Look for a circular building separate from the center. ♦ M-Sa 10AM-9PM; Su 10AM-6PM. 98-1005 Moanalua Rd, Pearl City

*Arizona
Memorial*

182 Arizona Memorial It was early Sunday morning, 7 December 1941, and most of Honolulu was still sleeping when America's defense outpost in the Pacific was savaged by a wave of Japanese bombers. Several ships were hit, but the **USS Arizona** is perhaps the most notable. It sank in five minutes at its mooring blocks in 40 feet of water. The remains of 1,102 officers and sailors are entombed inside its rusting hull.

In 1962, after a benefit concert by **Elvis Presley,** a gracefully arched white structure was built over the *USS Arizona.* The memorial, designed by Honolulu architect **Alfred Preis,** became a national shrine, with the

Oahu

names of the 1,177 US Navy men and Marines killed in the attack engraved on a marble plaque. This is one of Hawaii's most popular tourist attractions. Before boarding one of the navy shuttleboats that carry passengers to the memorial, walk through the $5 million **Visitors Center,** where the "Day of Infamy" is recounted. The entire tour, including a documentary film and shuttle to the memorial, lasts about 75 minutes. ♦ Free to Visitors Center and navy shuttleboat passengers. (Tickets to the day's launches issued on a first-come, first-serve basis. Before noon there's often a one- to three-hour wait.) Visitors Center daily 7:30AM-5PM. Shuttle, weather permitting, 7:45AM-3PM. From Honolulu and Waikiki drive west on H1, past the Honolulu International Airport, take USS Arizona Memorial exit, and follow signs to the Visitors Center. Shirts and shoes required. 422.0561

183 Pacific Submarine Museum The 10,000-square-foot museum in **New Bowfin Submarine Park** adjacent to the Arizona Memorial opened in 1988. Collections include

sections of American and captured enemy submarines, defused torpedoes, and related military knickknacks. There's also a hands-on exhibit in which you're encouraged to experience the feel of underwater drama in an enclosed area. ♦ Admission. Daily 8AM-4PM. 11 Arizona Memorial Dr. 423.1341

184 Aloha Stadium Home of the **Hula Bowl** and **Pro Bowl** football games, which are televised nationwide every January. **Charles Luckman & Associates** designed the 50,000-seat stadium with movable stands that can be converted from a football to a baseball field. The stadium is home to the **University of Hawaii Rainbows,** the state's only college football team. It's also used for high school football games and for some of Honolulu's largest rock concerts. ♦ 99-500 Salt Lake Blvd, near Pearl Harbor. 486.9300

185 Aloha Stadium Flea Market On Wednesday and weekends the stadium parking lot becomes a giant flea market, with new and secondhand goods. Scores of vendors sell jewelry, kids' clothes, food, muumuus, aloha shirts, slippers, toys, you name it. Shuttles to the flea market pick up at the major hotels, so check with your hotel for more information. ♦ W, Sa-Su 6AM-3PM. 99-500 Salt Lake Blvd near Pearl Harbor. 955.4050, 486.1529

185 Honolulu International Country Club This course, which opened in the late seventies, was designed in part by **Arnold Palmer** and built on what was known as "Salt Lake," where hundreds of balls were lost in various water traps. Par 71, 5,995 yards, 70.2 rating. Members and guests only. ♦ West of downtown Honolulu at 1690 Ala Puumalu, Salt Lake. Pro shop. 833.4541

186 Moanalua Gardens The huge monkeypod trees on this sprawling 26-acre picnic-playground first capture the attention of westbound motorists on H1 Fwy. The park is open to the public; a quiet location for nature lovers. An old cottage where **King Kamehameha V** entertained his friends, and the Chinese Hall built in the early 1900s by

Samuel Mills Damon, are the only buildings that remain in the gardens. Each spring, the gardens host the **Prince Lot Hula Festival,** honoring the prince (who became King Kamehameha V) for reviving the ancient hula during his 1863-72 reign, ending more than four decades of a missionary-imposed ban. The nearby **Moanalua Valley** has petroglyphs and other historic sights. ♦ Donation. Gardens daily 7:30AM-6PM. Nature hike into valley twice monthly. Call for dates and reservations. From Moanalua Fwy, take Moanalua Gardens exit near Tripler Army Hospital. 839.5334

187 Bishop Museum and Planetarium When **Charles Reed Bishop** founded the museum in 1889 in honor of the Hawaiian heritage of his wife, **Princess Bernice Pauahi,** he hoped it would rank along the great museums of the world. Often called the "Smithsonian of the Pacific," the Bishop Museum houses the world's greatest collection of Hawaiian cultural and natural history artifacts and is a highly regarded center for Pacific area studies. Museum director **W. Donald Duckworth,** who came to Honolulu from the Smithsonian museum in Washington DC in the early eighties, continues to expand the exhibition and publication programs. Walking in, you can't miss the 55-foot-long sperm whale skeleton, half covered in papier-mâché, suspended above an authentic grass house. The museum's centerpiece is **Hawaiian Hall,** three floors of Hawaiian artifacts, including carved war gods and feather cloaks that illuminate the pre-European world of the Islands, mementos of the 19th-century monarchs, and valuable Polynesian artifacts. The **Hall of Hawaiian Natural History** has fascinating displays on the Islands' fiery geological origin, including a lava tube with its own ecosystem.

Children are free to feel lava or try their hands at making a grass hut in the **Hall of Discovery,** just across the lawn from the main gallery building. Next door to this is the **Planetarium and Science Center,** and the **Shop Pacifica,** which stocks an outstanding inventory of books on Hawaiian and Polynesian history. You can also purchase Niihau shell leis, authentic reproductions of museum pieces such as *lauhala* bags and hats, and Hawaiian quilts. ♦ Daily 9AM-5PM. Tours daily 10AM and noon. Planetarium shows M-Th, Su 11AM and 2PM; F-Sa 7PM.

1525 Bernice St, Honolulu. 847.3511. For information about current programs and other schedules, call 848.4129. For planetarium reservations, call 847.8201

Oahu's Highlights

Sunset walks around **Kapiolana Park,** and jogging or walking through **Ala Moana Beach Park** on weekends.

The view from **Makapuu Point.**

Listening to **Hookena** or **Olomana,** popular Hawaiian entertainers, at an oceanside Waikiki venue.

Guided tours at the **Lyon Arboretum.**

An afternoon at **Waimanalo Beach.**

Lei Day (May Day) concert by the **Brothers Cazimero.**

A picnic at a Sunday polo game at **Mokuleia Beach Park** (March through August).

Ancient hula at the **Prince Lot Hula Festival.**

Iolani Palace tours.

Glider flights at **Dillingham Field.**

Hawaii's Best

Roy Yamaguchi
Chef/Owner, Roy's Restaurant, Honolulu

Fish feeding at **Hanauma Bay,** Oahu.

Having pig's feet soup with extra ginger and two scoops of rice at **Zippy's,** a 24-hour restaurant on several of the Islands.

Oahu

Watching the sunset from **Ko Olina,** Oahu.

Enjoying the panoramic view of Oahu's windward side while driving down the Pali Hwy.

Taking a quick spin between **Sandy Beach** and **Roy's Restaurant** along the Oahu coast on the way to work.

Brett A. Uprichard
Editor, *Hawaii Drive Guides*
Associate Editor, *Honolulu Magazine*

Sunset drinks at the Moana Hotel's **Banyan Tree Bar** on Oahu—very relaxing and beautiful, with views of surfers and canoes.

A morning hike to the top of **Diamond Head Crater** on Oahu—the very best view of Waikiki and the beach.

Any Hawaiian luau at an old beachside house. *Kalua* pig never tastes as good anywhere else, and usually the amateur entertainment is terrific.

A midnight stroll on **Lanikai Beach** on Oahu during a full moon—very romantic when the moon lights up Mokulua Island.

Teriyaki steak on a stick at the Punahou or McKinley High School carnivals on Oahu.

Restaurants/Clubs: Red	Hotels: Blue
Shops/ 🎋 Outdoors: Green	Sights/Culture: Black

Kauai

The leading lady of the Hawaiian Islands, Kauai (ka-*why*-ee or ka-*why*) anchors the northernmost post in the chain. This is also the oldest of the islands, and with its head start on the shaping and coloring of its volcanic mountains, canyons, valleys, rivers, and beaches, many view Kauai as the most beautiful island. Others see it as the wettest and dullest island. They're both right and wrong. The 5,200-foot peak of **Mount Waialeale** has more rainy days per year than any other spot on earth. It receives 450 to 600 inches of rain annually, causing many visitors to think (incorrectly) that the whole island has more rainy days than any place on earth. Actually, on the east side of the island it is generally sunnier southwest of the county seat of **Lihue**, and less reliable to the northwest. The **Wailua** region is climatically somewhere in between.

Kauai has another misleading reputation. Among some people, you are likely to hear the snide remark: "Kauai is lovely. But what do you do on the second day?" This island has considerably less structured activities than Oahu, Maui, or the Big Island—which is precisely one of its charms. It's relaxing. Life moves at a slower pace. There wasn't even a

Map labels: Na Pali Coast · Valley of the Lost Tribe · 26 · Kokee · Waimea Canyon State Park · 550 · Polihale State Park 25 · Mana · 50 Kaumualii Hwy · Kokee Rd. · 550 · Waimea Canyon Dr. · Waimea River · 24 · Kekaha · Waimea 23 · Kaulakahi Channel · Waimea Bay · Infinities Surfing Spot · Kaui

traffic light until 1973. But any perception of Kauai as unexciting is wholly inaccurate. Excitement is here, but it is not found via conventional routes.

To see and experience the best of Kauai you have to get up in the air, on top of the water, under the water, or strike out on foot. A dramatic alternative, and a controversial one, is the helicopter. A helicopter tour of Kauai, soaring above the Waimea Canyon and the Na Pali Coast, is the pièce de résistance for those up in the air—but it is the bane of hikers below. Those who have trekked and sweated their way to the well-deserved solitude of remote valleys and vantage points are understandably annoyed to meet up with the intrusion of helicopters. The other side of the coin is that no ordinary beach can match an isolated, picture-perfect stretch of remote Kauai shoreline or the monumental cliffs of the island's interior, which are only visible by helicopter. Kauai has Hawaii's only navigable rivers—but forget the rush on the Wailua River to the crowded Fern Grotto. Instead, discover the exotic underwater world by snorkeling or scuba-diving with guides from one of the excellent dive shops.

If you seek out Kauai (as so many do) for nothing more adventurous than a day of peace and quiet, the following four areas are where you'll find it. Excellent beaches, good snorkeling, and by far the best weather is in the

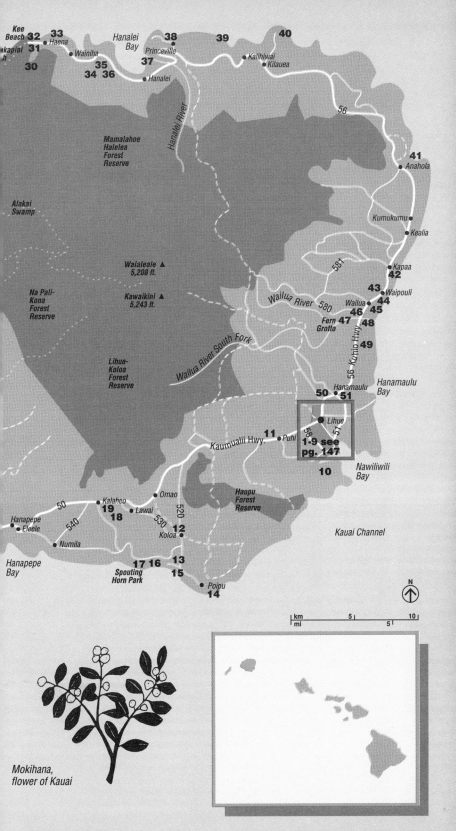

Kee Beach **32** **33** Haena · Hanalei Bay **38** **39** **40**
kapiai **31** · Wainiha Princeville **37** · Kalihiwai
30 **35** Kilauea
34 **36** · Hanalei

Hanalei River

Mamalahoe
Halelea
Forest
Reserve

56

41 · Anahola

Alakai
Swamp

Kumukumu · Kealia

Waialeale ▲
5,208 ft.

Na Pali-
Kona
Forest
Reserve

Kawaikini ▲
5,243 ft.

581

· Kapaa
42

Wailua River 580

43 · Waipouli
44
Wailua **45**
Fern **47** **46**
Grotto **48**
49

Wailua River South Fork

56 Kuhio Hwy.

Lihue-
Koloa
Forest
Reserve

Hanamaulu Bay

50 Hanamaulu ·
51

· Lihue

58
51

Kaumualii Hwy. **11** · Puhi

**1-9 see
pg. 147**

10 Nawiliwili
Bay

Kauai Channel

50 · Kalaheo Omao
19 · Lawai 520
18 530
540 · Koloa
· Numila **12**
Haupu
Forest
Reserve

Hanapepe
· Eleele

Hanapepe
Bay

17 **16** **13**
Spouting **15**
Horn Park · Poipu
14

N

km
mi 5 10
5

145

Mokihana,
flower of Kauai

Poipu Beach area, on the southern tip, where rainfall averages no more than the precipitation at famous dry spots such as Waikiki (Oahu), Wailea (Maui), and Kona (the Big Island). Traditionally casual, Poipu has become more luxurious and more crowded with the arrival of bigger and more expensive hotels and condominiums and the area's first golf course, but the sunshine-and-beach factor remains unequaled.

In Lihue, a thoroughly uninteresting town, the old Kauai Surf Hotel has metamorphosed into the Westin Kauai, another flamboyant resort by developer **Chris Hemmeter.** Among its most prominent features are the hundred-plus horses that pull guests in open-air carriages along eight miles of winding paths.

The Wailua area, past the mouth of the Wailua River, is dominated by the presence of the Coco Palms Resort Hotel, along with a string of hotels, condominiums, and shopping strips. Wailua beaches are windy, and because of the strong current, swimming is often dangerous.

When you round the island and reach the North Shore, you'll see the new Princeville Hotel, which takes center stage at the Princeville Resort, alongside the spectacular golf courses, roomy condominiums, luscious scenery, limited beach access, and unreliable weather. A fortunate few are able to land vacation beach-house rentals beyond Princeville in the bucolic Hanalei Valley. In between the resorts is a profusion of the kind of tropical beauty that gives Kauai its sobriquet, "the Garden Island." Seeing the island by automobile is restricted to the outer rim, since there are no paved roads into the rugged interior; thus, Kauai has more helicopter tour companies (16 of them) than any other island.

Be aware that this is a proud, fiercely independent little island. It was the only island that Kamehameha I failed to conquer with his invading armies in the 1790s. Kauai ceded to Kamehameha's rule 15 years after he conquered the others, and secession came only after Kauai's King Kaumualii conspired with Russia to seize control of all Hawaii. Today, the citizens of Kauai (numbering more

than 51,000) protect their island as if every inch of it were an extension of their personal backyards. Controlled growth is not a slogan on Kauai, it's a war cry. A four-story height limitation on building (which is no taller than a coconut tree) is strictly enforced. Any proposal for a hotel or condominium in the wrong place—which lately has meant just about any place on the island—is met with immediate, well-organized community protests. This is not, however, an inhospitable island. There's a warm welcome here, at least for those who come and go without altering the face of the island. It could be that Kauaians regard exaggerations about too much rain and too little to do on their island as pleasant myths worthy of encouragement. One problem that is not a myth, however, is the traffic. The one highway that encircles the island has fallen prey to the classic snafu—rush-hour traffic jams.

Kauai Helicopter Sightseeing There is no experience quite like flying over a ridge in a helicopter and suddenly seeing the Waimea Canyon sprawled out in technicolor splendor; soaring into a valley along the lush Na Pali Coast; probing shadowy and ominous Mount Waialeale on a rare day when the clouds have lifted; or hovering by a silvery streak of waterfall anywhere on the island. Companies offer short tours to specific sights and longer tours of around-the-island ventures that take in all the picture-book attractions. Most of the helicopters supply passengers with headphones for listening to music while thrilling to the views. Bring plenty of film. Helicopter companies include:

Air-1 Inter-Island Helicopters, Hanapepe...............................335.5009

Air Kauai Helicopter Tours, Lihue.....246.4666

Bali Hai Helicopters, Hanapepe......335.3166

Bruce Needham Helicopters, Eleele 335.3115

Discount Heli-Tours, Koloa 742.7100

Island Helicopters, Lihue 245.8588

Jack Harter Helicopters, Lihue......245.3774

Kenai Helicopters, Lihue................245.8591

Na Pali Helicopters, Lihue.............245.6959

Niihau Helicopter Inc., Hanapepe 335.3500

Ohana Helicopters, Lihue...............245.3996

Papillon Helicopters, Princeville ....826.6591 Lihue..245.9644

Rainbow Helicopters, Lihue 245.7541

Safari Helicopter Tours, Lihue 246.0136

South Sea Helicopters, Lihue........245.7781

Will Squyres Helicopter Service, Lihue 245.7541

Kauai Underwater It's been a well-kept secret for years that some of the finest snorkeling and scuba-diving playgrounds in the Islands are on Kauai's south shore, where the water is generally calm and the visibility excellent. But word has gotten out, and divers who used to go to Maui are now venturing to Kauai. Beginners who've decided to take the plunge are discovering that they can enjoy tropical fish and coral formations with minimal effort at convenient shoreline locations. Diving firms offer introductory courses and their guides take small groups of snorkelers and divers to enchanting locations to gaze at shipwrecks, explore caverns, and go nose-to-nose with rainbow-colored fish. Week-long visitors to Kauai may want to consider becoming certified divers, which will allow them to dive in deeper waters and see more spectacular sights. **Fathom Five Professional Divers** in Koloa (742.6991) will take

divers to meet "Grandpa," a white-mouthed moray eel, and "Tripod," a friendly 450-pound Hawaiian green turtle. Other diving companies include **Sea Sage Diving Centers,** Kapaa, 822.3841, 800/659.DIVE; and **Aquatics Kauai,** 733 Kuhio Hwy, 822.9213. All rent underwater gear.

Kauai By Raft One of the best ways to see Kauai's spectacular Na Pali Coast. On a Na Pali Zodiac rubber raft, you'll skim across the waves, explore sea caves, and visit deserted beaches, a unique way to experience a most amazing coastline. For more information and reservations, see page 159.

1 Barbecue Inn ★$$ One of Lihue's most popular cheap-eats joints for more than a quarter century. Their reputation is built on complete dinners from the American/ Japanese menu. ♦ American/Japanese ♦ M-Sa 7:30AM-1:30PM, 4:30-8:30PM. 2982 Kress St. 245.2921

1 Restaurant Kiibo $$$ Enjoy authentic Japanese specialties such as teriyaki steak, sashimi, sushi, bento lunch, tempura, and sukiyaki at this old-time favorite. Rustic oriental atmosphere adds to the charm. ♦ Japanese ♦ M-Sa 11AM-1:30PM, 5:30-9PM. 2991 Umi St. 245.2650

2 Hamura's ★$ All over the Islands locals line up for saimin, a traditional Hawaiian noodle soup that is the ethnic equivalent of hamburgers and fries. Saimin is a part of many social rituals in Hawaii; it's the snack of choice after football games, parties, and late-night gatherings. And Hamura's, with its narrow Formica counters and steaming slices of teriyaki beef, spoons out some of the best

noodles in Kauai. From dressed-up, chichi partygoers to kids with sandy feet on the way home from the beach, you'll find them all at Hamura's. ♦ Hawaiian ♦ M-Th 10AM-2AM; F-Sa 10AM-4AM; Su 10AM-11PM. 2956 Kress St. 245.3271

3 Eggbert's ★★$$ Excellent food and friendly service at reasonable prices. Omelets are the specialty, and there's a lengthy list of salads, sandwiches, burgers, fresh local seafood, and other Island foods. One of Lihue's best diners. ♦ Eclectic ♦ M-Sa 7AM-3PM; Su 7AM-2PM. 4483 Rice St. 245.6325

3 Casa Italiana ★$$$ The menu here is so large, literally and figuratively, that just ordering your meal can wear you out. Kauai's original Italian restaurant, it offers plenty of pasta (made fresh daily) and burgers. The dinner menu features cannelloni and manicotti, cioppino, chicken, veal, baked ziti (pasta), fish, and steaks. A casual atmosphere in what used to be one of the old Lihue plantation homes. ♦ Italian ♦ Daily 5-9:30PM; happy hour daily 2-4PM. 2989 Haleko Rd (Rice St) 245.9586

4 Kauai Museum The story of Kauai and Niihau, from the first volcanic eruptions more than six million years ago through the 19th century, is told in a permanent exhibit in the **William Hyde Rice Building,** named for the last appointed governor of Kauai under the Hawaiian monarchy. In the **Albert Spencer Wilcox Building,** which was named for the son of missionary teachers and was originally the Kauai Public Library, you'll find changing exhibits of Kauai art and historic artifacts. If you don't have the opportunity to take a helicopter tour of Kauai, the museum shows a film taken from one that captures some of the beautiful and generally inaccessible sights of the island. ♦ Fee. M-F 9AM-4:30PM; Sa 9AM-1PM. 428 Rice St. 245.6931

TIP☕TOP

5 Tip Top Motel, Cafe, & Bakery Long-noted by local residents and visitors from the outer islands as *the* breakfast place in Lihue for a stack of macadamia nut or banana pancakes, side orders of spicy Portuguese sausage, and papaya with morning eggs. This favorite meeting place of Kauai's politicians, journalists, and other movers and shakers is also well-known for its Island-style, fresh-baked cookies, cakes, and pies. Back in the old days, Tip Top was the only bakery making macadamia nut cookies, which have since become the ubiquitous item for inter-island gift giving. ♦ Daily 7AM-8:30PM. 3173 Akahi St. 245.2333

6 Grove Farm This is a slice of life of the real Kauai, so authentic one would think people really live here. Grove Farm was a self-contained sugar plantation founded in 1864 by **George N. Wilcox,** a New England missionary descendant-turned-engineer. When his niece **Mabel Wilcox,** the last Wilcox to live on the plantation, died in 1978, Grove Farm became a nonprofit educational organization dedicated to preserving the history of plantation life on Kauai. Well-versed guides take visitors on small, quiet tours through the main plantation home, the cottages where George Wilcox lived and guests stayed, and the small camp houses of the workers. The farm seems to have been preserved in suspended animation: Miss Mabel's clothes still hang in her closet, her sister **Elsie's** silver-handled hairbrushes remain on her dresser, their uncle's collection of canes and hats are in his cottage, and two housekeepers regularly dust the furniture, replace the flowers, bake cookies, and make iced mint tea for the visitors. This is one of the most tastefully arranged and genuinely unique attractions on Kauai and, for that matter, in all of Hawaii. ♦ Admission. Tours M, W-Th 10AM, 1:15PM. No children under age five. Reservations required (sometimes one week in advance). Tours are cancelled on rainy days. Nawiliwili Rd, Lihue. 245.3202

7 Rosita's ★★$$ A contender for best

Mexican restaurant, though more popular with tourists than locals. Rosita's goes beyond the obligatory Mexican fare of enchiladas, tostadas, and guacamole to such dishes as crabmeat-filled enchiladas and deep-fried, bacon-wrapped shrimp topped with Spanish sauce. Drinks have colorful names like Tijuana Taxi and Adios Mother. ♦ Mexican ♦ M-Sa 11:30AM-10PM; Su 11:30AM-5:30PM. Hwy 51, Kukui Grove Center. 245.8561

8 JJ's Broiler $$$ Kauai's original steak house has reopened in the new Anchor Cove complex at Nawiliwili. Even *Gourmet Magazine* couldn't pry open owner **Jim Jasper's** lips for the secret sauce on his famous garlic-flavored Slavonic steak. Mahimahi and lobster join the beefy stars served in this handsome establishment. ♦ Steak ♦ Daily 11AM-10PM. Anchor Cove. 246.4422

8 Nawiliwili Park The swimming at Kalapaki Beach is superb and the waves are suitable for novice surfers. Old-timers remember the days when Hawaiian beachboys steered their canoes through the surf here while the Kauai Surf Hotel (now the Westin Kauai) guests screeched with delight. ♦ Hwy 51, Nawiliwili

8 Club Jetty One of Kauai's oldest, most unusual, and most popular Cantonese restaurants recently closed down to focus on the club's late-night disco action. An old standby with a strong local flavor, though decidedly raunchy in some ways. A guitarist plays nightly. Dress code. ♦ W-Su 9PM-4AM. At Nawiliwili Harbor, Lihue. 245.4970

8 Kauai Chop Suey ★★$$ The enormous menu here has its following among the lunchtime crowd hungering for chow mein, shrimp with black beans, and the nearly a hundred Cantonese offerings. The "Kauai Chow Mein" is the house specialty: a steaming plate of noodles, chicken, shrimp, *char siu* (barbeque pork), and lots of vegetables. ♦ Chinese ♦ Tu-Sa 11AM-2PM, 4:30-9PM; Su 4:30-9PM. Pacific Ocean Plaza, Nawiliwili. 245.8790

Sweet Talk

Could be that the sugar used to sweeten your coffee or tea came from Hawaii. Since the end of Hawaii's whaling days in the 1860s, the Islands' economy has relied heavily on sugar as its cash crop. Hawaiian fields yield 849,000 tons of sugar a year, more than 12 percent of the sugar produced in the entire US.

Hawaii first exported unrefined sugar to America during the gold rush, when Northern California's sudden population boom made sugar a profitable commodity. Since then sugarcane has blossomed into a $353 million-a-year business, and it remains one of the state's leading industries.

The wandering Polynesians, who settled in Hawaii about 1,500 years ago, planted the first sugarcane. They carried it with them because the thick stalks

Kauai

held their water. And Hawaii's rich lava soil and wet climate, coupled with plenty of warm sunshine, proved to be the perfect fertile ground for the cane.

The sugar industry is also primarily responsible for Hawaii's diverse racial mixture. Native Hawaiians, spoiled by the Islands' rich resources, shunned the backbreaking labor required to harvest sugar, so peasant labor was imported from China, Japan, Korea, Portugal, South America, and many other areas.

8 Pink Pepper ★★$$ Spicy, savory curries from Indonesia, Thailand, and Vietnam are served from an open kitchen. Basil, coconut milk, lemon grass, cilantro, and heaps of fresh herbs flavor the dishes and scent the surroundings. Great food, very exotic, a welcome addition to Kauai. ♦ Eclectic ♦ M, W-Su 5-10PM. Pacific Ocean Plaza, Nawiliwili. 246.0266

Kauai didn't get its first traffic lights until 1973. They were placed on Rice St at the intersections of Umi and Kalena Sts, near the Kauai Museum.

9 Westin Kauai $$$$

Along with the Hyatt Regency Waikoloa on the Big Island and the Westin Maui, the Westin Kauai was one of the big three **Chris Hemmeter** projects to open on the Islands in 1987 and 1988. Whether you call them "experiences," as Hemmeter does, or simply hotels, they are flamboyant and very controversial. Take the Westin Kauai, the result of a $350 million metamorphosis of the **Kauai Surf Hotel.** It features a stable filled with purebred Clydesdales, Belgians, and Percherons that pull 35 carriages along eight miles of paths. And for guests who have something more serious in mind, a team of white horses harnessed to a white carriage stands ready to whisk them off to the resort's own seaside wedding chapel. The horse theme is carved in stone in the Versailles-like palace court, a 2.1-acre reflecting lagoon with seven white marble horses charging from the fountain in the center. Within this lagoon are islands where kangaroos, wallabies, gazelles, zebras, monkeys, turkeys, and llamas live.

If you would rather swim than sail, you might find more room in the Westin Kauai's main swimming pool than the ocean; it is one of the largest in Hawaii, with 26,000 square feet of water surface and a lining of 1.8 million blue and white mosaic tiles. If you prefer the sea, however, Hemmeter designed an eleva-

Kauai

tor inside a hundred-foot cliff to take you to the sandy beach below.

The hotel features five towers with 847 well-appointed guest rooms. The bathrooms are marble, the towels fluffy, and the beds comfortable. The resort is linked to Lihue Airport by its own two-mile road. ◆ Kalapaki Beach, Lihue. 245.5050, 800/228.3000; fax 246.5097

Within the Westin Kauai:

Terrace $$ Light spa cuisine is served in this indoor/outdoor restaurant that overlooks the swimming pool at the Golf and Racquet Club. ◆ Continental ◆ Daily 7AM-3PM. 245.5050

Inn on the Cliffs $$$$ Perched atop the cliffs of Ninini Point, this seafood and pasta house can only be reached by horse-drawn carriage or boat. The atmosphere is casual, with an upstairs bar, fireplace, and outdoor terrace. Fresh Island fish (broiled or grilled *ono, opakapaka, onaga*) and Hawaiian spiny lobster are some of the specialties, but the Inn's highlight is its 200-degree ocean view. ◆ Seafood ◆ Daily 5PM-midnight. 245.5050

Paddling Club A five-level discothèque, with a large dance floor on the ground floor. ◆ W-Th 9PM-2AM; F-Sa 9PM-4AM. In the Royal Boathouse and Paddling Court, at the edge of Kalapaki Beach. 245.5050

Duke's Canoe Club $$$ Named after Hawaii's famous turn-of-the-century athlete, **Duke Kahanamoku,** the restaurant is decorated with memorabilia from Duke's era, and the view is of his passion—the beach. Noted for fresh Island fish, Hawaiian lobster tails, steak, and prime rib. In the beachside lounge, the Kau Kau Grill serves burgers, sandwiches, appetizers, and cocktails. ◆ Steak/Seafood ◆ Upstairs restaurant: daily 5:30-10PM; Grill: daily 11:30AM-11PM. 246.9599

Kalapaki Grill $$ The open-air grill at the hotel's lavish pool features casual dining with an array of sandwiches, salads, desserts, and a full bar. ◆ American ◆ Daily 11AM-10PM. 245.5050

Sharky's Fish Market ★★$$$ This market and resturant located on the cliffs above Kalapaki Bay, has a wonderful open-air view of the hotel's beach, Nawiliwili Harbor, and the Haupu Mountains that rise above Menehune Fish Pond. There's excellent fresh seafood to match the view: oysters, clams, crab, shrimp, and the fresh catch of the day. Diners cannot wear swimsuits, but the casual atmosphere of the old Hawaiian fish market makes it popular for lunch, dinner, and cocktails. ◆ Seafood ◆ Daily 11:30AM-10PM. 246.4470

Prince Bill's $$$ There are views in every direction from the top of the Surf Tower. The breakfast buffet features an omelet station, fresh fruits, pastries, and grilled items, and grilled steaks and seafood are available for dinner. ◆ Continental ◆ Daily 5:30-10PM; champagne brunch Su 9AM-2PM. 245.5050

Tempura Gardens $$$ Set among waterfalls, koi (carp) ponds, and sculptured statuary in the hotel's Japanese garden is a restaurant featuring Japanese cuisine. The staff was trained by the Kyoto Culinary Institute in Japan, and the specialties are the tempura and the sushi. ◆ Japanese ◆ Daily 6-10PM. 245.5050

Cook's at the Beach Indoor/outdoor coffee shop-style dining fronting the Westin's pool complex. Casual. ♦ American ♦ Daily 6:30AM-11PM. 245.5050

🌳 **Kauai Lagoons Golf and Racquet Club** Thirty-six holes designed by **Jack Nicklaus**. The championship Kiele Course is created for tournament play, and the Kauai Lagoons Course, designed in the traditional links style, is for all levels. The club also has a swimming pool, health spas, and eight tennis courts, including a stadium court. ♦ 245.5050

10 Alakoko Fish Pond (also known as the Menehune Fish Pond) According to folk legend, the Menehune were two-foot-tall people who occupied Kauai long before the Polynesians and accomplished enormous physical feats whose remains are still visible. They're credited with building this 900-foot-long wall to cut off a bend in the Huleia River to make this mullet pond at Niumalu Beach Park. It's considered a forerunner of the aquaculture industry (ancient Hawaiians farmed fish in ponds built from rocks). Legend also says that a princess and her brother asked the Menehune to undertake this task, and they agreed as long as the two didn't watch them built it. Naturally, they did watch, and quite unnaturally, they were turned to stone as a result. The twin pillars near the fish pond are said to be the dearly departed. ♦ Overlook on Niumalu Rd, south of the Westin Kauai Hotel

11 Kilohana When **Gaylord Parke Wilcox,** the head of the Grove Farm Plantation, built his Tudor-style dream house in 1935 (pictured above), he probably never imagined that his old office would one day be turned into a jewelry shop. But times do change. His great, old plantation house has been lovingly restored and it is well worth a walk through the beautifully designed home. Along with the original woodwork, Gump's furnishings, and an Art Deco gallery hall are shops and restaurants. In addition to the **Jewelry Box** in Wilcox's old office, the library now houses the **Hemmeter Collection,** fine art from Asia and the Pacific. The master bedroom is now a gallery featuring the works of leading Hawaiian artists. ♦ M-Sa 9:30AM-9:30PM; Su 9:30AM-5PM. Rt 50, just outside Lihue in Puhi. General information: 245.5608

Within Kilohana:

Gaylord's

Gaylord's Restaurant ★★★$$$ Named after **Gaylord Wilcox** of the prominent missionary family, the restaurant offers alfresco dining in one of the most pleasing surroundings on the island. A courtyard overlooks the sprawling lawns of the plantation estate while a private dining room retains the luxury and splendor of the plantation heyday. Specialties include fresh Island seafood, prime rib, lamb with exotic chutneys, and everything from burgers to omelets. ♦ Continental ♦ Daily 11AM-10PM; Su brunch 10AM-3PM. 245.9593

12 Old Koloa Town There is more than bodysurfing to attract visitors to the Poipu area, especially since the restoration of the tour of Koloa was completed in 1984. This $2 million project was the idea of **Robert H. Gerell** of Koloa Town Associates, who negotiated a 67-year lease from the **Mabel P. Waterhouse Trust** and acquired three acres and about 1,000 feet of frontage road in Koloa. With a bent for renovating old structures such as the Stangenwald and the Mendoca buildings in downtown Honolulu, Gerell set to work refurbishing the weathered, termite-ridden storefronts that creaked from one end of Koloa to the other, dressing them in an 1800s look. Some of the historical structures restored are a stone mill stack from the first sugar plantation, **Grove Farm,** which was established here

Kauai

in 1835; the Koloa Hotel (Kauai's first hotel), an 1898 one-story building; and the 1900 **Yamamoto Store.** Among the dozens of other businesses that have opened behind the renovated (and commercial-looking) storefronts are D.J.'s Pizza, Lappert's Ice Cream, Pancho & Lefty's (where you can chow down on Mexican food), the Ralston Gallery, and a Crazy Shirts store. Unfortunately, several *kamaaina* (longtime residents) who couldn't afford the rents had to leave their cozy hometown storefronts.

12 Koloa Ice House ★$ The best quick-stop restaurant on the island for sandwiches, shave ice, frozen yogurt (Honey Hill), and shakes made with fresh Island fruits and homemade ice cream. ♦ Daily 9AM-9:30PM. 54832 Koloa Rd, Old Koloa town. 742.6063

Kauai is the oldest of the Hawaiian Islands and the first one discovered by British **Captain James Cook** in 1778.

Restaurants/Clubs: Red   Hotels: Blue
Shops/🌳 Outdoors: Green   Sights/Culture: Black

12 Koloa Broiler ★$$ Save some money and broil your own steak at this casual and rather quaint little restaurant in rustic Koloa. Fish and chicken are also reasonably priced and include the salad bar and baked beans. (Part of the **Chuck's Steak House** chain.) ♦ Steak ♦ Daily 11AM-10PM. Koloa Rd, Koloa. 742.9122

13 Poipu Beach Drive Kauai's rugged, mountainous interior is inaccessible by car, and there's no road that completely circles the island. The most popular drive from the Wailua or Lihue areas is to the sunny south shore and Poipu Beach. The **Tunnel of Trees** on Hwy 520, a grove of eucalyptus trees that form a natural archway above the road, is the most distinctive landmark along the way. Poipu Beach Park is a choice picnic area and all of Poipu Beach is generally reliable for sunbathing, swimming, and snorkeling, with quality bodysurfing at **Brennecke Beach.** The Poipu area's most famous natural attraction, beyond the fine beaches, is **Spouting Horn,** a geyser-like lava tube with a reputation that exceeds its performance. ♦ Approximately 14 miles from Lihue to Poipu Beach (about 20 minutes driving time)

Kauai

14 Brennecke's Beach Broiler ★★$$ Fresh fish from the *kiawe*-wood broiler, excellent wine by the glass, a sampling of local specialties, and the ocean view, especially at sunset, have made Brennecke's something of a local institution. Try their *pupu* (appetizer) assortment before dinner or with cocktails. ♦ Seafood ♦ Daily noon-10PM. Hoone Rd, directly across from Poipu Beach Park, Poipu. 742.7588

14 Poipu Kai Condominiums $$$ The large, comfortably appointed resort has 250 units on 110 lavishly landscaped acres along the beach. Pools, tennis, and Poipu's first championship golf course are nearby. A Colony Resorts condominium. ♦ 1941 Poipu Rd. 742.6464, 800/367.6046; fax 742.7865

14 Hyatt Regency Kauai $$$$ Built at a cost of $220 million, the South Shore's newest resort sits on 50 acres of choice oceanfront property on **Keoneloa Bay.** The remarkable architecture draws inspiration from Island homes, allowing outdoor elements to come indoors. Interior features include gorgeous, hand-crafted koa wood furnishings. Designed by Honolulu architects **Wimberly Allison Tong & Goo** (exterior) and Santa Monica designers **Hirsch-Bedner & Associates** (interior), the Hyatt is spendidly landscaped with a re-created shipwreck and a five-acre lagoon that faces Keoneloa, commonly called "Shipwreck's Beach." Watersports include scuba diving, snorkeling, and windsurfing. There are four tennis courts and a pro shop. A new **Robert Trent Jones Jr.** 27-hole golf course and driving range are being developed. And the resort is close to facilities for sailing, horseback riding, kayak excursions, and helicopter tours. In addition, the hotel's "Discover Kauai" program, under the auspices of the Kauai Historical Society and Na Hula O Kaohikukapulani, is free to hotel guests. The program's activities include the history and lore of hula (with demonstrations), the history of the Koloa area, and a dune walk featuring the endemic plants and sea life of the Poipu Beach area. The Hyatt Regency is a classy addition to the island. ♦ 1571 Poipu Rd, Koloa. 742.1234, 800/233.1234; fax 742.1557

Within the Hyatt Regency Kauai:

Dondero's ★★$$$$ Northern Italian cuisine in a formal dining atmosphere. Specialties include lemon pasta with shrimp, cioppino, and veal saltimbocca with spinach and buffalo mozzarella. They're very proud of the Moceri wines, from the chef's family vineyards in California. ♦ Italian ♦ Daily 6-10PM. 742.1234

Tidepools ★★$$$$ Fine dining near the saltwater lagoon, overlooking the bay. Entrées include charbroiled steaks and chops, fresh Pacific seafood, lobster in season, and the ever-popular mahimahi baked on *kiawe* (mesquite-grilled) bread. ♦ Continental ♦ Daily 5:30-10:30PM. 742.1234

Ilima Terrace ★$$$ This is the Hyatt's full-service restaurant, centrally located, with open-air dining for breakfast, lunch, and dinner. Pacific Rim cuisine is the specialty here, with Thai spring rolls, lemon-barbecued chicken salad, and stir-fried chicken. Great sandwiches and lighter fare are also available. ♦ Pacific Rim ♦ Daily 6:30AM-10:30PM. 742.1234

The Dock $$ Casual poolside dining for meals on the run or for sedentary sun-worshippers. Sandwiches and quick meals. ♦ American ♦ Daily 6:30AM-5:30PM. 742.1234

Kuhio's For late-night dancing in an Art Nouveau atmosphere, a disco with a dress code. ♦ M-Th, Su 9PM-2AM; F-Sa 9PM-4AM. 742.1234

14 Flamingo Cantina ★$$$ A nice addition to the meager offering of Mexican restaurants on the island, this family-style restaurant specializes in fajitas, which arrive at your table with sizzling gusto. Selections also include fresh fish and seafood, chimichangas, and other standard Mexican fare. ♦ Mexican ♦ Daily 5-9:30PM. Take Nalo Rd from Hoone. 742.9505

15 Sheraton Kauai $$$$ This must be one of the few resort hotels in the world divided by a road. For all practical purposes, there are now two Sheraton Kauai hotels: the original two-story low-rise **Ocean Wing,** anchored on a crescent-shaped white sand beach (perhaps the best beach location of any Poipu hotel) with all of the 220 rooms overlooking the beach and ocean; and the 238-room **Garden Wing,** opened in 1982, with four-story pitched-roofed buildings arranged amid fragrant tropical foliage, meandering lagoons, and a large pool area.

The Sheraton quickly recovered and rebuilt after the wrath of Hurricane Iwa in 1982, and emerged with better facilities than ever. The Garden Wing is a superior bargain because the rooms are about half the price of the Ocean Wing rooms. Although they have garden or mountain views instead of ocean views, the Garden Wing rooms have private lanais, clock radios, and excellent wheelchair access. All of the rooms in both wings have refrigerators and minibars, and each wing has its own pool, plus a wading pool for children. The hotel also features three new tennis courts and a nearby golf course. ♦ 2440 Hoonani Rd, Koloa. 742.1661, 800/325.3535; fax 742.9777

Ancient Hawaiians chewed *ilima* blossoms for their laxative effect, and used breadfruit sap for sores and other skin conditions.

The Outrigger Room ★★$$$$ The hotel's main dining room overlooks the beach and serves pricey Island fish, venison, and prawns. The seafood buffet on Friday nights is worth every penny. Typical Polynesian shows Wednesday and Sunday at 6PM. ♦ Continental ♦ Daily 6:30-9:30PM; prime rib buffet M 6:30-9PM; Su brunch 10AM-2PM. 742.1661

Naniwa $$$$ Traditional Japanese food and sushi bar, with a buffet on Saturday night featuring Japanese salad, miso soup, sashimi, tempura, and sushi. ♦ Japanese ♦ M-Sa 6-10PM. 742.1661

Breakers $$$ An upbeat, contemporary steakhouse with a *kiawe*-wood broiler for Cajun-style fish, steaks, and tiger prawns. ♦ Steak/Seafood ♦ M-Tu, Th-Su 5:30-9:30PM. 742.1661

15 Kiahuna Plantation Condominiums $$$ This first-class resort has plantation-style buildings set on rambling acreage beside Poipu Beach. It is an excellent place to settle while enjoying Kauai's sunniest shoreline. The property is generously landscaped with broad, manicured lawns, trees, and bougainvillea, and pathways and tiny, Japanese-style bridges that lead to the beach. A most serene setting. While the units most in demand are

Kauai

those on the beach, the ones fronted by lawns are quite pleasant. Pool, tennis, TVs. ♦ 2253 Poipu Rd, Koloa. 742.6411, 800/367.7052; fax 742.1047

15 Plantation Gardens ★★$$$ The Hawaiian plantation-home setting has been preserved here by one of Kauai's famous restaurants. After a period of upscale dining, Plantation Gardens has returned to a more familiar menu of Island fish, mainland US seafoods, and a few beef items, though it's all still rather pricey. Desserts, such as the naughty hula pie (ice cream, chocolate, and coconut), are Plantation Gardens classics. This intriguing structure, surrounded by lavish gardens planted with everything from tropical flowers to cacti, was the home of the last manager of the Koloa Sugar Company. ♦ Steak/Seafood ♦ Daily 5:30-10PM. Kiahuna Plantation, Poipu. 742.1695

Honopu Valley on Kauai became known as the Valley of the Lost Tribe when human bones were discovered there. Some speculate that the valley was once home to a Hawaiian tribe.

15 Kiahuna Plantation Golf Course Poipu's first championship 18-hole course, designed by **Robert Trent Jones Jr.,** was completed in 1983. It was bought by a Japanese sports company in 1986 and plans are in the works to add nine more holes. Par 70, 6,440 yards. ♦ 2545 Kiahuna Plantation Dr, Koloa, neighboring the Kiahuna Plantation Condominiums. 742.9595

15 Poipu Beach Hotel $$ Located on one of the island's loveliest and most popular beaches. Now managed by **Stouffer,** this hotel has 138 rooms in low-rise three-story buildings arranged in horseshoe fashion around a courtyard and pool, opening toward the ocean. Rooms have Japanese shoji sliding doors, customary tropical decor, and are equipped with kitchenettes and refrigerators. The hotel's neighbor, also managed by Stouffer, is the comfortably luxurious **Waiohai,** which shares tennis facilities with the Poipu Beach Hotel. ♦ 2249 Poipu Rd, Koloa. 742.1681, 800/426.4122; fax 742.6799

15 Stouffer Waiohai Beach Resort $$$$ Some hearts were broken when the 47 charming cottages of the old Waiohai were replaced with a $60-million, four-story, *W*-shaped, 434-room luxury resort in 1981—Kauai's first luxury hotel. But it didn't take long for visitors to fall in love with **Amfac Hotels'** showcase property. The Stouffer-managed resort continues to reign as one of the best (it used to be *the* best before the Hyatt Kauai opened in 1991).

The mood is luxurious but not pretentiously so, with a brass and marble lobby where iced

mint tea is served in the lobby when you check-in, 11 acres of gorgeously landscaped gardens, ocean-view rooms and suites, and high-class restaurants. But the Waiohai's enduring assets are location and weather. It's next to what many consider the best casual swimming and snorkeling beach on the island, and there is no argument over Poipu Beach's record for being the driest and sunniest locale on Kauai. The resort also has three swimming pools, a Jacuzzi serving as a tropical hot tub, six restaurants and lounges, a fitness center, six tennis courts, and a quiet, inviting library generously stocked with books on Hawaii. The architectural design, by **Arthur Y. Mori & Associates** of Honolulu, was criticized because many of the rooms face each other from inside the *W*-shaped wings. But this design maximizes the number of ocean-view rooms, and the lateral views have improved as the interior gardens have matured. Rooms are filled with special amenities, such as minibars

and refrigerators. ♦ 2249 Poipu Rd, Koloa. 742.9511, 800/426.4122; fax 742.6799

Within the Stouffer Waiohai Beach Resort:

Tamarind ★★★$$$$ Kauai's number one swank restaurant with a menu to match. Thai silk banners are strung above a room gleaming with rich woods, brass, etched glass, and large oriental lamps. Promising beginnings include caviar, pâté, a sensational clam bisque, and a sweetbreads appetizer capable of passing as an entrée. Fresh Island fish is prepared several ways. There is nouvelle cuisine and intriguing dishes with Asian influences, such as pressed duck, firecracker shrimp, and smoked-tea duck. The Tamarind's wine list, once outrageously expensive, has been toned down and carries an excellent selection of California wines. The service is quite professional. ♦ Continental ♦ Tu-Sa 6-10PM. 742.9511

Waiohai Terrace $$$ The Waiohai's all-purpose dining area takes full advantage of its splendid setting on the beach, presenting a large, comfortable, open-air terrace at the water's edge. There's a superior selection of breakfast specials, fresh fish is among the equally versatile luncheon offerings, and dinner features everything from Kauai prawns to prime rib. ♦ Continental ♦ Daily 6:30AM-10PM. 742.9511

Waiohai Sunday Brunch ★★★$$$$ No reservations are taken and the lines can be quite long since this spectacular brunch, served on the oceanside Waiohai Terrace, has become the primary Sunday attraction on Kauai. There are the traditional brunch offerings of fresh fruits and salads, hot dishes, and mouth-watering displays of sinful desserts. But there are also omelets made to order, fresh-made fruit crepes, and a stunning selection of Island delicacies: sashimi, *poke* (marinated raw fish), octopus, smoked fish, plus several other ethnic dishes. This is a grand opportunity to sample a variety of Kauai foods, especially the exotic local seafood. Champagne and serenading by Hawaiian musicians included. ♦ Continental ♦ Su 10AM-2PM. 742.9511

15 Poipu Beach Park Best swimming beach on the island and one of the most beautiful. Children, swimmers, bodysurfers, snorkelers, and volleyball players all take full advantage of the waters and park area. The shallow pool is inviting for children, the sea breeze is laced with the smell of family barbecues, and the stellar south shore sunsets never fail to please. Picnic and public facilities. ♦ Take Hoowili Rd from Poipu Rd

15 Brennecke Beach Poipu Beach Park's neighbor and the best bodysurfing on the island. ♦ Take Honowili Rd from Poipu Rd

16 Beach House ★$$$ Sunsets were made for the Beach House, which sits right on the water. The very casual, woodsy, pleasant dining room has enormous windows affording spectacular views of the Poipu surf (and surfers), the coastline, and, of course, the sunsets. Surely the best of the ocean-view settings on Kauai. The fresh fish is good, the apple-banana muffins are delicious and hot, the service is excellent, and the sunsets are the icing on the cake. Sit at the bar for some scenic sipping. ♦ American ♦ Daily 5:30-10PM. 5022 Lawai Beach Rd, on the road to Spouting Horn. 742.7575

17 Spouting Horn Park The starring attraction, visible from an oceanside hill, is a gush of ocean water that soars its highest through a lava tube when the waves are strongest, sometimes causing a moaning sound. Legend has it that the groan is from a lizard that was trapped in the tube. Spouting Horn's reputation far exceeds its actual performance, which too often sounds more like a popgun than a horn. ♦ End of Lawai Rd, near Poipu

18 National Tropical Botanical Garden
It has survived hurricanes, storms, and floods and is one of Kauai's most enduring and important botanical jewels. The 186-acre garden protects and propagates plants that otherwise might become extinct. It is the only national, privately supported tropical botanical garden chartered by Congress, adding some 1,000 plants to its inventory each year.

In the tradition established by the early Polynesian settlers of Hawaii, who packed plants in their canoes, modern botanists and serious gardeners have brought cuttings from throughout the tropical regions of the world to Hawaii, where they have flourished and multiplied. Since the world's large tropical research gardens in the old Dutch and English colonies had begun to deteriorate, this tradition became of significant importance to the field of tropical botany.

When the then-Pacific Tropical Botanical Garden was chartered by Congress in 1964 in Hawaii, no one was more supportive than **Robert Allerton,** the son of a pioneer Chicago cattleman. By 1938, he and his adopted son, **John Gregg Allerton,** had transformed a hundred-acre estate in Lawai-Kai, Kauai, formerly a vacation domicile of Queen Emma, wife of King Kamehameha IV, into a garden showplace. With the help of hired gardeners, Allerton and son spent 20 years clearing the land of jungle growth and creating sweeping gardens around reflecting pools, fountains, and statues. Kauai's *kamaaina* (old-timers) gave them cuttings and seeds, and the Allertons scoured the islands of the South Pacific for more plants, introducing varieties never before seen on Kauai. With substantial funding from the late Robert Allerton, the Pacific Tropical Botanical Garden opened next door to his estate in 1971. And when John Gregg Allerton passed away, he left the beachside estate to the botanical garden.

Today visitors are able to tour the garden and Allerton Estates, guided by the volunteers of Na Lima Kokua (helping hands). If you can bear being slightly warm in the back of a van with eight or nine other people, you will learn a great deal about the plant life of the tropics. ♦ Fee. Call well in advance (sometimes six months is required) for reservations. Tours offered daily 9AM, 1PM. Write: Box 340, Lawai, Kauai HI 96765. From Hwy 50 take the Lawai turnoff to Lawai Valley. 332.7361

19 Brick Oven Pizza ★★$$ Best-known name in pizza on the island and one of the few places to eat in this area on the way to Waimea Canyon. The dough is made fresh daily, and, naturally, there's a pineapple pizza,

plus a vegetarian pizza on whole wheat dough, sandwiches, and salads. To-go orders available. ♦ Pizza ♦ Tu-Su 11AM-10:30PM. Hwy 50, Kalaheo. 332.8561

20 Salt Pond Beach Park This beach is named for the nearby ancient ponds where the Hawaiians harvested salt from drying beds. **Hui Hana Pa'akai 'O Hanapepe** (The Hanapepe Association to Work With Salt) annually carries on the tradition, letting ocean water dry in the ponds, then collecting the prized salt crystals for use at home or to give to friends. Sometimes referred to as "Hanapepe salt," it has a reddish tint and is coveted by Hawaiians, who consider the colored salt the best for healing and seasoning. However, because of state health regulations, it can't be sold commercially. There's also good swimming, fishing, and shelling at this beach. Picnic and public facilities. ♦ From Hwy 50 take Lele Rd, west of Hanapepe

Restaurants/Clubs: Red   Hotels: Blue
Shops/ ♥ Outdoors: Green   **Sights/Culture:** Black

One of Hawaii's best surfing sites is **Infinities** in west Kauai, named after its 6- to 12-foot summer waves that offer long rides.

21 Russian Fort Officially known as **Fort Elizabeth,** this is another example of how everybody tried to get into the act in Hawaii. In 1817, a German doctor named **Georg Anton Scheffer** arrived in Kauai on business as an agent of Russia. He immediately got other ideas. Convincing Kauai's **King Kaumualii** that they could bring the other islands under their subjugation, a Russian-style fort named after the Czar's daughter was built in the shape of a star on the banks of the Waimea River, and the Russian flag flew over it. However, **Czar Nicholas** didn't share Scheffer's enthusiasm (he preferred to concentrate on conquering Alaska), and the ambitious Russian doctor eventually left. Remnants of the lava stone fort remain buried in the brush, and the state government makes periodic announcements that it will be restored. ♦ Trail to the fort on the beachside of Hwy 50, west of Waimea

22 Green Garden Restaurant ★★★$$ **Sue Hamabata** and her daughter **Gwen** continue the family tradition started in 1948 of serving abundant amounts of delicious Asian, American, and Hawaiian food in the greenery-filled dining room that was once the family's home. Locals and visitors alike thrive on the festive atmosphere and good food. Draped in her signature cascade of Niihau shell leis, Sue Hamabata greets guests, helps with the serving, and offers advice on meals tailored to your taste and budget. Start with a fresh lilikoi (passion fruit) or other tropical fruit daiquiris and don't dare leave without finishing off a piece of the famous lilikoi chiffon pie. ♦ American/Hawaiian ♦ M, W-Su 7AM-2PM, 5-9PM; Tu 7AM-2PM. Hwy 50, Hanapepe. 335.5422

Kauai

22 Lappert's Aloha Ice Cream $ The hula pie ice cream—a concoction of coffee and fudge with a hint of coconut and macadamia—is one of the irresistible flavors created by ice cream wizard **Walter Lappert,** who came to Kauai to retire in 1981 and instead found himself churning out batches of this creamy dessert. Soon the hobby snowballed into a 13,000-gallon-a-month business. His sweet success is spreading to local merchants as well, who supply him with crates of papayas, guavas, coconuts, pineapples, and mangos, and about 8,000 pounds of macadamia nuts a month, not to mention the pure cane sugar, which he whips into more than 70 flavors of ice cream. You can buy it from the small white factory in Hanapepe and throughout the Islands. ♦ M-F 10AM-5PM; Sa-Su 10AM-6PM. Hanapepe Factory and Retail, 1-3555 Kaumualii Hwy 50, just past Hanapepe. 335.6121

Mokihana, a rare, fragrant, berry-sized fruit that grows only on Kauai, is used to make exotic leis; however, *mokihana* leis cannot be worn on bare skin because the fruit is so potent it burns.

23 Wrangler's Restaurant $$ Dining selections are slim in quiet Waimea town, but Wrangler's manages to handle both the local business lunch crowd and the tourists with a wide variety of selections that make up for the sometimes average fare: seafood enchiladas, *kalbi* ribs, burgers, sandwiches, salads, fresh fish, and nine local-style plate lunches. ♦ Eclectic ♦ M-Th 11AM-9PM; F-Sa 11AM-10PM. Hwy 50, Waimea. 338.1218

23 Menehune Ditch Kauai schoolchildren learn shortly after they can talk that if something goes wrong and they don't want to be held responsible for it, blame it on the Menehune, the mysterious and mischievous people who have long endeared themselves to Hawaii's lore-mongers (see "Alakoko [Menehune] Fish Pond" on page 151). The less romantic say they were a pygmy-size class of Polynesian laborers brought to Kauai by the old Hawaiians. True believers credit them with magical powers and maintain that the ones who left Kauai did so on a floating island. The Menehune Ditch is a prodigious work, probably their most famous. What's left of the interlocking stones, a unique form of fitted stonework not found anywhere else in Hawaii, was at one time an aqueduct built by the Menehune at the request of a Kauai king, who wanted to irrigate nearby taro patches. Legend says the king was so pleased with their work he rewarded them with a feast of shrimp, along with their favorite food: sweet potatoes and *haupia* (coconut pudding). ♦ From Hwy 50 in Waimea, follow Menehune Rd one and a half miles to a swinging footbridge across from the ditch

24 Waimea Canyon The Waimea Canyon is out of step with the rest of this lush, green island, which prides itself on having more vegetation per square foot than any place else in Hawaii. This 10-mile canyon (plummeting 3,657 feet at its deepest point along the western side of Kauai) is a rough, inhospitable cut—the jagged terrain is fit only for goats and birds. For lack of a better comparison, it is called the "Grand Canyon of the Pacific"—a worn-out exaggeration. That Waimea is no match for the Grand Canyon, however, does not lessen its importance as one of Hawaii's greatest attractions.

People come to Kauai expecting beaches, sun, flowers, and palm trees...and they find them. But then there are the unexpected sights, such as volcanoes spewing lava, a snow-covered mountain, and this technicolor canyon. The canyon is one of Hawaii's most photographed attractions; colors may

Fruit Facts

The first **papayas** were brought to the Islands in 1778, when **Captain James Cook** offered a handful of papaya seeds to the Hawaiian king. The mellow fruit  ERIC J.W. LEE became a favorite among rulers, who exchanged papayas as gifts. Its rosy, golden meat is reminiscent of the cantaloupe and peach, yet it has its own exotic flavor. Also called "pawpaws," papayas grow in clusters on tall trees that look like a cross between breadfruit trees and palms. These trees are divided into three sexes—male, female, and hermaphrodite. The hermaphrodite fruit combines the juiciness of the female fruit with the leanness of the male fruit, and is considered the tastiest. Not only are papayas delicious, they're also commercially important to Hawaii, which grows millions every year in sprawling papaya groves. It's sold whole or pureed as a multiuse pulp, which is low in calories and rich with vitamins. The enzyme papain, found in papaya juice, is used in the manufacture of digestants and meat tenderizers.

The **coconut,** by comparison, looks like the ugly stepsister of the fruit family. Yet its thick hairy shell, however unattractive, protects delicious creamy milk and sweet meat. The Polynesians brought the first coconuts to Hawaii, and planted a tree for every child that was born to provide a lifelong source of the fruit. Sailors, explorers, and traders kept them at hand for sustenance. Today, fresh and packaged coconut are Island staples.

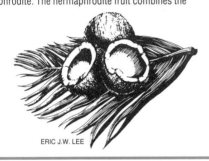

ERIC J.W. LEE

Papaya Tree

---

range from gold to purple, red, and green, and when the canyon depths are clouded by mist, the effect is even more dramatic.

The main overlook offers a sprawling landscape, where white-tailed tropic birds soar overhead and the echoes of bleating, faraway goats can often be heard. Hardy hikers can tackle trails that zigzag down the canyon's wall, but the Iliau Nature Loop north of the lookout is best for casual strollers. Treat Waimea as an all-day excursion because of the interesting towns that invite exploring along the way and the occasionally slow-moving traffic that causes delays. Once there, you'll want to continue on to Kokee State Park for a peek into the verdant and mysterious Kalalau Valley. ◆ From Hwy 50, take Waimea Canyon Dr. From Kekaha, take Kokee Rd (Hwy 550) up to the canyon lookout, marked by a Hawaii Visitors Bureau sign. Check your gas gauge before heading up to the canyon, and bring a wrap for the higher elevation and enough edibles for a brisk picnic. From Lihue, it's about a 35-mile trip

24 Waimea Canyon Drive The road from Lihue passes through sugarcane country, presenting charming views of the rolling green countryside and unspoken invitations to stop and linger in the sleepy coastal towns of Hanapepe and Waimea. The winding ascent from Waimea town to the canyon offers views of Niihau, West Kauai, and multicolored ravines of native flora. Forget your American Express card on this day trip, but don't leave

home without a fully loaded camera. ◆ About one hour driving time from Lihue

25 Polihale State Park The most remote beach on Kauai that can be reached by car. Take the road just beyond the turnoff to Waimea Canyon that winds through the cane field. Good summer swimming, but rough the rest of the year. Restrooms, showers, grills.

26 Kokee State Park and Kokee Lodge Situated eight miles from the canyon lookout in the northern reaches of Waimea, the park's cooler temperatures attract Islanders who tire of the same perfect weather day in and day out. At a 4,000-foot elevation, the 4,345-acre park is a cool, crisp nature-lover's bonanza, with rare honeycreepers, native flora, streams, and trails aplenty. Twelve rental cabins, completely furnished, must be booked well in advance. The hiking trails are abundant (45 miles worth), with one for just about every level of expertise. From the end

157

of June through August, the park's island-famous plums are free for the picking, although there's a 10-pound limit per person. Anglers will be delighted to know they can fish for rainbow trout in Kokee's cool streams from August through September (a license is required). The fish eggs were flown in from the mainland, hatched on Oahu, and released for sportfishing at Kokee. In the forest setting are a lodge, the **Kokee Natural History Museum,** a gift shop, bar, restaurant, and information center. The **Kokee Lodge Restaurant** is now managed by Kokee Ventures, Inc. ◆ Restaurant: M-Th 8:30AM-5:30PM; F-Sa 8:30AM-5:30PM, 6-9PM. Write to: Kokee Lodge, Box 819, Waimea, Kauai HI 96769. 335.6061

27 Kalalau Valley Lookout Timing is everything at this 4,000-foot-high lookout, where the view is usually clear in the early morning but mist and clouds gather to obscure the panoramic vista by afternoon. Many a sightseer has made the long ascent to Kalalau only to find the fabled view hidden by the clouds. When the clouds part, even if just for a moment, the effect is startling. Honeycreepers feed on lehua blossoms and waterfalls and fluted cliffs stand before you. Until early this century, the valley—the largest on the Na Pali Coast—was occupied by hundreds of Hawaiians who lived on the abundant fruits and vegetables grown here. No one lives in this valley now. Experienced hikers can reach Kalalau from Haena on the north shore, but there is no trail from the lookout because of the dangerous terrain. ◆ The lookout is located at the end of winding Hwy 550

Kauai

28 Na Pali Coast State Park From 1380 until 1919, a small group of Hawaiians lived in Nu'alolo, a part of the rugged Na Pali Coast State Park. Remains of their pole-and-thatch houses and *heiau* (an ancient temple) can be seen along the historic trail. The former residents worked the agricultural fields of Nu'alolo 'Aina, then traveled to the reefs by way of a cliff trail to collect fish. ◆ For more information about hiking in the park and required camping permits, call the Department of Land and Natural Resources, 241.3444. **Na Pali Zodiac** offers a hiker's drop-off raft service for an 11-mile hike to Kalalau (see Na Pali Zodiac on page **TK**)

29 Hanakapiai Beach Hike a two-mile, mildly arduous hike from Haena Point, with spectacular views at every turn. Pandanus, wild watercress, guava, fragrant laua'e ferns, kukui, and countless other flora are fed by mountain streams and tiny springlets. White-tailed tropic birds circle against the cliffs and porpoises can sometimes be seen if the trail is close enough to sea level. This trail reveals the marvels of erosion and the beauty of Na

Pali, one of Hawaii's stellar, unforgettable natural sights. Be careful of the strong currents and riptide at the beach; swimming is not recommended here.

30 Waikapalae and Waikanaloa Wet Caves According to Hawaiian legend, the fire goddess **Pele** made a vain attempt to find a home on the north shore of Kauai—but all she found were these wet caves. She didn't need water, so she packed her flames and went to Kilauea on the Big Island. Some people swim in the caves, but it can be dangerous. It is worth a quick visit to see the exterior. ◆ One mile west of Haena Beach Park on Hwy 56

31 Maniniholo Dry Cave This is the first of a trio of caves past Haena Beach Park. Maniniholo is named for a Menehune fisher (see "Alakoko [Menehune] Fish Pond" on page 151) and is really a mile-long lava tube running under a cliff. ◆ Hwy 56, Haena

32 Haena State Beach Park A set designer couldn't create a more beautiful beach than this one, curving sensuously among palm trees backed by lush mountains. Haena Beach is a Kauai legend, used for the Bali Hai setting in the movie *South Pacific.* Swimming is unsafe here. Picnic and camping facilities. ◆ Kuhio Hwy, Haena

33 Haena Point This is the famous "end of the road" on Kauai. It is also the beginning of the hiking trail into spectacular Kalalau Valley. Ke'e Beach is here and it is normally a safe place to swim, but be cautious. During summer months, when the waters are calm, the snorkeling can be wonderful. ◆ At the end of Hwy 56

34 Hanalei Colony Resort Condominiums The only resort development in the majestic Hanalei Valley that spreads along the coastline from the town of Hanalei to Haena. This scenic, isolated hideaway has 46 two-bedroom condominiums, a pool, and beach, but no TVs, phones, or air conditioning. Minimum stay is three days. ◆ Kuhio Hwy, near Haena. 826.6235, 800/628.3004

B&Bs in Paradise

Discriminating travelers who want to be personally matched to a bed-and-breakfast inn should contact **Barbara Campbell,** who is ruthlessly fussy in screening her host properties, and only recommends the very best cottages and homes. She'll ask you about your needs and preferences and give you her recommendations for a $10 fee. Only about 45 properties on Oahu, Kauai, Maui, and the Big Island have made her list, so you know she's very selective. Campbell's 20 years in the hotel business and her first-rate, personalized service make this Hawaii's best B&B referral service, hands down. For more information, write to Campbell at: Box 563, Kamuela HI 96743, or call 885.4550 or 800/262.9912.

34 Captain Zodiac Raft Expeditions
A Zodiac raft ride is a unique and thrilling experience that offers a spectacular view of the soaring **Na Pali Coast** cliffs. You'll also weave in and out of sea caves, ride around (and sometimes through) waterfalls that spill into the ocean. Captain Zodiac (aka **Clancy Greff**) and his band of enthusiastic guides know every inch of the coast and narrate the expedition with Hawaiian history, legends, and even gossip about the local celebrities. A dolphin or sea turtle might swim alongside the raft, or you can try to get even closer to the marine life on one of their snorkel-and-raft trips. Be aware that the front of the raft hits all the bumps, so sit at the rear if you want a smoother ride. Zodiac also offers drop-off and pick-up raft service to backpackers from May through September for the beautiful (if not downright stunning) 11-mile hike through the Na Pali Coast State Park from Haena to Kalalau Valley. Raft trips are sometimes canceled when the weather's rough, particularly during the winter months. ♦ Fee. Excursions leave from Bali Hai Beach (also called Tunnels Beach) Haena. Reservations 826.9371, 826.9772, 800/422.7824

34 Charo's ★$$
The effervescent entertainer of "cuchi cuchi" and **Xavier Cugat** fame bought a place on the North Shore and liked it so much that she set up her own business here. **Charo Rasten's** lovely little restaurant sits on the beach at Haena and has a view of the roaring surf. It's the place to visit on the way around the North Shore for a fresh Island fishburger lunch, a pupus (snack) and chi chi (drink), and a paella dinner (her secret blend of seafood, chicken, and aromatic Spanish saffron). Charo's replaced the former Sandgroper restaurant, which has not been missed. ♦ Continental ♦ Daily 11AM-10PM. Hanalei Colony Resort, near Haena. 826.6422

35 Hanalei-to-Haena Drive
For packing the most into the shortest distance, this may be the best little drive in Hawaii. It begins when you cross the Hanalei River on the 1912 **Hanalei Bridge** and dead-ends nine miles later, west at **Haena Beach Park** (also called Ke'e Beach). Along the way you'll rumble across the 10 little bridges of Hanalei Valley, some of them wooden and most of them only one-lane wide, and past stunning scenery. Taro fields fan out across the valley, then the road swings closer to the steep cliffs overgrown with tropical foliage. You'll also see a succession of sandy beaches nuzzled by foamy waves. The thickly forested **Na Pali Coast Range** is rich with eucalyptus, paperbark, giant tree ferns, banana and coconut trees, and many native trees. Waterfalls plunge hundreds of feet down the mountain slopes, cattle graze in long green valleys extending from the base of the mountains, and side roads dart off through tunnels of trees leading to silent beaches. There are wet caves and dry caves, tumbledown green clapboard houses with saddles straddled across porch rails, and expensive, chalet-style vacation homes trying to hide in the thickly wooded areas guarding the long, empty beaches. The drive is only nine miles long and you'll hate to see it end, so take your time. The only consolation in reaching the end of the road is that you'll have to turn around and drive the same beautiful route all over again. ♦ 18 miles (about 40 minutes total) roundtrip

36 Lumahai Beach
One of the most photographed beaches in Hawaii, with no small assist from its starring role in the movie *South Pacific*. ♦ Two swimming areas: to get to the first, turn after Hanalei Bay, then follow the trail; the second spot, which is dangerous, especially if the surf is up, is farther down the road by the river. Hwy 56, near Hanalei

37 Hanalei Bay
This is one of Kauai's most stunning beaches, a wide, picture-perfect arc of sand cradled by the sharp flanks of Waialeale in the background. Popular for picnics, sunbathing, and local beach gatherings, and sought after by Hollywood, which discovered it in all its splendor in the movie *South Pacific*. Swimming is dangerous here during the winter. Public facilities. ♦ Weke Rd off Kuhio Hwy, Hanalei

37 Tahiti Nui $
When owner **Louise Marston** leans against the front door of her funky bar and eating salon and says: "Sit, you sit," hopefully she'll be telling you to sit on the front porch (not fancy enough to qualify as a veranda), where you can drink something tall and cool and gaze at the passing Hanalei parade. Otherwise, she'll be directing you inside (not nearly as nice) where there's a thatched ceiling, woodcarvings, and Polynesian fabric-covered walls. Entertainment nightly. Luau on Wednesday and Friday nights. ♦ Hawaiian ♦ M-Tu, Th, Sa-Su 11AM-2:30PM, 6-9:30PM; W, F 11AM-2:30PM. Reservations required. Hwy 56, Hanalei. 826.6277

159

37 Shell House $ Seafood, burgers, Italian dishes, French fries with melted cheese, clam chowder, and an array of macadamia nut pies are all served in a homey atmosphere. ♦ American ♦ Daily 8AM-10:30PM. Aku Rd and Kuhio Hwy, Hanalei. 826.7977

38 Chuck's Steak House ★$$$ A few notches above the Joe Surfer ambience of the chain's earlier restaurants, this one is smartly designed and offers a more interesting menu. Ask for a table outside on the lanai and settle down for a fish sandwich or a hot entrée at lunch; seafood, steak, ribs, and salad are served at night. Daily blackboard specials are often your best bet. ♦ Steak/Seafood ♦ M-F 11:30AM-2:30PM, 6-10PM; Sa-Su 6-10PM. Princeville Shopping Center, Princeville Resort. 826.6211

38 Lanai Restaurant at Princeville $$$ A grand, open-air dining room overlooking the Princeville Resort's large pool and golf course. Pleasant for cocktails, dinner, and watching the sunset. Fresh seafood is a specialty, and the soup and salad bar is an option for light eaters. Also serves steaks, pastas, and veal. ♦ Steak/Seafood ♦ Daily 6-9:30PM; cocktails 4PM. Princeville Resort. 826.6226

Kauai

38 Princeville Condominiums $$$ The Princeville Hotel, a newcomer, is getting all the attention now, but there are also some exceptionally roomy and peaceful condominiums scattered throughout this scenic, 2,000-acre resort on the bluffs high above Hanalei Bay and the Pacific. The main attractions are the 27-hole, par 72, 6,600-yard **Makai Course** and the 18-hole, par 73, 7,000-yard **Prince Course,** as well as the gorgeous beaches and mountains of the Hanalei area. The newly opened 66,000-square-foot **Prince Golf and Country Club** serves the Prince Course and has its own restaurant and lounge. There are good beaches nearby, but access is not easy. The various condominiums all have pools; there are tennis courts, horseback riding, and best of all, a peaceful air infused with tropical beauty. ♦ Many real estate companies handle vacation rentals of condos and homes in the Princeville area; a good one to call for information is Princeville Travel Services, 826.9661, 800/445.6253. Hawaiian Islands Resorts handles rentals for **Pali Ke Kua** (one of the finest projects in Princeville) and **Pu'u Poa,** 531.7595, 800/367.7042

38 Beamreach ★$$$ Dinner begins with a salad for everyone seated at the table and loaves of fresh cracked wheat and honey bread, followed by a choice of chicken, fresh fish, or beef—their steaks are the best on the north shore. ♦ Steak/Seafood ♦ Daily 5-10PM. At the Pali Ke Kua Condominiums, Princeville Resort. 826.9131

38 Princeville Hotel $$$$ In 1985 **Sheraton Hotels** decided to venture where no major hotel had dared to go before: to the extraordinary setting and sometimes unreliable climate of the North Shore. The hotel holds the plum location in the Princeville development on the lookout point at Hanalei Bay. The original architects designed a simple hotel in a series of three terraces descending the face of Pu'u Poa Point down to a long stretch of white sand beach. There were two problems with the new hotel: a demand for more upscale accommodations and more ocean views. So the architects went back to the drawing board for a major renovation, which was completed in 1991.

It cost about $100 million to completely refurbish the property to meet the demanding standards of a five-star hotel, but now all public areas, including the lobby, lounge, and restaurants, offer a clear view of the 23-acre site. The new **Prince Suites,** about one and a half times larger than the king and double rooms, accommodate a formal entry hall, an oversize bathroom with a spa tub, 18th-century Italian-style furniture, floor-to-ceiling bronze mirrors in the bedroom, and an additional living room. Special services and amenities include butler and valet service, 24-hour room service, and complimentary transportation to the golf course and tennis courts. Facilities include a luxurious pool, exercise room, beauty salon, and beach kiosks for snorkeling and windsurfing. Guests also have preferred starting times and charge privileges at the adjacent Princeville Resort facilities, including the **Princeville Makai Golf Course** and tennis courts. ♦ Princeville, Hanalei. 826.9644, 800/826.4400; fax 826.1166

Within the Princeville Hotel:

Cafe Hanalei ★★$$$ Fronting a large reflective pond, this cafe has a soaring three-story-high ceiling crowned by three enormous chandeliers. Although the interior is quite luxurious, the atmosphere is casual, with dining available inside or on a covered lanai. Breakfast choices include a buffet and à la carte items. Lunch and dinner features steaks and seafood, such as charbroiled ahi. The Friday night seafood buffet, which gained a popular following before the renovations, promises to be even more spectacular. ♦ Steak/Seafood ♦ Daily 6:30AM-3PM, 5-10PM. 826.9644

La Cascata ★★★$$$$ Modelled after a restaurant in the town of San Pedro along Italy's Amalfi Coast, the interior features terracotta floors, trompe l'oeil paintings, and a traditional ballroom complete with 18th-century Italian gilded consoles. Named for the waterfalls that often grace the mountains beyond Hanalei, La Cascata brings a bit of the Mediterranean to the Pacific, with offerings such as swordfish carpaccio, pan-fried lamb loin, and a traditional Sunday brunch with an Italian twist. There's also a wide selection of pastas, seafood, veal dishes, and other favorites. ♦ Italian ♦ Daily 6-10PM; Su brunch 10AM-2PM. 826.9644

The Beach Restaurant $$ Light poolside meals and snacks, featuring American and local favorites: burgers, smoked turkey sandwiches, teriyaki chicken, fruit plates. ♦ American ♦ Daily 6:30AM-sunset. 826.9644

38 Hanalei Bay Resort Condominiums $$$ Originally built as an exclusive condominium project, the 200 units were converted into a hotel-style operation complete with a full-service restaurant, eight tennis courts, and a full-time, on-site tennis pro. A million-dollar renovation recently spruced up the operation even more. Two- and three-story buildings with one-, two- and three-bedroom suites overlook Hanalei Bay and the ocean, with stunning landscaping and all the romance of Bali Hai. With the Princeville courses nearby, this is an attractive choice for golf, as well as tennis buffs. Spacious units offer quality accommodations, including kitchens. There's a pool, but access to the beach is difficult. ♦ At Princeville Resort. 5380 Honoiki Rd, Princeville, Hanalei. 826.6522, 800/827.4427; fax 826.6680

38 Bali Hai ★★$$$ One of the most sophisticated restaurants on the North Shore in both decor and menu. The light and airy dining room, beautifully embellished with batik banners, overlooks the Hanalei Bay Resort's tennis courts and the Pacific in the distance. Poached salmon, rack of lamb, scampi, ginger chicken, and cannelloni are among the selections on the extensive menu. Entertainment nightly. ♦ Continental ♦ Daily 7-11AM, 11:30AM-2PM, 5:30-10PM. Hanalei Bay Resort, Princeville. 826.6522

38 Princeville Golf Courses These sensationally scenic 45 holes of golf (27 holes at Makai Course, 18 at Prince) were designed by **Robert Trent Jones Jr.** (who owns a home in nearby Hanalei). The course is spread out on a lush plateau high above Hanalei Bay with a view of Mount Waialeale, plunging waterfalls, and the ocean. The ocean holes are the

most spectacular, but the lake and woods holes also offer superb blends of golf and scenery. Princeville's only drawback is the threat of rain, especially during winter and spring months, though there were no rain-out days here in a recent three-year period. ♦ Makai Course: 27 holes, par 72, 6,600 yards. Prince Course: 18 holes, par 73, 7,000 yards. Expensive green fees; preferred starting times and rates for Princeville Resort guests. Pro shop. 826.3580

38 Hanalei Dolphin ★★$$$ For many years the most popular restaurant on the North Shore (and for many years, just about the only restaurant on the North Shore). Although it's located in a tranquil setting on the banks of the Hanalei River, the view is confined to great margaritas, grilled steaks, seafood, and chicken. ♦ Continental ♦ Daily 6-10PM. Hwy 56, Hanalei. 826.6113

38 Hanalei Museum Snack Shop $ The museum has closed but this tiny cafe is still popular for its local-style plate lunches. ♦ Hawaiian ♦ M-F 10AM-4PM. On Hwy 56, Hanalei. 826.6783

38 Waioli Mission House Museum This two-story cottage was brought to Hawaii in prefabricated sections in 1836 by New England missionaries who didn't want to go native. It's a pleasant sojourn into the past, replete with furniture of that period. There used to be a pole-and-thatch meeting house on this site in the early 1830s, when traditional, prehistoric tools were still being made and used in Hanalei. The church's present frame, built in 1841, represents the first time plaster, nails, and western frame construction were

used in Hawaii. (Wooden floors weren't used until 1861.) Lovely gardens flourish in the back, and it's easy to imagine the days when the **Wilcoxes,** the island's prominent missionary family, arrived on Kauai in the early 1800s. ♦ Donations welcome. Tu, Th, Sa 9AM-3PM. Half-hour guided tours; advance reservations required for groups. Hanalei. 245.3202

39 Anini Beach Well protected and offers good swimming, great windsurfing and camping facilities. Leave the winter surfing to the experts. Picnic facilities. ♦ Take Anini Rd from Kuhio Hwy, near Kalihiwai

40 Jacques Bakery ★$ Kauai's famous bakery has heavenly French pastries, pies, cookies, and rye and molasses bread. Jacques' bread turns ordinary sandwiches into gourmet meals and is served in some of the islands' finer restaurants. ♦ Daily 6AM-6PM. In Kilauea, en route to Kilauea Lighthouse. 828.1393

Restaurants/Clubs: Red	Hotels: Blue
Shops/ 🌴 Outdoors: Green	**Sights/Culture:** Black

40 Kong Lung Caveat emptor: Kauai's "Gump's of the Pacific" is dangerous to your pocketbook. An old plantation store converted to a charming, modern-day gift shop, Kong Lung offers only the most tasteful and appealing items, from top-quality men's and women's sportswear to unique children's books and gifts. Rare, luxurious soaps are tempting, as are the fine china, jewelry, accessories, and unusual gift items made by master artists across the country. ◆ M-Sa 9AM-6PM; Su 9AM-5PM. Kilauea Plantation Center, Kilauea. 828.1822

40 Kilauea Point National Wildlife Refuge Lighthouses are customarily located in rugged, remote areas that are unspoiled and spectacularly beautiful. This setting is no exception; in fact, it's one of the best. The lighthouse was built in 1913 and the building is on the National Register of Historic Places. Its light could be seen 20 miles from shore. The US Coast Guard stopped operating the Kilauea Lighthouse when an automated light was installed in 1967, and now the **US Fish and Wildlife Service** runs the 169-acre preserve. Look for the red-footed boobies and wedge-tailed shearwaters soaring above; and from the lookout point, try to spot the sea turtles and porpoises. This windswept, isolated corner of the island is a nature-lover's refuge. From December through April, it's a wonderful vantage point for humpback whale watching. ◆ Fee. Daily 10AM-4PM. Turn at Kolo Rd in Kilauea, then left on Kilauea Rd Park where the road ends. Drive through the open gate and park in the parking lot. 828.1413

Kauai

41 Anahola Beach Park The swimming is excellent here. Anahola's shallow waters are loved by fishers and families alike. Picnic facilities. ◆ Take Aliomanu Rd from Kuhio Hwy near Anahola

42 Jimmy's Grill $$ Jimmy, the son of **Jim Jasper** who owns **JJ's Broiler**, has followed in his dad's footsteps, breaking new ground with this hip restaurant that appeals to the under-50 crowd. From its sandy beach, ground-floor bar to its surfboard decorated second-floor restaurant, Jimmy's says "Relax, have fun, and enjoy the good food." Some think it's overpriced, though, and the steep stairs can be difficult for the elderly. Favorites are burgers, giant ribs, salads, fish, and steaks. ◆ American ◆ Daily 11AM-10PM. Hwy 56, Kapaa. 822.7000

42 Norberto's El Cafe $$ The third Mexican restaurant to enter the arena in tiny Kapaa is giving the competition a run for its money with good size portions and tasty selections including tacos, burritos, rellenos, and enchiladas. A welcome addition to the rather scant south-of-the-border offerings on this island. A small, crowded, and fun environment. ◆ Mexican ◆ Daily 5:30-9PM. 4710 Kukui St, off Hwy 56, Kapaa. 822.3362

42 Kountry Kitchen ★$$ From the breakfast omelets (including the outrageous Polynesian omelet with kim chee—spicy, pickled cabbage—and Portuguese sausage) to the quarter-pound burgers on giant sesame seed buns and the complete steak, chicken, and fish dinners this dependable little diner keeps big eaters happy without devouring the wallet. Great family restaurant with one of the best breakfasts in town. ◆ American ◆ Daily 6AM-2:30PM, 5-8:30PM. Hwy 56, Kapaa. 822.3511

42 Ono Family Restaurant $$ After becoming famous for their Ono Beef Charburgers, they've expanded into a fancy little three-meals-a-day dining room and there's often a line waiting to get in for dinner. Low prices (rock-bottom rates compared to the resort areas) and solid American food, from fresh snapper to pork chops with mushroom gravy and the Ono burgers (something all cheeseburger connoisseurs must sample). And then there are the one-of-a-kind items: buffalo burgers, buffalo steaks, and occasionally stir fry buffalo specials made from bison raised in Hanalei on the North Shore. There's a takeout window, too. ◆ American ◆ Daily 7AM-9PM. 41-292 Kuhio Hwy, Kapaa. 822.1710

42 Kapaa Fish and Chowder House ★★$$ Good seafood fettuccine, chowders, and kabobs anchor the menu of this restaurant in a plantation-era-turned-nautical building with battleship-gray walls adorned with ship's wheels. The lilikoi (passion fruit) daiquiris are not to be missed. ◆ Seafood ◆ M-F noon-9:30PM; Sa-Su 5-9:30PM. 4-1639 Kuhio Hwy, at the north end of Kapaa. 822.7488

42 Kapaa Beach Park Good swimming and picnic facilities for an East Kauai beach, but it's not as spectacular as the north and west beaches. ◆ Hwy 56, Kapaa

43 Tropical Taco ★$ The famous green van where tacos were sold in Hanalei for years gave birth to this stationary version of Tropical Taco. Line up indoors for the same gargantuan tacos and humongous burritos. ◆ Mexican ◆ M-Sa 11AM-9:30PM. Hwy 56, next to the post office in Kapaa. 822.3622

43 A Pacific Cafe ★★★★$$$ Owner/chef **Jean-Marie Josselin,** formerly of the Hotel Hana-Maui and the Coco Palms Resort, opened this restaurant in 1990 and lost no time adding to his already considerable reputation. In his hands, Pacific Rim cuisine takes on new life; try the grilled Hawaiian *aku* (tuna) with papaya-black bean relish, deep-fried sashimi with *wana* (sea urchin) sauce, sautéed crab cakes with mango-ginger sauce, or Kauai-grown clams in coconut milk and red curry. Kauai farmers truck in the fresh produce daily—90 percent of his produce is from the island and soon even the oysters will be Kauai-grown. The Chinese peas in the black bean sauce are a must, and vegetarians will love the potato-tofu lasagna. A stylish, cheerful restaurant, with tropical decor and ceramic plates made by Josselin's wife, **Sophaonia.** ♦ Pacific Rim ♦ M, W-Su 5:30-10PM. Kauai Village, Hwy 56, Kapaa. 822.0013

43 Zippy's $ The Oahu fast-food chain's Kauai entry, fortifying Islanders with Zippy's famous chili, saimin (noodles in broth), and the usual burgers, fries, and shakes. ♦ American ♦ 24hrs. 4-919 Kuhio Hwy, Kapaa. 822.9866

43 Aloha Diner ★$ Strictly local-style, a small diner with saimin and the best Hawaiian food on the Island. This small family operation is a local institution, where folks line up for fried *akule* (scad), *lomi* salmon, *lau lau* (pork in taro and *ti* leaves), and poi. Don't get your hopes up if you're a *malihini* (newcomer), as Hawaiian food is usually an acquired taste. ♦ Hawaiian ♦ M-Sa 10:30AM-3PM, 5:30-9PM. 971-F Kuhio Hwy, Kapaa. 822.3851

44 Bull Shed ★$$$ Many swear by it, others swear at it, but there's no argument over the Bull Shed's choice location on the beach, where the surf marches toward the windows on the windy eastern shores of Kauai. A heroic cut of prime rib stands out on a short menu of beef, lamb, chicken, fish, and a salad bar. Usually crowded and service can be haphazard. ♦ American ♦ Daily 5:30-10PM. 796 Kuhio Hwy, Kapaa. 822.3791

45 Sea Shell Restaurant $$ You can almost hear the surf better than you can see it at this strangely designed, oddly located restaurant set back from the beach across the street from the Coco Palms Resort Hotel. If you think the room is boring, wait until you see the menu. The specialty is fresh fish and a salad buffet. ♦ Seafood ♦ Daily 5:30-10PM. Wailua Beach, across the street from Coco Palms. 822.3632

45 Wailua Beach Good swimming when the waves are small. Strong currents pose a danger in the big surf.

45 JJ's Boiler Room $$$ The offspring of the original **JJ's Broiler** dropped the *r* out of the name, but not the popular Slavonic steak. Same steak and seafood menu as the original, but in a glossier location. ♦ Steak/Seafood ♦ Daily 5-9:30PM. Hwy 56, Coconut Marketplace. Wailua. 822.4411

Kauai's **Wailua River** area is dotted with several *heiaus* (ancient temples) that ascend from the mouth of the river toward the mountains.

46 Coco Palms Resort Hotel $$$ A bright

color scheme, a mile-long jogging path through the coconut grove, and the island's first clay tennis courts are just a few of the changes made by **Park Lane Hotels International** of San Francisco since taking over the Coco Palms in 1985. And just in time, it seems. Park Lane began a much-needed $7 million facelift the minute it took over, and happily, the Coco Palms is looking better today. The long, three-story structure (390 rooms) blends gracefully into the carefully preserved grove of 200,000-year-old coconut trees that wave above a long lily-dotted lagoon, surrounded by thatched-roof honeymoon cottages. Room decor carries out the Polynesian theme with huge clamshell wash basins in the **Sea Shell Rooms** and wrought iron and rattan in the **Alii Kai** wing. The schmaltzy evening show at the Coco Palms is legendary. Every night, a hush settles over the lagoon area as the history of the torchlighting ceremony is recited. During the dramatic narration, conch shells sound, drums beat, and barefoot youths run along the banks of the lagoon leaving a trail of lighted torches. A big disappointment is that **Grace Guslander,** the general manager since 1953 and acknowledged founder of the torchlighting ceremony in Hawaii, has retired, leaving a certain spirit and excitement at the gate. Her vision of what a resort hotel in Hawaii should be like helped make the Coco Palms Kauai's

most successful hotel for many years. A sandy beach is located across the road (watch out for speeding traffic), but it is often windswept and not very suitable for swimming. ♦ 4-241 Kuhio Hwy, Hwy 56, Wailua. 822.4921, 800/338.1338; fax 822.7189

Within the Coco Palms Resort Hotel:

Lagoon Dining Room $$$ Open air with front-row views of the lagoon and the evening torchlighting ceremony. Menu changes slightly each night, but the basics are beef and seafood with some Hawaiian and Polynesian offerings, such as *lomi* salmon, charcoal-roasted pig, shrimp tempura, and curries. Hawaiian entertainment is offered on alternate nights. ♦ American/Polynesian ♦ M-Sa 6AM-2PM, 6-9PM; Su 10AM-2PM, 6-9PM. 822.4921

47 Fern Grotto The Wailua River, the best known river in Hawaii, leads to Fern Grotto, a visitor attraction that has achieved the supreme status of being a must-do (a must-not-do if you don't like crowds and a circus-like atmosphere). Cruise boats glide up the river as entertainers do the hula and perform the standard Hawaiian songs to the accompaniment of ukuleles. The boats land and visitors walk through the jungle to the grotto, a cool cave filled with giant cascading ferns. Inside, the hired help recount legends to the accompaniment of more Hawaiian music. The trip back is highlighted by a Hawaiian sing-a-long. The grotto is a popular site for weddings, replete with the traditional singing of the "Hawaiian Wedding Song," a guaranteed tear-jerker. ♦ Cruise fee. Cruises daily 9AM-4PM. Boats leave Wailua Marina on Hwy 56, Wailua. **Smith's Motor Boat Service** 822.4111; **Waialeale Boat Tours** 822.4908

48 Kintaro ★★$$$ Sleek, elegant, and authentically decorated with kimono and Japanese screens. This Japanese restaurant is as good as anything you'd find in Waikiki, with an impressive selection of sashimi, sushi, *zaru soba, nabemono, teppanyaki*, and other exquisite selections. Be adventurous and try fresh-water eel grilled with sweet sauce over rice. ♦ Japanese ♦ Daily 5:30-9:30PM. Hwy 56, near Wailua. 822.3341

48 Lydgate State Park Lydgate is a favorite among local families and others who enjoy the pleasant combination of beach, protected pools, picnic pavilions, and tree-shaded park land beside the Wailua River. Picnic and public facilities. ♦ Hwy 56, Wailua

48 Wailua Marina Restaurant $$ Crowded during the day with **Fern Grotto** tourists, but there's a little more breathing room during

Kauai

dinner hours in this huge, very touristy restaurant. Fish, steak, chicken, and pork dishes carry reasonable price tags. Free pickup for dinner guests staying at Wailua area hotels. ♦ American ♦ Daily 9AM-2PM, 5-9PM. Hwy 56, Wailua Marina. 822.4311

48 Colony's Kauai Beachboy Hotel $$ Built within the **Coconut Plantation** development, this 243-room hotel is on a mile-long stretch of Waipouli Beach, which is better for wading and beachcombing than for swimming. The lackluster, no-nonsense rooms have refrigerators and lanais with ocean or mountain views. Serious shoppers are well-located here: it's not far from the **Coconut Marketplace,** a shopping complex with some 70 shops, restaurants, and movie theaters, most of them pretty touristy. Pool, tennis. A Colony Resort Hotel. ♦ 484 Kuhio Hwy, Kapaa. 822.3441, 800/327.3305 (HI), 800/777.1700 (US and Canada) fax 822.0843

Restaurants/Clubs: Red   **Hotels:** Blue
Shops/ 🌳 Outdoors: Green   **Sights/Culture:** Black

48 Sheraton Coconut Beach Hotel $$$$ The Sheraton chain took over this former Holiday Inn in 1981 and brought in one of their top hotel managers to upgrade it at all levels. The 309-room, multi-winged building has an airy, garden-like atmosphere that benefits generously from its setting amidst nearly 11 acres of coconut trees along Waipouli Beach. The stained glass and tapestry decor of the public areas is highlighted by a 40-foot waterfall cascading into a reflection pool. All rooms have lanais, most with ocean views. A pool and excellent tennis courts highlight the nonbeach activities. The beach is scenic, but often windy, and not good for swimming because of rocky conditions. Shops and restaurants are nearby. ♦ Coconut Plantation Marketplace, Kuhio Hwy, near Kapaa. 822.3455, 800/325.3535; fax 822.1830

Within the Sheraton Coconut Beach Hotel:

Voyage Room ★$$$ The main dining room offers buffets and à la carte selections at breakfast and lunch, with a comfortable open-air setting looking across the pool and lawn areas toward the beach and ocean. The menu features such specialties as fresh Oahu oysters and a chowder made with four types of fish. You should also try the shrimp, lightly breaded with coconut, deep-fried, and served with papaya chutney. A dessert star is the "Plantation Coupe," sliced Island bananas and macadamia nuts baked in ices and liqueurs, then served over French vanilla ice cream. ♦ Continental ♦ Daily 6:30AM-2PM, 6-9:30PM. 822.3455

Sheraton Coconut Beach Luau $$$ One of the Island's better hotel luaus, thanks in part to its superb location. The rustic luau *hale* (house) is an open-air, wood-beamed structure built in a grove of coconut palms that was once the playground of Hawaiian royalty. Limited seating enhances the intimate atmosphere. **Bill Lemn,** who learned the *imu* (earthen oven) traditions from his Hawaiian grandmother, adds to the family-like mood by explaining the traditions of the feast with the guests. The Polynesian show following the luau is another family affair, led by **Victor** and **Kuulei Punua.** ♦ Luaus Tu-Su evening. 822.3455

49 Wailua Golf Course *Golf Digest* rated this seaside course as one of the top 10 public courses in America, and with inexpensive green fees, it's unquestionably the best golf bargain in Hawaii. Extending more than a mile along Wailua Beach, the course was built in 1920 among sand dunes and ironwood trees. The ocean comes into play on three holes, and the demanding back nine is highlighted by the famous Sea Beach Hole at the par-three 17th, where too much club will put a ball in the Pacific. Par 72, 6,665 yards, 71.9 rating. ♦ Hwy 56, Wailua. 245.2163

49 Kaha Lani Condominiums $$$ Secluded on the beach at Wailua, the 74 units have ocean-view lanais. Managed by the always-reliable **Aston Resorts.** Pool, tennis, golf. ♦ Near Wailua. 822.9331, 800/922.7866; fax 922.8785

49 Kauai Hilton and Beach Villas $$$
Along Kauai's Coconut Coast, the new Westin Kauai is taking top honors for glitz, glamour, and grandiose amenities. But the Hilton, which opened in 1986, is holding its own a few miles up the coast with a regular (as opposed to super) resort hotel. The Hilton's series of low-rise, four-story buildings are oriented toward a long strip of sandy beach and the ocean. Because of the undertow, the beach is only suitable for sunning, but there is plenty of water in the three swimming pools, including the main pool area, which is landscaped with caves, trickling waterfalls, fountains, and lots of greenery.

There are 350 guest rooms with lanais in the main hotel, as well as 150 older one- and two-bedroom villas with kitchens and laundry facilities (a terrific bargain, especially for families). The **Wailua Golf Course** is a short, free shuttle ride away. Warning for those who prefer peace and quiet: groups and conventions are big at this Hilton. ♦ 4331 Kauai Beach Dr, Kapaa. 245.1955, 800/HILTONS; fax 246.9085

Within the Kauai Hilton and Beach Villas:

Gilligan's Pinch yourself if you think you're in Acapulco. This is Kauai's hottest new disco, complete with a long line of people on the weekends, and state-of-the-art audio and video entertainment jacked up so high that Kauai's King Kaumualii is probably dancing in his grave. Strict dress code. ♦ M-Th 9PM-2AM; F-Sa 9PM-4AM. 245.1955

50 Wailua Falls If there's been substantial rain, you'll see two falls (Wailua means "twin waters") tumbling over an 80-foot cliff, which Hawaiian chiefs used to dive off of to prove their courage. The lookout for the falls is four miles west of Kapaia along one of those side roads you might be tempted to take to satisfy your wanderlust. Pass on the lookout unless you don't mind the monotonous ride to get there. ♦ From Hwy 56 north of Lihue, take Hwy 583 (Maalo Rd) near Kapaia

51 Hanamaulu Cafe & Tea House ★★$$
Kick the Kauai salad bar habit and spend a unique Island evening in one of the garden rooms (by reservation only) at this large Japanese/Chinese restaurant, a local favorite that has been lining 'em up for more than 60 years. The chef's nine-course dinners (including snow crab claws, spare ribs, and ginger-seasoned fried chicken) are memorable, and Hanamaulu adds its special flavor to lobster, baking it in a rich butter sauce with bread crumbs. ♦ Japanese/Chinese ♦ M-F 9:30-11AM, 4:30-9PM; Sa-Su 4:30-9PM. On Hwy 56 in old Hanamaulu Town. 245.2511

Kauai's Highlights

Helicopter tours of the **Na Pali Coast, Waimea Canyon,** and **Mount Waialeale** (Papillon, Ohana, and Jack Harter offer the best tours).

A tour of **Grove Farm,** a former sugar plantation in Lihue.

Bodysurfing at **Brennecke Beach** in Poipu.

Visiting **Waimea Canyon.**

A tour of the **National Tropical Botanical Garden** and the **Allerton Estates** in the Lawai Valley.

The hike into **Kalalau Valley.**

Trail riding in Hanalei with **Pooku Stable** horses.

The view of Kalalau Valley and the Na Pali Coast from the **Kalalau Lookout.**

A visit to **Hanalei Bay** and the nine-mile drive from Hanalei to Haena.

Zodiac raft rides on the Na Pali Coast with **Captain Zodiac Raft Expeditions.**

Hawaii's Best

JoAnn A. Yukimura
Mayor, County of Kauai

A guided hike up Crater Hill, which is part of the **Kilauea National Wildlife Refuge** on Kauai, will reveal some of the most spectacular coastline in the world.

Experience the essence of Kauai by spending a week at the **Mokihana Festival,** which features a

Kauai

statewide hula competition and a remarkable songfest showcasing the best local composers.

A walk through old **Hanapepe Town,** one of the small-town treasures of our west side, filled with the history and spirit of Kauai's people.

The view of **Hanalei Bay** off Kauai as you descend into the Hanalei Valley is picture-perfect. Picnic areas at **Black Pot Park** make this a favorite spot for local family gatherings. The **Hanalei Pier** is a picturesque landmark on the bay.

The Wailua area on the east coast of Kauai is a storehouse of Hawaiian history and culture. A museum at the **Coco Palms** houses old Hawaiian books and artifacts. Several *heiaus* (ancient temples) are located within the area and many legends and events of historical significance are centered here.

For the visitor interested in Hawaiian history: The **Kauai Museum,** displaying Kauai antiquities, is located in the county seat, Lihue; the **Waioli Mission,** built and furnished by missionaries in 1834, is in Hanalei Valley; and the **Grove Farm Museum,** with an operating diesel engine and other plantation artifacts, is in Puhi.

Niihau

The island of Niihau (*nee*-how) holds as much intrigue for Hawaiian residents as it does for visitors. Strict controls on access to this 73-square-mile island and even on information about Niihau have given rise to its nickname, The Forbidden Island.

Niihau's small population, most of them pure-blooded Hawaiians, lives in chosen isolation. They speak Hawaiian fluently and spend their days fishing, swimming, shelling, and herding cattle or sheep. There are no hotels, no telephones, few modern appliances, some guns, little liquor, no jails, and lots of transistor radios. Horses and pickup trucks are the modes of transportation, and occasional entertainment includes a portable TV that's plopped down on the sands of a beach or hooked up to a generator that provides electricity to some of the homes.

In the 1860s, **King Kamehameha IV** sold Niihau for $10,000 to a Scottish family. The descendants, the **Robinsons**, who reside on nearby Kauai, still own the island and have resisted all efforts by outside agencies to purchase it. Niihau operates by a very simple tenet: no one is allowed on the island unless invited. The residents (230 in the 1990 census, up by four from 1980), most of whom were born and raised on Niihau, are free to invite neighbor-island friends and relatives to visit. Children attend Niihau's only public school, then move to Kauai for the upper grades. Many of them return to Niihau once their schooling years are over to live there permanently. The people of Niihau are employed by the Robinsons to work on the ranch lands. Food and other supplies are regularly brought to the island by boat. A serious pastime

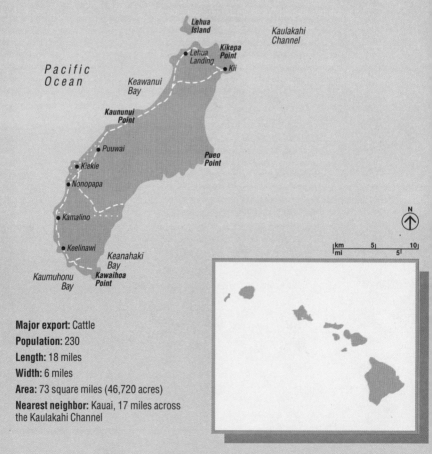

Major export: Cattle
Population: 230
Length: 18 miles
Width: 6 miles
Area: 73 square miles (46,720 acres)
Nearest neighbor: Kauai, 17 miles across the Kaulakahi Channel

among the women is the gathering of tiny, perfect shells that wash up on the beaches and are fashioned into the famous Niihau shell leis. These are delicate, rare, and quite expensive leis, and many are of museum quality and are coveted by private collectors. In fact, Niihau shell leis are one of the most treasured possessions of the Hawaiian people.

Life on Niihau is said to be free from the stresses and problems of modern-day life. There are miles and miles of white-sand beaches and, except for the residents' modest bungalow-type dwellings, the island remains in its natural state. As the last enclave of the Hawaiian race, Niihau was the only precinct in Hawaii to reject statehood in the general plebiscite of 1959.

Hula Kahiko: The Return of the Traditional Hawaiian Dance

According to a popular Hawaiian legend, the first hula was performed by **Laka**, the goddess of dance, to entertain her fiery sister **Pele,** the volcano goddess. Pele reacted by lighting up the sky with delight, and *hula kahiko* (ancient hula) then became a sacred part of Hawaiian religion, and was performed by men and women in honor of the gods. Hundreds of interpretive dances telling stories of Hawaiian history and life were passed on from generation to generation. **Nathaniel Emerson,** author of *The Unwritten Literature of Hawaii,* called the hula "the door to the heart of the people." But when missionaries arrived in the 19th century, they were disgusted by the ritual dance. They found the costumes (men in loincloths and topless women in *kapa* skirts) and the thrusting *opu* (pelvic) movements sexually explicit and vulgar, and promptly banned the dance.

Hawaiians responded to the ban by dancing in secret, which kept the ancient ceremony alive until **King Kalakaua** came to power in 1883 and brought it out of hiding, albeit with a few changes. Women were consigned to wearing long skirts under their ti-leaf skirts and long-sleeved, high-necked tops, though men remained dressed in their loincloths.

When mass tourism descended upon the Islands in the 20th century, the hula dance became a major tourist attraction, and its traditional meaning got lost somewhere between the swaying grass skirts

and the ukuleles. But in the last 15 years, the inner spirit of the hula has returned in full force, and the ancient dance is once again performed for historical and cultural reasons. Dance celebrations such as the **Prince Lot Hula Festival** at the Moanalua Gardens on Oahu and the **Merrie Monarch** in Hilo on the Big Island are flourishing. The hula is also being kept alive in public schools, where hula competitions are almost as popular as football games.

Niihau

Introductory hula classes are available on the activity rosters of many hotels. If you are watching—or learning—the hula, think hands, not hips. The body is supposed to sway gracefully to the rhythm of the music, while the hands and facial expressions tell the story.

MICHAEL BLUM

History of Hawaii

AD 500

Polynesians discover Hawaii and begin to settle on the Islands.

Hawaii, an isolated chain of islands more than 2,400 miles from its nearest neighbor, was inviolate until mariners from cannibal islands in eastern Polynesia arrived. It's believed the seafaring settlers migrated from the **Marquesas Islands** in Southeast Asia. These people became the first Hawaiians, and lived on the Islands for 1,400 years before any Caucasians set foot in their paradise. The different tribes lived peacefully, and cannibalism soon died out.

1100

Tahitian settlers enslave Hawaii's first inhabitants.

Tahitians arrived in Hawaii during the 12th century and conquered the natives. As Tahitian migration continued through the 14th century, dogs, pigs, chickens, and other domestic animals were introduced to the Islands. The natives also saw the arrival of taros, coconuts, bananas, sugarcane, sweet potatoes, and several other plants. And along with the food came the first rats.

1400s

Primitive Hawaiian culture begins to emerge.

Three social groups began to formalize during the 15th century: Tribal kings and queens (or *alii*) led the people; priests, doctors, navigators, and other professionals formed a class called "kahuna"; and the rest were common laborers and fishers. Their divergent standards of living were reminiscent of feudal Europe.

Religion was the fiber of life in ancient Hawaii, governing birth, education, occupation, family, marriage, illness, war, and death. The primary gods were **Kane,** the god of life and water; **Lono,** the god of harvest, wind, and fertility; **Ku,** the god of war, sorcery, and fishing; and **Kanaloa,** the ruler of the dead. There were also minor gods such as **Pele,** the still popular

goddess of the volcano; and **Mani,** the god of the sun.

Hawaiians worshipped profusely in private, elaborate ceremonies held at the village *heiau* (ancient temple). The *heiau,* surrounded by a stone wall and filled with drums, gourds, and carved idols, was often used for human sacrifice to the god Ku.

Kapu (meaning "taboo") was a strict legal system that kept order in this early culture. Its negative, primitive, and arbitrary laws were probably based on the whims of past kings and sorcerers; for example, women and men were not allowed to eat together; women were forbidden to eat pork, coconut, or white shark; and commoners were punished if they cast a shadow upon the house of a chief.

Only men in early Hawaii were permitted to make poi (pudding) from the taro plant, a skill that was physical-

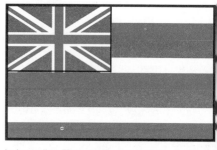

ly demanding. The paddylike taro fields required a constant water supply, so the natives developed ingenious irrigation systems. After harvesting, the plants were steamed, pounded into paste, diluted with water, and mixed into a bland pudding. This was the Islanders' dietary staple.

Punishment for breaking a law was vicious—often death by stoning, beating, or strangulation. Although if an accused *kapu* breaker was lucky enough to escape to a *pu'uhonua* (a designated city of refuge), he or she was considered safe from punishment.

In general, these early Hawaiians enjoyed a life free of disease. They lived along the coast, where seafood was abundant, and they made homes out of bark and coconut fronds. Paper mulberry was used to create *kapa* cloth, a process that evolved into an exquisite Island art form. Men wore simple loincloths; women wore short skirts.

For art and adornment, they wore intricately detailed *kapa* robes and tattooed their bodies, although the process was extremely slow and painful. Feather capes and helmets became popular—perhaps an influence of Spanish visitors—and they fashioned jewelry from shells, bones, hair, and sometimes human teeth.

A rich oral tradition grew over the centuries, providing the native language with a vocabulary of more than 20,000 words. Memorized poems, musical chants, and narratives kept the history of the earliest Hawaiians alive.

Early Hawaiians were avid athletes. They surfed, swam, boxed, wrestled, and played darts and board games in their leisure time.

War was another competitive diversion. The Islands were split into many tribes, and civil wars raged between kings battling for land and resources as overcrowding put a strain on the food supply.

1500s

The Spanish make their mark on the Islands.

Although **Captain James Cook** is credited with the discovery of Hawaii in 1778, many historians argue that Spanish navigator **Juan Gaetano** deserves that distinction. Spanish galleons had been exploring the South Pacific almost 250 years before Cook's ships anchored off Kauai, so there is a strong possibility that at some point (perhaps as early as 1555) Gaetano landed on Hawaii. (There is also considerable opposition to use of the term "discovery" these days, because the Hawaiian people and their culture were thriving before any Westerner set foot on their shores.)

In the mid-16th century, the Spanish were looking for the legendary cities of gold in the "southern continent." (Ancient geographers had speculated that the earth was balanced—each northern continent having a southern counterpart.) In their search, the Spanish developed routes through the South Pacific and traded goods with Acapulco, Guam, and Manila.

Historians cite other evidence of Spanish influence in the Islands. The native history, passed down orally for generations, tells of light-skinned people arriving in Hawaii (early Western visitors noted light skin and Caucasian features among some Hawaiians). And bright costumes with helmets, cloaks, and daggers were adopted in Hawaii but nowhere else in Polynesia. These styles mimic those of 17th-century Europe; even the colors most favored by Hawaiians—red and green—were the royal colors of Spain. In addition, several artifacts with distinctly Western origins, including fragments of material thought to be sailcloth, have been found among the contents of primitive Island tombs.

1778

Captain Cook lands on Kauai.

Captain James Cook of the British Royal Navy discovered the island Kauai on 17 January 1778, opening Hawaii to the west. This was the last major land discovery by Europe's seafaring empires.

Natives sighted the billowing sails of Cook's *Discovery* and *Resolution* and called the huge ships "floating islands." The sails resembled the banners used to honor **Lono,** the god of harvest, and the natives thought they were witnessing the god's legendary return, so they gathered by the hundreds to greet Cook and his crew. The two ships spent a fortnight on Kauai replenishing their supplies. They discovered that Hawaiians were familiar with metals, and coveted iron; in fact, sailors could trade a single nail for a fat Hawaiian pig.

Cook introduced melon and pumpkin seeds and goats to the Islands. Although his crew was strictly forbidden to mingle with the native women, the Westerners soon spread venereal and other diseases among the natives. Hawaiian people had no natural immunity to these inflictions, and within the next century, 260,000 Hawaiians (80 percent of the population) died of poxes, measles, and other non-native illnesses.

The Islands were originally named for a great Polynesian chief, **Hawaii Loa,** who supposedly discovered Hawaii. Cook renamed them the **Sandwich Islands** (for naval patron John Montague, the **Earl of Sandwich**) and declared them a part of the British Empire. He then sailed on to continue his search for the Northwest Passage. Returning some months later, Cook chose to land at Maui's Kealakekua Bay, known as the "Pathway of the Gods." His arrival coincided with *makahiki,* an annual tribute to Lono, the god with whom he was associated. Thousands filled the bay to greet their returning god. Flower-filled canoes met Cook's two ships, and when the men finally landed, provisions and honors were bestowed upon them.

1779

Captain Cook is killed.

In early February, Cook and his men again set sail, but a winter storm battered their ships, forcing them back to Hawaii. This time the natives were not happy with their return. They were tired of the constant demands placed on them by the outsiders and, with the death of one of Cook's crewmembers, no longer believed the *haoles* (Caucasians) were immortal gods.

On 13 February a small boat was stolen from the *Discovery,* sparking a tragic chain of events. Cook immediately stockaded the bay and went ashore with nine men to kidnap the local chief and hold him ransom for the boat. A skirmish broke out and angry natives attacked Cook and his men with rocks and clubs. Only five of Cook's party returned, and Captain Cook was not among them.

Parts of Cook's body, mutilated and possibly used in sacrifice, were later returned to his crew by sympathetic Hawaiians. The Europeans were so angered by the savage treatment of their leader that, shortly before leaving the Hawaiian waters, they sent barrages of cannon fire into the Island villages, killing scores of innocent natives. Cook's men sailed from Hawaii on 22 February.

1786

Western ships visit Hawaii for the first time since Cook's death.

Within 10 years of Cook's landing, British and French traders had adopted the Sandwich Islands into their eastern routes. Soon Russia, Spain, and the US were taking advantage of the convenient location. Fur trappers along America's northwest coast stopped here and rested on round-trips to China, where they traded for silk and tea.

1790

Kamehameha I begins a drive to unite Hawaii.

For some time, Hawaii had been split by intense tribal rivalries (the Big Island alone had four chiefs), and wars for power were constantly erupting. The various

newcomers greatly aggravated an already bloody situation by using cannons and guns to court the favors of local chiefs.

The central figure in these civil wars was a large, unattractive chieftain named **Kamehameha,** known as "The Lonely One." Since, as a child, he had witnessed Cook's arrival, Kamehameha was curious about European firearms. While other Hawaiians sat in awe, Kamehameha carefully studied the men, the ships, and their weapons.

Kamehameha's careful attention to Cook's weapons soon paid off. By 1790, after wars with his cousin, Kamehameha ruled the entire Big Island. Advised by his British friend **Captain George Vancouver,** Kamehameha mounted a cannon onto a platform that floated on two canoes and began his wars to unite all the Islands.

1794

Kamehameha I conquers other Islands.

Soon the king admitted more foreigners into his confidence and began to attack the neighboring Islands. To the west, King Kahekili controlled Maui, Molokai, and Lanai. Kamehameha defeated Kahekili at the Battle of Iao Valley on Maui, and then moved on to conquer Oahu, Kauai, and Niihau.

In 1803 Kamehameha chose Lahaina, Maui, as his seat of power. It was there that he built the "Brick Palace," Hawaii's first permanent building, to house his royal court. A small ruin of the structure is all that remains.

1810

The Hawaiian Islands are unified for the first time.

Settled under one king, the unified Islands began to enjoy a new popularity with Pacific shipping fleets. Kamehameha began exploiting the Islands' sandalwood groves, driving common laborers into the mountains to gather the wood that was greatly valued in China. Within a little more than a decade, the king's greed exhausted nearly the entire crop of native sandalwood.

Kamehameha has been called everything from "the George Washington of the Islands" to "the Hawaiian Napoleon." He forced his will upon the Islands, building his own wealth and arms supplies while denying those rights to other chiefs or visitors.

Despite his autocratic rule, "The Lonely One" gave the Islands peace and stability after years of bloody, savage civil wars; created a stable government that would rule until statehood; and brought an end to foreign manipulation and intrigue.

1819

Kamehameha I dies.

When Kamehameha died on 8 May 1819, his son **Liholiho** became the second Kamehameha, but shared his power with his father's favorite wife, the

History

charismatic **Kaahumanu.** (Legend has it that Kaahumanu won her king's heart with her brashness; she openly ate forbidden foods and was unfaithful to Kamehameha. When he executed her lovers, she ran away and flouted his power. But the king remained smitten by the bold and witty beauty.) When Liholiho turned out to be a drunken weakling, Kaahumanu named herself regent, took control of the government, and acted as the country's prime minister.

Under Kaahumanu, three dramatic changes took place that would form the basis of modern Hawaiian culture: Christianity gained a powerful foothold it would never relinquish; *kapu*, the Island order of forbidden practices, was shattered when Liholiho sat down and ate with women; and under the Westerners' direction, a form of parliamentary government was introduced.

1820

Missionaries arrive on the Big Island.

Led by the **Reverend Hiram Bingham,** a band of 14 Calvinist missionaries (seven married couples) from Boston arrived at Kailua on the Big Island on 4 April 1820. The missionaries reportedly cried when they first saw the barely clothed and seemingly destitute and degraded natives.

Despite reservations, Liholiho agreed to let the missionaries preach their foreign religion on a one-year trial basis. Kaahumanu was initially tolerant of, then amused by, and finally won over by the curious Calvinists. She was also fascinated by the women's clothing. Eventually Kaahumanu became the strongest ally of the Christian Protestants, helping them gain government advisory positions throughout the Islands.

In the 1820s, a tremendous influx of Yankee whalers set Hawaii's economic pace as a trade center for the next half century. As more and more ships visited Hawaiian ports—mainly Honolulu on Oahu and Lahaina on Maui—the Island economy became increasingly dependent on the US whale oil market.

1823

Kamehameha II visits London.

In 1823, Kamehameha II (Liholiho) left Hawaii to visit **King George IV** in London to discuss a mutual defense treaty. He and his queen (his favorite wife, **Kamamalu**) were lavishly greeted, entertained at court, and both promptly died of the measles.

1824

Christianity is more readily accepted.

Kapiolani, an important priestess, defied Pele, the goddess of the volcano, on the edge of the Halemaumau firepit by holding a Christian service there. When nothing happened, it was considered a good omen for Christians.

1825

Kauikeaouli becomes Kamehameha III.

On 6 May 1825, the bodies of Kamehameha II and his wife Kamamalu were returned from London to Honolulu for burial, and **Kauikeaouli** (Liholiho's younger brother) became king. Ascending to the throne at age 10, Kauikeaouli had the longest reign of the Kamehameha dynasty—29 years. Protected and schooled by Kaahumanu and other recent Christian converts in the government, he became Hawaii's most progressive ruler.

Also during this year, the first Catholic missionaries arrived in Hawaii but were soon driven out by Kaahumanu, who was by this time a devout Protestant.

1830

Protestant missionaries gain a firm hold on Hawaiian politics.

With the death of Liholiho and the ascension of young Kauikeaouli, the Protestant missionaries set out to transform the established feudal system into a democracy with new laws, schools, churches, and roads for each major settlement. They spread the use of the newly created Hawaiian written language by printing religious tracts, and using them to teach young Hawaiians how to read. They also tried to change the Islanders' customs. The hula was considered obscene and was outlawed, and the semi-nude natives were shamed and forced into Western-style clothing. By the mid-1800s, half the Islands had converted to the Christian religion.

1832

Kaahumanu dies.

With the death of this Protestant leader and advocate, the Protestant monopoly on Island religion ended.

1835

The first sugar plantation is created.

The original sugar plantation was on Kauai, were it is still in production as part of the **McBryde Sugar Company.**

During the next 15 years, 180,000 Japanese, 125,000 Filipinos, 50,000 Chinese, and 20,000 Portuguese immigrants were imported for plantation labor.

1839

Catholic missionaries return to Hawaii.

After the death of Kaahumanu, the Catholic missionaries made a second trip to the Islands. They also negotiated a protection agreement with France, which allowed the importation of French wines and brandies into the Islands.

1840

Kamehameha III introduces Hawaii's first constitution.

After growing up under Western teachings, **Kamehameha III** (Kauikeaouli) was determined to share democratic ideas with his country. He instructed his ruling chieftains on political history and theory, and in 1840 gave the people of Hawaii their first constitution. This established a two-house assembly (one for royalty, the other for elected commoners), created a supreme court, and adopted responsibility for running a public school system. Earlier in his reign, Kamehameha III had granted his subjects a Code of Civil Law and Declaration of Civil Rights. Former missionary **Gerrit Judd** became chief minister of the Hawaiian government.

At this time, the entire Island economy was based on whaling and the servicing of whaling fleets (more than 500 ships visited Honolulu on Oahu and Lahaina on Maui yearly). Tension also started building between missionaries and Islanders.

1845

The capital is moved from Lahaina, Maui, to Honolulu, Oahu.

1848

Kamehameha III divides the land.

The biggest reform of Kamehameha III's rule was the land reform called the **Great Mahele,** which divided Hawaii into three equal parts: one-third for the king and his heirs, one-third for the government, and one-third for the native people. This seemingly monumental break for common Hawaiians was in reality a *haole*-backed ploy to make land available for agricultural expansion. Two years after the Great Mahele, laws were passed allowing foreign ownership of Hawaiian land.

1852

The monarchy passes the Masters and Servants Act to import plantation workers.

The act was designed to aid plantation owners who desperately need contract laborers to work the sugar fields. The first envoy of Chinese to arrive were from the region of Amoy in southern China. The conditions they were forced to work under were brutally harsh. Subsequently, as their contracts expired, the Chinese laborers immediately pursued other business opportunities for themselves.

1854

Kamehameha III dies.

Kamehameha III's nephews **Alexander** and **Lot** had toured America with Gerrit Judd as part of their education. They were subject to intense discrimination in the US, and came home with a severe dislike for the country, feelings that were reinforced by the heavy-handed role Americans generally played in the power structure on the Islands. When Kamehameha III died in 1854, Alexander ascended the throne.

1860

Sugar grows as an export industry.

By the time **Kamehameha IV** (Alexander) came to power, the whaling industry was virtually extinct. The shortage of whales and the introduction of new sources of oil seriously threatened the Island's economy, until there was a dramatic increase in the demand for sugar. In 1860, 1.5 million pounds of sugar was exported, and boatloads of immigrants came to work on the plantations.

Leprosy, also called **Hansen's disease,** appeared in the Islands and grew to be a serious menace during

the 1860s. Makanalua Peninsula was chosen as the area in which to isolate the stricken, and suspected lepers were immediately exiled to that beautiful but lonely area of Molokai.

1863

Kamehameha IV dies.

The king died on 30 November 1863. His successor, Alexander's brother, **Lot,** also reigned for nine years, and he created the **Bureau of Immigration** to import more laborers for the sugar industry.

It was Kamehameha V who finally bowed to the inevitability of Western domination. By creating the Bureau of Immigration, he assured the future of sugar on the land bought by descendants of missionaries. Eventually the Caucasians would own four times as much land as the natives.

1864

Kamehameha V abolishes the constitution.

The king declared a special constitutional convention in 1864 and abolished the constitution of 1840. His act diminished the monarch's power and liberalized the government.

1872

Kamehameha V dies.

The king's death on 11 November 1872 marked 77 years of rule by the dynasty founded by Kamehameha I, who is often referred to as Kamehameha the Great.

1873

Hawaii holds its first election.

After a bitter political struggle, **Prince William Lunalilo,** a descendant of Kamehameha I, defeated high chief **David Kalakaua** and was elected by the legislature on 1 January 1873 to lead the country. He did little during the 13 months before he died in office.

1874

David Kalakaua becomes king.

Queen Emma, widow of Kamehameha IV, fought with Kalakaua, a former rival of Prince Lunalilo, for the crown, and her backers rioted when Kalakaua was elected king on 12 February 1874. British and American troops were asked to restore order.

1875

The Reciprocity Treaty paves the way for the sugar empires' expansion.

Soon after taking power, King Kalakaua traveled to Washington DC, where he and **President Ulysses S. Grant** negotiated a long-sought Reciprocity Treaty. The US granted Hawaii trade concessions and a reduced tariff, which escalated sugar profits.

1887

Hawaiians revolt against Kalakaua.

History

King Kalakaua, who was nicknamed "The Merry Monarch," adopted an extravagant monarchy. He built himself a $360,000 palace, left the country on a round-the-world tour (becoming the first monarch to circumnavigate the globe), and upon his return, gave himself and his queen an extensive and lavish coronation celebration.

Political scandal rocked the king's fragile hold on Hawaii. His name was linked to unethical real estate sales and cash bribes concerning an opium concession in the Islands. During the first 10 years of his reign, the national debt increased fivefold. The Caucasian plantation owners, whose wealth and power grew as sugar exports rose, resented the thought that their taxes were supporting a cor-

rupt regime, and a group of them secretly formed a reform party called the **Hawaiian League.** In June 1887 they led an open revolt, forcing the acceptance of a new constitution, referred to as the **Bayonet Constitution,** which severely limited the power of the monarch and any nonlandholder (about three-fourths of the native Hawaiians did not own land). **Sanford B. Dole** led the new party in renegotiating the Reciprocity Treaty to grant the US exclusive use of Pearl Harbor.

1891

Kalakaua dies in exile in California.

Upon the death of Kalakaua on 20 January 1891, **Queen Lydia Liliuokalani** (Kalakaua's sister) became the next (and the last) Hawaiian monarch. With severe nativist loyalties, she distressed the men in power by announcing her plans to dissolve the legislature and create a new constitution, which would return power to the monarch and the native Hawaiians.

1893

The monarchy is overthrown.

A coup led by pro-annexation and provisional forces ended with one casualty (a Hawaiian police officer) on 17 January 1893. Queen Liliuokalani surrendered to avoid further bloodshed.

1898

The Joint Resolution of Annexation passes the US Congress.

The annexation agreement was signed by **President William McKinley** on 7 July 1898. **Sanford B. Dole,** acting as president of the new Republic of Hawaii, officially handed the Island nation over to the US in a ceremony reportedly snubbed by all descendants of the original Hawaiians. Within hours of the annexation ceremony, US troops were on the Islands. On 16 August they began breaking ground for a new military installation, which became **Camp McKinley.**

Not all plantation owners on Hawaii favored annexation, since, under a democratic government, their laborers would have considerable freedom and power.

1900

Hawaii officially becomes a US territory.

By 1900, five percent of the Island population was white and owned most of the land. As a US territory, full civil rights were extended to all Hawaiian citizens.

1901

The Hawaiian Pineapple Company, Ltd. is organized.

When **James D. Dole** desided to start growing pineapples on his homestead in Wahiawa, Oahu, he envisioned—correctly—a big future in canned fruit. By 1922 his **Hawaiian Pineapple Company** was so big that Dole bought the entire island of Lanai, and established the largest pineapple plantation in the world.

1912

Sanford B. Dole is appointed governor of the Hawaii territory.

In American Hawaii, business stabilized, then boomed. Dole became governor and other pro-annexation leaders earned top appointments. Five plantation owners who played major parts in the annexation became known as the Big Five. This cartel included the **Doles, Thurstons, Alexanders, Baldwins,** and **Cookes,** among others, and controlled the land, the sugar and pineapple industries, the factories and docks, and many of the merchant stores on the Islands. In effect, these few families became the new Island monarchy.

The new order created a major division of wealth in Hawaii. A few Japanese and Chinese had started small businesses, but the majority of people were poor and dependent upon the Big Five for their wages. Land was no longer open to fishing, hunting, or farming, and the Islands were becoming increasingly urbanized. In the cities, many people lived in shacks.

The Big Five's firm hold on politics allowed them to appoint their governors and legislatures. All attempts by Hawaiians to create their own power block failed.

In this same year, Hawaii got its first international sports hero when Duke Kahanamoku set a record in the 100-meter swim competition at the Olympics. The famous waterman later introduced surfing to the mainland and Australia.

1917

Liliuokalani, Hawaii's last ruling monarch, dies.

1935

Unions are legalized.

With the legalization of unions and collective bargaining, local workers finally began to gain power.

1941

Japan attacks Pearl Harbor.

The Japanese attack on Pearl Harbor, Oahu, on 7 December 1941 stunned the Islands; 3,435 Americans were killed, martial law was declared, and the US entered WWII.

1949

Unions take over.

Throughout the 1940s, management and labor struggled for power in Hawaii. In 1949, a crippling strike led by the International Longshoremen and Warehousemen's Union finally turned the tide, and unions replaced the plantation cartel as *the* power on the Islands.

1954

Japanese-Americans gain control of Hawaii's legislature.

By the early 1950s, labor had solidified its political position in Hawaii. With help from the GI bill, many natives gained new professional status. The Japanese-Americans, the Islands' largest racial group, asserted their majority power. By 1954, the Japanese-Americans and labor had formed a coalition that backed Democratic candidates. Led by ex-policeman **Jack Burns,** they gained control of the state legislature, with Japanese descendants filling half the seats.

1959

Hawaii becomes a state.

This year Hawaii became the 50th state in the US, and the first Boeing 707 landed on the Islands. With the Boeing 707, air travel from the mainland was reduced to only four-and-a-half hours. Hawaii's population and tourism soon boomed. Statehood and the democratic government moved the sleepy territory into the modern era. Honolulu blossomed into a metropolis, and the Island's economy diversified, with tourism replacing jobs lost to agricultural mechanization.

1970s

The war against drugs begins.

Hawaii's multimillion-dollar marijuana industry prompted intensive anti-drug campaigns.

1974

George R. Ariyoshi becomes the governor of Hawaii—the first Japanese-American to be elected governor of a US state.

1977

Tourists outnumber inhabitants by four to one.

By this year almost a dozen large US airlines (and other small ones) flew to the Islands, giving the tourism industry a huge boost.

1983

The population of Hawaii reaches one million.

1984

Hawaii celebrates its 25th anniversary as a state .

1990

Kahoolawe is no longer used as a US Navy bombing target.

President George Bush ended 49 years of using Kahoolawe as a military practice range, and established a federal commission to recommend the conditions for returning the island to the people of Hawaii.

Index

Restaurants

Only restaurants with star ratings are listed below. All restaurants are listed alphabetically in the main (preceeding) index. Always call in advance to ensure a restaurant has not closed, changed its hours, or booked its tables for a private party.

★★★★

Canoe House $$$ **24**
Dining Room at the Lodge at Koele $$$$ **92**
Haliimaile General Store $$$ **78**
Kona Village Luau $$$ **26**
La Mer $$$$ **104**
La Perouse $$$$ **68**
Pacific Cafe $$$ **162**
Pacific Grill $$$ **69**
Prince Court (Makena) $$$$ **72**
Roy's Restaurant $$$ **134**
Seasons $$$$ **69**

★★★

Avalon $$$ **59**
Banyan Veranda $$ **110**
Bay Club $$$ **47**
Cafe Pesto $$ **21**
Casanova Italian Restaurant $$ **77**
David Paul's Lahaina Grill $$$ **62**
Furusato $$$ **111**
Gaylord's Restaurant $$$ **151**
Gerard's $$$ **63**
Green Garden Restaurant $$ **156**
Hakone (Honolulu) $$$$ **98**
Hakone (Makena) $$$ **72**
Harrington's (Kawaihae) $$$ **21**
Hotel Hana-Maui Dining Room $$$$ **75**
Keo's $$$ **118**
Kyo-ya $$$$ **101**
La Bretagne $$$ **57**
La Cascata $$$$ **161**
Leilani's on the Beach $$$ **54**
Le Soleil $$$$ **24**
Maile Restaurant $$$$ **119**
Makawao Steak House $$$ **77**
Mekong I $$ **123**
Merriman's $$$ **18**
Michel's $$$$ **115**
Mid Nite Inn $$ **84**
Old Lahaina Luau $$$ **57**
Orchids $$$ **104**
Parc Cafe $$$ **104**
Prince Court (Honolulu) $$$$ **98**

Raffles $$$$ **68**
Restaurant Miwa $$ **11**
Restaurant Suntory $$$ **106**
Roussels $$$ **12**
Scaroles $$$ **61**
Secret $$$$ **113**
Sergio's $$$ **108**
Swan Court $$$ **56**
Tamarind $$$$ **154**
Waiohai Sunday Brunch $$$$ **154**
Yanagi Sushi $$$ **126**

★★

Al Dente $$$ **134**
Alex's Hole in the Wall $$$ **60**
Aloha Theater Cafe $ **34**
Azteca Mexican Restaurant $$ **118**
Ba-le Sandwich Shop 1 $ **133**
Bali by the Sea $$$ **101**
Bali Hai $$$ **161**
Bay Terrace $$$ **24**
Beijing Chinese Seafood Restaurant $$$ **106**
Bon Appetit $$$ **97**
Brennecke's Beach Broiler $$ **152**
Brick Oven Pizza $$ **155**
Cafe Hanalei $$$ **160**
Cafe Sibu $ **28**
California Pizza Kitchen (Honolulu) $$ **118**
California Pizza Kitchen (Waikiki) $$ **100**
Charley's Restaurant and Saloon $$ **78**
Chart House at Haleiwa $$$ **140**
Che Pasta $$$ **118**
Chris' Smokehouse $$ **60**
Coffee Manoa $$ **120**
Dondero's $$$$ **152**
Doong Kong Lau-Hakka Restaurant $$ **133**
Eclipse $$$ **31**
Edelweiss $$ **18**
Eggbert's $$ **148**
Eggs 'n Things $$ **100**
El Crab Catcher (Lahaina) $$$ **54**
Gabel's $$$ **66**
Gallery $$ **24**
Greek Island Taverna $$$ **122**
Grill & Bar $$$ **46**
Hajji Baba's $$$ **118**
Hala Terrace $$ **119**
Hale Moana $$$ **25**
Hale Samoa $$$$ **26**
Hale Vietnam $$ **118**

Hanalei Dolphin $$$ **161**
Hanamaulu Cafe & Tea House $$ **165**
Hard Rock Cafe (Honolulu) $$ **122**
Hard Rock Cafe (Lahaina) $$ **59**
Harrington's (Hilo) $$$ **9**
Harry's Cafe and Deli $$$ **136**
Hau Tree Lanai $$ **114**
Hotel Lanai Dining Room $$ **92**
House Without a Key $$ **104**
Hy's Steak House $$$ **111**
India Bazaar Madras Cafe $ **122**
Island Fish House $$$ **66**
Jameson's by the Sea (Haleiwa) $$$ **140**
Jameson's by the Sea (Kailua-Kona) $$ **32**
John Dominis $$$$ **126**
Kacho $$$ **104**
Kapaa Fish and Chowder House $$$ **162**
Kauai Chop Suey $$ **149**
Kimo's $$$ **61**
King Tsin $$ **122**
Kintaro $$$ **164**
Knickers $$ **24**
Kona Ranch House $$$ **26**
Kua Aina Sandwich Shop $ **140**
La Bourgogne $$$ **33**
Lahaina Coolers $$ **60**
Lahaina Fish Co. $$$ **59**
Lehua's Bay City Bar and Grill $$ **12**
Los Arcos $$$ **136**
Maple Garden $$$ **122**
Mama's Fish House $$$ **79**
Matteo's $$$ **108**
Mauna Kea Luau $$ **22**
Ming Yuen $$ **43**
Miyo's $ **11**
Nick's Fishmarket $$$ **101**
Nikko Steak House $$$ **55**

Page	Entry #	Notes

Page	Entry #	Notes

Page	Entry #	Notes

ACCESS® Travel Diary

Page	Entry #	Notes

ACCESS® Travel Diary

Page	Entry #	Notes

age	Entry #	Notes

ACCESS® Travel Diary

Page	Entry #	Notes